# WORLD TELEVISION

To my wife, Sandra, and my children, Julia, Rolf and Chris, who have contributed vastly to my learning about and enjoyment of many of the places where this research took place.

# WORLD TELEVISION

## From Global to Local

Joseph D. Straubhaar
*The University of Texas at Austin*

**SAGE Publications**
Los Angeles • London • New Delhi • Singapore

*For information:*

Sage Publications, Inc.
2455 Teller Road
Thousand Oaks, California 91320
E-mail: order@sagepub.com

Sage Publications India Pvt. Ltd.
B 1/I 1 Mohan Cooperative
Industrial Area
Mathura Road, New Delhi 110 044
India

Sage Publications Ltd.
1 Oliver's Yard
55 City Road
London EC1Y 1SP
United Kingdom

Sage Publications Asia-Pacific Pte. Ltd.
33 Pekin Street #02-01
Far East Square
Singapore 048763

*Library of Congress Cataloging-in-Publication Data*

Straubhaar, Joseph D.
World television : from global to local / Joseph D. Straubhaar.
    p. cm.
Includes bibliographical references and index.
ISBN 978-0-8039-5462-5 (cloth)
ISBN 978-0-8039-5463-2 (pbk.)
    1. Television—Social aspects. 2. Group identity. I. Title.
PN1992.6.S765 2007
384.55—dc22

2006102718

07  08  09  10  11  10  9  8  7  6  5  4  3  2  1

| | |
|---|---|
| *Acquiring Editor:* | Todd R. Armstrong |
| *Editorial Assistant:* | Katie Grim |
| *Project Editor:* | Astrid Virding |
| *Copy Editor:* | Jacqueline Tasch |
| *Typesetter:* | C&M Digitals (P) Ltd. |
| *Proofreader:* | Anne Rogers |
| *Indexer:* | Ellen Slavitz |
| *Cover Designer:* | Bryan Fishman |
| *Marketing Manager:* | Amberlyn Erzinger |

# Contents

*Upper-Middle- and Upper-Class Cultural Identity*
*Some Broadly Shared Globalization via Television*
Hybridization: Race and Ethnic Identity
Gender Identity and Television
*Telenovelas, Gender, Sexuality,*
*National Values, and Local Values*
Layers of Identity as Boundaries for
Choices and Understandings
Layers of Identities as Mediators of Media Meaning
Reconfiguration and Synthesis of Identities

# Preface

This book reflects work conducted since the mid-1970s by the author and more recently by him and several colleagues. The interests reflected here started in a 1972 undergraduate class on mass media and national development at Stanford University. Lectures by Emile McAnany and others kindled a strong interest that led me to graduate school at the Fletcher School of Law and Diplomacy, where Rosemary Rogers, Hewson Ryan, Ithiel de Sola Pool, and others I met or studied with gave me a strong basic sense of the importance of development and international relations issues in media.

Although I had been very involved with anti-Vietnam politics, I had also been raised with a strong sense of interest in public service. So with some mistaken idealism about helping improve communications between countries, and with the more concrete goal of learning Spanish or Portuguese very well and having time to do extended fieldwork for a dissertation, I joined the U.S. Information Service (the culture and press service, which was then separate from the State Department). I spent three years in Brazil and five in Washington, where many colleagues, including Rodolfo Valentini, Bob Brown, Bob Cross, David Gibson, Charles Spencer, James McGregor, and Norman Painter helped me learn a great deal about language, culture, Brazil, and social research methods, as did colleagues at a University of Michigan summer institute in survey research, which the USIS Office of Research enabled me to attend. All these forms of support (and the considerable patience of my wife, Sandy, who was working on her own dissertation at the time) enabled me to finish my Ph.D. dissertation in 1981 while working at the USIS Office of Research. So one of my first real acknowledgments of crucial support must be to the U.S. Foreign Service and the former USIS, which was foolishly scaled back and folded into the State Department in the late 1990s.

In Brazil, I also met academic friends and colleagues who still influence me to this day: José Marques de Melo, Fred Litto, Carlos Eduardo Lins da Silva, Anamaria Fadul, Luis Fernando Santoro, Sergio Mattos, Ethevaldo Siqueira, and others. I also began to benefit enormously from the generosity of Brazilian media professionals, including Paulo Mora and Orjan Olsen of the Instituto Brasileiro de Opinião Publica e Estatistica (IBOPE) and Homero Sanchez Icaza of TV Globo, who shared a great deal of knowledge with me over the years.

Going from promoting human rights in Brazil under Jimmy Carter to supposedly helping the Reagan Administration understand foreign public opinion about the United States and its policies turned out to be very difficult—a sort of ideological whiplash. The Reagan people didn't particularly want to know that Latin Americans had actually liked the previous human rights policy. So I acted on my original impulses, left USIS, and went back to academic life.

I benefited enormously from a very fortunate first academic job at Michigan State University (MSU), where I learned a great deal about social research from Brad Greenberg, Carrie Heeter, Tom Baldwin, Bella Mody, Chuck Atkin, Tom Muth, Bob LaRose, and many others over 11 years, from 1983 to 1994. I also learned a great deal from colleagues in Latin American and International Studies there, such as Scott Whiteford, Jonas Zoninsein, Leni Silverstein, and David Wiley. MSU Latin American Studies led me to get involved in work in the Dominican Republic, through programs supported by the Partners of the Americas and the Universidad Católica Madre y Maestra. I took a Fulbright Fellowship to the latter in 1987. I was becoming interested in places smaller and less culturally autonomous than Brazil. Those grants and times for fieldwork in the Dominican Republic permitted me to do one sample survey about social class and use of broadcast versus cable television (Straubhaar & Viscasillas, 1991) and one in-depth interviewing project (Straubhaar, 1991) that enabled me to begin to understand connections between social class and preferences for foreign versus local television, breaking down social class connections into more useful components based on Bourdieu's (1984) ideas of economic and cultural capital. That insight came via feedback on a paper I gave at the International Communication Association (ICA), a nurturing and enlightening forum for testing out ideas and learning new ones from others.

I was able to resume fieldwork in Brazil and learn about ethnography by participating in an anthropological study grant (from 1985 to 1986) with Conrad Kottak about television's impact in Brazil. A University Affiliation/Exchange grant from the Institute for International Education/USIS in communications studies between MSU and the University of São Paulo also supported several research trips with similar results. I spent a sabbatical in São Paulo, Brazil, in 1989 and 1990, supported by MSU and that Institute for

International Education grant; I spent that year teaching at the University of São Paulo's School of Communication and Arts under Professor Marques de Melo and leading a study-abroad group for MSU. During my sabbatical, I began the ongoing in-depth interviewing in Brazil that is reported at length in Chapters 8 and 9 of this volume. In 1994, I found myself in the very enlightening position of being the trailing spouse and followed my wife, Sandy, to Brigham Young University. There I benefited greatly from four years of excellent research and travel support from the Department of Communication. I also enjoyed the stimulating intellectual company of Dan Stout, Allen Palmer, Steve Thompson, and Scott Hammond. The latter introduced me to complexity theory approaches to communications, which inform this book strongly.

More broadly, I benefited greatly from innumerable conversations at meetings of the International Communication Association (ICA), the International Association for Media and Communication Research (IAMCR), the Broadcast Education Association (BEA), and, more recently, the Global Fusion conference network. Doug Boyd, one of my most important mentors and friends, steered me toward active participation in these venues. Once a year at ICA, I see some of my more valued intellectual colleagues and friends: Doug Boyd, Don Browne, John Mayo, and many others who have been enormously influential and have made intellectual growth enjoyable. Another valuable intellectual resource has been the series of Global Fusion meetings on international communication, attended not only by U.S. scholars but also by international ones, such as Marwan Kraidy and Hussein Amin.

My continued work in Brazil and other Latin American countries has also benefited enormously from conference invitations, speaking visits, and seminar opportunities that colleagues there have extended to me. Just as I found ICA to be a nurturing U.S. conference home, so I have learned a great deal from attending more than a dozen annual meetings of INTERCOM, the Brazilian Association for Interdisciplinary Research in Communications, and a number of meetings of the Latin American Association for Communication Research (ALAIC). Beyond the Brazilian colleagues I originally met and mentioned above, I have met Immacolata Lopes, Cesar Bolaño, Mauro Porto, Sylvia Borelli, Othon Jambeiro, Marcos Palacios, and Sonia Virgínia Moreira. With Sonia Virginia and Immacolata, I have helped organize a series of bilateral Brazil-U.S. research meetings that have been financed by INTERCOM, Fulbright, and University of Texas's College of Communications and Institute for Latin American Studies. At ALAIC, I have also met a number of valued colleagues: Enrique Sanchez Ruiz, Raul Fuentes, Jorge Gonzalez, Delia Crovi, and José Carlos Lozano in Mexico, Guilhermo

Mastrini in Argentina; and Lucia Castellon in Chile; as well as Gaetan Tremblay of Montreal, whom I see frequently at these Latin American meetings. Lucia Castellon in particularly pushed me to start working more in Spanish and invited me to Chile several times to help make that happen faster. I have also learned a great deal by participating in the Association of Portuguese-Speaking Communication Researchers (LUSOCOM), where I have met Helena Souza and Manuel Pinto of the University of Minho in Portugal and Eduardo Namburete of the Eduardo Mondlane University in Mozambique, among many others. Grants from their universities, the Portuguese-American Society, and the U.S. Agency for International Development have enabled me to participate in several important meetings and to begin research on how media flow among the Lusophone countries.

I have developed several key research partnerships. One of the longest is with the University of São Paulo, particularly its School of Communications under Jose Marque de Melo, and its School of the Future, with Fred Litto and Brasilena Passarelli. Our work on both television and the digital divide has been financed by Institute for International Education exchange and USIS American Participant grants, the Fulbright Commission, MSU, the University of Texas, and other grants. Another major partnership has been with Othon Jambeiro and Marcos Palacios, with whom I am still working to compare information about knowledge societies in Brazil and the United States, supported in part by a grant from the Brazilian Commission for the Improvement of Higher Education (CAPES) and the University of Texas. Another important research partner is Jorge Gonzalez, now at the Autonomous University of Mexico. His work with me in Austin was largely financed by the University of Texas's Title VI grant and the Tinker Foundation. Quite of bit of the work on U.S. Latinos discussed in Chapter 9 developed in this partnership. Another has been with Lucia Castellon, former dean of journalism at the Universidad Diego Portales in Santiago, Chile, financed by their seminars and the University of Texas. Another connection, growing in importance to my work in Texas, has been with Jose Carlos Lozano and his colleagues at the Technological Institute of Monterrey, Mexico, who have supported several conferences and visits, with grants from the Televisa and Monterrey Technological Institute research chairs.

Another important relationship has been with Helena Souza and Manuel Pinto at the University of Minho in Portugal; they have enabled me to participate in several events about the Lusophone cultural linguistic sphere of communications, supported in part by the Portuguese-American Foundation. Giovanni Bechelloni and Milly Buonanno of the University of Florence, Per Jauert of the University of Aarhus in Denmark, and Kaarle Nordenstreng of the University of Tampere in Finland have opened a number of doors to my participating in European research meetings on television and media research. Their universities, Ellen Wartella and Rod Hart as deans of communication at University of Texas, and the Amon G. Carter, Sr., Professorship of Communication at University of Texas, have all helped support that.

Professors Lee Tain Dow of Taiwan, Georgette Wang of Hong Kong, and Joseph Man Chan of Hong Kong have all helped me participate in meetings and research on television in Asia. Those meetings helped introduce me to the work of Koichi Iwabuchi, Yoichi Ito, Eric Ma, and other Asian scholars. Most recently, I am particularly grateful to Professor Ang Peng Hwa, chair of communications at Nanyang Technological University in Singapore, who arranged for me to spend a month there as the Wee Kim Wee Distinguished Professor of Communication in 2006, which greatly facilitated research on Asian television for this book.

At the University of Texas, I have been blessed with remarkably interesting colleagues and good institutional support. Dean Ellen Wartella helped sponsor several conferences on communication in NAFTA and Mercosur, on the digital divide, and on global television, which enabled me to work with colleagues from Latin America, Asia, and Europe. Partners in Latin America, including Jose Marques de Melo (Brazil); Delia Crovi, Enrique Sanchez, and Jose Carlos Lozano (Mexico); Guillermo Mastrini (Argentina); and Gaetan Tremblay (Canada) have organized similar meetings and enabled me to participate in them. The College of Communication awarded me the Amon G. Carter, Sr., Centennial Professorship in Communication, which has supported some of my travel, some conferences, and graduate student work on projects, all of which has been invaluable. I am very grateful to the Amon G. Carter, Sr., family for that support. The Department of Radio-Television-Film under the chairs John Downing, Tom Schatz, and Sharon Strover has also been supportive. I have been well-supported by the Lozano Long Institute of Latin American Studies (LLILAS), under Nick Shumway and Brian Roberts, which has helped support travel, conferences at the University of Texas, and research networks with Latin American colleagues. I have had great colleagues in the Brazil Center of LLILAS, which I directed for 3 years, supported in part by the Brazilian government. Strong support for access to books and materials has come from the University of Texas Benson Collection on Latin America, under Anne Hartness. Much of my time on the ground during a number of summers in Brazil has come in connection with study-abroad programs, first at MSU, then at Brigham Young, and most recently at the University of Texas; these programs have been strongly supported by Helena Wilkins-Versalovic and John Sunnygard at Texas and others.

Last but not least, my colleagues and graduate students have provided enormous insight and joy in learning. Aside from colleagues mentioned above, many of my current Texas colleagues—Karin Wilkins, Rosental Alves, Shanti Kumar, Madhavi Mallapragada, Steve Reese, Joe Potter, and Bob Wilson—along with former colleagues John Downing, Nikhil Sinha, Chuck Whitney, and Horace Newcombe have been influential in this work. Equally important have been former graduate students, now colleagues: Antonio La Pastina, Viviana Rojas, Luiz Guilherme Duarte, Consuelo Campbell, Patricia McCormick, and Michael Elasmar. Current graduate students, Martha Fuentes, Juan Pinon, Jeremiah Spence, and Nobuya Inagaki, have also contributed materially to the research and ideas represented in this book. I would also like to thank Todd Armstrong and his staff at Sage Publications for providing encouragement and support throughout this project.

Sage Publications gratefully acknowledges the following reviewers: Divya C. McMillin, University of Washington Tacoma; Nitin Govil, University of California, San Diego; Timothy Havens, The University of Iowa; and James Hay, University of Illinois—Urbana-Champaign.

# 1

# A Multilayered World of Television

## An Overview

Television in our world is an increasingly complex system with global, transnational, translocal, national, regional, metropolitan, and local spaces, dynamics, players, and flows. The rapid global extension of economic and technological changes has reframed the possibilities of television around the world. However, the realization of those possibilities is a much more complex historical process, involving the hybridization of various global and local elements and influences over time. What emerges is multiple spaces or levels of television production, flow, and reception, corresponding to multiple levels of culture and identity.

Television is the focus of this book because it continues to be the main source of news and entertainment for most people in the world. Hesmondalgh (in press) noted that cultural industries are still central to our lives because they create the media texts that influence our understanding of the world. And, for most people in most countries, television remains the central element in their consumption of the cultural industries. A television set (or a better television set) is the main consumer priority for most people in the developing world (and still a high priority elsewhere, as large recent spending on digital high-definition television sets in the richer countries also shows).

A key first note is what is meant by *television*. Allen (2004) mentioned several possibilities for what might be included in studies of television, including technological elements, programming, forms of narrative such as genre, a set of institutions, and a social experience for both producers and audiences. In this book, I look primarily at broadcast television because, taking a global view, that is what the large majority of the world's television viewers still watch; however, in several chapters, I also discuss satellite, cable, and Internet-based television because those are growing in importance for many. Programming is closely examined in terms of production, flows between cultures, and genres, whereas I include readings of specific television narratives only as examples. Some excellent global television studies books examine specific narratives—for example, Kumar (2006); I take a more systemic focus. I look extensively at the institutions of television, particularly broadcast television, but also transnational satellite television corporations and institutions, such as Rupert Murdoch's News Corporation or the BBC. I also look theoretically and practically at the experience of producers, and I look extensively at audience experience, their identities, their choices, the ideas that inform their choices, and the sense they make of what they watch. So I take a fairly holistic approach, as urged by critical scholars from Schiller (1969) to Miller (2005), except for the close reading of texts. This analysis tries to bridge international communication and cultural studies, as excellent recent work by Kraidy (2005) and others have done, but the approach is probably more sociological than literary.

One of the key arguments of this book is that television, particularly national broadcast television channels, is still the dominant framework for news and for cultural forums (Newcomb & Hirsch, 1994) and discussions, for most people in most cultures and nations. Television still forms a dominant layer of media experience for most people, although admittedly it is supplemented more and more by other layers and other media. Television also means very different things to people in various cultures and countries, as I will begin to map out in this book.

Television is changing, both globally and nationally. The dominance of national public or state broadcasters in most nations has eroded but not disappeared. In particular, Western Europe is making a real effort to hang on to what are often passionately felt to be the benefits of public television. The new technologies for producing and distributing television have expanded to almost all countries in the past few decades, enabling a number of new channels to appear. However, in many of the lowest income countries, very few people have access to more than a few broadcast channels, and many do not even have effective access at home to those. The capitalist or market model of economics has also expanded to almost all the world, which tends to make television a commercial vehicle for advertising and tilt its content toward entertainment in most countries. However, the meaning of capitalism and commercial media varies a great deal between China, the United States, and Russia, for example. Much of what is called globalization centers on these forces of economy and technology (Castells, 1997), which have expanded quickly across the world, leading many to focus on the recent geographic or spatial extension of global forces. However, as these forces move into a new country or cultural space, they hybridize, becoming part of the ongoing history of that country, interacting with previous forces, and becoming localized, enacted, and received by local people with their own identities, histories, and agendas. New trends in economy and technology can be drastically rolled back; Russia, for example, has converted several major independent commercial television networks back to state enterprises to better control them politically (Mydans, 2004).

Television is a very plural phenomenon for many, with cable and satellite television dominant in the richest countries, having more than 80% penetration in the United States, for example. For the minority who have access to the Internet, television is becoming even more diverse, with all kinds of clips and short programs offered by a wide diversity of amateur as well as professional producers. For many, those new channels often come from outside their nation or culture. However, for many, if not most people around the world, television is still primarily broadcast television coming from national networks, supplemented in some places by regional networks at the provincial or local level. Many of the programs carried on satellite, Internet or DVD originated as nationally based broadcast or satellite/cable programs. However, many national programs are based on global or regional models, so national television itself must be problematized and understood in new hybrid or *glocal* (local adaptations of global) forms.

## Central Issues

This book is divided into chapters that address aspects of an overall argument. This first chapter gives an overview of that argument and lays out some underlying theoretical premises on which the whole book builds.

In the first section of the book, I examine historical patterns of cultural development, patterns of control often referred to as political-economic, and global versus national struggles to define and construct the use of the technologies, economic models, and cultural frameworks that define what television means in a given place and time. It follows this chain of arguments.

1. Nearly all television systems work within long-term patterns of language and culture that sometimes coincide with nation-states but are frequently either larger—the Arabic-speaking world—or smaller—several states in India that have distinctive systems of language, culture, religion, and television. (Chapter 2)

2. As nation-states were created or became independent of colonial powers from the late 1700s on, most of those states tried to create a sense of nationality or imagined national community (Anderson, 1983), using media. Since 1950, television has often been the primary tool in this effort, giving it a national focus. (Chapter 3)

3. That national focus of control has been strongly challenged, but not necessarily overturned, by the processes often referred to as globalization since the 1980s or 1990s. (Chapter 4)

In the next section, I take a more contemporary focus on specific uses of technology, patterns of program development and flow, genres of television, the interaction of producers and audiences, and patterns of audience choice among emerging alternatives. The book's chain of arguments resumes:

4. Two potentially contradictory roles of satellite, cable, and Internet technologies have permitted greater flows of television across cultures, with implications often described as cultural imperialism or homogenization. However, computer and other television production technologies have also made it possible for television production and distribution to take place at ever smaller and simpler levels by radically increased numbers of people and groups. For example, Osama bin Laden may be videotaped in a cave in Afghanistan and broadcast by a regional Arabic network, Al-Jazeera, challenging the prior global dominance of both U.S. political and media power. (Chapter 5)

5. Producers and networks have developed diverse production formats and genres that fit their understanding of the cultural nature of their audiences or markets, so that, in effect, culture defines markets, principally at local, national, regional, and cultural linguistic levels. Producers and audiences interact in the production and evolution of genres: globally, within nations, and across cultural-linguistic regions. Television production and flow has changed toward greater national and transnational cultural-linguistic or regional production consumption, particularly in certain specific genres such as variety and talk shows. (Chapter 6)

6. The dominant global exports of the United States and other major exporters are increasingly focused in certain genres, such as action-adventure

television series and drama or feature films, where higher production costs make widespread production prohibitive. Global and transnational satellite channels also cross borders but have to adapt to their audiences. Instead of canned programs, genres and licensed television formats increasingly flow across borders. They are adapted to local, national, and regional cultures but still bring complex transnational influences with them. (Chapter 7)

Finally, the last section of the book examines how the audience for these evolving forms of television is structured, how the audience itself restructures production and genres through its choices and reactions, what cultural patterns underlie audience choices, and how these forces or patterns of television have an impact on both cultural formations and individual identities. The chain of arguments concludes:

7. Audiences feel competing sets of proximities or attractions to programs from different places; the Latin American telenovela is one example. Audiences are structured both by the evolving cultures they live in and by structures of class, race, gender, and cultural geography in terms of the program choices and interpretations they make of local, national, regional, and global television programs. The primary example discussed is the diverse audiences in Brazil, where the author and his colleagues have done fieldwork for 30 years. (Chapter 8)

8. The cultural impacts and uses of television can be understood in terms of a twin process of hybridization and formation of multiple layers of identity among audiences, which guides audience choices and structures impacts on them. The chapter draws on fieldwork by the author and colleagues in Brazil and among Latinos in Texas. (Chapter 9)

## Globalization and Culture

Some fear that globalization implies a global cultural homogenization. Appadurai (1996) thought extensive cultural homogenization was unlikely and cited as opposing evidence the anthropological record, what he called

> the archive of lived actualities, found in all sorts of ethnographies . . . This archive, and the sensibility that it produces in the professional anthropologist, predisposes me strongly toward the idea that globalization is not the story of cultural homogenization. (p. 11)

More likely is a varied kind of cultural globalization that is perhaps better theorized as *hybridization* or *glocalization*. In hybridization, global forces bring change, but that change is adapted into existing ways of doing things via a historical process in which existing local forces mix with new global ones, producing neither global homogenization nor authentic local culture, but a complex new hybrid with multiple layers of culture, where older, traditional forms may persist alongside new ones. This situation is neither a complete resistance to rejoice about nor a complete loss of identity to despair about, but a complex contradiction of both continuity and change.

Globalization is different in various world regions. For example, although most European and African countries continue to import television programs primarily from the United States and relatively little from each other, that is less true in Latin America and the Middle East, where cultural trade within cultural-linguistic regions is large and growing. East Asian countries, which also used to import television almost exclusively from the United States, have begun to import more from each other in the past few years. Between 2002 and 2006, for example, the hot new phenomenon in television imports in East Asia was dramas from South Korea, not Hollywood. Latin American television markets are more likely to import American production ideas and genres than American programs in prime time, although they still import many U.S. programs to fill up the rest of the 24-hour broadcast day. So they are still engaged in globalization, but in a very different way.

One of the main limits on globalization in media and culture is that relatively few people have a primarily global identity. There is a small, important global professional elite, who move easily between cultures, who probably identify more with the company or nongovernmental organization (NGO) that employs them or the cause they espouse than the nation in which they were born. For most people, however, identity still tends to be based in language, religion, geography, history, ethnicity, collective memory, and political power apparatuses (Castells, 1997). Those elements of identity tend to correspond to smaller, more discrete levels of culture than the global. Many people increasingly have multiple levels of identity, but most are still local, metropolitan, subnational/provincial (like Quebec), or national. However, many are also migrating or otherwise adding strong layers of transitional identity, which can stretch within a geocultural region. For example, a Mexican family migrates to the United States and begins to add a layer of U.S. cultural influence. At the same time, members stretch out or back within a cultural-linguistic space or market, when that family watches Mexican telenovelas on Hispanic U.S. channels to stay in touch with their cultural roots (Rojas, Straubhaar, Fuentes, & Piñon, 2004).

Given the forces for continuity of local and national identities, as well as for globalization, one sees contradictory trends; for example, the expression of local identity via an imported genre, as when the American soap opera is transformed into the Latin American *telenovela*. Robertson (1995) aptly noted that people now tend to see the global replication of ideas and models for how to express locality and local identity, a process he terms *glocalization*. However, even when a form of television is imported for explicitly commercial purposes, such as the licensing and local production of the reality show *Big Brother* in a number of countries, it may still end up expressing local culture to many in its audience. Young *Big Brother* fans in France, Italy, and Portugal were often pleased to see young people on screen that they felt they could identify with, even though some critics of those versions of *Big Brother* showed that these "local" productions imported global stereotypes in those same characters (based on reviews from those countries).

In many developing countries, media, particularly radio and television, have been powerful recent forces for consolidating national identities that had previously been nascent or fragile. In the second half of the 20th century, television took up and extended the role ascribed to newspapers and novels in the 19th century (Anderson, 1983). This reflects a strong priority by most developing nation-states to try to use electronic media to push or even create a sense of national identity (Katz & Wedell, 1976).

In this book, I argue that national cultures, national markets supported by national governments, and national television networks still dominate the television viewing reality of most audiences. Note that this is more true of television more than other media. In a new study of Brazil, the author is discovering that film, by contrast, tends to be more of a globalizing force and that music, in recordings or on the radio, tends to be a complex force with truly local, national, and global elements all strongly visible.

One can also see the development of regions or markets, based on both geography and cultural-linguistic identity groupings, which are less than global but more than national. In fact, two types of cultural-linguistic spaces or markets can be distinguished. Geocultural markets are cultural-linguistic spaces that are also contiguous or closely linked by geography. Transnational cultural-linguistic markets can be spread all over the planet by colonization—for example, the former Portuguese empire, which has produced the modern Lusophone cultural-linguistic market for television—or by massive migration, such as the Chinese, Indian, or Turkish diasporas across continents. In this book, I argue that in television, this trend toward geocultural and transnational cultural-linguistic regions or spaces is perhaps just as crucial as globalization per se. In Latin America, Asia, and the Middle East, hundreds of millions of people regularly watch transnational regional soap operas, comedies, news, and variety shows—far more than watch the truly global channels, such as CNN, Discovery, HBO, or MTV. Although it is still less important in most countries due to costs, subnational provincial or local television also grows in importance in many larger countries.

## Complexity, Structuration, and Cultural Agents

In this book, I propose an analytical structure for understanding global, regional, national, metropolitan, and provincial culture industry systems such as television. The analysis focuses on three main ideas. First, that television creation, flow, and reception are bounded but not determined by political, economic, and institutional structures. Second, those structures, plus similar structures of technology, provide resources as well as constraints for cultural agents, such as television producers and consumers. Third, that rules and patterns grow within those boundaries but are shaped both by institutions and those who work within them. The argument draws on common elements from Raymond Williams's (1980) analysis of base and superstructure, complexity theory (Prigogine & Stengers, 1984; Urry, 2003), and Anthony Giddens's (1984) analysis of structuration.

The main structuring elements for world television are: economic frameworks, technological bases, institutional forms of organization and operation, genres and forms of television content, and enduring cultural definitions and values. In terms of structuration theory (Giddens, 1984), these structural elements form boundaries within which cultural forces and agents, such as television producers, distributors, and viewers, operate. The structures of television limit what is possible. For example, commercial television systems tend to produce few documentaries, educational programs, or one-episode dramas. However, within those boundaries, the same structures also provide resources to cultural forces and agents to create and consume quite a few other kinds of television programs and other cultural products (Giddens, 1984).

Complexity theory argues against linear notions of cause and effect. Overly linear and deterministic analyses of both economic structures and technological impacts have hampered understanding (Prigogine & Stengers, 1984; Urry, 2003). A number of the main theories of international structural and cultural interaction, such as cultural imperialism and cultural dependency, have offered great insight while being at the same time overly linear and deterministic. This characteristic is shared by a number of analyses of the international and domestic impacts of technology, whether of television, satellite and cable television, or, more recently, the Internet. What complexity theory offers is a sense of complex possibilities, hard to predict exactly but bounded by certain factors, such as technology and economics, and patterned by others, such as cultural formations like genres that flow among television systems.

Complexity theory focuses on people, groups, and institutions as agents who employ strategies based on their experience with previous variations of work, watching, producing, interacting with and learning from others, and selecting/refining strategies as they go along (Axelrod & Cohen, 2000). These agents work within boundaries established by structural forces, such as economic and technological change, and previous cultural patterns that accumulate out of the history of their shared group experiences. They work with patterns established over time, which complexity theorists sometimes call fractals, small patterns that reflect larger wholes, the way a soap opera can contain both enjoyable cultural themes and commercial imperatives to buy more soap (González, 1987, 1997). For example, the historical interaction of Latin Americans with Spain and Portugal established a pattern in which media were owned by major elite families. After the nations of Latin America achieved independence, their subsequent interactions with U.S. advertisers, agencies, and networks introduced ideas of how to construct commercial television networks, based on American patterns but adapted over time to Latin American commercial realities. U.S. companies, such as Colgate-Palmolive, introduced specific genres—for example, radio and television soap operas—into Latin America to sell their soap (or other products), but local agents (producers, writers, etc.) mixed that genre with ongoing local traditions of melodrama, testing variations on audiences; over time, this resulted in the telenovela (Martín-Barbero, 1993). The telenovela bears a familial resemblance to U.S. soaps but has emerged over time as a quite distinctive form, innovative to the point where U.S. soap producers now borrow format ideas back from it (Bielby & Harrington, 2005).

Structuration is remarkably similar in key points. This theory is Giddens's (1984) effort to reconcile the effects of structures and institutions on society with the existence of agency exercised by individuals and groups, which often seem to go against the determining effects of the structures). Giddens "proposes that we consider structure as a duality including constraining rules and enabling resources" (Mosco, 1996). Working within constraining rules or boundaries imposed by structures and institutions, but with enabling resources and guiding patterns often provided by those same structures, individuals and groups produce cultural products like television, move them around the globe, and make meaning of them within other patterns provided by culture.

A complementary set of ideas comes from another sociologist, Pierre Bourdieu. He establishes several ideas that I use in this book. One is that agents can acquire and use cultural, economic, and other forms of capital from education, family, and social networks (Bourdieu, 1984, 1986). Another is that people and groups acquire and use such capital competitively in certain specific fields of endeavor, such as cultural production (Johnson, 1993) or journalism (Marlière, 1998). Another is that individuals acquire certain dispositions over time about how to acquire and use capital, and groups acquire collective dispositions that Bourdieu (1998) referred to as class or group *habitus*. Many of these ideas are useful for examining both television producers and audiences in terms of how they work within the social structures they inhabit and how they make decisions about what to produce and what to watch.

Another compatible set of ideas comes from Raymond Williams (1980), especially his discussion of classic Marxist and post-Marxist problems of structure or materialism and culture. Williams wanted to rethink Marxist analysis in which the economic bases of society were seen as determining culture outcomes; he thought this view was simplistic. As an alternative, Williams discussed the role of institutions and structures in creating rules and resources for cultural agents; television producers work with them, and audiences interpret cultural products. He also tended to view industrialization and commodification of culture as complex, constraining some forms of culture and enabling others (Hesmondalgh, in press).

Putting several of these ideas from complexity theory, Bourdieu, Giddens, and Williams together, I will emphasize several key underlying theoretical constructs. The first set has to do with different processes in how structures of economy, technology, and institutional organization affect the production of culture for television and its consumption by audiences.

*Boundaries.* A number of kinds of forces tend to create boundaries that limit, guide, and constrain (Urry, 2003). These tend be material, for example, economic or geographic limits, but can be both economic and social, such as the access of different groups of class, age, gender, and ethnicity to certain kinds of media in nonlocal languages. Common boundaries are the wealth available to finance television, access to technology for production or distribution, and limits on producers imposed by institutional models. Complexity theory emphasizes how discovering the key boundaries to a phenomenon enables understanding the limits within which that phenomenon will play out, even if the result is not precisely predictable.

*Cultural constraints or dispositions.* Culture can restrain use of a technology, as Williams (1980) observed, or an economic model. For example, some Islamic ideas on the use of human images restricted the initial use of television in Saudi Arabia and led to its abolition in Afghanistan under the Taliban. Ideology can limit acceptability of a new idea. Social democratic governments in Europe long resisted commercial television in favor of publicly owned television. Cultural dispositions, building on Bourdieu, can also lead individuals, groups, and societies in certain directions; for example, the policy tradition of the United States tends to prefer private initiatives over public ones, even when either would be acceptable under law.

*Rules.* Cultural systems tend to have either formal rules, as Williams (1980) observed, or patterns of behavior, as described by complexity theory, that condition or guide the way that culture is created. For example, professional socialization of producers/editors, institutional rules by networks or governments, and ground rules set by religion and culture all tend to define what is news or what makes for a good soap opera.

*Enabling forces and conditions.* Although any kind of structure imposes boundaries, limits, and conditions, it also tends to bring with it new ideas or resources (Williams, 1980) for cultural production and broadcasting. Advertising-based, privately owned commercial networks can disrupt an existing public service television system, but they can also bring in new resources to make more production possible, within the new limits.

*Resources.* Similarly, institutions and structures place boundaries and rules around what cultural producers can do, but they also provide resources to work with, an idea common to Williams, Giddens, and complexity theory. So the classic Hollywood studio production system might have seemed a straitjacket on creativity to some, but those who were able to work within that system made quite a remarkable number and variety of films, showing what some called "the genius of the system" (Schatz, 1988).

The second set of processes and actors has to do with how cultural actors, both producers and audiences, work within structures and how actions by those cultural agents or actors cumulate into larger patterns of culture.

*Cultural agents.* These include both producers and consumers of cultural products like television. Although people work within structures, they also constitute and recreate what is thought of as structure (Giddens, 1984). The structures of television require buildings and equipment, but the real structure is the organization and actions, person by person, of the productive processes that use the buildings and equipment.

*Patterns.* Although it isn't always easy to predict what kinds of cultural forms television will produce or what forms television institutions will take, there are patterns that tend to replicate globally, then adapt to regional, national, or local situations, as complexity theory describes for various complex systems (Urry, 2003). Patterns can be strong institutional models—for example, the pattern of commercial broadcasting that is being driven globally by economic changes—or they can be smaller patterns within that larger one, for example, the global predominance now of soap operas, music videos, talk shows, reality shows, and variety shows because these work well as program formats with newly commercialized networks and stations.

*Continuity.* Cultural patterns tend to show both stability and change. Much anthropological work tends to show a bias toward continuity in cultures despite global pressures for change (Appadurai, 1996). However, cultures are also constantly changing, both from internal forces and from external ones (Nederveen Pieterse, 2004).

*Emergent change.* Even without radical breakthroughs from outside, cultural systems tend to show gradual change from within (Urry, 2003). This is accomplished both from internal creation as people and institutions change and have ideas and from slow and gradual absorption of ideas from outside, so that change is slow and tends to be incorporated into ongoing continuities. Japan is often cited as an example of deliberate, gradual absorption of changes from outside, as when it takes American cultural forms and adapts them (Iwabuchi, 1997).

*Hybridization.* New elements from outside a culture, whether from slow gradual contact or major threshold change, tend to be adapted to local culture over time. All of the preceding forces tend to interact in a way that fosters hybridization, in most cases. Hybridization can be a genuine synthesis of different culture elements into some new culture, as with the emergence of new Latin American cultures from indigenous, African, and European roots.

*Multilayered cultures and identities.* Instead of genuine synthesis between cultural elements or parallel to it, multilayered cultures and identities can also coexist; older cultural elements survive in somewhat coherent layers while new ones are imposed or adopted over them in new layers. So cultures change in both hybrid and sedimentary ways as layers build, interact, change, and persist.

*Threshold events.* Outside forces of new technology or ideas (what Rogers, 1983, might have called *innovations*) can cause major ruptures and changes in cultural systems, like other complex systems. The structures shift after a new force enables new infrastructure with new technologies such as satellite distribution, or after new models such as commercial television change how television is conceived of and produced. Analyses of globalization emphasize many recent threshold events.

*Cataclysmic change.* Complexity theory sees some changes as extremely rapid, completely changing boundaries and patterns. Although cultures tend to persist and hang on, in many cases, change imposed from outside is cataclysmic, such that small fragile cultures simply die out or are absorbed into other larger or more powerful cultures. Dozens of small indigenous languages have died out in the past decade as speakers of the language either die off or are absorbed into other culture and language groups.

In this analysis, the chief structural factors are technological, economic, and institutional. Technology tends to enable new developments. It can also present constraints, but the result over time tends to be a layering, additive effect of new possibilities. New technologies, such as broadcast or satellite television, don't necessarily eliminate other options based on earlier technologies. For example, although VCRs and satellite/cable television make accessible to developing countries many new U.S. movies and television programs, only a small number can afford access to these technologies, and many of them don't necessarily use such technologies to watch the "new" U.S. or global content. Economic factors also both enable and limit cultural developments. Economic relations with other countries and economic growth can create new possibilities, such as bringing television broadcasting into a country. However, economic relations can also create dependencies that narrow possibilities.

At the cultural level, I focus on the formation of language and cultural communities and the creation and flow of media, particularly television, within and across those communities. The key elements in the formation of communities are their own historical dynamics, particularly the development of language and cultural themes, the creation and maintenance of group cultural identities as a locus of meaning, and cross-cultural interpersonal interactions such as travel and migration between communities. The media, the main focus of this study, build on, reinforce, and, by dint of the agency of both media producers and consumers, sometimes contradict both this cultural context and the larger structural context of economics, technology, and institutions. Both structuration and complexity emphasize that human agency and even aggregate social forces are sometimes hard to predict based on structural or even cultural forces.

Culture is clearly more than a force acted on by technologies such as television and economic patterns such as advertising. Social forces, such as the migration of people across countries and regions, have powerful effects on the cultural and social context of television, economic actors, and forces. Although these social and cultural forces are driven by economic and political factors, they also have powerful effects of their own, once set in motion. Appadurai (1996), for example, saw the major social ruptures and transformations attributed to modernization and globalization as driven by migration and media. Chapter 2 explores this process of hybridization, the synthesis of local cultures with the imported elements of culture brought in by globalization, through specific processes such as electronic media, migration, inflow of genres and models, and entrepreneurial action of global or regional companies.

An important question is whether the different levels raised here are relatively independent or whether some are rather more conditioned, if not determined, by others. Appadurai (1996) argued that media interactions diverge—or are disjunct, in his terms—from economics, technology, politics, and people flows. He noted,

> Global flows occur in and through the growing disjunctures among ethn-oscapes, technoscapes, financescapes, mediascapes and ideoscapes. This formulation, the core of my model of global cultural flow, needs some explanation. First, people, machinery, money, images, and ideas now follow increasingly non-isomorphic paths; of course, there have been some disjunctures in the flows of these things, but the sheer speed, scale, and volume of these flows now are so great that the disjunctures become central to the politics of global culture. (Appadurai, 1996, p. 37)

In this book, I argue, however, that cultural factors such as migration and media content flows are not truly independent from structural factors such as economics, technology, and institutional structures. There are separate developments and relative degrees of autonomy, owing to the kind of complexity and disjuncture that Appadurai perceives. But factors such as economics and technology affect cultural factors such as migration, historical development, and media relatively more often than vice versa. Political economists certainly argue the primacy of economics, and a number of scholars from McLuhan (1994) to Postman (1986) have argued for the primacy of technology as a determining factor.

This current chapter presents a tentative model that summarizes the relative positioning of the structural and cultural factors. In this model, the structural and cultural factors influence each other, but the relative weight of the structural factors is slightly higher. This is deliberately intended to be not a strong statement of determination but a more complex statement of the asymmetric interdependence of factors that influence each other at multiple levels. Structural factors, such as economic conditions or technological changes, are more likely to either limit or enable changes in cultural factors than vice versa. A new technology like the printing press creates a series of new social possibilities. However, cultural factors affect structural factors, too. Some technological changes have been put off by cultures that could not absorb them or found that they clashed too strongly with cultural values.

For example, the printing press was much more revolutionary in Western Europe, where a series of economic and cultural factors favored it, than in China or Korea, where it was also invented but where cultural and other factors did not favor its rapid diffusion. Even more dramatically, Japanese military culture largely gave up use of guns between 1543 and 1879, even after they had been proven decisively useful in battle, because they strongly threatened the dominant samurai culture (Perrin, 1979).

These structural and cultural factors interact. They often affect each other strongly, with some primacy to the structural factors. Both sets of factors influence and condition both structural and cultural interactions. Structural interactions might range from colonialism or imperialism to interdependence. Cultural interactions might range from homogenization to hybridization.

There are several important structural and cultural factors. These factors both bound and enable developments in the cultural factors. Within cultural factors, I emphasize migration, media, and cultural history or internal development of cultures over time. Although these factors are bounded and enabled by the structural factors, the cultural factors also form patterns that can bound or enable structural developments.

There are also a number of possible modes of interaction at both structural and cultural levels. This book examines several possible modes of structural interaction between societies, including colonialism, imperialism, dependency, and the mode that this study sees as ascendant in increasing numbers of interactions between societies, asymmetrical interdependence. These structural forms of interaction also create boundaries that limit forms of culture. This book also examines several possible modes of cultural interaction between and within cultures. These include penetration, one-way flows of products and influences, homogenization, interpenetration or two-way flows, hybridization, and the formation of multiple layers of culture. In complexity terms, these could be seen as patterns of interaction that tend to play out and replicate at different levels of the world television system.

All of these forms of interaction can be found in the relationships between different societies at this time. A few societies are still in a colonial relationship with a dominant state; for example, Guam, Surinam, and a number of small island societies. Many recently independent countries, such as the French-speaking countries of West Africa, still find themselves dependent in both structural and cultural relations with former colonial powers, in this case, France. Even countries with longer histories of independence, such as those of Latin America, often find themselves dependent in many ways, not necessarily on former colonial powers such as Spain or Portugal, but on currently dominant powers such as the United States. However, I argue that although imperialism and dependency may characterize the structural relations of a significant number of societies, the tendency over time is toward asymmetrical interdependence: relationships that are increasingly interactive or interdependent but often highly unequal. Societies' relations also change so that a country may well move from colonial status to dependency on the former colonial power to a more interdependent but still unequal or asymmetrical relationship. These trajectories vary. In the early growth period of television in the 1960s, Brazil imported much of its television programming from the United States. Imports declined in the 1970s and 1980s as Brazil's own productive capacity grew; Brazil produced large numbers of television programs and began to export them. Brazil is now a dominant exporter to Portugal of cultural products. Mozambique, another former Portuguese colony, is far more dependent on Portugal (than is Brazil) and even somewhat dependent, especially in cultural imports, on Brazil.

At the cultural level, interactions between societies also clearly vary. Almost all societies are now penetrated by outside cultures, but many increasingly put some influence back out to those that have penetrated them, in a form of asymmetric cultural interpenetration. Robertson (1995) talked about the cultural interpenetration of the global or universal and the local or particular as one of the predominant cultural patterns of current globalization. Many countries have been and still are on the receiving end of largely one-way flows of culture and information. This was highlighted during the New World Information and Communication Order debate in the 1970s and 1980s, which noted that flows of television, film, music, news, and data between countries tended to be very unequal, even one-way (UNESCO, 1980). In some areas, notably feature film and news, this extremely asymmetric flow still seems to predominate. However, since the 1970s, an increasing number of countries have begun to create more of their own television, video, music, blogs, and Web sites, to produce local, national, or regional cultural goods. In some cases, these smaller producers can export cultural goods back into the world or regional systems. In this book, I argue that few cultures are effectively homogenized by outside forces, but that hybridization of local and foreign cultural elements and forms is increasingly common. This builds on the idea of Robertson (1995) that cultures are increasingly *glocal,* placing local elements within globalized forms or other combinations of the global and the local.

## Structural and Cultural Process Frameworks for World Television

This book looks at globalizing, regionalizing, nationalizing, and localizing forces that include both structure and culture. At all of these levels, alternative structural process or interaction frameworks ought to be considered. These include a number of the theoretical models that have been created to analyze international media interactions: colonialism, imperialism, dependency, and asymmetrical interdependence. Several alternative cultural process types have also tried to capture the essence of cross-cultural interaction via media. These include the initial penetration of cultures by outside cultures, homogenization, one-way flow or interaction, interpenetration, cultural proximity, and hybridization.

## Colonialism and Imperialism

Cultures have rarely been completely isolated. Even before the European expansion in the 1400s, there was considerable trade and contact between many, if not most cultures. Abu-Lughod (1993) is among the scholars who have argued that, before 1492, there was in fact a world system of loosely interconnected regional empires in what are now Africa, the Arabic world, central Asia, China, Egypt, Europe, India, Iran, Japan, Russia, and Southeast Asia, a point discussed further in Chapter 2 of this book.

From 1492 (or earlier, in the case of Portuguese expansion into Africa) onward, however, the European powers raced to create empires, which in several cases spanned the globe. They colonized many formerly independent areas as well as many that were already parts of other empires. These European empires greatly affected the earlier regional and national cultures, but that impact varied. The European empires went further, in some cases, creating new areas and nations with hybrid cultures, such as English-speaking North America and Spanish-speaking South America. Chapter 2 also describes this cultural hybridization process and how it forms a number of the other major cultural-linguistic markets for television.

## Cultural Imperialism

One dominant tendency in international television research has been to examine the global development of media as cultural aspects of U.S. and European imperialism. This builds on the idea that although most countries are now independent of the formal colonialism that once characterized most of the world's societies, even these technically independent countries are caught up in a postcolonial web of cultural imperialism. In this view, deriving from Marx and from Lenin's analysis of imperialism, culture and communication are seen as the ideological superstructure of the world capitalist economy's expansion.

In this relationship of cultural imperialism, the role of culture, including television production, is both economic and ideological. Television can be seen as another product sold at high prices by First World producers to Third World consumers, although as we shall see, the reality of international television sales and flows is considerably more complex than that. The ideological role of television is to make Third World residents content with their lot as lower paid consumers of First World products.

Cultural imperialism usually makes strong claims about the social or behavioral effects of media, advertising, and other cultural forces. This theoretical concept tends to see culture as only part of a holistic system, in which imported television programs, local adaptations of U.S. genres, local and imported advertising, and commercial media models all combine to produce an attitude favoring increased consumption among viewers (Schiller, 1991). The main specific critiques, according to Tomlinson (1991), are that capitalism is a homogenizing culture force and that capitalism produces and reproduces a culture of consumerism. I agree that these to be very likely macro or high-level effects of the globalization of television within a capitalist world system. However, Chapter 3 argues that these complex effects operate differently among various nations and various classes within nations.

## Postcolonial National Television

In almost all countries, television formed part of postcolonial development. Regular television broadcasting began to arrive in the 1940s in some of the world's most industrialized countries. Some began to pass their patterns of broadcasting on to their colonies or former colonies. However, most countries began television later, as post–World War II economic development permitted them to afford it. This meant that television in most newly independent countries was, in fact, still highly dependent on their former colonial powers or others.

After independence, most countries fell into structural relationships that could be characterized as dependent. Most of the countries in Africa, Asia, Latin America, and the Middle East were described this way, as were some smaller European countries. These nations depended on the industrialized world for capital, technology, models, and most imported goods. Speaking primarily of Latin America, Fox (1992) observed that "cultural dependency generally was taken to mean the domination of content, financing, and advertising of the domestic media by foreign, specifically U.S. companies" (p. 4).

Some theorists veered away from the holistic explanations and the degree of economic determinism implied in dependency and cultural imperialism theories, but they wished to build on many of these ideas. Lee (1980) focused on several interrelated factors: financial or ownership involvement by First World companies in Third World media, the adoption and use of First

World media models, the uneven flow of media products (particularly television) from First World to Third World, and the effect of both imported models and programs on Third World cultures. Chapter 3 examines how television developed in a variety of nations, with different levels of dependency or growth and autonomy, along with varying forms of adaptation and hybridization of foreign influences.

Another key research tradition focuses on cultural industries. The original research by Horkheimer and Adorno (2001) focused strongly on the power and integration of what they saw as a monolithic culture industry that tended to change culture into a mass culture that reinforces capitalist consumer ideology. This research analysis had a powerful effect in Latin America, Europe, and the United States, where powerful national cultural industries were growing. Quite a bit of current research on the conglomeration and integration of cultural industries such as Time Warner follows this theme (McChesney, 1999). However, Latin American scholars (Martín-Barbero, 1993) and others have also begun to use this basic framework to look at aspects other than power and conglomeration: the way national production has grown in some countries rather than others and incorporation of global models in national industries (Sinclair, 1995). Chapter 3 also looks at this body of research.

## Globalization

Many observers from journalism, industry, and the academy have noticed a rapid global penetration of recent economic and technological changes. For many, and from diverse angles, globalization is now the new dominant paradigm. They look at "flows of goods, people, information, knowledge and images" which "gain autonomy at a global level" and at "third cultures" of people who are more than national or bilateral in orientation (Featherstone, 1990a, p. 1). For those who stress political economy, globalization is the extension to the whole world of capitalism, the consumer economy, advertising, and concentrated ownership of media groups such as Bertelsmann, Sony, and Murdoch (Herman & McChesney, 1997). Featherstone (1990a) saw globalization as "cultural integration and disintegration processes which take place not only on an inter-state level but processes which transcend the state-society unit and can therefore be held to occur on a transnational or transocietal level" (p. 1). Writing about globalization tends also to incorporate postmodern perspectives in focusing less on homogenizing processes, such as media imperialism or Americanization, and more on a diverse set of processes, codes, symbols, and cultural products that can be both local and globalized (Featherstone, 1990a).

A good example of this process is advertising. The roots of the current global trends in advertising can be traced to the U.S. advertising industry, which created a prototype of organization; models for newspaper, radio, and television ads; and a general model of how advertising might fit into an industrial economy and a consumer society. This model and the specific ad prototypes have been widely diffused, first by U.S. firms moving into new markets where they wanted to advertise, then by U.S. advertising agencies that followed their clients, and finally by professionals from other countries who were trained by U.S. firms and advertising agencies. This process struck a number of observers as direct Americanization and dependency on the United States (Fox, 1975; Janus, 1977). However, various countries, including China and Japan (Iwabuchi, 2002), have modified advertising-based media models and further diffused those modified models to other countries. The modifications feed back into the increasing number of global actors, U.S., European, Japanese, and others. A slightly different global style emerges, along with very different adaptations of the advertising idea. All of these models still serve to promote an increasingly global consumer economy, but they are both generalized to the world and specified to various localities, well beyond direct dependence on the original U.S. companies, agencies, and models.

There is a general movement away from deterministic views of the political economy of television (Martín-Barbero, 1993). In this book, I use complexity theory and structuration as means of considering structural power without falling into determinism. It is important to neither under- nor overestimate structural power because these political economy analyses correctly stress the importance of ownership, class relations, and other economic factors in the shaping of television at world, regional, and local levels. Chapter 4, which discusses the creation of global media firms and the new global patterns and models for television, covers in more depth theories of globalization and presents a model for understanding the asymmetrical interdependence of world television.

## Roles and Impacts of Technology

Chapter 4 focuses primarily on the political-economic aspects of globalization, which are usually seen as fundamental for understanding the resulting recent rapid changes. However, equally central to most analyses of globalization is the equally rapid, widespread impact of technologies of communication, covered in Chapter 5. Since the mid-1990s, much of that fascination with technological globalization has focused on the Internet. However, before many knew of the Internet, the new technologies of satellite and cable television held the world's attention and fears for decades (de Sola Pool, 1983). Many expected technologies such as satellites to facilitate the next wave of cultural imperialism (de Sola Pool, 1979; Jayakar, 1993; Oliveira, 1986), and indeed, many still fear exactly that, although now most speak of a more complex scenario of both global and regional satellite forces, such as the relationship between global CNN and regional Al-Jazeera (Kraidy, 2002).

Much of the fear of change focused on satellite and cable television distribution, particularly their potential for carrying television programs and channels across borders. However, equally significant is the technological potential in changes that enable much cheaper and more flexible production and distribution. Production technology in video and sound has dropped dramatically in cost and gone up dramatically in quality. For example, a broadcast-quality production camera, which is also portable enough for exterior production, can be had for well under $5,000. A broadcast-quality editing system can be had for $5,000 or less. High-quality sound recording and simple but adequate mixing equipment can be had for under $3,000.

Another key issue with technology impacts as part of globalization is to ascertain who in what culture actually has access to what technology. When speaking of computers and the Internet, statements from world forums like the World Summit on the Information Society (2003–2005) clearly see that most people in the world do not have access to these new communication technologies, which greatly diminishes the potential impact they have as part of globalization (ITU, 2006). However, many of those concerned about impacts of satellite and cable television technology fail to recognize that most people in the world do not have access to them either because they cannot afford them, because governments like China restrict access to them, or because they are sufficiently satisfied with broadcast television that they choose not to pay for access to them.

## Asymmetrical Interdependence and Asymmetrical Cultural Interpenetration: A Proposed Model

To move beyond the original limitations of dependency and imperialism theories, some of their main points were incorporated while complexity was added to their approaches. In this book, I reinterpret the term *asymmetrical interdependence* (Galtung, 1971) to refer to the variety of possible relationships in which countries find themselves unequal but possessing variable degrees of power and initiative in politics, economics, technological capability, and culture (Straubhaar, 1991). This view builds on the concept of dependent development, in which dependency may direct or limit national growth but growth or development can take place (Cardoso, 1973; Salinas & Paldan, 1979). While the structural context, problems, and constraints for much of the world's media that dependency theory pointed out should be analyzed, consideration must also be given to the development of cultural industries that show increasing aspects of interdependence by creating more cultural products, adapting and changing cultural product models, and exporting both. This concept also builds on ideas of globalization, viewing global, regional, national, and local actors as part of an interdependency that is dynamic but asymmetrical, with growth and change in uneven and changing degrees. Nation-states and national-level actors have a continuing role, but so do local, supranational, regional, and transnational actors.

This vision moves beyond looking at world cultural and economic relations using dichotomies between dependence and independence or narrow typologies, such as core, semiperipheral, and peripheral countries. In this book, I anticipate a broad range of possibilities between relative autonomy of the sort enjoyed by the United States and relatively strong dependence such as that suffered by the smaller countries of the Caribbean. Rather than one range of possibilities, several interrelated levels or kinds of relationships between nations or cultures were considered, on dimensions analogous to Appadurai's (1990) scapes. For example, a nation like Brazil might depend on others for the manufacture of the more sophisticated information and communication technologies, which restricts its possibilities, but still be relatively autonomous in using the communications and cultural content of those imported technologies as enabling tools to create new forms of culture. Other nations might predominantly import both technologies and content, but perhaps from very different countries; for example, the Dominican Republic imports technology from the United States and Japan and content from the United States and Mexico.

Building on Appadurai's (1990) idea of disjuncture, I propose several levels of interaction between cultures in the world: political-economic, technological, cultural production, content, content flows, and reception of culture. Many previous analyses of these problems fail in part because they look only at one level, such as political economy or media effects, without considering the others. On the other hand, Appadurai's analysis may overestimate the disjuncture or separation between these levels of interaction. There are relationships between political and economic systems, technologies, cultural producers and media institutions, and receivers of cultural and media products. Correspondingly, there is a range of levels of causation or explanation for both structural and cultural issues.

Having reviewed some of the main international structural interaction models, I must examine some of the cultural models or theories that have tried to capture the essence of cross-cultural interaction via media, including television flows and television genre development, television producer-audience understandings and interactions, cultural proximity, theories of cultural action and choice (such as Bourdieu), hybridization, and the formation of multilayered cultures and identities. The question of the emergence of hybrid and multiple identities among television viewers is covered more thoroughly in Chapter 9.

## Imported TV Versus Local and National: Producers Localize, Glocalize, and Hybridize

Nearly all societies and cultures have been affected by outside cultural influences, and few have ever been free from outside cultural influence. Extensive contacts between cultures (Nederveen Pieterse, 2004) have long existed. A combination of economic and technological changes in the 20th century have enabled mass media to reach many, if not most of the people in the world. Radio, film, television, satellite TV, and the Internet have all increased the rate of contact between societies. Radio and television, in particular, have brought most people into greater contact with the worlds outside their culture.

By the 1960s and 1970s, this technological penetration seemed to have resulted in dramatically increased, largely one-way flows of film, music, news, and television programs from the United States and Europe to other countries (Guback & Varis, 1986; Nordenstreng & Schiller, 1979; Nordenstreng & Varis, 1974; Stevenson & Shaw, 1984). In 1974, Nordenstreng and Varis concluded that most of the world imported most its television programming, which was mostly entertainment and mostly from the United States. These one-way flows seemed a primary symptom of cultural dependence and media imperialism (Beltran & Fox de Cardona, 1979; Lee, 1980).

However, there is evidence, as the tables in the Appendix reveal, that the flows of television have changed considerably in the past 30 years. This study of 26 countries in 1962, 1972, 1982, 1992, and 2002 shows that television schedules in most countries, particularly during the prime-time hours, are increasingly filled by programming from within the country in question or from within its cultural-linguistic region or space.

Some commercial program genres in television and music have become relatively cheap to record and produce. Some genres, such as talk shows, live local news, live music, and live variety shows, are often cheaper for a poor country than importing a situation comedy from the United States, according to interviews with producers in the Dominican Republic and Mozambique.

These genres have replicated as patterns across countries and are adapted to fit local circumstances, budgets, and audience interests

Chapter 6 examines how national or local producers have worked within cultural industries to produce television. It examines several more theories of globalization, localization, glocalization, reconfiguration (Ricoeur, 1984), and hybridization, relating them directly to how television producers and programmers might think about what to produce, what to import, where to import it from, what to export, and how to adapt television produced for one culture to the interests and demands of the audiences in another one.

Chapter 7 looks at the production and exportation of programs, genres and even whole channels, such as MTV or Discovery. It examines some theories of how programs get altered for export, such as delocalization, and it reviews what is still primarily exported from the United States both in terms of total flow and of genres. The turn from exporting programs and channels to exporting formats, such as *Jeopardy* or *American Idol,* is also covered.

Increasingly, when poor countries import much of their programming, it no longer primarily comes in a one-way flow from the United States. The Dominican Republic has imported many genres, such as comedies, variety shows, and news, from Mexico (Rogers & Schement, 1984; Straubhaar & Viscasillas, 1991), just as Mozambique imports entertainment from both Brazil and the United States. This constitutes a more complex flow. Programming now flows horizontally from one developing country to another quite frequently. Some programs even flow back to the United States and Europe. Brazilian television now tends to dominate the prime-time programming of its former colonial power, Portugal (Marques de Melo, 1988, 1992; Pinto & Sousa, 2004). Mexico has long dominated the television and radio programming of the Hispanic audience in the United States (Fernández & Paxman, 2001). The overall flow is still asymmetric, but there is now an interpenetration of cultures, both by migration and by media, which flows largely from developed North to the developing South but increasingly flows back as well.

Many countries now import television genres for national production almost as much (or in some cases, more) than they import television programs. Some genre imports come as formal economic contracts, licensing formats such as *Big Brother.* Others are simply imported and glocalized or adapted by local producers, as Chapters 6 and 7 document. When countries produce more and import less, at least for broadcast television, the flow of television genres such as the soap opera and, recently, prepackaged television formats such as *American Idol* becomes even more important. Instead of importing an entire canned program, networks today tend to import a genre idea to develop themselves, or a virtually turnkey package for a program like *Survivor* or *Popstars,* which provides a complete formula for a local production or version. The question, then, is how much global economic or cultural baggage comes along with such a formula and how relevant to local culture the resulting production is. Chapter 7 addresses these issues.

This book reports the decline of importation into many of these countries of television programming from the former centers of media flow, the United States and Europe. A more subtle reading of the pattern over time seems to indicate that relatively new television broadcasting operations, particularly commercial ones, tend to use more imported U.S. programming because it is cheap and they lack programming resources, personnel, and experience. Smaller, poorer markets import more television for the same reasons. As television becomes more firmly established, national stations and networks tend to produce more of their own material. However, since the rise of transnational format licensing, an increasing amount of that local or national production is based on local adaptation of transnational formats, such as *American Idol* (Moran, 2004).

Regional producers also tend to grow in the kinds of major television production centers that Curtin (2003) calls media capitals. These global television centers—Cairo, Hong Kong, Mexico City, and Tokyo—produce for their own national markets but also export to their cultural-linguistic markets and, increasingly, to networks around the world. So for smaller national and local networks, increasing amounts of imported programming tends to come from within their own cultural-linguistic regions (Sinclair, 1994, 1995). Chapters 6 and 7 examine these changing patterns of broadcast television flow.

In film and news, the flows are still more consistently one-way. Film distribution in most countries is still dominated by the United States. Similarly, screen time in most countries is still largely North American (Miller et al., 2005). U.S., British, and French news agencies, plus a few new satellite and television services such as CNN and the BBC, still dominate global news flows, although regional rivals like Al-Jazeera now dominate some cultural-linguistic or regional news spaces. Particularly with the Internet, more diverse flows of news material seems possible, although critics note that many Internet news readers visit the same dominant corporate sites, such as CNN or the *New York Times* (McChesney, 1999). More sources for news stories are available, but it is not clear that news media are really using them yet.

## Cultural Identification and Proximity

Competing with the idea of cultural imperialism have been the ideas of cultural identification with various cultures, nations, and regions and cultural proximity (Straubhaar, 1991), which would lead people to choose local, nonimperial cultural products. In some ways, this is the cultural analog of the structural idea of asymmetrical interdependence. Cultures tend to interact, even though unevenly and in conditions of even more unequal political and economic power. Although a powerful culture can impose on a less powerful one, forcing it to adopt certain customs, ideas, and forms such as television programs and genres, the less powerful culture can often still resist and maintain much of its original form and content. This has been discussed even more in terms of hybridity, which is examined below.

One theoretical description and explanation for this change to more local, national, and cultural-linguistic regional program production revolves around cultural proximity. This is a seemingly common attraction audiences feel for cultural products, such as television or music, that are close in cultural content and style to the audience's own culture(s). Most audiences seem to prefer television programs that are as close to them as possible in language, ethnic appearance, dress, style, humor, historical reference, and shared topical knowledge. This is not necessarily a national phenomenon. Audiences can be attracted or feel proximities to local culture, regional cultures within their nation, national culture, and transnational cultural regions or spaces. This is explored further in Chapters 8 and 9.

The clearest line of demarcation in cultural proximity is language. Schlesinger (1987) showed in Europe, for example, that differences of language and culture create effective barriers to television program trade between countries, even when the larger European Community is promoting intra-European television trade and pan-European productions. For programs that rely more on language-based understanding, such as talk shows, game shows, soap operas, comedies, and variety shows, much of the audience in most cultures does not have the cultural capital to understand and enjoy such programs from another culture or country, even when they are dubbed and language, per se, is not a problem. This kind of cultural capital is the familiarity based in language, education, or travel that enables someone to understand a language- and culture-based (as opposed to more purely visual) program from elsewhere. For example, many Americans just don't get British humor on television, even when it has a strong visual component, like Monty Python, because the cultural references are beyond their sense of comfort and interest, based in their cultural capital. The author interviewed one Brazilian satellite entrepreneur who planned in the 1980s to create a pan–Latin American television channel in English, based on U.S. talk and news magazine shows such as *Oprah* and *20/20*. When asked about her intended audience, she specified those who had fluent English, traveled once or twice a year to the United States, and had probably lived, worked, or studied in the United State or those who aspired to do so—in essence, a small and elite group with quite unusual and quite U.S.-focused cultural capital for people within the Latin American cultural context. This intended audience was much too small to be profitable, and her satellite venture failed.

Studies in Brazil (Duarte, 1997; Straubhaar, 1991, 2003), Dominican Republic (Straubhaar, 1991), and Namibia (Veii, 1988) all indicate that aside from a small elite with truly globalized cultural capital, most audiences of the lower middle class and below are more interested in cultural products, particularly television and music (but seemingly not necessarily film), which are as culturally relevant or proximate as possible. This seems to indicate a preference, first, for local, provincial, or national material when available; and second, for material from within a region defined by culture and language, where cultural products will also be more similar to the cultural capital or cultural frame of the audience than cultural imports from outside the region, like those from the United States or Europe.

This tendency toward guiding cultural choices based on cultural proximity seems strong, but most members of a society are also interested in some amount of diversity and difference as well. A certain number of television programs or songs from completely outside seem to continue to be popular, in part because they represent a source of novelty and new ideas. Even in countries with strong production industries and cultural markets strongly oriented toward national products—for example, Brazil—a few imported programs and films can usually be found on television, even in prime time, because they have interest value or competing senses of proximity for the audience, even though they no longer represent a dominant trend of one-way importation. The increasingly complex relationship between audiences with multiple levels or identity and interest, and the multiple genre offerings of different levels of world television, are examined in Chapter 8.

## Cultural Hybridization

Within certain economic constraints and influenced by successful global patterns, however, regional and national cultures still tend to assert their own content strongly. What emerges is often a strongly localized or hybridized adaptation of global patterns (Kraidy, 2005). For example, there is much current discussion of an Asian approach to modernity. In Taiwan, Iwabuchi (1997, 2002), interviewing young people, found that they were more likely to choose and identify with popular music and television from Japan than from China because the Japanese material was viewed as modern while still recognizably familiar within an Asian context. He argued that Japanese popular culture successfully adapts or "Asianizes" U.S. popular culture genres into more localized or regionalized forms.

One useful theorization is to reconsider globalization as a set of regionally differentiated patterns of modernization. Japanese popular culture and cultural industry represents a transformation from the perception of the 1970s that "the media are American" (Tunstall, 1977). Instead, globalized and regionalized patterns of modernity build on, but also transform U.S. patterns of modernity, in this case in media, that seemed so specifically American in the first wave of U.S. television program export dominance in the 1960s and 1970s. For example, Iwabuchi (1997), in "*The Sweet Scent of Asian Modernity,*" described the Japanese adaptation of cultural industry globalization as de-Westernized modernization (Iwabuchi, 1997). This is a hybrid localization or regionalization of a global pattern.

Hybridization has been one of the ideas most strongly developed and argued over within globalization and postcolonial theories about culture. It was formulated in several major variations. The form most worked with in this book is by Canclini (1995), who looked at how hybrid cultures, along with racial miscegenation or *mestizaje,* had emerged in Latin America throughout its 300 or more years of Spanish and Portuguese colonial history. He observed a great deal of complex blending of cultures that continues, changing as new forms of interaction, such as mass media, come into the process. Another important strand is from Bhabha (1994), who examined the complex hybrid identities and roles of intellectuals and cultural producers in postcolonial situations, where they must deal with multiple cultural forces whether they remained in their homelands or immigrated to economic core nations, such as the United States or Great Britain. Kraidy (2005) saw hybridization as the essential mechanism of cultural globalization.

Notably, some examples that were seen as archetypes of cultural hybridization, or the related syncretism of religions, are being rethought. Brazilian *candomblé,* for example, was thought to be a classic example of genuine synthesis between some of the religious traditions of West Africa and Portuguese Catholicism (Bastide, 1978). *Candomblé,* however, is varied. Although some groups intend to make a genuine synthesis of these elements, others see the European elements as a protective covering for African practices, which were useful when the groups were repressed by religious or civil authorities but which can be discarded or minimized now, in favor of a pursuit of a more roots-oriented, Afrocentric practice. That cultural practice and identity exist in parallel to other layers of practice and identity.

In turn, Chapter 9 develops a theoretical notion of multiple cultural strands, television flows and identities that tend to work out alongside hybridization, or in some cases, in place of hybridization. This reflects the fact that people interviewed for Chapters 8 and 9 often describe their own complex identities as multilayered areas of interest and identification. People are likely to have local television viewing interests, corresponding to local identifications, as well as regional, national, and transnational or global ones. They are also likely to have viewing interests that reflect class, ethnic, gender, religious, and other identities. To some degree, these identifications reflect positions that have been structured for them, such as class. In a post-colonial situation, identities are often structured in interaction with colonial powers, including religious and ethnic identities, whereas other identities may correspond to rapidly changing social movements. All are dynamic, not static. None can be essentialized or frozen in time.

# 2

# Hybridization and the Roots of Transnational, Geocultural, and Cultural-Linguistic Markets

Much current globalization research looks at the spatial or geographic extension of change across the world, driven by technology and economics. How do those global forces interact with the structures, cultures, and tendencies already present? Sometimes, fascination with globalization leads scholars to overestimate its force relative to other historical forces already in play (Ferguson, 1992). Other views argue that the synthesis or hybridization over time of local historical forces and new international or global forces is the fundamental aspect of globalization (Kraidy, 2005; Nederveen Pieterse, 2004).

In this chapter, I focus first on the already ongoing historical patterns of culture, social structure, and economy into which global change arrives. The new forces expanding across space meet older forces developed locally across time. According to Giddens (1991), Robertson (1995), and others, globalization has both a spatial and a temporal dimension. Social structures that have been taken for granted for centuries in many places—for example, the nation-state—are nevertheless built over much earlier social structures: kingdoms, empires, and flows of people, ideas, and technologies. Nederveen Pieterse (2004) noted, "We come to see nation states as a *grid* [emphasis in the original] that has been temporarily superimposed upon a deeper and ongoing stratum of human migrations and diasporas" (p. 34).

Second, I focus in this chapter on hybridization and multiple layers and flows of culture. Television works at a variety of levels, including global, regional, national, and local. I particularly examine the roots of geocultural and transnational cultural-linguistic markets in prenational and colonial history. However, defining culture at all these levels is the process of hybridization. In many ways, this is the most fundamental and enduring of the processes that surround world television. Most of the cultures that produce or receive world television reflect centuries or more of mixing and synthesizing together a variety of local and foreign cultural forces.

Hybridization is key to understanding the historical dimension of globalization. I build here on Nederveen Pieterse (2004), who argued that in the long run *(longue durée),* which is to say historically and over time, globalization essentially *is* hybridity. This reflects a perspective based in two sets of theory. First, culture is viewed as one of the forces that helps structure society, placing boundaries, creating resources, and setting patterns that guide social actors (Giddens, 1984; Williams, 1980). Second, a gradual process of cultural construction of society over time is posited (Berger & Luckmann, 1967), particularly the cultural and social construction or shaping of how technologies are actually implemented (Dutton, 1999).

Specifically, cultures have evolved historically at several levels. Historically, local cultures come first. In many times and places, local culture in a village or an extended family was all that people knew. And local culture is still important to almost everyone; even those who spend a lot of time traveling live in neighborhoods somewhere, and usually cherish local music, restaurants, pubs, coffeehouses, or other aspects of the local life. Next to arrive are subnational regional cultures, which were the dominant force in many eras, often persisting as tribal cultures that subsume a number of localities or as religious, ethnic, or linguistic minorities that give a state or province a distinct identity; for example, Catalonia within Spain, Kerala or Tamil Nadu within India, or Quebec within Canada. These cultures and identities seem to be resurging in importance, as subnational conflicts in areas like the former Yugoslavia reflect. In fact, the forces of identity formation linked to those cultures are often more powerful than the collective identities of the nations that have tried to subsume them, as the experience of the former Yugoslavia also reflects. In other places, the nation survives, but long-standing local identities drive the rising importance of television systems at the state level, as in India since the 1990s (Kumar, 2006).

Coming third historically are larger transnational cultural-linguistic regions, which take in several current nations (Wilkinson, 1995). Some of these are geographically defined, contiguous geocultural regions, like greater China or the Arabic-speaking world, which share borders, history, language, and often religions, government traditions, and so on. Such regions often historically precede the nations that have been subsequently carved out of them. In many ways, these regions continue to evolve cultural conditions to which nations or more recent global actors must respond. The common Spanish heritage of most of Latin America creates conditions for a cultural-linguistic market, and both national television powers, such as Televisa of Mexico, or global ones, such as Rupert Murdoch's communications empire (partnered with Televisa in Sky Latin America), must respond. Similarly, the combined heritage of Arabic language and development within the Islamic religion and culture(s) created a cultural-linguistic market within which Al-Jazeera or Orbit can operate. Beside these kinds of geocultural spaces, there are also geographically disconnected, transnational cultural-linguistic markets, connected by language, colonial cultural heritages, inherited philosophical and administrative traditions, and so on but not necessarily by ethnicity, religion, or regional culture; an example is all the places that speak English as a first language.

Fourth on the time line are national cultures, asserted by some nation-states since early recorded history (China or Egypt), by several since the end of the Middle Ages in Europe, and by many former colonies after World War II. Much has been written about how globalization challenges and reduces the powers of the nation-state. However, my empirical research, described in Chapter 7, indicates that most broadcast television is still produced and watched at the national level, even as the other levels, such as local or global, make slow inroads into national primacy over television. In fact, production and viewing of television seem to be increasing faster at the national level than at the others, as smaller and poorer nations begin to make more of their own television.

Fifth in line are transnational institutions, companies, and flows of people (as migrants), media products, religions, and values. These act across the borders of a world that has been dominated since 1945 by many nation-states. Their importance comes both from the continuance of prenational geocultural forces, such as the languages and cultures of greater China, and from new entities that see the need or opportunity to address people across national borders, which often seem artificial. These new entities include non-profit or nongovernmental organizations (NGOs), for example, the regional human rights groups in Asia or Eastern Europe, and companies that see an opportunity for new business, for example, Indian businessmen who broadcast television via satellite back to India from Singapore to get around national restrictions on commercial channels.

Finally come global actors and flows of technology, finance, and culture. There are even increasing indications of a global culture, per se, particularly when focused specifically on areas such as global consumer culture or global youth culture. More often, however, global technologies, resources, and ways of doing things are combined with cultures and forces from other levels, in what Robertson (1995) calls *glocalization* and others call *hybridity* (Canclini, 1995).

## Precolonial Cultural History and Television

Abu-Lughod (1993) argued that too much of the analysis of globalization focuses on the effects of European colonialism: the world after 1492. There were significant cultures before 1492 at local, national, and cultural-linguistic or regional levels, and these still define many of the essential characteristics of the cultural markets for television in 2006.

There were partially overlapping regional systems of empire, trade, and religious and cultural influence. Some of these constituted significant empires of millions of people, influencing cultures in profound ways. The Islamic world stretched from Indonesia to Spain, a world system of its own that invaded Europe and actively combated and survived the spread of European colonialism. China was the center of a vast geocultural system that profoundly influenced cultures from Southeast Asia to parts of what is now Russia to Japan. The Hindu religion, social system, and culture of what is now India was the center of another geocultural system in South and Southeast Asia, interpenetrated in many places with Islam. These regional systems created the historical roots of some of the main geocultural television markets in the world today: the Arab world, Hindi South Asia, greater China, East Asia, and Southeast Asia. All of them build on spatially defined regional developments that preceded European colonialism. Most of the other regional or transnational systems, such as Latin America, the Anglophone world (United States, Canada, Australia, and so on), the Francophone states (France, parts of West Africa, and so on), and the Lusophone world (Brazil, Portugal, Angola, Mozambique), were in fact largely the result of European colonial expansion. Some of those are geocultural geographic units, but several are dispersed transnational cultural-linguistic markets usually defined by colonial language groups: Anglophone, Francophone, and Lusophone.

In fact, until quite recently, it made more sense to talk of geocultural or cultural-linguistic regions than nations in many parts of the world. The idea of the nation-state developed in Western Europe after 1492, in fact, and spread slowly to other parts of the world (Smith, 1993). So while scholars can talk of the early regional roots of modern Indian culture, they have to recognize that India, Brazil, and other national units are recent, modern creations. In fact, that is why this book starts historically with local cultures and geocultural and cultural-linguistic regions (in this chapter) and only then turns to nations and their modern cultural industries (Chapter 3).

Looking at the world before 1492 also shows how the pattern of hybridization developed historically and how it functions. There are several prototypes of hybridization, ranging from cataclysmic shocks and conquests to gradual contacts. As peoples, languages, religions, and cultures moved, they encountered existing peoples and societies. The Aztecs the Spanish conquered in Mexico had themselves taken over lands and people from other indigenous cultures just a little earlier.

Few of these earlier conquests and empires were achieved particularly peacefully. Many of these movements and impositions of peoples, religions, and cultures were forceful and bloody. Many North Americans are descended from Celts who were driven from central Europe through Western Europe to Spain to the edges of the British Isles, pushed by other warlike tribes. However, over time, these cultures blended as well as conquered. The Norsemen who conquered parts of France after 911 c.e. became Normans who conquered England in 1066 c.e., but ultimately, they blended into both places. Although some conquered cultures were literally wiped out, others persisted under the new rulers in a way that provided one of the fundamental prototypes for the kind of hybridization still seen in the world. Change was rapid, almost cataclysmic, breaking boundaries and patterns of culture, but a surprising amount often remained, hybridized into the new dominant culture or surviving in subcultures.

A more gradual or emergent hybridization prototype is based on more gradual contacts between cultures. Even before the European conquests after 1492, almost all human cultures were touched by some form of trade, by small-scale movements of people, and by the movement of tools, ideas, stories, and religious ideas—in short, of culture. Although some primitive groups remained truly isolated, most peoples were slowly changing as these new forces gradually moved in (Nederveen Pieterse, 2004). For example, religious movements are often key to both gradual and rapid cultural change. Missionaries sometimes came with the backing of armies, as did Christians in Latin America and Muslims in Africa, southern Europe, and South Asia. Often, however, religious ideas moved slowly as a few individuals or organizations spread their ideas one by one, with increasing effect over time.

This gradual process can also be quite revolutionary in its impacts. Changes in tools and economic systems alter cultures powerfully over time. However, cultures also resist and push back. Some tools and economic ideas are ignored or even specifically rejected because they are too alien or threatening to the receiving culture. An often cited example is the way that Japan stopped using firearms for hundreds of years because such weapons were too threatening to the position of the warrior class, the samurai (Perrin, 1979). Although firearms in the hands of peasant soldiers were equally threatening to European knights, who became an anachronism on the battlefield, other dynamics in Europe pushed the development and use of firearms forward, so that they became a major tool of subsequent European conquests.

Because we are interested primarily in recent change connected with media, particularly television, which of these two basic models is more applicable? Some writers think about television as an invasion, almost as if media were missionaries backed by the force of armies of conquest, armies now of economic and technological change (Herman & McChesney, 1997). But is world television really as powerful in changing culture as the movement of peoples, literal conquests by force, and the massive spread of new religions, by both conversion and conquest?

Some other writers see gradual, incremental change as a better prototype for the kind of impact that modern world television systems have (Pool, 1977). Rather than an overwhelming force, is television a more subtle part of long-term changes, interacting with the cultures that receive and use the forms and technologies of television? This sort of prototype is often analyzed with the theory of hybridity (Bhabha, 1994; Canclini, 1995, 2001; Kraidy, 2005; Nederveen Pieterse, 2004). Throughout this chapter, I further define models of hybridization and give concrete examples of how complex cultural hybridization occurs. I discuss the role of television and show how it affects or accelerates the ongoing process of hybridization in a variety of countries.

## Hybridization

Hybridization was developed first as a theory applied to Latin America, where the national populations and cultures are almost all historically clear hybrids of indigenous, European, and African elements. These hybrid cultures built up from movements of people—the Iberian conquests, African slavery, and subsequent immigrations—that occurred before mass media arrived, but hybridization as a model may help us understand cultural contact via television and other media, as well.

One of the main theorists of hybridity, Canclini (1997) noted, "I found this term better suited for grasping diverse intercultural mixtures than '*mestizaje*,' which is limited to racial mixings, or 'syncretism,' which almost always refers to religious combinations or to traditional symbolic movements" (pp. 22–23)

He also considered traditional/modern and elite/popular/mass culture blends as more current aspects of hybridity. He thought that in many cases, both elites and masses are conscious agents of hybridity, blending "the desired modernity" with "traditions they do not wish to cast away" (p. 23).

Another major theorist, Bhabha (1990, 1994) also saw hybridity as an active process in which cultures interact, transgress previous boundaries, and transform each other; people can work within borders and in in-between spaces to (re)assert their idea of their culture. Bhabha saw this process as complex and unpredictable, unequal but not exhibiting the classic domination of center over periphery, which he considered an overly simple binary. Compared to Canclini's focus on popular culture, Bhabha focused more on language and literature. He tended to think that critique and subversive use of language can effect change. Not surprisingly, critics accused him of ignoring the realities of existing power differentials between cultures and nations (Dirlik, 1994).

Bhabha emphasized the hybrid cultures created by migrants, often colonial subjects relocated back to the capitals of the colonial powers. In fact, critics of the area of postcolonial literary theory, where Bhabha is a central figure, thought the movement focused too much on migrant writers rather than on the production in the former colonial areas (Moore-Gilbert, 1997). Others emphasized how those who remain in former colonies adapt to the 20th-century penetration of their countries by media and the globalization of their economies. In this regard, the Latin American experience may be seen as a prototype of the current media aspects of hybridization. U.S. multinational corporations and U.S. mass media exports penetrated Latin America, starting in the 1920s and 1930s and with increasing intensity, before they reached much of the rest of the world (Fejes, 1980). As a result, Latin American cultures began the media phase of hybridization earlier than the much of rest of the world, which noticed the U.S. outflow of culture primarily after the 1950s (Smith, 1990). Kraidy (2005) and others particularly have warned that hybrid forms of culture can easily be co-opted and commodified by what Kraidy called *corporate transculturalism*. He urged a more cautious and critical approach to analyzing and managing the process of hybridity.

Earlier media imperialism studies tended to see cultural hybridization as the linear imposition of the cultures of the strong on the weak, or of industrial centers on less developed peripheries (Hamelink, 1983; Schiller, 1969). Canclini (1997) moved away from what he called such "Manichean perspectives" toward an emphasis on "the reciprocal borrowings that take place in the midst of differences and inequalities" (p. 23). He cited Stuart Hall to the effect that "the hegemony of the United States is not understandable solely as the elimination of difference, rather he observes, there are multiple ways that Latin American cultures can be 'repenetrated, absorbed, reshaped, negotiated, without absolutely destroying what is specific and particular to them'" (Hall, 1991, pp. 28–29, cited in Canclini, 1997, p. 23). One of Canclini's major studies, for example, showed how traditional indigenous artisans in Mexico adapted pre-Colombian crafts and styles to modern Mexican and foreign tourist markets.

> By incorporating contemporary scenes into the devils of Ocumicho and the amate paintings of Ameyaltepec, by learning English and traveling by air, or by using credit cards, they acquire the money that allows them to modernize their ancient traditions and ceremonies. (Canclini, 1997, p. 24)

Some Latin American critics of hybridization have said that the type of modernization Canclini observed constitutes severe change in the culture and economy of the formerly traditional artisans, that fundamental continuities have been broken. This raises a key question, for hybridity is admittedly not preservation but clear change. For Canclini's artisans, their art is no longer pure or completely traditional, but is it any less authentic? Is an underlying continuity of culture that lasted for centuries now being broken by air travel, credit cards, modern tools, and media? In other words, does the rapid recent push of all these new forces combine to create much stronger impacts on cultures, impacts that might justify the labels or charges of cultural imperialism, homogenization, and destruction of traditional cultures?

Latin American cultural theorist Jesus Martín-Barbero (1993) preferred to use the term *mestizajé* for cultural as well as ethnic mixture, rather than the concept of hybridity. He emphasized that considerable authenticity and continuity tends to survive the encounter of traditional cultures with modernization. Using complexity theory terms, I would argue that such traditional artisans work within cultural and economic patterns that have been ruptured by modern economic forces or threshold conditions so that new patterns emerge. However, these new patterns of working conditions do not blot out the culture of the artisans. Anthropological work has noted a tendency in cultures to maintain as much continuity as possible, to resist complete change by preserving much of old cultural patterns and fitting them into the changed boundaries of their local economy, creating effectively a new wave or layer of patterns of hybridzation, where much of the old is still visible.

Hybridization is used to describe several kinds of cultural mixtures. Canclini and other Latin Americans have tended to focus on the intrinsic historical hybridity of their cultures, which have been mixed since the Iberian conquests with several different ethnic stocks: Latin, indigenous, and African.

This might be seen as a situation where hybridity is one of the results of the critical initial conditions for a culture, such as conquest, migration, enforced immigration of slaves, religious change by conquest, and so on. In this form, new cultures are created from forced mixtures, such as *mestizaje* or the mixture of races, characteristic of Latin America.

Many other cultures result from similar processes of conquest, migration, and mixture. Singapore, for example, would not exist in anything like its current form without British colonization. The British deliberately created a new port city and either brought people to it, such as South Asian traders and civil servants, or created free trade policies that brought others, such as Chinese, Malays, and Europeans, to create a multiethnic society. Such cases are the clearest examples of hybridity—where hybridity is clearly visible at the origin of the current dominant cultural pattern.

However, another style of hybridization involves resistance to colonialism. In this mode, much more of the original populations survive. Local power structures are not completely broken, whether among indigenous peoples or imported slaves. There is a great deal of cultural continuity. In fact, a kind of superficial hybridity may serve to mask underlying continuity, so that overlays of adopted culture are seen, rather than true mixtures. In this mode, the inner core of traditional culture remains substantially intact. Scott (1999) described how subaltern, forcibly subordinated populations can resist cultural colonialization in often small, subtle ways, which he viewed as hidden transcripts of discourse, backstage talk, and manipulative action that lulls the colonizers into thinking they have imposed their own culture, when the original local culture may be simply hiding to survive. I will discuss this later as one of the bases for multiple layers of identity and culture that often emerge in hybrid cultures, where instead of a genuine hybrid blend of cultures, much of the original indigenous culture survives, hidden by masks of superficial hybridity.

One example might be India, where many aspects of education, government, bureaucratic organization, and the language of elites changed with English colonialism, but others—class and caste structure, religion, popular culture (as opposed to elite culture), material culture such as cooking, and vernacular home languages—showed considerable continuity (Appadurai, 1988). For South Asian theorists of hybridity, such as Homi Bhabha (1990, 1994), the concept is useful for this situation, where the continuity of Indian cultures is not so completely broken by English colonialism but where the effects are still deep. Bhabha looked to see what kind of literature and other culture comes out of the postcolonial blend of British and Indian elements.

In another style or mode of hybridity, often attributed to Japan and the United States, dominant cultures incorporate the other without breaking their own continuity. They incorporate or appropriate cultures from minorities and immigrants, as when the dominant U.S. Anglo culture absorbs other elements, such as African music rhythms. The incorporation of foreign cultures is often selective, as when Japan absorbs elements from China, Western Europe, or the United States.

At the other extreme, many very vulnerable cultures absorb flows and restructuring without much control or ability to resist. In many cultures, for example, the structures of the capitalist economy change the material bases for local cultural production and labor and class relations. Such cultures are vulnerable to media flows, immigration inflows, and religious or ideological movements. Their local languages are overtaken by outside languages, usually national languages of unification (and broadcasting). Some cultures simply break under such strain, resulting in the ongoing extinction of dozens of small languages and cultures.

Overall, there appear to be two dominant forms of what might be termed *hybridity*: (1) a genuinely new mixture and (2) relations between multiple layers of culture. Both forms come from a process of hybridization that includes flows and encounters of peoples. The interpenetration of cultures results, and multiple layers form, resulting in resistance or in mixture (forced, voluntary, or selective). Key elements of those hybridizations include populations, racial or ethnic groups, religions and value systems, languages, social classes, and forms of political economy.

## Emergent Change Versus Hybridization

If the definition of hybridization is too broad, then all cultures are constantly hybridizing, mixing, changing if you will. But as I have previously discussed, complexity theory offers two types of change, only one of which results in hybridization. The first kind of change is emergent, the cyclical change inherent in any patterned system (Urry, 2003). The summer weather outside the window as I write this chapter is changing. There is a breeze and a few clouds. Perhaps there will be a shower tonight, but tomorrow, the sky will be blue again. All cultural systems are changing, emergent as well. But hybridization requires a higher order of change. Over time, events occur to shift the overall pattern of the weather, to move from warming to cooling, from tropical times to the ice age. But occasionally there is a cataclysm where a volcano erupts, sending ash into the atmosphere and drastically reducing the amount of light that comes into the lower atmosphere, causing the known weather pattern to adopt a new, hybrid pattern (Straubhaar & Hammond, 1997).

In culture, events such as the landing of Columbus, the proliferation of television, or the spread of commercial television systems create cataclysmic or sudden and dramatic change. When the change occurs at a system level as a result of the clash of two strong patterns, then a hybrid pattern that contains key elements of the previous patterns often emerges.

Complex hybridization seems to have accelerated in the 20th century with postcolonial migrations, increased travel, transnational mass media, and economic globalization. A number of current theorists, particularly those, like Bhabha (1994), whose personal or family history centers on postcolonial migrations, focus on the postcolonial period as the critical period of hybridity. Canclini (1997), for instance, questions whether some of Bhabha's work can be applied to Latin America because it focuses too much on postcolonial as opposed to colonial era hybridity. The kind of hybridity under discussion is important because different kinds relate to very different political-economic structures of colonialism, postcolonial migration, and globalization.

As epochs in hybridization, the colonial era, the era of postcolonial migrations, the era of mass media, and the era of economic globalization are all important. Not every country experienced a deep form of hybridization with colonialism or postcolonial migration. With mass media and economic globalization, however, almost all countries are caught up in some type of increased cultural contact, resulting in some degree of hybridization. By many accounts, the dominant form of increased cultural contact has been mass media, both national and international.

Bhabha (1994) noted that "the very concepts of homogenous national cultures, the consensual or contiguous transmission of historical traditions, or 'organic' ethnic communities . . . are in a profound process of redefinition" (p. 5). As an explanation, he observed a set of forces that seem to affect many countries in this century.

> For the demography of the new internationalism is the history of postcolonial migration, the narratives of cultural and political diaspora, the major social displacements of peasant and aboriginal communities, the poetics of exile, the grim prose of political and economic refugees. (p. 5)

## Hybridity and Television

One form of hybridization takes place in the production of cultural products such as television. Formats are commonly copied and adapted. The North American soap opera format was introduced into Cuba and other countries and gradually was turned into the current telenovela (Straubhaar, 1982).

Kraidy (2005) uses the example of Mexican television producers who created their own version of the *Teletubbies* called *Tele Chobbies* because another network already had the license to import the original series. Such adaptation is discussed more extensively in Chapters 7 and 8.

Another form of hybridity takes place in the consumption or configuration of culture by audiences. Canclini (1995) noted that consumption is the appropriation of products; it is more than passive reception or consumerism. Consumption, as a form of hybridity, represents a struggle for meanings between classes within countries, between high and popular cultures, and between local, national, and imported cultural traditions. This is parallel to the type of active meaning construction that Fiske and others describe among television audiences in developed countries (Curran, 1990; Fiske, 1987). As Ricoeur (1984) observed, this kind of active reception or configuration of culture by audiences feeds back into the collective culture, in what he called reconfiguration, so that meanings made by audiences become part of the cultural context for the next round of television production.

Canclini (1995) pointed out that hybrid cultural products resulting from the rearticulation of popular or folk traditions within transnational companies or markets actually serve to expand overall consumption of goods and cultural products. Kraidy (2005) saw such deliberate corporate transculturation as increasingly common and warned researchers to be cautious about accepting it as part of a normalized cultural process. Thus, modernization and even internationalization of local and national markets does not interfere with and may even serve the interests of transnational capital. To some critics, this is another damning characteristic of cultural hybridization: that it takes place within an increasingly commercialized context, often no longer under full national control (Oliveira, 1993). Certainly, the growth of a transnational, even global form of cultural production, in which television is commercially based, created via privately owned networks, and oriented toward mass audiences, creates a pattern of economic boundary conditions that will limit to some substantial degree what can be produced. It will also tend to promote consumerism in audiences (Canclini, 2001).

# The Roots of Transnational, Geocultural, and Cultural-Linguistic Regions and Markets

Most of the main transnational geocultural and cultural-linguistic markets for television in today's world system of television have their roots in the religious and cultural systems that predate European colonialism, which began in the 1400s in Africa and 1492 in Latin America. Many of the cultural and linguistic factors that create geocultural markets result from shared regional histories of cultural hybridization, such as the long spread of Chinese cultural influence through Asia; again, they predate European colonialism and imperialism. In many cases, the colonial experience added new historical ties that pulled neighboring countries together.

These cultural similarities and common histories come together to define cultural markets, to which television responds. Populations defined by these kinds of characteristics tend to seek out cultural products, such as television programs or music, that are most similar or proximate to them. Whereas some scholars used to fear that the intrinsic attraction of U.S. cultural products would result in "wall-to-wall *Dallas*" around the world (Collins, 1986), it seems more likely that most audiences are really looking for cultural proximity (Straubhaar, 1991), to see people and styles they recognize, jokes that are funny without explanation, and so on. Cultural-linguistic markets are unified by language, even though different accents and dialects may divide countries somewhat (Wilkinson, 1995). However, these markets go beyond language to include history, religion, ethnicity (in many cases), and culture in several senses: shared identity, gestures and nonverbal communication, what is considered funny or serious or even sacred, clothing styles, living patterns, climate influences, and other relationships with the environment. Cultural-linguistic markets are often centered in a geographic region, hence, the tendency to call them first regional, then geocultural markets, but they have also been spread globally by colonization, slavery, and migration. These cultural linguistic spaces or regions are closely related to the ideas of cultural identity, cultural proximity, and multilayeredness that will be developed throughout this book.

## Precolonial Forces: Before 1492

Regional or geolinguistic cultures and their effects on local cultural identity have existed throughout recorded history (and even before). These include Arab, Aztec, Chinese, Incan, Mongol, Persian, Malay, Turkish, Semitic, Greek, Roman, and many other expanding ethnic groups and empires. Broad religions movements such as Buddhism, Christianity, and Islam still show up in the historical bases for current cultural markets.

Greek colonies spread Greek culture through the Mediterranean and Asian world during the Hellenistic era. The Roman Empire spread its systems and influences even further into northern Europe and the Mediterranean. Christianity spread via the empire in its latter stages. Chinese civilization also spread political systems, economic forms, and culture in early recorded history, from Southeast Asia to Japan. Semitic, Greek, Roman, Christian, and Islamic empires spread their systems and influences around the Mediterranean, North Africa, and Europe. Somewhat later, the spread of Islam reached from southern Europe to India and Southeast Asia.

These empires had strong impacts, often spreading religion and culture beyond any boundaries of conquest, as with the spread of Buddhism well beyond India into much of Asia or of Chinese customs through much of Asia. In a discussion of cultural imperialism, several Asian graduate students once joked with the author that current Western influence on Asia was nothing compared to earlier Chinese cultural imperialism.

Japan represents an interesting example of pre-European hybridity. Japanese culture borrowed a great deal from China over thousands of years before the first European colonial contact by the Portuguese in the 1500s. Japan borrowed its system of writing, many aspects of its aesthetics for poetry and painting, its styles of dress, and its weapons directly from China, and one of its major religious forms, Buddhism, came to it via China from India. These were gradual borrowings from contacts that remained largely under Japanese control, rather than being imposed by conquerors. The Japanese expelled the Portuguese in 1639, limited European trade, and were only forcibly opened to the West by U.S. Admiral Perry in 1853; even then, Japan retained strong political independence and exerted strong control over the process of adoption and hybridization.

## European Colonialism

The most visible processes of hybridization are related to the European conquests that began in the 1400s. Although the major European colonization that began in the 1400s is often thought of as globalizing, spreading Western culture throughout much of the world, Europeans also contributed to current patterns of regional and geolinguistic culture. Geolinguistic cultures such as the Arab world or the widespread Chinese diaspora have formed in part in interaction with and reaction to the Western culture spread by European colonization. The current dominant position of Hindi in India grew under the British, who pushed for linguistic unification or simplification.

European colonization often had more drastic effects. As European people migrated to most parts of the world, they sometimes overwhelmed the indigenous local inhabitants and essentially imposed almost all aspects of their own culture, as in the United States or Australia. At the other extreme, in countries like Mozambique, the physical presence of the Portuguese was felt only in a few port and trading areas for most of the colonial period. In the middle of this range of possible colonial experiences, Latin America represents a case where large numbers of Europeans settled but tended to mix extensively with indigenous people and imported African slaves, producing the racial mixture called *mestizaje*.

During the period of European colonization and political hegemony around the world, European culture was exported widely, above and beyond the migration of peoples. European-style schooling was brought in, reinforcing the learning of European languages, at least among local elites. European print media, music, and later film and radio poured out to the colonies, in part to sustain the expatriates who lived there, but often deliberately spread to local elites to bring them into fuller cooperation with foreign governors and economic managers.

Most influential, in some cases, were new forms of religion, a key aspect of cultural hybridization in many places; this is often specifically referred to as *religious syncretization* between imported religions, such as Christianity, and local beliefs. The Europeans, ironically, also brought other competing beliefs with them as they encouraged or forced the migration of African slaves, South Asian administrators and traders, and others who brought influential non-Christian belief structures with them. In Brazil, Cuba, and Haiti, for example, the most powerful elements of religious syncretization, which also fed cultural hybridization, were European Catholicism and African pantheons of gods and spirits from Nigeria and elsewhere, producing the religions called *voudon, candomblé, santeria, macumba,* and so on (Bastide, 1978). More recently, especially since World War II, many Koreans, Chinese Singaporeans, West Africans, and others have become Christian. This can be seen as part of an intensive postwar wave of Western influence, but it is also something more hybrid and complex. Rapidly growing, increasingly global Protestant churches are based in South Korea, Brazil, Nigeria, and elsewhere.

One of the effects of this pattern of cultural export was to draw an increasing gulf between local elites and local masses in the colonies. Indians who learned English, went to English-style schools, and read English-language Indian newspapers created an elite subculture that stood apart both from the British themselves, particularly as this Indian elite began to push for independence, and from the masses of people who spoke vernacular local languages (Parameswaran, 1995). Although the masses of people were often touched by imported colonial culture, the assumption of some cultural imperialism theorists that they were massively affected is questionable.

A more interesting assertion is made by Robertson (1995) and others: that colonialization, like earlier patterns of contact, circulated global patterns in which indigenous identities were reconstructed or constructed. The institutional and cultural structures of colonization and postcolonial relations between countries such as Great Britain and India or Hong Kong created new boundaries for cultural production. Old forms of culture were discouraged, while new ones were imported or hybridized between old and new. Unequal opportunities were given different to groups of social actors. Some elites were permitted and encouraged to re-create themselves in the mold of colonial culture, whereas other groups were systematically excluded. Both created new forms of culture that reacted to and incorporated colonial culture in different ways.

Local or indigenous peoples varied greatly in how they fared under colonial conquest. In the Americas, a large number of peoples, languages, and cultures were essentially wiped out. Islands like Hispaniola (the Dominican Republic and Haiti) were essentially depopulated of indigenous people in the 1500s. Other groups, for example, the once-numerous Tupi-Gurani of Brazil, were pushed out of most of the territory and reduced from tens of millions in 1500 to tens of thousands by 2000. However, even as they were catastrophically reduced from their original numbers, groups like the Tupi and Guarani intermarried or interbred to contribute to the gene pool of Brazil. They also contributed legends and stories, place names, foods, methods of farming, images, religious ideas and spirits, music, and so on to what emerged as Brazilian culture. Different scholars view these events in a range from the almost benign (Freyre, 1964) to the genocidal (Galeano, 1988), but the sheer decline in numbers of indigenous people after the conquests reflects an awful era of enslavement, forced labor, eviction from lands, starvation, plagues, disease, and religious conversion on pain of death, which nonetheless fed into one of the world's most vibrant hybrid cultures—a vivid reminder of the sometimes horrifying contradictions entailed in the process of hybridization.

In many countries, indigenous populations survived far more intact from their encounter with colonialism. The local or indigenous populations often contributed the dominant means of agriculture and economy. Local power structures often survived, although usually manipulated by colonizers. Social institutions, forms of culture, and religions also survived remarkably intact in many places, particularly when few Europeans were living among many local people.

Japan is again an interesting example. Portuguese traders and Christian missionaries obtained an initial foothold in Japan in 1542, spreading technology such as European-style firearms. When they were expelled in 1639, after the Japanese began to fear that their influence was becoming too strong, local Christian converts were forced to recant or be killed. Much of the technology introduced, including firearms, were also ultimately repressed or given up.

## Imperialism

Seldom did colonial powers encourage the kind of industrial development that would also facilitate the growth of modern cultural industries or other media institutions. A number of countries got stuck in unfavorable economic positions in the course of European imperialism. Colonies were often seen as sources of raw materials, markets for exported goods, and in some cases opportunities for investment to take advantage of cheap labor or other specific resources (Magdoff, 1969).

Restrictions on colonies' abilities to trade independently and industrialize were part of what led to the American Revolution. Restrictions were even more severe elsewhere, including specific restrictions by many colonial powers on the development of both print and electronic media. For example, the Portuguese suppressed printing in Brazil until 1808. Such restrictions were often resisted and resented, contributing to revolutions in Latin America after 1820 and in much of the rest of the world after World War II. However, such restrictions worked all too well in many places. This held back many of the structural bases required for media: a general industrial infrastructure, a specific infrastructure for printing, infrastructure for transportation and telecommunication (essential for distributing media), commercial and industrial jobs that would lead to increased incomes to be spent on media, and the increased literacy that tends to go with such jobs.

Some colonial powers did permit radio to develop in the 1920s and 1930s, usually as part of colonial administration. The Dutch started in 1927, Germany in 1929, France in 1931, and Britain in 1932 (Head, 1985). This radio programming was often aimed at expatriates serving colonial administration and at middle and administrative classes among the local population, which the colonial administrators wanted to draw into their political, economic, and cultural hegemony.

That is to say, colonial electronic and print media attempted to bring the emerging middle classes of various colonies into an acceptance of the superiority of the colonial power's culture. Numerous analyses and works of fiction have considered how Indian intellectuals were led to admire British culture or how West Africans were drawn into the cultural paradigms of France (Fair, 2003). Although the inclusion of colonial subjects in the colonial power's cultural world might be a more or less natural consequence of the redrawing of cultural boundaries, it also has very real consequences in terms of economic and political power. Those colonial subjects who accepted the culture of the colonial power were also perhaps more willing to accept their political and economy hegemony, according to writers like Fanon (1967).

However, this is a complex process. Parameswaran (1995) discusses how Indian women sometimes found English-language stories more liberating than local ones. Bourdieu and Wacquandt (1999) accused U.S. organizations such as the Ford Foundation of cultural imperialism when they went to Brazil to promote American definitions of who is "black" linked to specific notions of black power and civil rights. However, black Brazilians had their own reasons for finding those American ideas useful or even liberating (Telles, 2004). It is a mistake to not recognize the agency of local people in negotiating with such forces, even as it is a mistake not to recognize the powerful ideological forces of such transnational institutions as the Ford Foundation.

## Broadcasting Models: From Colonial to Postcolonial

Starting with radio in the 1930s and 1940s, many countries began broadcasting, often taking their models from colonial and postcolonial powers (Katz & Wedell, 1976). In British and French colonies, radio was both a direct colonial imposition and a more subtle drawing of colonial elites into accepting such models as part of a logical hegemony of how to do "modern" things. In countries that were already independent politically, yet dependent economically on postcolonial powers such as the United States, the latter approach, drawing local elites into a hegemonically logical approach to media, was prevalent (Schwoch, 1990). For elites in most of Latin America, it seemed only logical to adopt a commercial media approach, given the postindependence capitalist development project in which they were already engaged, in an asymmetrical interdependence with the United States, France, and Great Britain. The postcolonial experience of a number of other developing countries was foreshadowed already in the 1930s in the way that most of Latin America adopted and adapted the U.S. model of broadcasting. That experience will be examined in much detail in the next chapter, which focuses on the growth of television in postcolonial (inter)dependency.

The United States quickly developed a distinct broadcasting model. After some experimentation, the country had by 1927 a clear pattern of advertiser-supported and privately owned radio, loosely regulated by a federal agency, the Federal Communication Commission, essentially to allocate licenses and avoid frequency interference (Streeter, 1996). To reach maximum audiences, stations and networks developed programming that was largely entertainment, with some news. National commercial networks developed to create a national audience for advertisers and to develop economies of scale in programming, covering as many people as possible with the same centrally produced shows (Barnouw, 1977). This model was very attractive to advertisers in either developed or emerging capitalist economies, so both transnational and national advertisers (and advertising agencies) tended to foster it in places like Latin America (Fejes, 1980). It was also attractive in principle to governments that wanted to stress capitalist models for development, although for many, the French model of government-owned or -controlled media that carried advertising was even more interesting because it combined capitalist development with political control.

The United Kingdom also developed a distinct model early in the 1920s. A 1922 report by the British post office on the American experiment with commercial broadcasting recommended a strong contrast: a public monopoly oriented to education and culture (Smith, 1973). The British Broadcasting Corporation (BBC) evolved as a public entity, governed by an autonomous board to maintain independence. It was financed by license fees levied on all households with radio (or television) sets (Briggs, 1995). That was to keep the BBC financially independent of government budget control as well as advertiser control. In Great Britain, this model worked very well, maintaining substantial independence from government even during World War II, with finances adequate to support high-quality programming. Both the United States and the United Kingdom promoted their models and, to some degree, defined their broadcasting model against the other, showing that even such seemingly fundamental paradigms or models were developed in international interaction not national isolation (Hilmes, 2003). A number of northern European countries adapted the BBC model, as did Japan under Allied pressure after World War II (Smith, 1973). Most who adopted it were former colonies, Commonwealth countries, and members of the resulting cultural-linguistic markets. Developing countries found the BBC model much harder to build and sustain, both because it depended on political stability that was not always easy to ensure and because many governments found it hard to collect license fees (Katz & Wedell, 1976).

The British experience with television shows that the early radio models were apt to change as societies developed new forms, such as the emergence of a consumer society linked to advertising in Britain after World War II. Even with a model as powerful and prestigious as the BBC, emergent change is almost inevitable as economic boundaries shift and new patterns such as commercial broadcasting and advertising spread. So even the home sources of major models of media, such as Great Britain, reflect emergent change toward hybridization of ongoing national trends and new global forces. In this case, a new model emerged, the "duopoly" of a strong public sector in the BBC and a growing private sector under the Independent Television Authority. Consistent with ongoing British patterns, its private sector was far more heavily regulated than was private television in the United States. That pattern, a duopoly with strong regulation, became attractive to a number of countries, including Japan, whose system is quite similar in many ways.

France had largely private radio until World War II, when governments ran both Nazi-controlled and Vichy French stations. The state took over the company, SOFIRAD, which had operated private radio stations (Browne, 1989). After the war, Radiodiffusion-Télévision Française (RTF) was started as a government department. When Charles de Gaulle took office in 1958, he saw television as a major political tool (Smith, 1973): "de Gaulle believed in the need for a strong hand to 'guide' (some would say 'order') French broadcasting" (Browne, 1989). An effort to create an independent oversight board in 1962 collapsed in 1968 during an effort to control political coverage of the student rebellion. Television stayed under tight political control until the Mitterrand government. Mitterrand felt that he had suffered under Gaullist control of television news, so he loosened political controls over television news in 1982 and authorized private networks in 1985. Politically, this pre-1982 French model indicated to many nations that it was all right to maintain control over television content, particularly news, to maintain the stability of the state, a point that de Gaulle had made clear. Economically, the French model also showed how state-owned television could be supported in part by direct state subsidy and in part by advertising, a pragmatic hybrid that appealed to many developing countries.

The Soviet Union developed broadcasting explicitly as a tool for mobilizing support for the Soviet Revolution after 1917 (Paulu, 1974). Beginning with Lenin, Soviet governments saw media as so powerful that they must remain a monopoly of the state. In particular, media were to be a tool for the Communist Party to accomplish its development program for the country. To ensure this, the party retained exclusive ownership and control over media, which were run as part of government (Mickiewicz, 1988). In some ways, the history of the Union of Soviet Socialist Republics (USSR) was a striking experiment in testing a strong belief that media could help a government transform its citizens and mobilize their support. Because the USSR was in many ways a large, underdeveloped, mostly rural country in 1917, this experiment was particularly relevant to the task that faced many other developing countries; particularly those governments had taken over through revolution and saw themselves as revolutionary vanguards, responsible for radically and rapidly changing their countries.

These different models influenced most countries in Africa, Asia, Europe, and Latin America as they developed radio in the 1930s through 1950s. However, local people often took initiatives that were quite important. For example, radio started in Egypt (and many other countries) with independent amateurs but was consolidated at the national level by the British-controlled government, which gave a contract to Marconi, a British company, to operate "national" radio (Boyd, 1993). These imported models often set boundaries and patterns for thinking about media that would last until television broadcasting arrived after World War II.

Regular television broadcasting began to arrive in the 1940s in some of the most industrialized countries, such as the Soviet Union (1945), Great Britain (1946), and the United States (1946). However, most countries began television later, as postwar economic development permitted them to afford it. Fifty countries, including the rest of Europe, most of Latin America, and parts of other regions began television in the 1950s (Head, 1985). Others followed later. Many newly independent nations undertook the development of television in unfavorable circumstances as part of postcolonial development. They were also building models for television and other media in the middle of the intense ideological conflict of the 1948–1991 Cold War between the USSR and the United States and their respective allies.

## The Cold War and the Major Models for Broadcasting

Linking the colonial period with the Cold War era was the dominance of a few key industrialized countries in the emerging world system of television. The United States, Great Britain, France, and the USSR dominated broadcasting in a number of ways that carried from radio into television. These countries were the dominant military powers, emerging from World War II as victors. They had geographic areas of influence linked to that military might as well as to previous colonial or postcolonial influences. So France and Great Britain continued to set patterns for much of Africa and parts of Asia, even after their former colonies became independent. The Soviet Union emerged with a post–World War II area of direct control in Eastern Europe, as well as wide influence as a model over new socialist governments in China and Yugoslavia, which seized control by revolution after the war. As other revolutionary regimes emerged in Africa, Asia, and Latin America, the USSR was a logical model and ally. The United States was the only one of the four models and powers not directly touched by the war, its economy energized by war production. With the prestige that was attached to its perceived success, the United States emerged as the power and model that would most successfully swing other countries in its direction.

Opponents or critics of the USSR during the Cold War often misunderstood or ignored the appeal that the Soviet model of broadcasting had for many other countries. The core Soviet idea of deliberately harnessing media as apparently powerful tools for economic, social, and political development appealed to other countries trying to accelerate their own development in these areas. The idea of overtly didactic programming that educated people about how to improve economic and social growth was attractive to many new nations with unschooled and traditional populations. Some revolutionary countries even liked the clearly ideological nature of Soviet programming because they also wanted to conduct ideological education among their audiences. Many countries were willing to assert government control over broadcasting to get its support for their efforts to mobilize their populations in support of government programs.

For many of the poorest nations, the government was the institution most easily able to create or mobilize resources to support broadcasting (Katz & Wedell, 1976). That made variations of the Soviet and French models attractive. However, as countries developed sufficient economic, personnel, and other resources to support an expansion of broadcasting, other would-be broadcasters, particularly in the private sphere, began to push to change monopoly models or to liberalize, so that licenses might be available to private competitors. In some ways, this move began with the pressure in Great Britain after World War II, to open up the new medium of television to both a public (BBC) sector and a new private sector, despite the prestige that the BBC had acquired for its acclaimed performance in World War II (Smith, 1973).

A number of countries, however, also shook off colonial models and attempted to go in their own directions. For example, the Free Officers Revolution in Egypt in 1952 took over radio as a government operation and redesigned it to mobilize support for the national revolution at home as well as the pan-Arab mobilization that President Gamel Abdel Nasser promoted throughout the Arabic-speaking countries (Boyd, 1993). First radio and then television were of crucial importance for new revolutionary governments as the prime means to communicate with national audiences who were often illiterate— 75% of the population in the case of Egypt in 1960 (Washington, 1964).

These imported models for organizing the goals, institutions, program forms, and even the language of television have proved to be a crucial frame or boundary in many countries. Most national administrators thinking about media goals and organization were shaped by colonial educational systems. Many media professionals were specifically trained by media institutions like the BBC in the former colonial powers' ways of organizing the institutions, reporting the news, writing drama, and so on (Golding & Murdock, 1997).

For a few other countries, for example, Japan, borrowings from European culture were more selective, under the guidance of a national government that tried to modernize more or less on its own terms and to absorb foreign cultural elements somewhat selectively. After World War II, Japan was pushed to reorganize broadcasting as a British-style system with both public and private systems, but adapted it to fit their own traditions and industrial interests. In fact, it is questionable whether the concept of hybridity really fits the Japanese pattern or whether some less far reaching, more partial and selective term is required.

A better term for the Japanese process might well be glocalization. As Robertson (1995) observed, that term originated within Japan as an effort to capture the nation's sense of how it selectively localized global influences into the ongoing direction of Japanese culture and society. Localization has similarly emerged as the cultural industries' own term for how global products and concepts are adapted to fit into local markets (Duarte, 2001). Still, theoretically hybridization remains the richer and broader term, if one that is admittedly problematic and highly criticized within the cultural studies literature. However, glocalization is useful to describe deliberate borrowings and adaptations of global forms by local, national, and regional actors.

## Hybridity and National Development

Taking careful account of the nuances of hybridization may help provide people in local cultures with analytical means for dealing with an increasingly globalized set of patterns for modernity (Kraidy, 2005). This was precisely Canclini's (1995) goal when he wrote a book titled *Hybrid Cultures: Strategies for Entering and Leaving Modernity*. Historical patterns of hybridization can help reveal what kinds of indigenous cultural elements survive in new hybrid forms. History also reveals what kinds of policy interventions can help guide the development of hybrid forms in cultural industries. Both states and cultural industries, as well as their producers and audiences, collectively frame and guide the reterritorialization of international patterns, such as soap opera, within national industries, such as Brazilian or Mexican television. That particularly is the focus of Chapter 3, which covers the role of the state in cultural industries within patterns of dependent development.

# 3

# Creating National and Regional Television and Cultural Industries

This chapter focuses historically on the efforts by nations around the world to develop national television systems, particularly from the 1950s through the 1980s, before the era of globalization. Nations poured much of the effort to unify their peoples and to become modern into developing national television, which is eclipsed now in some countries by a much more fragmented, postmodern form of television. However, this chapter develops the idea that the cultural industries of television are often best understood historically as national industries that worked within national markets defined in a reciprocal relationship with government policy and national identity. A number of national systems later turned into regional or transnational exporters and, by the era of satellite broadcasting, an increasing number of translocal and regional broadcasters who produce and program for specific nations outside their borders.

Most of the networks or channels that are thought of as regional or global, such as CNN or MTV, have expanded from an initial base in a single country, where they are most often still strongest and most profitable. Some exceptions are a steadily increasing number of U.S.-based satellite/cable TV channels created to target either global or regional audiences, for example, the AXN channel, which carries selected American action television series to Latin America, or the Sony Channel, which carries American sitcoms to Latin America. Another set of new channels consists of the satellite networks, such as Star TV in Asia and Orbit or Al-Jazeera in the Middle East, which were explicitly started since the 1980s to be regional television networks. Another new category is the local or regional channels that work with cultural-linguistic markets smaller than the nation-state, such as Catalonian television within Spain or Telegu-language television within India.

Through a political economy and historical view, this chapter focuses on some of the main structural elements for the national bases of world television: economic frameworks, ownership bases, governmental regulations and controls, and institutional forms of organization and operation. In terms of complexity theory, these structural elements form boundaries within which cultural forces and agents, such as television producers, distributors, and viewers, operate. The structures of television limit what cultural agents can do, but within those limits, agency may create different patterns. In terms of Giddens's (1984) approach to structuration, these same structural elements form limits within which television producers, distributors, and viewers operate but also provide the resources that can be used to produce, distribute, and consume television.

## Dependency, the Cold War, and Television Industry Production

Even after their formal independence, many developing countries still depend on the industrialized world for many things, as detailed later (Hamelink, 1983). This is a structural legacy of imperialism that many countries have struggled with and which only a few countries have substantially overcome.

For quite a long time, these postindependence issues were analyzed in terms of world systems theory and dependency theory. In world systems theory, a core of industrial nations controls the essential dynamics of the world capitalist system. A large number of nations, most of the developing world, are peripheral or essentially dependent, and a smaller number of nations, which Wallerstein (1979) calls semiperipheral, achieve some growth and development. Semiperipheral states include the partially industrialized states of the Third World, Eastern Europe, and, at least before World War I, Russia (Wallerstein, 1991, pp. 88–89). In all of these cases, the world economy, still controlled by the core nations, is expanding and penetrating new states to draw in new raw materials and potential markets. Dependency theory takes a similar analysis, but more from the point of view of developing countries, which even after obtaining political independence, often saw themselves entangled in a series of dependent relations with either their former colonial powers or with competing international powers, such as the

United States or Great Britain. These lines of dependence tended to center on:

Finance: Many countries depended on outside powers for either investments or foreign aid;

Trade: Many countries remained locked in unfavorable trade relations with dominant countries, selling their raw materials cheaply and buying manufactured goods for high prices;

Politics: Countries often had to accept subordinate political alliances to obtain foreign aid or other benefits;

Culture: Countries often imported television, films, and news from either their former colonial power or the United States;

Education: National elites often spoke the languages of either former colonial powers such as France or of emerging global powers such as the United States (Cardoso, 1970).

Dependency varied greatly in regions of the world. The term itself was created by Latin American theorists, like Cardoso (1970), to describe the experience of Latin American countries after becoming independent in the 1820s, then forming powerful new relationships of dependency on Great Britain, France, and the United States. Most other developing countries became independent of colonialism much later, after the 1940s. However, the Latin American experience provided a useful set of prototypes and precedents for understanding dependency among other newly independent countries in other regions. However, regional experiences differed, and dependency developed and transformed in different ways around the world.

The reach of the industrialized nations continued to expand after World War II and to draw the newly independent nations into dependency. Even though the United States had been a literal colonial power in only a few countries, for example, Cuba and the Philippines, the United States now became a logical economic partner for developing country elites around the world. Both the United States and the USSR actively pursued alliances with elites in developing countries as part of the Cold War, so political and military concerns often overlapped or even opposed economic interests of the elites in both industrialized and developing countries.

Almost all national elites, whether in the economy, politics, or cultural industry, were seen as strongly linked to the economic interests of the core countries (dos Santos, 1973). These elites had been educated by the colonial powers, had learned the colonial languages, had often worked in or been trained by their companies, and often saw their economic fortunes as linked to the corporations and governments of the major core countries, even after independence. So as these elites created political systems, economic groups, and cultural industries, they often saw profit and stability in continuing ties to the core countries. A key example is the television broadcasting personnel in various countries, who have been trained in how to produce television and, implicitly, what television is or should be, by the BBC or other dominant media groups (Golding & Murdock, 1997). Cultural industry elites, in television or elsewhere, were particularly interested in creating and guiding markets for both their economic role and their ideological role in reproducing the systems of culture and information.

Many saw the ideological role of television under dependency as making Third World residents content with their lot as lower paid consumers of the First World products. The core nations saw advertising and the consumerism it promotes as a key vehicle of both economic and ideological expansion (Fox, 1975; Janus, 1981). However, some elites in politics, economics, and media were interested in increasing their own national power and reducing dependency. So a great deal of policy making came to focus on reducing dependency by addressing issues such as enabling countries to produce more of their own media content and reducing imbalances of cultural imports (MacBride Commission, 1980).

## Cultural Imperialism and Media Imperialism

Building on dependency theories, another, perhaps more lasting body of theory was created: cultural imperialism. This theory identified several key problems that must be considered before further discussion of developments in national television. First, perhaps most fundamental, is the creation and reinforcement of commercial models for television. Herbert Schiller (1976) argued that the powerful U.S. communication industries had essentially forced global commercialization on most countries and on the international communication system as a whole. The spread of the commercial model of media, foreign investment in media, and the power of multinational advertisers were viewed as threatening to the use of media for nationally determined, development-oriented purposes (Beltran & Fox de Cardona, 1979; Janus, 1981).

A second key and related issue is the profound role of media in producing ideologies that favored capitalist market development over other possibilities, favoring the economic interests of the United States and other advanced industrial nations (Schiller, 1969). In this view, the ideological role of media is primarily as part of the cultural superstructure that results from the more basic structural economic relations of dependency. In this pattern, which is related to dependency and world systems theories, the peripheral or developing countries depend on the industrialized world for capital, technology, and most manufactured goods, while tending to export low-cost primary products or cheap manufactures, which add little benefit to the local economy. The role of culture is to make Third World residents content with their lot, an idea similar to, but in many formulations less sophisticated than Gramsci's (1971) concept of hegemony, in which elites and sometimes others compete to use media and other cultural or informational structures to set a dominant ideology that the members of society tend to accept.

A third key issue in cultural imperialism is the unbalanced flow of media products between countries. Several studies (Beltran, 1978; Beltran & Fox de Cardona, 1979; Nordenstreng & Varis, 1974) identified what was increasingly perceived as a one-way flow of television from a few countries of the First World out to the rest of the world, whereas other studies (Boyd-Barrett, 1980) observed a similar one-way flow of news controlled by the four large news agencies, Associated Press, United Press International, Agence France Presse, and Reuters. Studies (Guback, 1984; Schnitman, 1984) observed a possibly even more unbalanced flow of film from Hollywood to almost everywhere else, except India.

For cultural imperialism theorists, control of domestic media structures and the ideological role of advertising and imported news and media products were primary concerns. This view clearly sees structures and economic factors as determinant and does not give much attention to the interaction of the audience with the actual text or content of the cultural products. Media imperialism theory is somewhat less structural and Marxist in orientation and focuses more on imbalances of power and flows of media (Boyd-Barrett, 1977; Lee, 1980). Lee (1980), in particular, also tried to refine indicators or levels of media imperialism, which could be empirically examined. He focused on flow of television, foreign investment, adoption of foreign models, and impact on cultures. Critics particularly noted that he missed some of the connections between the larger context of dependency and media, particularly the influence of advertising (Mattos, 1984). Boyd-Barrett (1980) also relied on a largely empirical definition; he viewed media imperialism as essentially an unbalanced set of relationships between countries in the sphere of media.

## Local Cultural Production

One of the conclusions of Chapter 2 is that outside influences coming into a culture encounter and interact; they hybridize or layer with the institutions, identities, and cultural production that are already there. Before television came along in the 1950s or later, many countries and cultures already had traditions and highly productive institutions (or industries) of radio, theater, music, film, publishing, circus, dance, and other arts. Many of these contributed to the form and development of local or national television, interacting with the kinds of outside forces that were often the focus of dependency and cultural imperialism theorists. In fact, early theories of media development in the 1950s and 1960s focused almost exclusively on local media capabilities and how they could be grown and adapted to support development programs (Schramm, 1964). Dependency and imperialism theorists critiqued that work because it did not take the strong role of international forces into account (Schiller, 1969), but their work in turn tends to underestimate the local forces involved (Straubhaar, 1981).

Specifically, where other local cultural industries were well developed, they influenced television's development. In India, a well-developed film industry with massive annual production in not only Hindi but a number of regional languages such as Tamil and Telugu had several impacts on television. Although television started in developmentalist and political directions preferred by the national state, the Hindi film industry was able to push to have its films prominently featured in national Hindi-language broadcasts. Furthermore, the existence of strong state or regional level film industries made India one of the first countries to have strong local or province-level television networks (Kumar, 2006). In several parts of Latin American countries, the role of film was less direct, but directors, actors, writers, and other professionals from film and theater were crucial in providing a base for local production of programming, especially in television's early days of the 1950s and 1960s.

Existing local forms of media ownership and control were also important. One of the strengths of dependency theorists was to point out how both the state and local cultural industries prior to television had evolved in interaction with outside capital and other forces. In both Asia and Latin America, for example, family media empires had already been built in film, such as the Shaw Brothers film studio and interests that contributed to powerful Hong Kong producer TVRB, or in newspapers and radio, which supplied dominant media groups ready to develop television in Argentina, Brazil, and Venezuela.

## Cultural Imports

Despite the potential for local cultural production, a classic and enduring pattern of former colonial powers and other dominant economies is to export as much as possible to the nations that are still dependent on them, keeping the trade balance in their favor as much as possible. Goods exported by the core countries often include cultural products like television programs that are far cheaper for poor countries to import than to produce. This was probably most widely true in the late 1960s and early 1970s, as reflected in the 1974 Nordenstreng and Varis study, which showed that most countries then imported most of their television programs, mostly from the United States. So in some ways, television came to be seen as yet another product typically sold by First World producers to Third World consumers. Such unbalanced cultural imports also add to a pattern of cultural and media imperialism.

Especially for new television operations, importing television programs was always considerably cheaper than producing them at home. However, by the 1980s, studies began to show an increase in national production in several parts of the world (Antola & Rogers, 1984; Straubhaar, 1981; Straubhaar et al., 1992; Waterman & Rogers, 1994). I explore below the factors that made that possible. Conversely, many other countries were unable to produce much of their own television programming, which reveals the most crucial structural boundaries or barriers that blocked some cultural industries and institutions from growing.

Empirically, structural factors promoting national television production growth include market size and market characteristics, state intervention, entrepreneurial behavior, and ownership structures. This chapter will focus on specific structural forces, while subsequent chapters focus on questions related to cultural factors, such as producer behavior, genre development, and audience preferences.

## The Nation-State and Television

Television has differed crucially from music, film, radio, newspapers, and newer media in several crucial ways, some of which focus on the interest and the power of many nation-states to control or even own and operate television to ensure or at least pursue several key national goals.

First, radio and television are for the 20th century what the print media of newspapers and books were to the 19th century: the primary means of building and reinforcing national identity. Television becomes a crucial medium to unify geographically and ethnically dispersed and diverse peoples into a sense of nationhood. For example, writing of the history of Egyptian television, Abu-Lughod (2005) says that "in Egypt, public television was seen as an aggressive attempt to assimilate the distinct communities into a nation state" (p. 5).

Second, the state has unique powers to control radio and television by being able to decide who gets a license to use the radio spectrum to broadcast. Many states simply took over television themselves to promote national identity, to control national politics, to mobilize people to support government development programs, or to educate people in new ideas and ways of working or living that national states wanted to promote. India was a good example of a state that initially ran television directly under a state monopoly, Doordarshan, to achieve all these goals, even though television there eventually became much more complicated (Kumar, 2006). Other states, like Mexico, left broadcasting in private hands under a monopoly that worked closely with government to achieve most of the same goals (Fernández & Paxman, 2001).

Third, political, economic, and other leaders, both domestic and transnational, need the state to use television to carry out certain educational tasks that turn people not only into citizens of a nation but also into useful employees and consumers. Speaking of Turkey, Sengul (2006) said, "First of all, the need to integrate new migrant communities into the texture of western cities created both a need and a demand for programs that would serve as pedagogical and performative items to this end" (p. 10).

Fourth, television was initially so much more expensive than radio that it was more likely to remain a national project, clearly under the gaze of the national state. In fact, in much of the world, particularly large parts of the Arab world (Boyd, 1993), Africa (Head, 1974), and Asia (Lent, 1978), national government started television because no private actor had enough money.

## Dependency and Ownership

Direct foreign investment in media ownership first followed lines of colonialism and then dependency. For example, the logic of regional proximity led U.S. companies to become involved in Latin America from the 19th century on, first with resource extraction and trade, later with direct investment for manufacturing. So radio and television developed in Latin America in the context of a region that had already moved from mercantilist capitalism under Spain and Portugal to a capitalism dependent on trade, capital, investment, and corporate models from the United States and Europe. American advertisers and advertising agencies promoted commercial radio and television elsewhere because they wanted to have commercial media with which to work (Fox, 1975, 1997).

The United States, Britain, and France also made a considerable direct investment in colonial and other Third World newspapers in the 1920s, in movies in the 1920s–1930s, in radio in the 1930s and 1940s (Schwoch,

1990), and in television in the 1960s and 1970s (Beltran & Fox de Cardona, 1979). Early in the 20th century, as today, many local elites have found it convenient to grow their national industries through cooperative links with global corporations (Herman & McChesney, 1997). For example, Brazil's TV Globo is now one of the largest media corporations in the world outside the core industrial countries. But when Robert Marinho started it in Brazil in 1962, he was unsure of his own capabilities in a new medium. In classic industrial strategy, he sought to minimize his risk with an alliance for technology, capital, and management advice with Time-Life, which invested in TV Globo and advised him until 1968, when it was forced out by the government (Straubhaar, 1984). There was one initial wave of investment in foreign television companies in the 1960s, particularly by the United States in Latin America. However, most countries enacted laws that prohibited or limited direct foreign investment in television, even if it meant forcing out some of the investments made in the 1960s. "With a few minor exceptions, nationalism would prompt foreign governments to deny outsiders control of sensitive and powerful medium of television" (Duarte, 2001, p. 21).

Dependency theorists note that local families, often those already involved with print media, started most radio and television operations in Latin America, but they took these initiatives within a context of a capitalism that might be characterized as dependent (Fejes, 1981). These cultural industries were also hybrid. They blended national characteristics, such as family ownership and strong ties to the state, together with typically U.S. characteristics such as commercialization, professionalization of network management, production, and the development of truly national advertising markets with strong ties to national and global advertising agencies. Of the influences exerted on Brazil's TV Globo by Time-Life, for example, the most lasting were the reorganization of its production system, its network/affiliate management, and its relations with advertisers and ratings firms. In contrast, Time Life's programming advice was almost immediately rejected as useless within the Brazilian cultural market context, and program decisions were made by a combination of Brazilian advertising executives who knew the national market and program producers hired from other networks who knew which genres worked in that market (Straubhaar, 1981, 1984).

## The State as Owner

In Asia, the Middle East, and Africa, television was usually started by the state (Katz & Wedell, 1976). In many countries, including most of Asia, government acted to ensure its role in controlling a powerful medium. In some countries—for example, most of Africa—an additional reason was that only the state had enough money to start and operate television networks because the consumer markets were not rich enough to support commercial television. In a few places, such as Taiwan and South Korea, private television was permitted, but formal joint ownership with government agencies was required to ensure control. Former colonial powers had invested in electronic media in other parts of the world, but these media were also often nationalized in the 1960s and 1970s.

In dependency theory, not enough attention was paid to the national entrepreneurs or government elites who started television broadcasting. Several critics of dependency and of cultural imperialism argued that these theories did not attribute sufficient responsibility to national elites. As Sarti (1981) observed, Latin America has had enough time to develop its own systems and ideologies, traceable to indigenous class interests, and that to attribute too much influence to the other developed nations is to neglect analysis of internal class and group interests that also determine the nature of the system.

Fernando Henrique Cardoso (1973) described a scenario that foresees growth and development for some countries like Brazil or Chile within a context of dependence on developed countries, called *associated-dependent development*. Cardoso and Evans (1979) identified three groups as crucial to the process of dependent development: the state-owned enterprises of the developing countries, the multinational corporations that invest or sell in developing countries, and local firms, which are usually associated with either or both. Cardoso called these groups the tripod of dependent development, and Evans saw them as being in an alliance.

## The Economic and Political Role of States

The initial role of many Third World states has been to grant and, sometimes, control or regulate concessions to foreign exporters and investors. In this process, many smaller states have found themselves relatively powerless in dealing with multinational companies. Unlike the government of a large state like Brazil, smaller states do not have the information or bureaucratic expertise to negotiate adequately with multinationals. However, governments have often focused harder on media multinational investors than others because almost all states are leery of foreign control over media. In fact, until the 1990s, almost all states, including the United States, forbade direct foreign investment in television broadcasting.

Results from dependency and media imperialism analysis contributed in many ways to a wave of policy intervention against foreign investment in broadcasting and importation of foreign media products that was remarkably effective in many countries. Most countries enacted controls against foreign ownership of electronic media, either by nationalizing older foreign investments or by having the state initiate and control television broadcasting (Katz & Wedell, 1976). Clearly some states were more active and capable than others. Evans (1979) noted the state's role in financing local entrepreneurs in their dealings and joint ventures with multinational corporations. Evans also noted that the state in South Korea and other Asian countries had been very active in helping national firms negotiate and deal with outside multinationals, especially in the computer industries (Evans, 1992).

In Europe and Japan, the states deliberately built up public-sector broadcasting to ensure national cultural and informational sovereignty. During the 1960s and especially during the 1970s New World Information and Communication Order (NWICO) debate in the United Nations, the desirability of a greater role for public-policy and public-sector broadcasting was widely discussed (McPhail, 1989). However, economic support for new public or state-sector broadcasting projects was limited. Private-sector broadcast firms also vigorously opposed any change. So private ownership and control of broadcast industries continued to grow, even in Western Europe, where the public-sector model was stronger (McChesney, 1997).

## Import Substitution in Cultural Industries

In Asia, Europe, Latin America, and some other areas, one of the main strategies for reducing dependence has been import substitution industrialization: creating market reserve policies and tariff barriers to protect infant industries and promote the growth of national industries or national/ multinational joint ventures to supply national markets. A number of Latin American countries have been pursuing import substitution in various sectors since the 1930s (Baer, 1989). Initially focused on areas such as petroleum and steel, this policy was powerfully applied by several states to cultural products as well, such as radio in the 1930s and 1940s, film (Schnitman, 1984), and television (Straubhaar, 1981). Just after World War II, a number of Asian countries, such as Japan, South Korea, and India, also focused on import substitution for their own markets, including cultural industry markets (Ito, 1991). Many countries in Latin America, Asia, and Europe took various measures to increase national television production and reduce imports. This question of reducing television imports also figured strongly in the NWICO debate and other national communication policy discussions of the 1970s and 1980s.

A number of states, particularly in Europe and Asia, have relied extensively on requiring certain quotas of national production on television, especially on prime time (Grantham, 2000). Several Asian countries, such as Taiwan, South Korea, and Japan, set those quotas high, essentially requiring almost 90% national television production for most of the 1970s through the 1990s (Ito, 1991; Lee, 1980). Although they were more controversial in world policy debates, national content quotas in Canada and Western Europe were actually less stringent than those in several East Asian countries.

However, many countries were not able to do that kind of cultural import substitution. In other words, a crucial distinction appeared between those developing countries where certain key conditions facilitated a relatively autonomous approach to television institutions and industries and those where these conditions did not exist. Many would-be producers of television programming have been constrained by economic realities. The continuing results of conditions of dependency, such as low-income resources, lack of industrial infrastructure, lack of support by weak governments, inappropriate models for production, and lack of trained personnel, have kept a number of poorer countries from developing much local or national production, even if their audiences might prefer more national programs. This is particularly true for the smallest and poorest of nations, such as those in the English-speaking Caribbean (Brown, 1987).

## Adaptation and Glocalization of Foreign Models

The adoption and adaptation, or glocalization, of foreign models has gone through several phases. The studies of the 1970s, such as Katz and Wedell (1976), observed the first phase, a postcolonial era in which developing countries typically modeled the structures of former colonial powers or dominant economic partners. In this manner, former British Commonwealth countries tended to copy or adapt structures like the BBC, former French colonies modeled French institutions, and Latin America, the Philippines, and others that depended on the U.S. economy or experienced U.S. political intervention tended to model the U.S. commercial broadcasting system (Katz & Wedell, 1976; Lee, 1980). A number of countries also tried mixed models of public and private ownership.

Over time, however, even as postcolonial dependencies in developed world countries sorted out and shifted, an asymmetrical replication persisted of core capitalist country structures, especially those of the United States. Although some countries originally modeled British or French colonial systems, many have moved increasingly toward the U.S. model because it reflects an increasingly dominant, essentially capitalist economic model. This took place in part because of direct economic dependency on the United States and U.S. firms. The U.S. model spread well beyond its area of direct primary influence in Latin America, however, because as more countries shifted toward greater integration with the world capitalist economy, policy makers and would-be media owners both saw the U.S. model as a highly functional and commercially successful way of organizing television. That view was, needless to say, powerfully reinforced by both foreign and domestic advertisers, who wanted to see television become an advertising vehicle open to them (Fox, 1975). One of the weaknesses of the media imperialism model is that it did not recognize the power of advertising as a systemic influence, although some analyses of the era, particularly in Latin America, pointed that out (Fejes, 1980; Fox, 1975; Janus, 1977; Mattos, 1984).

For a number of contemporary writers, this focus on the U.S. model has transformed into a focus on a globalizing modernity that includes many aspects of U.S.-style capitalism (Giddens), but that has now lost some of its U.S. particularities precisely as it has become more universalized (Robertson, 1995). This widespread tendency to adopt a model of capitalist production, including in media, is then localized, or as Robertson hypothesizes, glocalized. Countries such as Japan make significant changes to such models, and those revised regional models then attract other developing economies (Iwabuchi, 2002). Iwabuchi (1997) evocatively called this attractiveness of the revised or glocalized model to other Asian cultures and economies "the sweet smell of Asian modernity."

## Advertising

When related to cultural dependency, particularly in television, most observers add advertising to the foreign economic influences observed by the dependent development paradigm in the general economy. Fejes (1980) emphasized the influence of multinational advertising on television industries throughout Latin America, both currently and historically. He noted that "it was the demands of advertising, particularly the advertising of multinational corporations, that shaped the commercial development of television in Latin America" (p. 25). Evans (personal interview, 1979) and Beltran and Fox de Cardona (1979, pp. 36–37) have observed that the television industry still depends on foreign financing in the form of advertising revenues from multinational corporations and advertising agencies.

By the 1980s, work in Brazil by Mattos (1984) and elsewhere noted that the state itself was a powerful advertiser. In much of Latin America and Asia in the 1970s and 1980s, a form of state capitalism prevailed in which various aspects of the national state, including commercial banks, development banks, trading companies, pension funds, investment funds, manufacturing firms, and military firms, were involved in as much as half of the national gross national product. By directing the advertising of all these state firms, governments in Brazil, Mexico, China, Korea, and Taiwan, among others, could reward cooperative media and punish critical media—a powerful tool for control, which often overshadowed the power of foreign advertisers.

## National Conglomerates and Competition

Fox (1997), McChesney (1999), and others also called attention to the importance of national economic conglomerates, including the media themselves, as advertisers. In Venezuela, for example, the Cisneros Group is involved in many activities other than broadcasting and can support itself with its own advertising to some degree. Even with media business, per se, national conglomerates can cross-promote their own cultural products. TV Globo and others, for example, make quite a bit of money by selling television program soundtracks that the programs themselves promote.

This is one example of a larger phenomenon. From the 1970s on, a number of the larger or wealthier national cultural markets began to show a tendency toward the development of concentrated and conglomerated cultural industries. Private television in Latin America and Asia became concentrated, with one or two firms usually achieving dominance over the market or the audience's viewing habits. In many cases, this was accomplished in part through cozy relationships with national governments, for example, the Brazilian military government's favored relationship with TV Globo or the ruling party's encouragement of a virtual monopoly over television in Mexico by Televisa (whose owners included a former president, Miguel Aleman). Similarly, governments favored or in some cases co-owned key private stations in Taiwan, South Korea, and Hong Kong. Monopolizing distribution to the audience is a form of horizontal integration (controlling most of one level of economic activity, like broadcasting or film distribution).

Most broadcasters outside the United States also produced most of their own programs in-house, a sort of vertical integration of production and distribution. In part, this is because many countries did not have institutions like Hollywood film studios to fall back on for production of programs, as the U.S. television networks did. In part, this also centralized all profit for the broadcasters, instead of splitting it between producers and broadcasters. This horizontal and vertical integration also made control over production easier for government authorities that wanted to keep track of content. In many other cases, the state owned and operated television networks. These government broadcasters even more naturally tended to both horizontal and vertical integration.

## The Cultural Role of States: National Security and National Identity

It is clear that the core countries try to assert political and cultural hegemonies over other nations. At the most obvious level, there are also regional economic hegemonies in which Japan asserts special relationships with Asian countries, the United States with North, Central, and South America, and some European states with nations in Africa, the Caribbean, the Middle East, and parts of Asia. However, other nations, at least the larger states in the Third World, have frequently resisted. Many nation-states intervene as gatekeepers to limit cultural inflows, to protect cultural industries, and to resist ideological domination.

Both industrial and cultural policies have led to the protection of national cultural industries. Control of media content and control over the direction of cultural discourse are also clearly important for political and even military reasons, as well. Extensive debates about communications and cultural policy in Latin America and elsewhere led to little affect or action, according to some observers (Fox, 1988). But, in fact, in a number of countries, economic policy and institutions, cultural policy and cultural industries, and the military all have a role in the function of national identity in national security policy. These bodies have combined to create formal and informal policies that promoted the protection of national cultural industries precisely to reinforce a certain sense of national identity. In many countries, such as Brazil, Mexico, Taiwan, and South Korea, an alliance of the state bureaucracy, political parties, private interests in the media industries, and, often, the military supported such cultural nationalism (Atwood & Mattos, 1982; Mattos, 1982; Sinclair, 1994).

In a number of places, radio and television have created unifying spoken languages that bring diverse dialects together. This happens within nations, as in Brazil or India, where Hindi is emerging as a dominant language for a variety of groups. It also happens across nations, as in the Arab world, where Nasser's *Voice of the Arabs* from Egypt began to unify speakers of different dialects of Arabic or where the Arabic adaptation of *Sesame Street* came up with an innovative, simplified common written Arabic to teach children. The unifying force of media can also be seen at a subnational level, as when television broadcasting in a local language, such as Catalan, reinforces that local identity against the national one (Moragas Spa, Garitaonaindia Garnacho, & Lopez, 1999).

At least until the 1990s, most television was watched via national systems. Furthermore, much if not most of that television was still produced at the national level, particularly programs in the prime-time hours when most people watch (see Table A.1, which looks at trends from 1962 to 2002). States have worked hard to create this outcome because national production of television reinforces a sense of identity that has a number of desirable aspects. National television can reinforce national political identity and loyalty among the citizens, sustain a sense of patriotism, conform to a military sense of national security, and reinforce a sense of being a national consumer within a national market, which also helps the state by strengthening national industry. When Katz and Wedell (1976) surveyed national ambitions for broadcasting in the 1970s, creation of a national identity was one of the highest aspirations for radio and television. That aspiration continues for many.

## Cultural Industries

For many countries, by the 1980s, the political economy of television had changed and nationalized, as both nation-states and national cultural industries had grown in power. In Cardoso's (1973) terms, in many countries, the tripod's legs of state and national capital had grown to match the third leg, foreign capital. That change was, interestingly, in some part due to a policy reaction to the earlier analyses of dependency theory. Some states had acted against dependency, so that theory had to change, in part, due to its own successes. However, this analysis best applies to the larger and more powerful states and cultural industries; some smaller, poorer countries remained heavily limited by the constraints or boundary conditions economic dependency imposed. Still, overall, another era of generally increased national television production began in the 1970s and 1980s.

Another school of thought in the 1980s tried to build on both the political economy and cultural studies schools of thought by looking at television as a cultural industry. Some saw cultural industries as virtually all-powerful actors in determining what people think (Guback & Varis, 1986). Others saw cultural industries as the home for several sets of actors with varying degrees of power, actors who are themselves but one part of a larger process of creating cultural products and making meaning (Sinclair, 1995).

The original literature on cultural industries comes from the Frankfurt School (Adorno, 1957), where they were seen as turning both high culture and folk culture into industrialized mass cultural products that strongly controlled the development of culture, arriving at a kind of mass man in a mass culture. This paradigm has been powerful, particularly in Latin America, where it fit nicely with an era of industrialization, urbanization, and massification of social life. During this period, traditional agrarian societies rapidly transformed into modern urban ones, and the common experience was now of the urban working class, as compared to the rural peasant. Cultural industry theory has converged with theories about economic determinism, economic dependence, and hegemony to see large cultural industries, both domestic and foreign, as overwhelming individuals and determining cultural outcomes (Beltran, 1978). Building further on the cultural industry literature and dependency theory, McAnany (1984) described how the commercial Brazilian television industry had grown beyond the limits originally predicted by dependency theory but was still constrained by structural problems of a limited, at least partially dependent economy and still working within organizational commercial media models imported from the United States.

This approach to cultural industries recognized the limits placed on many nations' media systems by operating within subordinate positions in the world economy, but it also recognized and gave analytical emphasis to the distinct dynamics of each nation or industry's historical development. Key national issues included conflicts between domestic and transnational elites, interests of key national elites, entrepreneurial competition, the agendas and actions of key production personnel, and the effects of state intervention, particularly as policy maker, provider of infrastructure, and advertiser (Mattelart & Mattelart, 1990; Mattos, 1982; Straubhaar, 1984; Vink, 1988). Larger nations saw an increasingly complex and dynamic development of local cultural industries. As technologies and economic developments permitted smaller-scale production, local radio, local newspapers or newsletters, local video productions, and so on enabled various cultural fronts or actors to produce culture in an increasingly industrialized way.

## Crucial Structural Conditions of National Cultural Industries

A number of crucial structural conditions made national media production more likely. These conditions enabled national cultural producers to resist the contrasting advantages of global and regional producers. In terms of complexity theory, these were crucial initial conditions, which shaped the boundaries of what was possible for the actors that operated inside those systems or institutions. In terms of structuration theory, these factors drew the limits on what is possible, set rules on how producers can operate, and provided the resources that would or would not permit extensive national cultural production.

*Market size* was crucial. Small countries generally produced less television, whereas most large countries eventually became significant producers of television. Larger markets enabled producers to achieve economies of scale and to attempt more complex and costly genres of production. "Producers in countries that belong to large natural language markets have a financial incentive to create larger budget films and programs that generally have greater intrinsic audience appeal, a clear advantage in international competition" (Wildman & Siwek, 1988, p. 68). Even a rich small country like Belgium or Norway had the total wealth to produce only a limited amount of television, whereas a large poor country like India could assemble the resources to do quite a bit.

The *relative wealth* of a market was also crucial. A relatively small or medium-size market, like Japan, Taiwan, or Hong Kong, could still produce quite a bit of television if it was wealthy enough. *The financial base* likewise placed boundaries around what kind of programming could be produced. Reliance on advertising constrained programming options to those that were commercially successful; that is, those that drew the largest or most economically attractive audiences. Government finance tended to give greater control over programming to government institutions and ruling political parties. License fees, used, for example, in Britain or Japan, tended to insulate programming against both government and commercial pressures. *Commercial structure* bounded or limited what kind of media products would be produced. If commercial success in a market was imperative, the most commercially successful program models would be adopted, whether they were local or foreign.

*Competition* among media in a national, regional, or global market may have promoted creativity, but it also tended to disperse resources among a number of competitors. Growth for television stations or networks was sometimes enhanced by limiting the number of competitors. Lord Reith decided in the 1920s that the BBC needed a monopoly over resources to produce a quantity of diverse, quality programming. Although thinking in the United States has always favored competition, many other countries in almost all regions opted instead for television monopolies in the early days of the medium, often to pool resources for production, although often simply to make television easier to control (Katz & Wedell, 1976).

*Government policies* could provide or deny crucial resources to television. It could enable television industries to act independently of foreign pressure. The state could be a media actor on its own, a facilitating or obstructive regulator, or the creator of favorable conditions, such as subsidy for construction, research and development, or other needs.

*Other cultural industries* could support or limit television industries. Television drew heavily on the strength of related local cultural industries (film, music, theater, recordings). If those were underdeveloped, too, that placed another boundary to television production. For example, most developing countries that became major television producers, such as Brazil, Egypt, or India, drew heavily on previously built-up film industries to do so. The fact that India had well-developed film industries in local languages such as Telugu made the emergence of strong, separate television networks at the local level much more possible than in most countries (Kumar, 2006).

*Producer behavior* often followed commercial imperatives, but it also responded to the demands of the domestic market or audience when resources allowed. However, in some cultures—for example, Russia since 2000—political imperatives were reimposed over what were successful commercial networks. Within the boundaries placed by these political economy structures, developments tended to be nonlinear and hard to predict, but patterns are discernable among the groups of actors involved. The key groups were those involved in the management and direction of television, the entrepreneurs; those involved in the actual program planning and production, the producers; and the receivers or audiences.

*Entrepreneurial* behavior by those who own or manage cultural industries likewise tailored operations to the programming interests of domestic (or regional or global) audiences and to domestic and foreign business needs and markets, with considerable differentiation among larger markets/systems.

*Audience behavior* not only reflected choices among what was offered, but also worked within a cultural context; the national culture could define audience tastes to dispose viewers toward choosing national productions over imported ones. National culture's appeal to domestic audiences was (and is) a crucial local advantage. National industries' ability to compete with foreign imports varied depending on the homogeneity of audiences and their acceptance of national culture.

Over time, the patterns of action and behavior by these kinds of actors tended to stabilize and form culturally defined boundaries. Among industry professionals, those took the form of "the way we do things here." Among audiences, they took the form of preferences for certain kinds of programming or genres.

## Achieving National Coverage via Satellite

Satellites have often been seen as an inherently globalizing technology by many scholars. However, their initial major impact was their use to distribute television channels from broadcast networks to affiliates and from cable channel producers to local cable system head-ends within national systems. I will take up their global role more in Chapter 5, but the main impact of satellites as a mass medium arguably continues to be this intermediate role of delivering signals from network producers to affiliates, retransmitters, and cable head-ends. For example, much of the population in many rural areas gets television by satellite dishes hooked to local retransmitters, not even affiliate stations, just literal retransmitters. For example, in rural Brazil, most small towns and villages have a municipal dish that pulls down the main commercial channel, TV Globo, and retransmits it to the local area. If residents want a second channel, they have to lobby the mayor to put up a second retransmitter or go get their own satellite dish so that they can receive the other national broadcast networks (La Pastina, 1999).

In 1975, HBO exemplified this stage of the process, achieving national impact by putting its channel on a satellite for distribution to cable systems all over the United States (Baldwin & McEvoy, 1988). The international impact of television satellites started about this same time, as cable systems in Canada, Mexico, and the Caribbean also began to pull down and distribute HBO and other channels primarily intended for domestic U.S. distribution.

In the 1970s, a number of governments around the world saw satellite distribution of national television channels as a crucial priority. The USSR invested massively in satellite distribution to reach across its seven time zones and two continents to deliver a centrally controlled message to its large, diverse population (Mickiewicz, 1988). India obtained early assistance from U.S. satellites to deliver television signals to a widespread rural audience under the Satellite Instructional Television Experiment (Singhal & Rogers, 1989). Brazil and Mexico both invested tens of millions of scarce, borrowed dollars in nationally owned satellite systems to ensure that they could subsidize the extension of their national television networks (Hudson, 1990). These systems initially reached rebroadcast transmitters and community viewing facilities, but eventually, many individuals also bought antennas so they could receive national television via satellite (Straubhaar, 2003).

## Supplementing National Coverage via Satellite: Translocal Television in the Nation

Many people have also bought antennas or subscribed to cable television systems to receive television that is aimed at the nation from outside via satellite, what Kumar (2006) calls translocal, technically transnational signals programmed outside the nation, which are aimed at its audience or cultures within it. One leading example is Zee TV and others in India (Thussu,

1998), which have used regional satellite platforms, starting with Star TV, to transmit alternative national- or local-language programming into India since 1991 (Star TV) and 1992 (Zee TV; Sinclair, 2005). This translocal television in India built on several factors. Like a number of other countries that experienced powerful impacts of translocal, transnational, or global television in the 1990s, the existing broadcast television in India was a government monopoly that had not diversified into some areas of strong potential interest, such as music video, in-depth news, and regional-language programming. Unlike some countries, where cable remained an expensive luxury for the middle classes, translocal television in India built on transmitting satellite signals to a rapidly growing local infrastructure of "cable-wallahs," local, often irregular cable systems. The latter grew from 150 operators in 1985 to 100,000 in 1995, when they were finally regulated, with perhaps 60,000 still in business by 2002 (Sinclair, 2005). Perhaps most important, translocal television was driven by both national and regional Indian entrepreneurs like those behind ZeeTV, which developed a national audience with entertainment in "Hinglish" (Sinclair, 2005), and those behind Sun TV (regional Tamil television) and Eenadu (regional Telegu television; Kumar, 2006).

In the early 1990s, translocal channels grew up in a number of parts of the world as entrepreneurs or émigré groups saw satellite television as a way of sending television back into their homelands for commercial, religious, or political purposes. A number of channels—music channels, as well as news, religious information, and ethnic channels aimed at groups like the Kurds—were broadcast into Turkey by groups wishing to challenge the state monopoly on broadcast television. Similar channels were initially broadcast from outside the Arabic-speaking world back into it, such as Middle Eastern Broadcasting Center (MBC). A number of satellite channels have also been broadcast back into Iran by various dissident groups and entrepreneurs (Semati, 2006).

Another variation on the translocal is outside channels aimed at national audiences and those who have migrated away, for example, Indians in the United States or Turks in Europe. For example, a number of channels have targeted both Turkey and Turkish audiences in Europe since the early 1990s (Aksoy & Robins, 2000; Oncu, 2000). In fact, Zee TV has also come to serve dispersed or diaspora Indian audiences across the globe, but I will talk more about Zee TV as a global medium in Chapter 4, about global television.

Like many other transnational forms of television, translocal television seems to depend on both national domestic trends and opportunities perceived by transnational actors; for example, the people who started Zee TV or Rupert Murdoch, who initially carried such programming into India on

Star TV. If major audience interests were not being met by national broadcast channels, then satellite technology provided a new technological option, starting in the early 1990s, for reaching those audiences and interests. In both India and Turkey, the state operated national television under clear but narrow mandates that excluded a number of things in which audiences were potentially quite interested, such as a wider range of entertainment options, including music videos, and minority-language television. In Turkey, Islamic-focused television was also attractive. In a number of cases, after the possibility of translocal television via satellite had broken the monopoly of former national broadcasters, a liberalization of competition occurred in the 1990s that permitted national and regional broadcasters to start business. (That overall process of liberalization, as an aspect of globalization, is covered more in the following chapter.)

## Television Above and Below the National Level

In places where the national state has not become a strong pole of identity, local and supranational regional cultural identities are often particularly strong. In much of Africa and parts of Asia and Latin America, national television does not reach much of the population, or it reaches them only in national languages that they do not speak comfortably. As a result, much of the population either ignores television, tries to create local productions, or seeks out television from neighboring or related countries in languages that they do speak.

For example, in Mozambique, only 25% to 35% of the population speaks Portuguese, roughly the same percentage that has access to television. Consequently, the reach of television is so limited that many people focus on local languages and local cultural forms, which are more likely to be expressed on radio than on television, if they appear in mass media at all. Given limited resources for production, television in Mozambique has always depended on imported programming for much of its schedule. Although many of those imports used to come from Europe or the United States, Mozambican television has turned increasingly to imports from Brazil, which exports a great deal of soap opera, music, and comedy. That Brazilian programming has the advantage of being in the national language, Portuguese, as well as drawing on a common cultural heritage of symbols, references, and even jokes that build on their common history as former Portuguese colonies. This situation contributes to the growth of a transnational Lusophone, or Portuguese-speaking cultural-linguistic market that includes Brazil, Mozambique, Portugal, and others. This kind of transnational development is covered more in Chapter 4.

In a few wealthy countries, such as Canada, Spain, or Great Britain, there are enough resources to permit local production in subnational languages, such as French (in Quebec), Catalan, Welsh, or Scottish (Moragas Spa et al., 1999), or a number of regional languages in India (Kumar, 2006). In some countries, minorities are part of large diasporas, such as the overseas Chinese in Malaysia or Canada. These immigrants tend to use a variety of technological options, from video to satellite channels to Web pages, Internet music downloads, and Internet streaming video to gain access to television produced in the languages they speak and reflecting the cultures with which they identify.

Local television is still more limited by costs of production. It is less developed in most countries than national television due to the need to spread costs across a larger audience to achieve economies of scale. Local television genres are also in a way limited by the need for a strong visual component, whereas musical genres can be remarkably varied. Television genres have developed remarkably over the past 20 to 30 years, however. A number of low-cost genres have evolved, which can be produced almost anywhere with the simplest and cheapest of equipment: news, talk, variety, live music, and games. More and more nations are producing an increasing proportion of their own programming using such genres. Table A.1 shows that a significant number of countries are doing more than half of their own programming, both in the total broadcast day and during prime time, where audience viewing is concentrated and the most popular programs are usually placed.

Some genres also lend themselves to more localized programming on provincial-level or municipal stations. Latin America, for example, has experienced an increase in local news and discussion programs on television stations. For public stations, such programs are a natural line of programming, if resources from public or state sources allow. For private stations, the viability of such local programming depends on costs of production balanced against audience demand and advertiser willingness to pay. Indications from an early study (Huesca, 1985) in one fairly poor Latin American country, Bolivia, is that local programming in news and public affairs varied considerably, particularly depending on who owned and controlled the station and what their resources were, but many stations were doing quite a bit. Furthermore, stations were able to draw on some resources and programs produced by alternative producers. Bolivia, like Brazil and a number of other countries, has had a growing tradition for several years of alternative video production by nongovernmental organizations, activist groups, church groups, unions, and so on (Alvarado, 1988). As one of the main alternative video producers then in Brazil, Luiz Santoro (1989), observed, many such groups saw alternative video as a means toward producing materials for television as local, provincial, or even national opportunities open up. Since then, alternative video producers have circulated materials on public access cable and, more recently, on the Internet. As alternative regional satellite broadcasters grow, alternative video or television may also find a possible outlet there (Downing, 2001). For example, the new regional satellite broadcast channel in Latin America, Telesur, sponsored by Venezuela and several other Latin American governments, has begun to use such materials to create alternatives to the existing regional commercial channels (Aharonian, 2006).

## Glocal Processes and National Identities

In television and in other cultural industries as well, people use globally distributed forms to create cultural products, which define and redefine the national and the local. Robertson (1995) observed that "globalization has involved the reconstruction, in a sense the production, of 'home,' 'community' and 'locality'" (p. 30). Cultural producers use forms and genres that have spread globally to express ideas of what home is like. There is a subtle interplay between the global, national, and local in television form and content.

It is increasingly hard to have a national idea that does not relate at least in part to global roots. In other words, the national productive apparatus for cultural industry described so far in this chapter produces many products that are national hybrids of a variety of influences, global, regional or cultural-linguistic, national, and local. The creative process that proceeds through these cultural industries reflects hybrid forms. Globalized ideas of how identities are expressed affect national and local cultures:

> Much of the apparatus of contemporary nations, including the *form* of the particularities—the construction of their unique identities—is very similar across the entire world (Meyer, 1980; Robertson, 1991), in spite of much variation in levels of "development." This is, perhaps, the most tangible of contemporary sites of the interpenetration of particularism and universalism. (Robertson, 1995, p. 34)

# 4

# Creating Global, U.S., and Transnational Television Spaces

For a number of theorists in the past 10 to 15 years, the primary macro-analytic framework for television and other media has become globalization (Giddens, 1991; Robertson, 1990). However, that word has also become overextended as a term of analysis, covering a number of contradictory analyses and points of view. I intend to talk about globalization primarily in the economic and technological areas where almost all analysts agree that it is fundamental. In this chapter, I talk about economic and political/institutional globalization and their impact on world television, especially after 1990. In the next chapter (Chapter 5), I examine technological globalization, along with its complexities and impacts.

Global forces have a powerful effect on communication, particularly television, by redefining many aspects of it at a systemic level. However, it is important to distinguish the dynamics of economic and technological forces, on the one hand, and cultural forces, per se, on the other. Appadurai (1990) did this by distinguishing between substantially disjunct *scapes* of finance, technology, and so on, which are globalized in different ways. Ortiz (1994, 2002) distinguished between globalization related to economic and technological changes and what he called *mundialização* or *mundialization*, "understood as the process where a process of world modernity is developing, but articulated and differentiated according to the particular historical circumstances of each country" (Stald & Tufte, 2002, p. 4). This builds on recent French theoretical work (Darling-Wolf, 2006).

Analysts are less agreed on the notion that globalization accurately describes the dominant forces directly acting within culture and on the specifically cultural contents of television. When globalization is the cover term for virtually everything international or transnational, how are phenomena that are indeed heavily globalized distinguished from those that may be less broadly encompassing? I believe that to define the overall tendency of television systems throughout the world as globalization gives global phenomena too much emphasis compared with phenomena that are more precisely transnational, geocultural, or cultural-linguistic—national, regional, or even local. For example, media entrepreneur Rupert Murdoch casts a long shadow over the world in many ways, but in most specific places, he and his companies are far less important to what is on the television than national powers like Roberto Marinho, owner of TV Globo in Brazil, or the Chinese government in China, which has managed to constrain Murdoch's desire to enter the Chinese cultural space and market. So in this chapter, I discuss various aspects of what is considered global, distinguishing what is perhaps more accurately or precisely thought of as transnational, geocultural, or cultural-linguistic.

Part of my uneasiness with globalization as a cover term is that some aspects of television are truly globalized and need to be highlighted, not lost in mixture with other, less globalized aspects. Discussing globalization, Castells (2005) noted that "in the strict sense, it is the process that results from the capacity of certain activities to function as a unit in real time on a planetary scale." In certain economic areas such as finance, foreign direct investment, the commercialization of television systems and program formats, the marketing of U.S. feature films and series, and the licensing of television formats (such as *Survivor*), I argue that the emphasis on globalization is correct. Even in areas where global flows move quickly and with great effect, however, many crucial things are still decided and controlled at the national level in many, if not most countries. Nederveen Pieterse (1995) observed, "Globalization can mean the reinforcement of both supranational and sub-national regionalism" (p. 50). Although a key argument in this chapter is that the role of cultural-linguistic regions warrants greater attention, such an emphasis can be fit into the more sophisticated interpretations of globalization that are emerging, such as this view of Nederveen Pieterse (1995, 2004).

I argue, then, that global television is a complex system operating in different layers. One set of layers is cultural and geographic: global, transnational, cultural-linguistic spaces, geocultural regions, nations, global metropolises, states/provinces, and localities. Another set is functional, rather like Appadurai's (1990) notion of scapes (finance, technology, ideology, people/migration, and ideology); these are disjunct and differentially globalized. The two sets of layers are related. The most densely globalized parts are those related to the effective global spread of the capitalist system, such as finance, the models for operating commercial networks and stations, and half a dozen truly global conglomerates with widespread ownership and influence. I argue that program models and genres circulate globally but are far more complex, a topic I will discuss extensively in later chapters. I argue that in key regions (or cultural-linguistic spheres), national and local producers tend to make culture-specific adaptations of global genres and models, which are then followed by a number of other producers and networks within their regions, as in Asia (Iwabuchi, 2002), the Arab world (Kraidy, in press), or Latin America (Straubhaar, 1991; Straubhaar & Viscasillas, 1991).

For the balance of the chapter, I examine economic, political, and social aspects of globalization that affect television. I then compare those global levels of analysis with transnational, cultural-linguistic, and geocultural levels of how television functions, not only as an economic system, but a cultural and social one, as well. (The last chapter included a discussion of national and local production capabilities, which I will return to later, as I look at program and genre production and flow.)

## Globalization Broadly Defined

Globalization is the worldwide spread, over both time and space, of a number of new ideas, institutions, culturally defined ways of doing things, and technologies. Harvey (2005) spoke of a compression of both time and space in the spread of capitalist modernity on a global scale. Giddens (1991) defined globalization as "the intensification of worldwide social relations [with] distant localities in such a way that local happenings are shaped by events occurring many miles away and vice versa" (p. 64). Giddens (1991) stressed four areas of globalization as primary: multilateralism, global division of labor, spread of capitalism, and military alliances. Appadurai (1990) talked of five scapes of globalization that cover migration, finance, technology, culture, and ideology. Closer to the focus here on the role of globalization in mediated communication, Tomlinson (1999) said, "globalization refers to the rapidly developing and ever-densening network of interconnections and interdependences that characterize modern social life" (p. 174).

Tomlinson (1999) said complex connectivity leads to a variety of proximities for people, beyond the local and national. Featherstone (in Featherstone & Lash, 1995) said that globalization undoes local cultural unities and creates cultural complexity, and I will argue that globalization adds more layers of culture for television production, flow, and consumption above the local and national. While that may reduce somewhat the salience of the local and national to many people, most people will continue to have strong local and national identities, even as they gain other layers as well.

## Economic Globalization

Economically, globalization is often seen as the spread of capitalism as a system (Wallerstein, 1979), as capitalist modernity (Tomlinson, 1999), as a specifically neoliberal form of capitalism (Harvey, 2005), as consumerism and commercialism in systemic models, and as social ethics, sometimes referred to as McDonaldization (Ritzer, 2004a, 2004b), and as the growing penetration and power of international corporations (Herman & McChesney, 1997). Economic analyses tend to focus on finance, on ownership and foreign investment, on models of operation, and on the ability of the state or others to regulate or control economic activity.

Business leaders (Wriston, 1988), pundits (Friedman, 1999), and others have noted how globalized finance has become overall and how quickly money moves around the world (Sassen, 2004). Television, however, is most often a stubbornly national system, even in terms of finance. Most television markets are still financed by nationally focused advertising, which operates under rules defined largely by nations, with advertising conceptualized in terms of national audiences, even if the advertiser is a multinational corporation with a global sales strategy. In ownership, even though foreign direct investment flows globally, television network ownership rules are still usually defined by national governments, as are those of cable television systems. Direct-to-home satellite television systems may try to bypass national governments, but if they wish to collect a subscription fee or work with national advertisers, they usually end up having to cooperate with national governments, which most often try to regulate such activities. Clearly, too, national governments vary enormously in their ability and will to regulate. At one pole, China quickly forced Murdoch's Star TV to submit to intense regulation, allowing very little into the country, and at the other are fragile states like Belize, where foreign satellite television preceded national television (Oliveira, 1986).

## Globalization as the Spread of Capitalist Modernity

Globalization can be seen as both spatial—the outward geographic spread of ideas and forms, particularly those related to capitalism—and temporal—changes over time within many locales, often portrayed as a process of hybridity (Kraidy, 2005; Nederveen Pieterse, 2004). "One way to attempt to simplify the level of complexity which the intensification of global flows is introducing in the figuration of competing nation-states and blocs, is to regard globalization as an outcome of the universal logic of modernity" (Featherstone & Lash, 1995, p. 2).

Inside the academic debate on communications—indeed, in most of the debate about change and development of nations—modernization was seen as an outmoded idea. Modernization, in the original sense of following a set of stages toward development derived from Western nations' experience (Lerner, 1958), was seen as unworkable, given structural differences between nations, such as the economic dependency of former colonies on their former colonial powers (Faletto & Cardoso, 1979). Modernization was also seen as introducing unnecessary Westernization or Americanization (Hamelink, 1983; Schiller, 1976). Outside the academic debate, however, many governments, particularly in East Asia and Latin America, were still pursuing a strategy of modernization, regardless of the cultural imperialism and dependency debates. However, in practice, many of their concrete policies and initiatives were, in fact, aimed at increasing autonomy and minimizing dependence. In pursuing autonomous mini- and microcomputer industries, for example, countries such as South Korea and Brazil were pursuing a practical antidependency policy (Evans, 1992).

Since the 1990s, academic debates have revived modernity as a key concept. Tomlinson (1991) argued that much of what was labeled cultural imperialism was in fact a broader spread of a globalized pattern of modernity. This discourse argued, in particular, that much of what was seen as Americanization or Westernization was a more general, deeper globalization of capitalism, "the broader discourse of cultural imperialism as *the spread of the culture of modernity itself*" (Tomlinson, 1991, pp. 89–90, italics in the original).

A related question is whether modernity is a singular tendency or one with many possible versions and outcomes. As I will show later, a number of aspects of globalization tend to standardize certain kinds of economic modernity, such as financial institutions, trade rules and regimes, and commercial media models. However, Tomlinson (1999) also argued later that a "decentering of capitalism from the West" was taking place (p. 140). A number of writers, such as Iwabuchi (2002), argued for distinct Asian or Japanese versions of both capitalism and media/cultural modernity. China has also steadily emerged as a major site and alternative form of capitalist production in the current neoliberal system (Harvey, 2005), with many features of current global capitalist modernity. The fact that China has refused

Western prescriptions of the sort of democracy that is supposed to accompany modern capitalist development presents a long list of contradictions to traditional notions of modernity.

One problem with this modernity-focused analysis, with relying on a rather systemic notion of modernity as the key concept, is losing sight of real issues of differential power between different parts of the world in economics, in politics, and in cultural industries like television. Some forms of cultural production, such as commercial television genres, for example, soap opera, could be analyzed either as forms of capitalist production or as manifestations of modern approaches to media. The two angles offer somewhat different insights. Both imply limits placed on—and resources available to—cultural producers (television networks) and cultural consumers (television audiences). One virtue of cultural imperialism is that it reminds academics to consider that different actors within the world system have different resources and levels of power.

One problem with classic, neo-Marxist approaches, in contrast, is that they tend to reduce too many things to linear conceptions of political economic power. For authors such as Schiller (1969) or Herman and McChesney (1997), the power of ownership is paramount, but as Murdoch's attempts to enter China show, simply owning something, even something as apparently powerful as Star TV, is no guarantee of obtaining access to a nation's audience. Building on Appadurai's (1996) notion of scapes, I must note that there is not a single dimension or continuum of action or power at work. A country might well be highly dependent on outside technology, while relatively autonomous in cultural production. The investigation of popular culture "requires taking the cultural sphere as neither derivative from the socio-economic, as a merely ideological phenomenon, nor as in some metaphysical sense, preceding it. Rather it (Barbero, 1988) is the decisive area where social conflicts are experienced and evaluated" (Rowe & Schelling, 1991, p. 12).

## Economic Neoliberalism and American Empire

There has been a reassertion in the past several years of the primacy of the political economy associated with globalization. In a broad review of the claims of globalization as a new paradigm, Sparks (2005) commented that "many of the phenomena we have reviewed are better understood as aspects of capitalist development than as the products of some new and distinct social phenomenon called 'globalization.'" One striking version of this refocus on the essentials of a world capitalist economy comes from several writers who have argued that a new world economic system of neoliberalism dominates world structures, relying on most of the actors noted below, but perhaps not centered enough to be called an empire (Harvey, 2005). Harvey (2005) argued that the current phase of capitalism is neoliberal imperialism orchestrated by finance capital and neoliberal states. The center is "the Wall Street-Treasury-IMF complex." The focus of this system is on privatization, liberalization of competition, opening up of closed economic sectors (including cultural industries like television and film in some countries) to outside trade, deregulation, and a focus on markets as the fundamental social process and on valuing for-profit companies as more efficient than public institutions (Gray, 2003). All of these aspects of neoliberalization can act on television, particularly in changing the rules at the national level (Sanchez-Ruiz, 2004).

Another recent analysis is that the current world system should be seen as a new kind of empire. Hardt and Negri (2001) saw the system as a decentered empire, primarily economic rather than political. The United States is a loose center of this empire, especially in military power, which is used to assert economic and some political interests, and in the primary formation of economic policy. However, almost equally important or central to this new form of empire are international organizations such as the International Monetary Fund (IMF), World Bank, and World Trade Organization (WTO), which can be seen as following the U.S. policy lead but also representing a consensus that is larger than the United States' own interests. Major global corporations are also central actors; they are still represented by their home nations and also represent themselves directly in places of interest such as the International Telecommunications Union (ITU) on issues like media and information technology standards. Hardt and Negri (2001) see communication and electronic networks as central, both as one of the hegemonic sectors of production in themselves (in products like television programs, satellite television networks, feature films, Web sites, and so on) and in the ways that they enable and modulate the flow of immaterial labor, such as outsourcing.

The empire idea has received many comments and critiques. One key observation is that this system is still centered (Arrighi, 2005) but not necessarily on the United States. Arrighi (2005) argued that the center of the system may be moving from the United States to China, particularly since the occupation of Iraq undermined U.S. centrality and strengthened the emergence of China as an alternative to U.S. leadership, based on a successful alternative form of capitalism, growth, and trade. A perceived U.S. shift to reliance on military force rather than political hegemony since 2000 has been destabilizing to those who previously saw the United States as an acceptable central power in the system, he said. Arrighi argued that North-South economic differences are still primary, that capital flows and infrastructure are still centered in the more industrialized North (those nations, usually in the northern hemisphere, in North America, Europe, and East Asia, which tend to be the center of the world economic system and figuratively including industrialized countries, such as Australia, that happen to be south of the equator), but some in the South (the largely less industrialized southern hemisphere, plus figuratively those less industrialized nations that happen to be north of the equator), such as China and the Asian tigers, which are acquiring capital and power.

The perceived power of global capitalist neoliberalism and liberalization has also been critiqued as too Western or perhaps too top-down a view, given the many forms of cooperation of public and private sectors in Asia, Latin America, and the Middle East. For example, some successful capitalist states, such as Singapore, maintain strong public sectors in all sorts of areas from media to housing (George, 2004). Interestingly, Hardt and Negri (2004) saw the same underlying factors of globalization within empire as also enabling contradictory opposition movements to it. They described a variety of groups and movements that use new economic forms, information channels (e.g., the Internet), and forms of organization (e.g., a variety of transnational nongovernmental organizations) to oppose empire; they are "the living alternative that grows within Empire" (Hardt & Negri, 2004, p. xv). Hardt and Negri referred to this opposition as "the Multitude," which encompasses all classes and groups that contest the dominance of empire. It is characterized by plurality and internal differences that form multiple networks of resistance (pp. xii–xvi), and it builds on the same electronic networks that empire uses, contradictory forces using the same tools.

## American Empire: Film and Television

In some ways, the U.S. creation, internationalization, and dominance of several new cultural industries in the 20th century provide an interesting prototype of Hardt and Negri's idea of empire. A number of studies starting in the 1970s described the 20th-century domination of world culture flows by the United States (Guback & Varis, 1986; Nordenstreng & Varis, 1974; Schiller, 1976). Starting with films, popular music, and then television, the United States has been the major exporter to the global market and remains so, even with increasing competition in various regions of the world. But cultural imperialism theorists have always argued that the United States was more than a dominant exporter (Schiller, 1976). They argued that beneath the visible imbalance of media flows, there was a deeper paradigm in which the United States created and spread patterns of cultural industry that ideologically supported the increasingly global capitalism that also benefited the United States more than any other country, at least after World War II (Beltran & Fox de Cardona, 1979; Horkheimer & Adorno, 2001).

Starting in the early 20th century, U.S. cultural industries capitalized on new technological possibilities, the size and wealth of the U.S. market, supportive government policies, and the cultural resources in its heterogeneous population. Taking advantage of new structural possibilities, U.S. cultural actors created products and patterns that helped define a new form of modernity related to new forms of industrial capitalist life. People in many countries could watch Charlie Chaplin get literally trapped in the gears of the new industrial life in *Modern Times*. This development expanded to pattern other cultures and economies as the new structural possibilities of the capitalist cultural industry that first characterized the United States spread globally. The U.S. national pattern of media industry, thus became a pattern that replicates and adapts to many other nations, first as the influence of U.S. media industries and their models traveled through those countries in the U.S. sphere of influence, such as Latin America in the 1920s and 1930s. U.S. models spread even further as economic globalization after the 1970s pushed countries toward commercial cultural industries and created structural conditions that make that pattern sensible in other national situations.

The U.S. government also strongly supported the spread of U.S. media, particularly film, into the rest of world. For example, the Webb-Pomerene Act of 1918 was U.S. federal legislation exempting certain exporter associations from certain antitrust regulations. One of the beneficiaries was the Motion Picture Export Association of America (MPEAA), which was permitted to act as a cartel abroad to allocate markets, set prices, and market together (Guback & Varis, 1986). The U.S. government saw Hollywood as a major asset in its efforts to conduct cultural diplomacy abroad (Dizard, 2004; Nye, 2004), so it facilitated Hollywood in a number of ways, particularly in countries where American movies were challenged by trade restrictions (Grantham, 2000) or where they needed help getting into a culture or market initially (Dizard, 2004). Overall, then, this is an interesting approximation of the Hardt and Negri (2001) empire idea: U.S. government policy and economic power facilitated a film empire that is primarily operated by global corporations, based in the United States. The Hollywood experience shows that this idea of U.S. empire is not entirely new; in this one particularly important area of media, it has been developing since the 1920s.

Another way to look at the U.S. position in global media structural models and media product flows is as a pilot case in both national hybridization and globalization of culture and cultural industries. The United States is part of an Anglo-European cultural base and is still part of a distinct Anglophone cultural-linguistic market. However, the success of its audiovisual products in broader global markets is largely due to the hybridization of those cultural roots with others. The Anglo-European threads were combined with the culture of African Americans and with other cultures that were part of late 19th- and 20th-century immigration: eastern European Jews, Arabs, Latin Americans, and Asians.

U.S. media drew on these diverse cultures and, even more important, had to appeal to all of them to succeed in the American national cultural marketplace (Read, 1976). Read (1976) and others noted that U.S. cultural products were then well-situated to succeed as exports because they had already achieved a kind of universalization or narrative transparency (Olsen, 1999) by the absorption of various elements and the need to appeal to diverse audiences. Tomlinson (1991) noted that fear of Americanization ironically assumes, perhaps falsely, that American culture is homogeneous. Gitlin (2001) persuasively argued that U.S. culture has become everyone else's second culture, but one of the interesting questions is indeed the coherence of "American" culture as it fragments among hundreds of cable channels, satellite radio channels, and thousands of films, some targeted at audiences as small as the roughly 5.5 million Mormons in the United States, targeted by the Mormon film production community in Utah, which has produced dozens of feature films for them since 2000 (Davis, 2006).

Olsen (1999) argued that it is not enough to trace the political economy of Hollywood's domination of other markets, abetted by the U.S. government and international organizations such as the WTO. Hollywood also developed forms of narrative transparency that made it easy for audiences around the world to enjoy U.S. feature films and, later, U.S. television programs.

> Transparency is defined as any textual apparatus that allows audiences to project indigenous values, beliefs, rites, and rituals into imported media or the use of those devices. This transparency effect means American cultural exports such as cinema, television, and related merchandise, manifest narrative structures that easily blend into other cultures. (pp. 5–6)

The other side of narrative transparency is the audience's ability to interpret Hollywood films and television programs in a way that makes sense to their own lives and cultures. Olsen questioned the strong effects of U.S. media that cultural imperialism theorists and others assumed to exist. Cultures that receive Hollywood products "are able to project their own narratives, values, myths, and meanings into the American iconic media, making those texts resonate with the same meanings they might have had if they were indigenous" (Olsen, 1999, p. 6). He noted that identity is complex and dynamic . . . It builds on prior readings and memories. Initial readings of imported media invite the projection of pre-existing cultural conceptions, particularly when the text is narratologically *transparent* and therefore conducive to polysemy (Olsen, 1999), but subsequent readings necessarily become dynamic hybrids of projection and reception. (Olsen, 2002, p. 2)

Another key argument came from Robertson (1995), who argued that globalization contains two relevant trends. One is that cultural elements particular to one culture can become universalized as they are spread around the world, what he called the universalization of the particular. This has clearly happened to U.S. cultural exports. People in many cultures have become so exposed to U.S. culture that over time, it has come to seem familiar, not necessarily as the first culture of someone living in Ghana or Russia, but as a familiar, acceptable second culture. Robertson referred to that process as the particularization of the universal, its adaptation to the particular circumstances in which diverse audiences find themselves. This corresponds to Gitlin's (2001) argument that U.S. popular culture is now the second culture of most people in the world. The same universalization of particular cultures seems likely to expand beyond U.S. films and television. Hong Kong martial arts films, Japanese anime, Mexican telenovelas, and Bollywood movies have all found large, continuing audiences beyond their national and regional boundaries, to reach broadly transnationally, nearly globally. Bannerjee (2002) called this the globalization of the local: "It is not the global which comes and envelops us. It is the local which goes global" (Soh, 2005, p. 2).

Still, almost no one disputes that Hollywood started with and maintains a considerable advantage in media trade. Hollywood used its initial cultural advantage relatively well. Producers developed interesting genres of film, music, and television. They began to draw in much of the world's talent, film directors, actors, writers, and singers from Europe and even Latin America (Read, 1976). This again heightened a certain type of transparency or ease of interpretation based on hybridization of American and other cultural elements.

The United States also capitalized on an emerging English linguistic hegemony, drawing on the global penetration of English under the British Empire, as well as the 20th-century expansion of the United States itself. As Hoskins and Mirus (1988) and others (Wildman & Siwek, 1988) have pointed out, the fact of production in English has given the United States an export advantage in the global market of the 20th century. There also may be an advantage to culturally diverse natural-language markets.

The variety of populations immersed in the melting pot of the United States gave U.S. producers a kind of microcosm of the developed world's population as a home market . . . their invention of a cultural form that is the closest to transnational acceptability of any yet contrived. (Collins, 1986, pp. 214–215)

Creating television for that audience trained U.S. producers in a certain form of programming that some call universal and others, "lowest common denominator." The United States also has the advantage of having several wealthy media markets, the United States itself, Canada, Great Britain, and Australia, all part of a narrower English-speaking or Anglophone geolinguistic market. In that market, the United States is even more dominant than in other markets, where language and culture present greater barriers to popular acceptance of American cultural products. So to some degree, the U.S. position represents a commercial pattern successful in national industry terms, within a particularly wealthy cultural-linguistic market and within a globalization that was shaped in part by U.S. power to serve its own commercial interests. Reviewing the imperialism and globalization debates, Chalaby (2006) noted that while the former was too strong in its estimation of U.S. cultural power, the latter may be too weak in estimating what he called U.S. cultural primacy.

## Rethinking Audiences for the U.S. Empire

One of the deeper issues of both cultural imperialism analyses and much of the globalization work, particularly in political economy, is the continued assumption of an unchallenged and undiminished global audience appetite for U.S. television programs and channels. Examining audiences more closely reveals that culture, reflected in audience choices, is a powerful factor placing limits on or boundaries around a phenomenon that seems logical, almost predetermined from political economic factors, such as U.S. dominance of both film and television flows across the world. Clearly, U.S. production appeals in many places; in particular, U.S. feature films dominate most worldwide box offices (Miller, 2005). However, empirical data, which will be presented in Chapters 6 and 7, along with the evidence visible in sources like *Variety Magazine,* show that local television programs dominate television prime-time listings and top-10 program lists in most countries. That seems to conflict with the large volume of television programs that Hollywood continues to sell around the world and its resulting profits (Miller, 2005). However, as early as 1992, O'Regan observed that,

To be sure, the U.S. accounted for 71 percent of the international trade in 1989 ($1.7 billion out of estimated total of $2.4 billion in television exports). But this dominance needs to be understood with reference to the very much larger sum of estimated world television production that never leaves its nation of origin. This nationally destined programming accounted for an estimated US$ 70 billion in 1989—29 times greater than the amount spent in international audio-visual exchange. (quoted in Moran, 2000, p. 5)

Adding another angle, in Chapter 7, I show that much of the U.S. sale and profit in television is not necessarily global, but rather concentrated in the Anglophone cultural-linguistic market, the Anglophone Caribbean, Australia, Canada, New Zealand, and the United Kingdom. Much of the rest is concentrated in Western Europe, where Hollywood has managed over decades of distribution dominance to cultivate a position as the familiar second culture that programmers turn to when they cannot, or choose not to, produce a certain genre (Buonanno, 2002). That dominance is eroding somewhat as programmers turn to importing licensed formulas in reality and game instead of imported programs, per se (Moran, 2004). Much of Hollywood's export volume fills up the off hours outside of prime time with old movies after midnight, old series in the early afternoon, and cartoons in morning and late afternoon. Although that racks up sales volume and some profit for Hollywood, it does not directly engage the bulk of the audience in prime time, as evidence in Chapters 6 and 7 demonstrates.

Several theoretical challenges have been posed by the ideas of (a) the cultural discount audiences apply toward media from dissimilar cultures (Hoskins & Mirus, 1988), (b) the cultural distance perceived toward television from different cultures (Galperin, 1999), (c) the cultural proximity audiences feel toward media from similar cultures (Straubhaar, 1991), and (d) regional market and cultural identity development among audiences (Sinclair, Jacka, & Cunningham, 1996; Wilkinson, 1995).

Audiences tend to reject cultural products like television programs that are too distant from their own cultural realities, leading to the ideas of cultural discount (Hoskins & McFayden, 1991; Hoskins & Mirus, 1988; Hoskins, Mirus, & Rozeboom, 1989) and cultural distance (Galperín, 1999), "the barriers in language, viewing habits, and genre preferences that hamper cultural products flow between two given nations" (Galperín, 1999, p. 2).

Conversely, audiences are attracted to cultural similarity or proximity (Straubhaar, 1991). Cultural proximity theory argued that countries and cultures would tend to prefer their own local or national productions first, due to factors such as the appeal of local stars, the local knowledge required to understand much television humor, the appeal of local themes and issues, the appeal of similar looking ethnic faces, and the familiarity of local styles and locales (Straubhaar, 1991). The argument was extended to say that if countries did not produce certain genres of television, then audiences would tend to prefer those kinds of programs from nearby or similar cultures and languages, rather than those of more distant producers such as the United

States. Iwabuchi (2002) is among the critics who strongly agreed with the basic argument but warned against being essentialist about cultures, observing that proximity, like the cultures themselves, was dynamic and changed over time. Iwabuchi (2002) raised some interesting further issues about the subtle, variable relations of cultural proximity. He said, "Complexity articulated in the intensification of intraregional cultural flows is closely related with the ambiguity of meaning of cultural intimacy and distance associated with locality" (p. 48).

There are some global audiences for U.S. feature films and cable and satellite channels. CNN, Discovery, MTV, and HBO all have truly global reach and impact on audiences. The CNN audience, while small, tends to include the world's political and economic elite, who are interested in truly global contents. Upper middle and middle classes in many countries tend to be increasingly segmented into interest areas, not unlike the U.S. audience. These middle classes, who can often afford pay television, either direct-to-home satellite television (DTH) or cable TV, show increasing interest in global segmented channels, such as Discovery, ESPN, MTV, or HBO.

To deepen this point about the importance of social class segmentation of audiences for global or national programming theoretically, going deeper into the ideas of Bourdieu (1984, 1986) is useful. He investigated why social class seemed to make a great deal of difference in the music that French people preferred (Bourdieu, 1984). He broke down social class into several useful components. Economic capital has a great deal to do with what people can afford to access; it also correlates strongly with the depth and quality of schooling parents can arrange for children and what kinds of enriching experiences they provide their offspring. The latter two, schooling and cultural experiences, bear directly on the cultural capital that people acquire. Closely related is the idea of disposition, what people are inclined to do with the economic and cultural capital they have accumulated. All these are closely connected to the kinds of choices that people make about cultural options. In his original study, Bourdieu (1984) found that those with greater cultural capital tended to prefer classical music to popular culture, which was preferred by those with less education or less elite family backgrounds; that is, with less cultural capital. Several studies have applied this to television, showing that people with more economic and cultural capital are more likely to choose to watch imported U.S. television shows, which often demand knowledge of U.S. or global culture. Those with less economic or cultural capital are more likely to choose local, national, or regional material, which is easier for them to understand (Straubhaar, 1991, 2003). This connection between cultural capital and cultural choices breaks down further by genre: The most popular U.S. genres are the least demanding of cultural knowledge about the United States (action-adventure, cartoons, and physical comedy). These arguments and supporting data are developed more in Chapters 6, 7, and 8, but I cite them here as a potential limit or boundary on the political economic forces being discussed.

## Globalization, Changing National Policy, and the State

Globalization constrains the ways in which the nation-state can direct and support cultural industries, a major force described in Chapter 2. A number of globalizing forces seem to reduce the autonomy of the nation-state. Major changes in trade regimes are essentially becoming shifts of power toward multilateral governance and regulation. There is a strong replication of global patterns, particularly those of commercial broadcasting, based on advertising. An underlying shift toward global capitalism promotes commercial operation and advertising finance. These tend to push national governments toward opening up or liberalizing competition, as well as privatizing media previously controlled by the state or public corporations, like the BBC. Highly concentrated, large global media firms have operations that penetrate most societies across the world and compete with national media that are often more under state control. Finally, satellite and cable TV channels and operations belonging to global firms reach directly into most societies in the world, sometimes bypassing state controls or even forcing them to open up terrestrial broadcasting to new stations.

New international trade approaches or regimes are enshrined in powerful agencies such as the World Trade Organization, the World Intellectual Property Organization, and the World Bank (Sinclair, 1995). These institutions challenge the legitimacy and legality of many of the mechanisms that states had used to protect and subsidize national cultural industries. Global financial institutions now move stock investments and currency transactions so quickly that states cannot control them (Friedman, 1999).

New international media conglomerates, for example, Rupert Murdoch's News Corporation or Time Warner, also integrate operations in many countries in ways that can often bypass state controls or regulations (Herman & McChesney, 1997). They also create operations such as direct satellite broadcast channels or Web sites that are capable of bypassing borders and controls. They also concentrate production of media in a few Western countries and then spread that content to many countries via the new technological channels of satellite and cable TV.

Satellites permit single companies or broadcast organizations, for example, the BBC, to cover the whole Earth, if they can afford and arrange the technology. However, even forms of television that seem likely to be highly global, like satellite pay television, require the cooperation of the nation-state to collect license fees, advertise, set up dishes, and so on. In perhaps the most spectacular example, Rupert Murdoch discovered that although he could technically broadcast from satellites into China from Hong Kong without the Peoples' Republic of China's (PRC) permission, he could not build an audience or make money without the PRC's cooperation. Global television companies such as HBO are U.S.-owned but have regional offices that carefully track and comply with national rules on both their content and the cable and satellite systems that deliver their content to audiences. For example, although HBO would make more money as a premium channel in Taiwan, with separate fees to subscribers (the way it operates in the United States), national Taiwanese regulators require it to be offered as a basic service channel, paid for as part of an overall fee to cable providers at a much lower price (Spink, personal communication, August 17, 2006).

## Deregulation, Liberalization, and Privatization

The push for liberalization and privatization of ownership since the 1980s represented a change in the international consensus or intellectual and policy regime about national economic activities and policies. Political economy analysts have correctly pointed out that this is an instance of renewed predominance of underlying economic policy changes, such as deregulation, which come to affect or even determine media policy changes. Both multilateral organizations, such as the World Bank and World Trade Organization, and core-country governments, like the United States and Great Britain, have promoted deregulation of industry, including cultural industries. Deregulation often includes liberalized entry of private firms into media, entry of foreign firms, increased concentration of ownership, increased vertical and horizontal integration of production and distribution, less protection of national content producers, and less concern about national control of management.

A number of countries have privatized national broadcasters by selling channels to private interests. Privatization has been pushed for a number of reasons, including reducing government's ability to control political content, acquiring investment capital to start or improve channels, and opening investment opportunities to powerful international companies.

The privatization of government television has often been promoted as a form of political opening, a movement from more authoritarian controls to more competitive and open private systems. A striking precedent came when French socialist President François Mitterrand began to liberalize competition in radio and television by allowing new private networks to enter the market in the 1980s. Mitterrand began privatizing TF-1, one of the major state networks, because he felt he had been politically disadvantaged by the political control of its newscasts when, as a state enterprise, its news orientation had been controlled by the Gaullist Party, prior to his defeat of them in an election. Interestingly, the process was continued and finalized by Jacques Chirac of the Gaullist Party, for similar reasons (Brants & Siune, 1992).

Other parties out of power have similarly pushed to privatize major news channels to reduce control over them by parties in power. This has ranged over several regions and several types of ideological control and rivalry. The Argentine military had taken control of the country's three networks when it took power by coup in 1976. When the military government collapsed after the Falklands/Malvinas war, the stations were put back in private hands as part of what was called a transition from authoritarianism to the rule of civil society. In several central and eastern European countries, part of the 1990s transition from Socialist or Communist Party rule was the privatization of television stations and networks. This has been pushed by domestic would-be private broadcasters, reflecting their own commercial interests, as well as by domestic anti-authoritarian political forces wishing to decentralize power and open up civil society. However, U.S. development policy and institutions of public diplomacy have also pushed hard for privatization of media in Eastern Europe, Afghanistan, Iraq, and elsewhere in the Arab world (Hartenberger, 2005; Iskander, 2006).

In some countries, liberalization of competition has primarily served to increase nationally owned and nationally focused television networks. New commercial television networks often turn first to importing globally popular programs, mostly from the United States but also sometimes including Latin American telenovelas or Bollywood films. Newly privatized operations often do not initially have all the factors discussed in Chapter 3 for beginning or increasing national production. However, they often start producing more national material because it is more popular with audiences and, hence, also more attractive to advertisers, who want the largest possible audience (Straubhaar, 1991). For example, Turkey now has three private networks in addition to the state/public channel, TRT. All four primarily program nationally produced serials, having gradually replaced imported serials, particularly U.S. soap operas and Latin American telenovelas, which had dominated prime time along with U.S. feature films until a few years ago (Sengul, 2006).

## Global Spread of Market Capitalism

Probably one of the most widely agreed upon ideas in economic globalization of media is that more and more countries are taking up commercial broadcast models under global pressures. Countries adopting a commercial model tend to use certain kinds of television program forms or genres and neglect or even avoid others. To use a concept found in parallel form in both complexity theory and structuration theory (Giddens, 1984), systemic changes such as a shift toward a more commercial, advertising-driven basis of financing broadcasting redraw the boundaries of what is possible within that system.

Commercial broadcasting is proliferating across the globe. This increasingly global commercial pattern for television is reinforced by several factors. Perhaps most powerfully, more and more countries are being drawn into a world capitalist or market economy (Herman & McChesney, 1997; Wallerstein, 1979). Within this global market economy, both national and global firms pressure broadcasters to allow, indeed to rely on, advertising (Fox, 1975; Herman & McChesney, 1997).

Lee (1980, p. 91) asserted that a crucial difference existed between endogenous or domestic pressures toward using a commercial broadcasting model and exogenous or foreign pressures. McAnany (1984) considered this too simplistic; in fact, he said, one must consider the role of domestic advertisers who are influenced by or dependent on foreign interests. However, in writing about Latin American cultural industries, particularly television in Brazil, McAnany was perhaps too pessimistic about the chances of domestic advertisers and other pressure groups acting independently of foreign pressure (Mattos, 1984; Straubhaar, 1984). Certainly the increasing commercialization of television in Britain results from a complex mixture of interests among both domestic and multinational advertisers. Poor countries like Mozambique often start with state-dominated, development-oriented media but find themselves pressured toward commercializing cultural industries by the loss of revenues available to the state. Ironically, they often turn to advertising out of need to support continued broadcasting but find that their markets are too poor to support much advertising. Many become newly dependent on donor countries in the West to support media, although support from development agencies can reverse pressures toward commercialization and refocus media on the development issues in which international donors are interested (interviews with international donor representatives, Maputo, April 2002).

When new systems started in the past 10 to 15 years, they were often commercial. A number of state and public systems in Europe, Asia, and Africa have also been fully or partially privatized, which nearly always results in commercial operation (Herman & McChesney, 1997). Some remaining public systems are essentially commercialized by a need to rely on advertising for support, even though the government or a public corporation is still the owner. For example, Radio Television Mozambique is still owned by the state but has increasingly sought advertising support since the early 1990s, even though it still tries to concentrate programming on development objectives (conversations with RTM executives and programmers, 2000).

In the 1990s, European countries, for instance, moved from largely non-commercial public service systems toward increasingly commercialized ones. A general movement toward liberalization of competition by private inter-ests and privatization of national public or state channels is discussed more thoroughly later. National commercial media interests wanted to enter the potentially profitable television business (Ferguson, 1995). The European Union (EU) was interested in creating a more dynamic set of media industries to compete in global markets and resist cultural imports into Europe (Schlesinger, 1993). Those commercial systems need to draw the largest possi-ble audiences to satisfy advertisers. As a result, several cherished forms of pro-gramming are diminished, including long-form documentaries, one-off or single-episode dramas, and high cultures, because they fall out of bounds in the new commercial logic of television (Herman & McChesney, 1997).

However, local or national cultural boundaries also shape the form media capitalism takes within any specific nation or culture. Experience in Latin America, Asia, and, recently, Eastern Europe shows that national govern-ments may maintain a great deal of power to shape private, commercial broadcasting by manipulating licensing of frequencies, by manipulating advertising (especially from government-controlled firms), by providing infrastructure, and by co-opting new commercial elites into power sharing (Morris & Waisbord, 2001). Cultural preferences themselves will push new commercial broadcasters toward providing what local audiences prefer, which tends to be local versions of popular global genres and formats (Moran, 2004).

## Global Economics and Advertising

One of the economic binding or boundary-setting forces most closely related to media and to cultural identity is advertising and the creation of con-sumer desires. Forces of economic globalization in almost all countries have established advertising as a dominant media economic base. Many companies want to sell the same goods or services throughout the globe. Janus (1981) and Mattelart (1991) argued that multinational firms had pushed particularly hard to commercialize systems and introduce advertising because they were used to promoting goods with advertising in other markets.

Major manufacturers and service groups conduct global marketing campaigns and global operations. Their desire to advertise global goods promotes the growth of advertising as the primary economic support for television in most countries (Janus, 1983; Mattelart, 1991). Viewing publics also tend to push for more programming choices, as with British television in the 1950s, and this demand is often met by allowing more commercial channels.

Commercial television systems, like commercial film studios before them, require that cultural products succeed in drawing a large, profitable audience. In television, like film before it, these demands for commercial success lead to the emergence and standardization of certain successful formulas. Schatz (1988) noted that Hollywood's early film experimentation settled into a pattern of standard formulas or genres for producing films on an industrial scale that had the best predictable success with the audience.

Although constraints from economic systems are a real issue, various critics of globalization believe overly simplistic assumptions are being made about the causality of economics, particularly the global spread of capitalism, in globalization. They fear a new wave of economic reductionism, which might oversimplify cultural phenomena (Boyne, 1990; Ferguson, 1992).

## Direct Investment and Partnerships

To a number of political economists in communication in the mid-1990s, globalization was most often seen as the globalization of ownership, creating "world barons of the mass media" (Herman & McChesney, 1997). Economists argued that the consolidation of ownership, accelerating in the 1990s, profoundly changed the face of the world media system. They saw massive amounts of control being centered in less than a dozen large global conglomerates: Time Warner, Disney-ABC, AT&T-TCI, Rupert Murdoch's News Corporation, Bertelsmann, Sony, and Vivendi-Universal (McChesney, 1999). Figure 4.1 gives a list of some of the largest global media conglomerates.

For some theorists, the power of these media conglomerates is symptomatic of a broader change toward a new form of empire, combining economic interests of major states, such as the United States, and the transnational media corporations.

> They tend to make nation-states merely instruments to record the flow of the commodities, monies, and populations they set in motion. The transnational corporations directly distribute labor power over various markets, functionally allocate resources, and organize hierarchically the various sectors of world production. (Hardt & Negri, 2001, pp. 31–32)

| Corporation | Nationality of Ownership | 2005 Revenue (U.S. $) |
|---|---|---|
| Time Warner | U.S. | $43.70 billion |
| Disney | U.S. | $31.9 billion |
| Vivendi | French | $25.98 billion |
| News Corporation | Australian/U.S. | $23.859 billion |
| Bertelsmann A.G. | German | $23.856 billion |
| Comcast | U.S. | $22.078 billion |
| CBS Corporation | U.S. | $14.536 billion |
| Sony Film/TV | Japan/U.S. | $12.6 billion |
| NBC Universal (General Electric Co.) | U.S. | $12.437 billion |
| DirecTV Group | U.S. | $12.216 billion |
| Viacom | U.S. | $9.609 billion |
| EchoStar | U.S. | $8,048 billion |
| Gannett Corporation | U.S. | $7.6 billion |
| BBC | British | $7.59 billion |
| Pearson, PLC | British | $7.514 billion |
| Cox Communications | U.S. | $7.054 billion |
| Tribune Company | U.S. | $5.73 billion |
| Fuji TV | Japan | $5.141 billion |
| Mediaset (Berlusconi) | Italy | $4.588 billion |
| ITV PLC | British | $4.31 billion |
| Axel Springer | Germany | $3.90 billion |
| EMI | British | $3.43 billion |
| Warner Music | Canada (Bronfman) | $3.50 billion |
| Nippon Television | Japan | $2.96 billion |
| Tokyo Broadcasting System | Japan | $2.665 billion |
| TV Globo | Brazil | $2.6 billion |
| Televisa | Mexico | $1.9 billion |
| TVB | Hong Hong | $0.53 billion |

**Figure 4.1**    Major Global Conglomerates

*Sources:* Corporate reports, Advertising Age Top 100, Variety Global 50.

Certainly global ownership, investment, and partnerships have created major global media operating entities and dispersed commercial media patterns. The United States, Britain, and France made considerable investments in colonial and other Third World newspapers in the 1920s, in movies in the 1920s and 1930s, in radio in the 1930s and 1940s (Schwoch, 1990), and in TV in the 1960s and 1970s (Beltran & Fox de Cardona, 1979). However, the most visible and probably most significant global consolidation via partnerships has taken place since the 1990s.

With the neoliberal trend toward deregulation in the 1990s, direct foreign investment in television picked up again in some countries (Herman & McChesney, 1997). However, the actual investment patterns in the 1990s and 2000s already show some change toward a postdependency diversity, with Hong Kong media investing in Indonesia and Malaysia, Mexican media corporations investing in Chile and Guatemala, and Brazilian television networks investing in Portugal and Mozambique. There are also resurgent postcolonial activities, such as Spain's Telefonica investing in Latin American telecommunications firms.

Rupert Murdoch is perhaps the most visible example of the current global media mogul, moving from a base in Australia to acquire a variety of print media in Britain and the United States. He has started or acquired broadcast media (Fox Channel); film production and distribution companies, and satellite and cable TV systems in Asia (Star TV, Channel V), Britain (Sky Channel, now B-Sky-B), and the United States (Fox Networks). He is also partnering with other major players, such as America's TCI, Mexico's Televisa, and Brazil's TV Globo in Sky Latin America. He has invested considerably in direct global reach via satellite television.

Time Warner has taken a different focus, directing global reach with a number of specific satellite channels (CNN, TBS, TNT, HBO, etc.), AOL's Internet operations, Warner films, music distribution, television program sales, and a number of key magazines. Disney also has direct global reach with satellite television channels (Disney, ESPN), film distribution, music distribution, and television program sales.

Not all conglomerate growth represents a lasting or sustainable accumulation of economic power. Vivendi Universal acquired satellite TV channels (Canal+, USA Networks), film distribution, considerable magazine and print distribution, a substantial share of global music distribution, and television program sales starting in the late 1990s but had to sell most of its media assets after 2002, when it lost more than $12 billion (Public Broadcasting Service, 2002).

Viacom has global reach with film distribution, publishing, and cable operations. Its major global television operation, MTV, started its own regional operations in Asia, Europe, and Hispanic/Latin America. It partnered with TV

Abril in Brazil for MTV Brasil and with Star TV for MTV Asia, then withdrew from Star TV to control its own operation, while Star TV adapted the concept in its own Channel V. Sony is heavily involved in global video game distribution, media and computer hardware sales, film, and music distribution.

These global giants tend to spread out into new national or regional markets in several ways. All sell their productions directly to a number of national and regional markets, usually the first step in international business operations (Duarte, 2001.) A number of other smaller companies now join in direct global sales: the BBC (Britain), TBS (Hong Kong), Televisa (Mexico), TV Globo (Brazil), and many others. Television program sales are still asymmetrical, dominated by a few global firms. However, entry to the program sales business is opening up, becoming less dominated by American firms and more open to a variety of firms from Europe, Asia, and Latin America.

The next step in internationalizing media business is to get involved in producing or distributing media abroad (Duarte, 2001). Companies can start their own operations, start a joint venture with a national or regional partner, or license their format or material to a local partner. Foreign investment is still asymmetrical, dominated by firms from the industrialized core nations.

Figure 4.1 shows 30 top media companies. It clearly shows that the largest conglomerates in media, noted above, are still U.S., European, or Japanese. However, that is changing somewhat, as companies from countries such as Mexico and Venezuela invest in broadcast or cable operations in countries such as Chile, Guatemala, or Argentina. Figure 4.1 also shows that a number of media companies in developing nations now figure in the world's top 30. Most of these kinds of investments could probably be considered regional, with the outside firm investing in markets within the cultural-linguistic region rather than in truly global operations. The asymmetry of investment and partnering is most visible at the global level and most likely to change within regional markets.

## Resisting Liberalization and Privatization

Some countries resisted pressures to privatize and liberalize. For example, in Egypt, the state has developed and still owns 30 television channels, which are addressed to national audiences, provinces within Egypt, and via satellite to other audiences throughout the Arabic-speaking world. In 1999, the information minister said, "The Egyptian media are not for sale. I'm not in favor of privatizing the media, nor for selling the tools that shape the Egyptian mind and protect it against the challenges facing our developing country" (Safwat Sheriff, quoted in Sabra, 1999). However, some content, such as some popular soap operas are produced by private groups. The state broadcaster retains distribution rights over such programs to protect its control and economic sustainability.

Some states have created corporations to operate their television networks while the state retains ownership. In this case, a state-owned institution becomes a commercial venture, seeking most or all of its revenue through advertising, sales, or other means typically ascribed to commercial media; these ventures are often required to show a profit, taking in more revenue than they spend in expenses. A good example of this is Singapore. It started radio as a British colony in 1936, started television as a government-owned national department within the Ministry of Culture in 1963, became a quasi-government corporation (Singapore Broadcasting Corporation) in 1980, and became a government-owned corporation (MediaCorp) in 1994, when limited competition was also allowed as part of overall economic liberalization (Pong, personal communication, 2006). Some states have liberalized or privatized only very recently. Cape Verde, one of the smallest African states, an island where Portuguese is spoken, announced its first private television channel and its first cable television system in 2006; these will compete with government-owned television (Infopress, 2006).

## Globalization via International Trade Regimes and Multilateral Governance

There is a good deal of accuracy in descriptions of the world economy as increasingly neoliberal. One of the main macroframes applied to analyses of global media flows and comparative media structures in the late 1980s and 1990s was changes in rules for production and trade, particularly under the banner of free trade. A number of the rules and techniques designed to foster national production and import substitution in television programs were ruled illegal or illegitimate, starting in the 1990s, especially after the World Trade Organization began to limit the previous exception to trade rules that had been given to cultural industries. This changed many of the national government practices for fostering cultural industries discussed in Chapter 3 (Roncagliolo, 1995; Sanchez-Ruiz, 2001; Sinclair, 2001).

New international trade rules discourage nation-states from subsidizing cultural industries. The impact of this has been most drastic for film industries because those in many developing countries and in Europe depended on considerable government subsidies (Grantham, 2000). Cuts in subsidies have also hurt television in some places, although it is often easier to hide subsidies to television in the form of state advertising and subsidized telecommunications infrastructure for distributing broadcasts around the country (Mattos, 1984).

New trade rules often prohibit quotas requiring certain proportions of national or regional production to be included in broadcasts or movie theaters. Again, this discussion has been most visible in the fight between Hollywood and some European countries, such as France, over quotas for theatrical film exhibition (Grantham, 2000). However, quotas for national content in television have been imposed by the European Union as a whole (Schlesinger, 1987) and by countries as diverse as Canada, China, Great Britain, South Korea, and Taiwan.

Changes in multilateral rules about media technology standards also reduce national government controls. States cannot use standards as trade barriers against imported hardware or software. Previously, a national television technical standard could be a tacit barrier against importing both television sets and television programs on video, for example. Now, nation-states cannot as easily promote certain producers as national champions or encourage import substitution. Widely shared technical standards also facilitate the direct flow of media, such as videotapes, satellite television, or the Internet, across borders.

The intellectual property aspects of new trade regimes also make it harder for national or regional cultural industries to simply borrow a good program idea from elsewhere and localize or adapt it to create a national or regional version. Considerable change has moved toward formal licensing agreements in which broadcasters actually pay for the formats they are adapting. The owners of such intellectual property now have considerably more power to require formal agreements and adequate payment. The World Intellectual Property Organization and the World Trade Organization have pressed developing countries to follow copyright rules to gain access to other trade benefits, such as lowered tariff barriers for developing countries' goods. To combat plagiarism and copying of such programs, the Formats Recognition and Protection Association (FRAPA) was formed in 2000 (Moran, 2004). The United States, the European Union, and other culture-exporting nations have pressed those international organizations to adopt these measures.

These examples show us that cultural factors work with economic ones. The next section looks at migration, which combines both major economic and cultural impacts.

## Migration as Globalization

One of the striking aspects of cultural globalization has been the migration of many groups of people to create cultural subgroups within other cultures. This is, in many ways, an old and ongoing process (Nederveen Pieterse, 2004), but it has accelerated in recent years, facilitated by many of the same technological and economic changes that enable other aspects of globalization. What is perhaps most different about the new migration is the degree to which migrants are often more able to stay in touch with their home cultures, both by travel and by media. Some have argued that a new kind of transnational community is formed by "the growing number of persons who live dual lives, speaking two languages, having homes in two countries, and making a living through continuous regular contact across national borders" (Portes, Guarnizo, & Landolt, 1999, p. 217). Such groups include Latino migrants in the United States, Chinese in Malaysia, Turks in Germany and the United Kingdom, and many others. Although Latinos and Chinese have been living in and moving to those areas for hundreds of years, the Turks are more recent migrants, so some of these new patterns are layered on old communities, whereas some are genuinely new within the past 100 years.

With more global reach for media such as film, videocassettes, direct satellite broadcasting, cable TV, and the Internet, migrant groups have an interesting role as hybrid audiences, trying to maintain contact with home while often using local media to acculturate at least partially into the dominant culture. Sometimes, they use media from home to resist acculturation. This phenomenon became clear in the 1980s with minority-language communities renting videotapes from back home at ethnic grocery stores (Dobrow, 1989). It accelerated with the proliferation of different translocal- and transnational-language channels in the 1990s, using satellite technology (Kumar, 2006), and others in the late 1990s and after using Web sites, music/video download sites, and streaming video (Mallapragada, 2006). Sometimes, migrants even create new ethnic media in their host cultures, for example, Iranian television programming in Los Angeles (Naficy, 1993), South Asian Web sites in Northern California (Mallapragada, 2006), or a variety of immigrant ethnic-language media in Australia (Cunningham, 2001; Sinclair & Cunningham, 2000).

A number of the world's current ethnic subgroups originally moved along with empire and conquest. The British not only went to India themselves, but also took Indian nationals with them to other parts of the empire, such as the Caribbean or South Africa, to work in the colonial bureaucracy and trade. Even more dramatically, colonizers in the Americas brought in millions of African slaves. The people who moved as part of the empire-building wave and their descendants became minority populations in countries like the United States, added to hybrid or mixed populations in countries like Brazil, and constituted majorities in countries like Haiti or Jamaica. In a few cases, particularly in Latin America, large populations grew up as a synthesis or miscegenation between populations. In Latin America, many people have mixed European, indigenous, and African parentage as discussed extensively in Chapter 2. Although the languages that emerged were often those of the European conquerors, the cultures were more mixed, such as the *mestizo* culture of Mexico (Rowe & Schelling, 1991).

Current economic and technological conditions allow for more and more dramatic migration. Most of the ethnic groups that once made up Western Europe had been there throughout recorded history, although some groups migrated from the Urals or the Middle East. Now, the ethnic face of Europe is changing more rapidly as new groups come in from Africa, Asia, and other areas. Such migration, current and past, is a result of structural possibilities created by political decisions, such as the tolerance or encouragement of slave importation, and economic and technological changes, such as economic colonization of Latin America and the diffusion of ships and planes. However, migration also redraws cultural and economic structures, which change the environment within which media operate.

## Transnational Television

For many aspects of television in the world, *transnational* is a more current and appropriate level of analysis than global, per se (Chalaby, 2005c). As a term, *transnational* has a merit over *international* in that actors are not confined to the nation-state or to nationally institutionalized organizations; they may range from individuals to various (non)profitable, transnationally connected organizations and groups, and the conception of culture implied is not limited to a national framework. As Hannerz (1996, p. 6) argued, the term transnational is "more humble, and often a more adequate label for phenonema which can be of quite variable scale and distribution" than the term *global,* which sounds too all-inclusive and decontextualized. Moreover, the term transnational

> draws attention in a more locally contextualized manner to the interconnections and asymmetries that are promoted by the multidirectional flow of information and images, and by the ongoing cultural mixing and infiltration of these messages; it effectively disregards nationally demarcated boundaries both from above and below, the most important of which are capital, people, and media/images. (Iwabuchi 2002, p. 17)

Chalaby (2005a) points out that the late 20th century produced many phenomena that were indeed globalizing. Satellite and optical fiber networks permitted companies and services to obtain global reach. Some television channels, such as CNN, became global in scope. Large integrated corporate empires such as Murdoch's News Corporation pushed for global reach, especially in advertising, where local firms partnered extensively with 10 or so dominant global firms.

However, some globalizing firms also pulled back, as SBC sold off overseas telecommunications acquisitions that had proved to be less profitable than expected or as Vivendi's board pulled out of its recent media empire amid multibillion-dollar losses in 2002. In response to a situation in which global organizations and strategies are not always most profitable, some global firms are decentralizing to become more diverse and regionalized, segmented, and adapted to various circumstances, more transnational than global (Chalaby, 2005a). MTV's diverse adaptations and partnerships around the world represent the transnationalization of what still is a global brand but now is structured as a "transnational network of local channels" (Chalaby, 2005c, p. 31).

Chalaby (2005b) argued that globalization from the central economies of the world continues but is now supplemented, perhaps supplanted in some areas, by a push into transnational activity by many firms and institutions that were not part of the dominant global firms. These new players often come from major developing country producers such as Zee TV in India (Thussu, 2005), Future TV in Lebanon (Kraidy, 2006), Al-Jazeera in Qatar (El-Nawawy & Iskandar, 2003), Channel News Asia in Singapore, or TVB in Hong Kong (Chan, 1996).

Audiences are also increasingly transnational. Diasporas of people from China, various African cultures, India, and Pakistan, among others around the world, now serve as audiences for producers from "home." However, as Sinclair and Cunningham (2000) pointed out, old distinctions between home countries of origin and new home countries of immigration are increasingly tenuous, as people circulate back and forth and create hybrid identities that bridge the two multilayered identities that include both in parallel.

Transnationalization points out the salience of forces that cross borders, but it also makes clear that borders persist. The use of transnational still strongly implies that in many areas, national borders exist to be crossed. Some writers, such as Nederveen Pieterse (2004), have provocatively asserted that in the long run, borders are difficult to maintain against the natural flow of culture across them. Clearly, the strength of national borders varies a great deal. Some countries, such as Canada, China, and France, work very hard at protecting and promoting national culture, with policies empowered to place barriers of tariffs, quotas, and other protections on cultural goods that might cross their borders (Grantham, 2000). Other countries have no policy at all about cultural sovereignty or the protection of national culture. Some countries, such as Brazil and Mexico, rely on strong internal cultural industries to displace cultural imports, rather than resorting to formal barriers.

Conceptualizing transnationalism presents a challenge. Some transnational television operations are governments or national broadcasters that primarily think of migrant or diaspora audiences who want to watch television from back home. Others are truly global institutions like the BBC, which have to think globally, transnationally, regionally, and nationally to reach all those they wish to reach. In between are various others. Translocal broadcasters often originally wanted to use transnational satellite technology to break into a home market that restricted new commercial competitors, such as India or Turkey.

Of the many types of transnational broadcasters, few have truly global reach. Chalaby (2005a) described four types of transnational broadcasters in Europe: ethnic channels, multiterritory operations, pan-European (or more broadly, regional) channels, and networks. Globally or transnationally owned and targeted channels or programs often have to be localized to be effective. This localization process is described more in Chapter 6.

## Geocultural or Cultural-Linguistic Regions

Iwabuchi (2002) argued for thinking of globalization as decentered. Instead of thinking of a globalization centered on the experience of the industrialized West, he added other centers of global power, such as Japan. One can see the development of geocultural regions or transnational cultural-linguistic markets that are less than global but more than national, based on both geography and cultural-linguistic identity groupings. These supranational cultural-linguistic regions are perhaps more crucial to many television viewers than globalization per se (Sinclair et al., 1996). Cultural-linguistic and geocultural television markets are typically unified by language (even though different accents and dialects may divide countries somewhat). Beyond language, however, such markets are also defined by history, religion, ethnicity (in some cases), and culture in several ways: (1) shared identity, gestures, and nonverbal communication; (2) ideas of what is considered funny or serious or even sacred; (3) clothing styles; (4) living patterns; and (5) climate influences and other relationships with the environment.

Indian movies are popular in the Arab world for such similarities; Brazilian *telenovelas* (evening serials or soaps) dubbed into Spanish are more popular than the American *Dallas* or *Dynasty* because of such similarities (Straubhaar & Viscasillas, 1991). Iwabuchi (1997) showed that Taiwanese young people see Japanese television and music as culturally proximate, sharing a sense of "Asian modernity," despite the language difference between Japanese and Chinese.

As an example of the role of cultural elements beyond language in this process, Chadha and Kavoori (2000) noted that even Asian audiences in countries where substantial minorities speak English, such as Hong Kong, India, and the Philippines, still prefer local television dramas to imported television dramas. They attributed this to the fact that Asian programs show similar lifestyles, norms, and sentiments.

In geocultural regions, such as Latin America, Asia, or the Middle East, regional cultural industries have been selling to regional cultural markets, based on language, religion, ethnicity, colonial heritage, historical roots, and so on, for hundreds of years. In Latin America, Asia, and the Middle East, hundreds of millions of people regularly watch regionally produced soap operas, comedies, and variety shows—far more than watch the truly global channels, such as CNN, Discovery, HBO, or MTV. These dynamics have resulted in many types of media development, resulting in a series of relationships that stretch across a continuum from rather complete dependency to dominant interdependence (even the United States has discovered that it is not independent). This range of relationships can be called a form of asymmetrical interdependence.

Sometimes, regional cultural industry is led by demand, when geocultural conditions permit markets to develop around shared cultural conditions in multiple cultures and countries. Sometimes, governments pursue them by trade agreements and other policy initiatives (Galperin, 1999). In 1989, the European Union Directive on Broadcasting set some rules to consolidate the single European Audiovisual Space. Their intention was to create a European market for "television without frontiers."

Aspects of shared history often draw countries together in cultural-linguistic markets. Media programmers or marketers can take such commonalties and consciously try to synthesize a cultural-linguistic market out of common elements, glossing over significant differences. For example, broadcasters and marketers in the United States have attempted to construct a pan-ethnic Hispanic audience to create a broader Latino market that would economically justify production of programming and generate broader potential sales. Rodriguez (1999) remarked, "This conceptualization of ethnicity ignores or submerges structural variables such as race and class, represented in differing U.S. immigration histories" (p. xx). As she further noted, this construction of a pan-ethnic Latino audience (submerging racial identities ranging from indigenous, black, or European to various combinations) has been consciously related to the creation of a broader Latin American market: "Latino panethnicity has been broadened in the construction of panamericanism, the notion that the U.S. Hispanic market is one segment—albeit the wealthiest segment—of a hemispheric market

that embraces Spanish speakers in North, Central, and South America"
(Rodriguez, 1999, p. xx).

## Asymmetrical Interdependence and World Television

It seems more theoretically sensible to place nations on a continuum between
fairly complete dependence on global actors, systems, and products, which
is still true for some of the world's smallest and poorest nations, and the
relatively dominant but still interdependent positions of the United States,
Japan, and the major European nations. It seems clear that there are many
gradations in between, not just three categories of periphery, semiperiphery
and core, as Wallerstein (1976) argued. As I argued in Chapter 1, this situation can be viewed as gradations in asymmetrical interdependence between
nations, cultures, and organizations such as companies.

In this analysis, I try to go further to look at the interdependencies and
mutual bounding of structural factors, such as economics, technology, and
culture. Receiving, borrowing, and adapting foreign models tends to perpet-
uate asymmetrical interdependence. For example, even if Hong Kong, Japan,
Mexico, or Brazil prospers in television exports using an adaptation of the
U.S. commercial network production model, their development is still somewhat conditioned by the lasting effects of that model. However, the interdependence aspect of the term is quite real, too. All of those countries adapt
and change the model in different ways. They even use their several adapted
versions of the commercial television model to successfully substitute for
and compete with U.S. exports, particularly within cultural-linguistic markets, where their versions of a given genre will often be more appealing. Their
adaptations of the soap opera, the drama, the music video, and the variety
show are more popular than the original U.S. prototypes (Sinclair, 1999).

There are limits on many of these globalizing forces. Many nations resist
trade regimes, and a number have obtained specific exemptions for cultural
products such as film and television. Global patterns of television are often
adapted and hybridized, recalling that new global forces undergo hybridization with local cultures just as older precolonial and colonial forces did.
Global capitalism is itself hybridized by cultural forces and regulated into
adaptation by many nation-states, which fight to retain this power. Several
states have worked hard to control seemingly difficult-to-control technologies such as satellite television (Chan, 1994) and the Internet (Kalathil &
Boas, 2001), most notably China, with some success. Admittedly, nation-
states vary enormously in their interest in and ability to exercise such controls, but quite a few attempt control and, to varying degrees, succeed.

Highly concentrated global media firms are also frequently contested successfully in national and regional markets by local media firms, although the latter also tend to be highly concentrated, even monopolistic. Serious questions about the exercise of political power remain, even when content is produced by a national commercial quasi-monopoly, such as Televisa in Mexico, rather than by the United States or other industrialized nation exporters. U.S. hegemony over television exports has been increasing contested by national, regional, and even global producers in a number of other countries. Many of the apparently global satellite and cable television channels have been localized or hybridized into something quite different than what their global owners or partners originally intended. Furthermore, many of the most successful satellite and cable channels are now regionally or nationally controlled, sometimes in partnership with global media giants, often not.

# 5

# Increasing Complexity

## The Technology of Creating Global and National Television Spaces

In this chapter, I will address the role that various technologies have played in the globalization of television. I argue that the emerging technologies of television, such as satellites, cable systems, and digital production, are making possible a complex world system of television. I will explore how technological changes in production equipment have enabled national production to increase in many countries and cultural markets. I will also explore how new television distribution technologies, such as satellites, have both encouraged a renewed flow of U.S., Japanese, and European programming via direct satellite broadcast and cable TV and also helped a number of large countries, such as Brazil and China, to reach their whole national populations. I also explore the considerable differences in technology available to different countries, regions, and cultures, which greatly restrict the impact of new television technologies or even broadcast television itself in many places.

The role of technology in world television is presented from several angles. At the most general level, technology forms the grounds of what Appadurai (1990) called the technoscape. Technology also enables the form of globalization that Tomlinson (1999) called complex connectivity. This is a level of interaction between nations and cultures that many see as one of the driving forces of current globalization.

Just as some writers tend to see economic relations as determinant of world cultural systems, including television, other writers have seen technology as the prime determinant (McLuhan, 1994). For cultural industries such as television, technological change greatly affects how television is produced, distributed, and consumed. As technological impacts became visible, some experts thought technology would let people create content that was localized and liberating (Pool, 1983). Scholars focused on social movements and alternative media often still perceive that possibility (Downing with Ford & Stein, 2001). Others, such as Mattelart and Schmucler (1985), thought that technologies such as satellite television and VCRs would expand the outflow and domination of U.S. television programming. This study sees both of these trends at work in a complex, contradictory process. Empirically, technology is increasing the outflow of U.S. television programs and films on VCR/DVD, cable TV, and direct broadcast satellites. It also is making local production cheaper and easier; recording and transmission equipment costs less, and the integration of television production with low-cost digital computer technologies is under way. I will try to both chart these trends empirically and to look for theoretical explanations.

## Television Technology as a Structuring Force

This study deliberately turns to technology after discussing the history and political economy of world television precisely because it sees the two as closely interwoven. The forces of globalization are all interdependent, interpenetrated. Economics, technology, and culture all facilitate, yet set bounds for each other. Along with other social and cultural conditions, economics adds greatly to what is currently called the social shaping of technology (Dutton, 1999), but technological change is also a structuring force. Technological change creates conditions for increasing complexity of communications. A new technology can permit what seems like epochal, even cataclysmic change, reshaping the boundaries of what is possible for actors in the system and permitting various resources to be employed in new ways. Technology can even restructure the possibilities of the economy, permitting the entry of new forces into an area of the media, making new economic activities possible, and making others too expensive to continue.

As Castells (1997) pointed out, the economic conditions of most African economies—the product of centuries of economic neglect and abuse by colonial powers, postcolonial multinational corporations, and local actors—virtually preclude the widespread use of the Internet. That, he noted, virtually precludes the incorporation of African companies and other actors in the global economy, which depends so heavily on that technology for almost all communications. As a result, African economies are increasingly excluded from the global economy for reasons that seem technological but really rest in the underlying global political economy.

For example, the economic resources available in Mozambique deeply limit the basic structural possibilities of television organization. In the mid-1990s, a group attempted to create a private, second television network to compete with the state network, Radio-Television Mozambique. However, given a small consumer economy in a poor nation damaged by civil war and natural disasters, there was not enough advertising available to support such a commercial effort, especially because the state network was also increasingly turning to advertising to support its own operations. There was not enough advertising revenue in the economy to support both, so the second, private network survived only by being purchased by a religious broadcasting group from Brazil, the Universal Church of the Reign of God. Television in a country like Mozambique is limited by global and national economic factors. However, as the economy grows and the number of consumers increases, then advertising might conceivably add new resources for television operation.

The political economy of the state and other national institutions is also crucial. The fact that a national economy like Mozambique does not have the structural potential yet for a widespread consumer economy increases the importance of the state as a facilitator of local media. Katz and Wedell (1976) observed in the 1970s that broadcasting in most African countries was undertaken by the state, in part because no other actors had emerged to do so. Because the underlying conditions have not changed radically, it is not surprising that the state remains the mainstay of many television operations, which are expensive, while competitive private commercial operations have developed much faster in radio, which is much less expensive. For example, in Mozambique, several commercial and community radio stations have found resources to broadcast, in addition to the state radio system.

Technology is constrained at the systemic level by the political economy of the nation or region and the institution or firm. It is also constrained at a more microlevel by the class stratification of television or other media audiences or users. Technology is constrained by what the collective mass of the audience or users can afford. A global elite can afford access to virtually everything, from satellite or cable TV to the Internet. The middle classes of technologically advanced and affluent nations likewise can afford access to the main television technologies and most of the new media. However, many people in large parts of the world are constrained by poverty from having access even to broadcast television, much less satellite or cable TV.

## Technologies Facilitate Pattern Ruptures

Within borders framed by factors like economics, other critical conditions, for example, the availability of certain new cultural technologies, may create or enable new possibilities. In complex cultural systems, technology often creates ruptures or cataclysmic changes that enable new cycles of radical change, and technology is prominent among the initial conditions that shape cultural patterns. For example, new digital video and audio production technologies have lowered costs for producing television programming so that a developing country's limited economic base may now permit a much larger quantity of television production. New forms of television delivery, such as videocassettes, DVDs, cable TV, direct-to-home satellite dishes, and the Internet create new options for those who can afford them.

Recent technological history is full of stories of seemingly insignificant technologies interacting with culture, geopolitical forces, and other technologies to create a significant but unpredictable wave of change. Technologies that have significant impact are not necessarily the latest or best in technical terms. There is a certain amount of randomness, which in effect means that some technologies will die, regardless of their technical superiority. The technical merits of a given technology interact with other social and symbolic factors within a cultural context and create what Ricoeur (1984) called a *cultural prefiguration*. He defined that as a set of cultural meanings and understandings that both creators and consumers of cultural products refer to and, in both the process of creating and interpreting, modify as well. In complexity terms, a cultural prefiguration could be seen as an initial symbolic condition, a set of cultural understandings that can both frame, bound, and pattern cultural practices such as television production and viewing. Bourdieu (1984) might have called it a collective disposition by a group to approach something in a certain way. It is the boundary of thought, the framing, if you will, of the individual, the group, or the culture. A particular use of a technology may be feasible, such as the creation of community-based radio to challenge a central authority's control over media, but not possible within the prefigured cultural or social boundaries of society. Then, it will not occur or may not be developed very far. One well-known example involves China and Korea, where major aspects of moveable type printing were invented centuries before Gutenberg in Germany. However, Gutenberg's printing press had a much more revolutionary impact in Europe because other critical initial or prefigurative conditions—a movement toward more massive literacy, a need for clerks for commerce, a latent demand for personal Bible reading, and protoindustrial technologies to facilitate printing—were available to coalesce in a pattern of mass printing and reading. This is a classic example of how social forces can shape the development and use of technology (Dutton, 1999). Conversely, given a prefigurative cultural and social disposition toward a particular technological concept or the cultural use of a particular technological possibility, then that technology is almost sure to emerge when conditions permit, in the way that television seemed to be almost simultaneously imagined and developed in several parts of the world from the early 1900s to the 1930s.

When the telegraph emerged as a technology, what complexity theory might call a rupture of patterns created the conditions for a new pattern to emerge. For the first time, humans could send messages faster than a messenger on horse, ship, or train could carry it (Carey, 1989). As a result, communication was dramatically reconceptualized as something that spanned distances quickly, an initial condition for new kinds of technologies, uses, and interactions. It is little wonder that many innovators began to move fairly quickly to telegraph without wires (radio), then wired telegraph with sound (telephone), and then radio with pictures (television), all building on the telegraph's paradigmatic breakthrough to a new level of speed and reach. As television moves into new distribution methods and enhanced quality projection, it is likely that continued fascination with the medium owes something to a prefigurative disposition toward visual and auditory communication over distances that began with the technological rupture of the telegraph. It is no surprise, then, that different ways of distributing and consuming television over the Internet have developed since 2000: for example, Web sites such as YouTube; services to download television programs or music videos over iTunes and MySpace; various forms of streaming video on major media sites such as CNN.com; individually produced video sites such as sendspace.com; or institutional sites such as the Singapore government site, where one can stream the hours-long but highly iconic and widely viewed National Day Parade.

## Cycles of Technology

The overall conditions of dependency and poverty faced by many nations greatly constrain what they can accomplish with communications technologies. Technological dependence is itself an importance aspect of the overall problem. Most developing countries were long dependent on imported technology for television production, transmission, computer effects, and so on from more fully industrialized countries (Mattelart & Schmucler, 1985). This has changed, in some countries since the 1970s, in others more recently. Hardware development still takes place in a few countries, although that list has grown as both China and India have become centers of technology research and development since 2000. Meanwhile, hardware manufacturing has diversified to many more countries. Mature technologies first moved to the East Asian and the Latin American Newly Industrializing Countries (NICs) for manufacturing; they have since moved further into developing areas. Brazil, China, India, Malaysia, Mexico, Singapore, South Korea, Taiwan, and quite a few others now produce VCRs, DVD players, satellite dishes, microcomputers, and minor production equipment. A larger number of countries now produce television sets, although increasingly free trade has ironically reconcentrated television set production in some of the highest-volume, lowest-cost, and most efficient producers. As Sony (Japan) displaced RCA (United States), so Samsung (South Korea) has severely challenged Sony on both price and quality of television sets, and other countries produce lower quality but cheaper sets, with more than 40 countries now assembling televisions, so sets also cost about one tenth of what they did in the mid-1950s (Mougayar, 2002).

However, the manufacture of hardware may not be a key cultural issue, aside from the economic desirability of gaining jobs for the national economy by building manufacturing industries that will employ workers and managers. A larger view of technology examines how it is employed and used, rather than just where it comes from. There is "soft" technology, or ways of using hardware to create other products, particularly television or video programming. Looked at more broadly, then, one can see an even larger absorption of mature technologies for the production of cultural content into many smaller industrial countries and developing countries.

Television sets, while almost ubiquitous in rich and middle-income countries, are still a scarce luxury in many poor or rural areas of much of the world. Some poorer developing countries are still struggling to absorb radio production and diffuse radio receivers to all their population. For instance, in Mozambique, only half of the population in areas surveyed had a radio at home, and roughly two thirds hear radio regularly (Craddock, 2003). Similar or lower levels are found in most other African countries. In India, radio also reaches slightly more than half of the population, while somewhat more than 100,000 households have television (Research, 2006). However, in Latin America and East and Southeast Asia, majorities of the population have both radio and television at home. Those who do not have television at home tend to see it frequently in public places. As discussed in Chapter 3, this audience growth tends to mean more money for regional, national, and local television, whether from advertising revenues, taxes, or license fees, and more money is available for regional, national, and local production.

## Technology and Production

The production media of the 1950s and 1960s were usually bulky, non-portable, expensive, and based in tube or early transistor technologies. The move to transistor solid-state technologies and then to digital technologies made equipment more inexpensive, flexible, and portable through miniaturization. Cameras, microphones, recorders, lights, and mixers are among the appliances that have become steadily smaller, lighter, and easier for television producers to take into the field to use existing locations and take advantage of live events. Those same pieces plus studio equipment such as cameras, lights, switchers, and special effects generators, have also become much cheaper. When I visited several Dominican Republic television networks in the mid-1980s, I found them doing a great deal of live programming out of one or two studios with two or three cameras, a few lights, a couple of microphones, and simple switchers. Several stations had put adequate studios together for less than $80,000. With those studios, they were often producing 8 hours of television a day or more, which helps explain some of the growth in national production that occurred in the 1980s in a number of countries (described in Chapter 6).

Production is being made much easier by sharp decreases in the cost of technology along with increases in portability, ease of use, flexibility, and other characteristics. One political activist and producer in Brazil, Luis Fernando Santoro, estimated that except perhaps for cameras, production equipment in 1990 cost about a quarter of what it cost in 1980 and that the equipment bought in the late 1980s was much easier to operate and use in field production (Santoro, personal interview, August 20, 1989).

This kind of elementary studio production relied on simple genres that could be produced live in front of a few cameras or a studio audience: live variety shows, live news readers, live discussions and panels, and live music. That helps explain some of the trends in genre development described in Chapter 6, too. It also enabled new producers to find local and national jobs, get experience, and begin to explore what they could do with the technology, money, genres, and other cultural resources available to them, which helps explain some of the developments described in Chapter 6.

With digitization, costs have gone down substantially further, supporting all manner of television production. Because most production can now be done with computer-based equipment, which also permits easier and cheaper editing, producers can go beyond live programming; their costs have gone down while options for production have increased. My visits to similar simple broadcast studios in the northeast of Brazil in 2002 through 2005 showed that the studios could now be mounted for even less, often less than $30,000, but creating much higher-quality visual images.

In Latin America and Asia, at least, the larger countries had already absorbed and dominated the use of television production technology by the 1980s, although that is still an ongoing process for the smaller and poorer countries. For example, major broadcasters in Brazil, especially TV Globo, have mastered and used television production increasingly efficiently and creatively since the 1960s. Domination of the technology arrived later in smaller developing countries, such as the Dominican Republic and Bolivia, where the decrease in costs of production technology and transmission led to a profusion of television stations in the 1980s and to a considerable increase in local production (Prada & Cuenco, 1986). Since the 1980s, there has been rapid growth in new commercial stations and networks. Private television networks are starting in several nations in Africa, where competition to existing state-owned broadcasters had been seen as economically unfeasible as recently as the late 1990s.

Technological change permitted more actors and institutions to enter music production, radio and television broadcasting, and other media because the costs of doing so declined considerably. Social actors who want to use a technology like television can creatively employ it within the limits imposed by economics, institutions, and culture. This enables more production by more producers at all levels, from the local, such as alternative video producers, social movements, universities, and local governments, up to sophisticated national and regional broadcasters (see Chapter 6). For example, public cable channels mandated by law in Brazil in the 1990s had gone undeveloped until radically lowered costs permitted universities to exponentially increase student television production, which now fills many of those channels.

This has increased even further after 2000, as thousands of groups and individuals across the world now create both simple and sophisticated video programs for distribution over the World Wide Web. Most of these television productions are short. Patterns on new distribution channels such as YouTube or Grouper show that few videos are longer than a few minutes, but some are much longer, and many are quite sophisticated, revealing careful use of computer editing and effects. Most are designed to be entertaining, but one can find anything from Al Qaeda instructional documentaries on how to make a bomb to development education on how to conduct oral rehydration therapy in African villages.

## Technology and Media Distribution and Flows

Some of the first writing on how technological changes in television would affect media imperialism and the flow of media products assumed the worst, assuming that technology would simply reinforce the unequal flow between countries by adding a new set of channels that would favor U.S. exports over other television possibilities (Mattelart & Schmucler, 1985). In fact, video-cassette recorders (VCRs), cable TV, and home satellite dishes did open new channels for the flow of U.S. feature films and, to lesser degree, U.S. television programs and music videos (Boyd, Straubhaar, & Lent, 1989).

However, the new distribution technologies also created a number of other possibilities. Satellite distribution of television signals has enabled a number of large countries, from the ex-USSR to Brazil, India, and Indonesia, to reach their geographically dispersed audiences with national programming (Hudson, 1985; Kraidy, 2002; Page & Crawley, 2001; Wang, 1993). VCRs and DVDs permit political, religious, ethnic, and other groups to circulate alternative video productions completely outside the formal world of broadcast television, a sort of electronic *samizdat* or underground video literature (Downing et al., 2001). Cable and direct-to-home satellite TV also permits the entry of new channels at the national level, opening the doors to new religious and musical expression in Turkey, new political views in Taiwan, national feature films in Brazil and Mexico, and news from home for migrants all over the world.

## Satellites

One of the theoretical misapprehensions of the satellite television phenomenon was to extend the mass media metaphor of the 1960s and 1970s, an era of national television networks, into the global sphere. Critics perceived a massive potential effect of cross-border satellite-based television in the 1960s and 1970s, long before direct satellite broadcasting or even satellite delivery to cable systems became technological realities (McPhail, 1989; Nordenstreng & Schiller, 1979). Fears that cross-border television controlled by other countries would find and affect mass audiences was reflected in policy debates in the U.N. Commission on the Peaceful Uses of Outer Space in the 1960s (de Sola Pool, 1979), in the New World Information and Communication Order debate in UNESCO and the International Telecommunication Union (ITU) in the 1970s (McPhail, 1989), and in academic work by Mattelart (e.g., Mattelart & Schmucler, 1985) and others in the 1970s and 1980s. Some studies indeed found effects of cross-border satellite television, particularly in small countries such as Belize or parts of the English-speaking Caribbean, where direct reception of foreign satellite television started before national broadcast television had begun (Oliveira, 1986).

The first major cross-border satellite-to-cable TV flows of programming took U.S. cable channels into Canada and the Caribbean in the early 1980s. U.S. cable programming had an extensive impact in English-speaking Canada (Raboy, 1990), the English-speaking Caribbean (Hoover & Britto, 1990), and Belize (Oliveira, 1986). It had less impact in the Spanish-speaking Caribbean, where it tended to be used only by English-speaking elites (Straubhaar, 1989b; Straubhaar & Viscasillas, 1991). When cable systems initially expanded in Europe, particularly in smaller countries such as Belgium or Switzerland, they often brought in channels and networks from other European countries in the same or similar languages, to add diversity to what those countries could afford to produce on broadcast television (Straubhaar, 1988).

Meanwhile, in many countries of the former Soviet Union, Latin America, South Asia, Southeast Asia, and North Asia, the primary initial impact of satellites was to permit dominant national broadcasters to achieve truly national coverage by relaying signals across large expanses of land (as in Brazil, India, or Russia) or ocean (as in Indonesia and Malaysia). The main overall impact of satellites, at least until the 1990s, probably has been this facilitation of national distribution, particularly in several large countries containing much of the world's population: Brazil, China, India, Indonesia, Mexico, Russia, and the United States, all of which developed early-generation national satellite systems precisely to cover their own national audiences. This was discussed more extensively in Chapter 3 but is important to recall in this global context (Sinclair, 2005). Still, because satellites can technologically cover a good part of the globe, many people expected them to produce a global village of the sort anticipated by Marshall McLuhan.

## From Cross-Border Spillover to Direct Satellite Broadcasting

The main global impact has probably been distribution of cable channels across borders but within regions. Starting in the 1970s and early 1980s, international spillover of satellite-based cable channels beyond the borders of their intended national audience took place from the United States to its North American and Caribbean neighbors, from Japan to Taiwan, and from

Europe to the Mediterranean region. Spillover continues to be an important part of international satellite impacts, accentuated as people in a number of countries covered by the footprints of television and cable distribution satellites acquired C-Band satellite (4 to 6GHz) dishes (1.5 to 2 meters across). These were large enough to permit individual homes to receive satellite signals directly, accidentally initiating the era of direct satellite broadcasting in the mid-1980s.

Direct broadcast satellites (DBS) had been anticipated since the 1960s but weren't seen as commercially viable then, at a time when individual satellite dish owners precipitated the de facto DBS known in the United States. as TVRO (TV receive-only dishes). In fact, DBS systems began to succeed commercially in a variety of countries in the mid- to late 1990s. Until then, direct reception from satellites on a wide scale was limited by receiving dish costs. In the early era of de facto DBS, C-Band dishes often cost at least $2,000 in the United States and more in other countries, although this cost declined as manufacturing achieved some economies of scale and spread across nations. (A C-band dish for picking up unscrambled national television distribution signals in Brazil cost about $300 in 2006.). In Brazil, thousands of small towns have spent municipal funds on satellite dishes and retransmitters to bring in national television signals, which are rebroadcast locally to provide television coverage (La Pastina, 1999).

Millions of such dishes sprouted across the globe to capture satellite spillover channels from other countries. Initially, only a few channels were distributed globally (such as CNN, the U.S. Armed Forces Radio-Television Network, and the U.S. Information Agency's WorldNet—see below), and regular national broadcast channels were distributed to affiliates by satellite, especially in large countries with vast rural areas not served by television—Brazil, India, Indonesia, and Mexico, for example. India's first major experience of widespread national television distribution and reception was via large satellite dishes to community reception centers and schools in the Satellite Instructional Television Experiment in 1975 to 1976.

Costs of DBS increased again in the late 1980s, when satellite channel distributors, such as the American cable channels, began to scramble their signals, requiring the purchase of a decoder and the payment of a monthly fee to permit reception. Costs decreased again in the 1990s with a new generation of smaller dishes, made to receive higher power signals broadcast in the Ku frequency band (12 to 14 GHz). In the United States, these new systems cost less than $200 by the late 1990s or were installed free after 2000 by such providers as DirecTV and Dish network to compete with cable-based systems. Dishes often cost slightly more in most other countries, plus at least $20 to $30 per month for programming fees. This level of price and accessibility has turned DBS into a mass medium in the United States, Great Britain, and a few other places but keeps it an elite or middle-class medium in much of the world. (This is discussed in detail below.)

Besides providing DBS reception to home dishes, satellites also deliver broadcast and cable channels for rebroadcast and retransmission over cable systems. In some places, not only broadcast channels but also cable channels such as CNN or MTV are locally retransmitted on either VHF or UHF channels after being downlinked from a satellite. MTV achieved most of its audience penetration in Brazil, for example, on newly opened UHF channels fed by a national satellite signal (Duarte, 1992).

## Satellites and Cable TV

Cable systems were and still are the dominant means by which satellite-delivered channels are actually carried to the viewer in most countries. Cable television systems often have substantially different dynamics than DBS; as a result, subscriber costs are lower, and cable became more of a mass-audience service in a number of countries. Cable was cheaper in cities or affluent towns, where many people could be wired up in dense areas, creating economies of scale (Baldwin & McEvoy, 1988), whereas satellite systems initially flourished primarily in rural areas or poorer regions and countries where only a few potential subscribers could afford them. Satellite systems have since decreased considerably in price, but cable systems have also increased in capability, providing an attractive base for broadband Internet connections, as well as increased numbers of cable channels.

Cable systems are cheaper in many countries, costing only a few dollars a month in some places, for example, India, where systems are informal or illegal. Governments as diverse as Canada, China, and France have favored cable systems over DBS because they offer greater national control for governments trying to mitigate the direct inflow of foreign culture or political information (Price, 1999; Straubhaar, 1988). Government policy can control dozens or hundreds of cable companies more easily than millions of individual home or apartment-block satellite dishes.

## Satellite TV at Global, Regional, and National Levels

All the major spheres or levels of television distribution—global, transnational, cultural-linguistic, geocultural, translocal, and national—are facilitated by satellites. CNN can cover the entire globe using three or four satellites, becoming a truly global phenomenon. Satellite TV can also be used to cover all or most of Latin America or Asia, as cultural-linguistic regions.

It can take programming aimed translocally from Singapore into India for Zee TV and send it further, with other satellites, toward a transnational diaspora of South Asians across North America, Europe, the Middle East, and Africa (Kumar, 2006). It can also be used to make sure that all Brazilians or Indonesians get a national television signal, either through DBS dishes or, more commonly, through receiving dishes hooked to local broadcast television retransmitters or cable TV systems.

Satellites and the increasing network of broadband undersea cables permit the increased delivery of globally segmented channels, such as Discovery, ESPN, MTV, or HBO. However, those global/U.S. channels have had to adapt to regional and even country-specific markets, focusing on much smaller areas than the broad footprint of a regional or even multiregional satellite beam.

Several notable attempts have been made to use the regional technical reach of satellites to create or address television audiences or markets, defined by geographic region, that span multiple cultures and languages. For example, the European Economic Community (EEC) has made a pronounced effort to promote a Europe-wide television market, beginning with its report, *Television without Frontiers: Green Paper on the Establishment of the Common Market for Broadcasting, Especially by Satellite and Cable* (Commission of the European Communities, 1984). Critics such as Schlesinger (1993) thought that the EEC efforts were unlikely to succeed because they are attempting to define as European what is in fact an economics-focused geographical alliance of several distinct language and cultural groups—English-, German-, and French-speaking groups, among others, which are found in both countries and subnational minority populations. Experiences to date with satellite-delivered cable TV or DBS programming in Europe indicates that it either faces considerable resistance unless it fits existing interests in either national programming, U.S. genres of interest, or certain genres, such as music, sports, and news, where regional channels seem to succeed better. For example, since 1954, Eurovision has provided a specific exchange mechanism in Europe, which functioned before satellites and came to focus on news item exchanges; live events such as sports, which were considerably facilitated by satellite technology; and the annual Eurovision Song Contest, which has become one quite visible point of Europe-wide cultural interaction (Agger, 2001). The Eurovision sports and news programs were popular enough to produce the specialized pan-European channels Eurosports and Euronews.

Although the technical capability of satellites has encouraged some—regional groups such as the European Union and companies such as Rupert Murdoch's Star TV—to assume that markets can be defined by technology, the evidence to date shows that television markets are defined by culture and language, instead. Some striking early results of satellite television were perhaps deceptive. For example, people were surprised by the degree to which audiences in both Canada and the Caribbean were drawn into watching more American television by the accidental spillover of the footprint of the first U.S. cable distribution satellites in the 1970s and 1980s (Lee, 1980; Oliveira, 1986). However, the effect was so strong in large part because many of those populations spoke English and were tied to the United States by trade and migration. Based on a series of in-depth interviews in the Dominican Republic between 1986 and 1988, I found that even Spanish-speakers felt closer to U.S. culture due to physical proximity to the United States and Puerto Rico and circular migration to and from the United States; hence, they were more likely to watch U.S. cable channels than were Brazilians whom I interviewed between 1989 and 1990 in São Paulo.

Global/U.S. channels often make regional adaptations, dubbing programs into languages that are widespread throughout regions, such as Mandarin Chinese or Spanish. They are also increasingly adjusting or localizing the selection of contents (films, documentaries, or music videos) to reflect regional tastes. For example, MTV channels in Asia, Europe, and Latin America play more local music and less American music to adapt to local taste. ESPN Brazil plays more soccer and less American football. This process of localization is discussed in more detail in Chapter 7.

Related is the capability of satellites to support cultural-linguistic markets that are either centered in one geographic region or spread across several. In Latin America and the Middle East, geocultural markets are in fact centered on a geographic region, although immigrants and migrant workers have carried the Arabic market into Europe and the Latin American market into North America. In Asia, a satellite permits a television channel to address the audience of greater China, even though the audiences in question are spread across East Asia, Southeast Asia, and the considerable extent of China itself (Man Chan, 1994; Curtin, 2003). Satellites have helped the growth of channels and networks aimed at cultural-linguistic markets, both those concentrated in single geographic regions and those that follow diasporas, like the overseas Chinese and the Indian or South Asian populations widely dispersed across Asia, North America, Europe, and elsewhere as well.

Overall, the primary initial impact of television satellites seems to have been to permit complete national distribution and penetration of television in a number of larger countries, such as Brazil, Canada, China, India, Mexico, and the former USSR. Next, it has permitted a number of channels to grow from national to global. Some of those have truly global ambition and reach, like Discovery or CNN. Perhaps more widely watched are those that supply programming from major producers to those who share a language and culture with them, whether in the country next door or in California's Silicon Valley.

A quite different effect, following a quite different logic of globalization, may be to permit upper and middle classes to become more distinguished from working and lower classes of their own nationality. That can happen on either a global or regional basis, as global and regional channels come to them via satellite through DBS or cable TV.

## TV Technology, Access, and Choice

One thing that emerges from studies of audiences for different kinds of television is the primacy of social class in explaining audience access and preferences. In particular, I propose that the use of new television technologies to gain access to the global flow of television outward from the United States or other core countries is most common among two groups: a globalized elite who speak English and are interested in CNN's perspective on world news and people in the Anglophone nations of the world, where U.S. television exports tend to be most popular (and best understood; Abram, 2004).

CNN is famous for having a global audience. However, a review by Sparks (1998) showed that the actual audiences for both CNN and BBC worldwide were quite small and that neither source provided a common core of information and perspective for what might be considered a potentially global public sphere. Both surveys and in-depth interviews I did in Brazil (Straubhaar, 1991, 2003), in the Dominican Republic (Straubhaar & Viscasillas, 1991), and among Latinos in central and south Texas (from 2003 through 2005) showed that relatively few people watched CNN. Many people explained that watching CNN was difficult because it demanded knowledge of current events and also knowledge of English, which very few had. Featherstone noted,

> Access to these, not imagined but virtual communities, to these neo-worlds constituted by the "iconic-symbolic" and "graphic/dictive" flows is exclusive. It is based on the power and ability to decode (and encode) the signals in the flows. Such decoding/encoding ability depends on the possession of particular, virtual-community-specific types of cultural capital. (in Featherstone & Lash, 1995, p. 11)

### Economic Capital and Access to Television Technologies

One theory relevant to the personal construction and use of information and communication technologies examines various forms of capital, how they are gained, the fields they are deployed in, and how they are accumulated in a larger group of class *habitus* (Bourdieu, 1984, 1986, 1998). Economic capital or disposable income basically determines what communications media a person can afford to access (Rojas, Straubhaar, Fuentes-Bautista, & Pinon, 2005). Cultural capital, such as education, family experiences, language ability, exposure to foreign cultures, and travel, is related more to what a person chooses to watch than to what they can afford. The economic capital aspect of social class has the greatest impact with the newest television technologies, such as satellite television or satellite-fed cable TV in the 1990s and computers or the Internet after 2000 (Rojas et al., 2005). For instance, whereas less than 10% of the audience had cable or satellite television in most of Latin America as of 2006, more than 80% of homes in increasingly middle-class Taiwan had cable (Oba & Chan-Olmsted, 2005). In many developing countries, including most of Latin America and Africa, direct satellite reception or cable television is a middle-class or even upper-middle-class technology, unavailable to most of the population. For example, cable or satellite-based pay television in Brazil and several other Latin American countries costs $20 to $30 per month, which greatly limits its penetration below the middle class (Porto, 2001).

One key limit on access to television in general is personal wealth or, as Bourdieu (1984) refers to it, economic capital. People must have enough income to buy a television set and, in rural areas, an expensive antenna or satellite dish. Even though people buy televisions before stoves, refrigerators, or indoor plumbing, hundreds of millions in the world still cannot afford a television. Perhaps 50% to 60% of people in Mozambique cannot. Perhaps 10% in the Dominican Republic cannot. Less than 5% in Brazil cannot. One reason that radio is still more widespread as the medium of the world's poorest is that radio receivers are still much cheaper to buy and radio signals much cheaper to transmit over greater distances. Radio transmitters are a much less expensive way to bring media transmissions or signals to where the people are. In places like Mozambique, as many as a third of the population cannot afford even simple receivers for AM radio or the batteries to keep them running.

However, in some countries, such as India, cable television was developed as a localized, often pirated technology that often cost only a few dollars (Sinclair, 2005). Cable has also been encouraged as a technology in some countries, such as Singapore, because it is more easily controlled than DBS television reception. Governments can weigh in on which channels will be offered and which will be excluded. Relatively low-cost cable television systems have been built up as part of an overall broadband telecommunications infrastructure in some areas, such as Hong Kong and Singapore. In some countries, cable TV developed as a mass-audience technology that reached below the middle class into the working class.

To date, DBS technologies are usually more expensive than cable TV, including the initial cost of the satellite dish. But nearly all countries have developed at least a small DBS industry to serve those who have both money and interest in programming that tends to lean heavily toward international channels. The exceptions are countries where DBS is politically forbidden as in China (Pashupati, Sun, & McDowell, 2003) and Singapore (Datta-Ray, 2006). Local or translocal channels for DBS services, such as Zee TV in India (Kumar, 2006), may develop when a mass audience, usually developed through lower cost cable television, justifies production of new material for the local audience.

## Cable and Satellite TV Relative to Broadcast TV

The other factor to take in account in understanding whether cable or satellite television has developed further as a mass-audience technology in a given country or region is the relationship to what has been offered to audiences via traditional broadcast television. In some countries, broadcast television developed as a robust multichannel system with both quality and diversity of offerings. Examples might include Great Britain and Japan, which have both strong public service systems and strong commercial networks and which have both offered such diverse channels that television households, even though they could afford either satellite or cable television, did not initially show much interest. Other examples might include Brazil and Mexico, where broadcast television was overwhelmingly commercial; they developed multichannel cable or satellite systems offering some diversity of choice as well as dominant channels that delivered high-quality entertainment, such as prime-time telenovelas, that also succeeded as export products to other countries (Sinclair, 1999).

My interviews with programmers at satellite and cable television systems in Brazil, Hong Kong, Singapore, and Taiwan show that they are aware of the need to increase the local content of satellite and cable systems to attract mass audiences. An example from the early 1990s was the local news and talk that made TVBS (a joint venture in Taiwan between local backers and TVB of Hong Kong) popular with the Taiwanese audience. These programmers recognized audience demand for cultural proximity as they sought to localize satellite channel programming, supplemented by programming from nearby producers within cultural-linguistic regions, such as TVBS's use of some crime drama, kung fu, and soap opera from TVB in Hong Kong. That process was well-established early in Taiwan, where more than one dozen local Taiwanese satellite-delivered cable TV channels were available as early as 1993, plus Chinese channels from elsewhere in the greater China cultural-linguistic region, mostly China and Hong Kong. Taiwan now has nearly 40 locally produced channels, showing the high level of audience response. Localization or translocalization of satellite/cable channels has also taken place in Argentina, India, South Korea, Turkey, and a number of other places, mostly countries with a large middle-class population and well-developed broadcast television systems that had been held back by government controls, at least until the 1990s, when most of this satellite channel development took off.

## Geography, Language, and Other Barriers to Satellite or Cable TV

Another main barrier for many people is sheer geographic distance from coverage by broadcast signals. A significant fraction of the world's people are still geographically isolated from the towns and cities that provide electronic media coverage, as well as the centers of education that would give them access to print media. Close to a fifth of Mozambique's people do not have reliable access to radio signals, and slightly over half have access to television signals. Some are too far away from the transmitters. In theory, they could listen to long-distance short-wave radio and use satellite dishes to get television, but those are both prohibitively expensive technologies for most rural dwellers. As some countries become more prosperous (and as some technologies become cheaper), satellite dishes are in fact proliferating in rural areas.

However, one of the most fundamental dynamics in many countries in the past century has been internal migration from rural areas to cities. Most people are increasingly migrating to or relocating in or near towns or cities, experiencing much more direct exposure to the electronic media. The first purchases of many new migrants are radios and televisions to permit them access to what they see as the modern media. (One of the most poignant interviews I have ever conducted was with a homeless man in 1989 in São Paulo, who was deeply shamed to admit that he did not have a television. He saw a television as the minimum possession required to be a "real Brazilian.")

Language is another aspect of access to television that tends to exclude many people in a number of countries. Many people speak certain television export languages, such as Chinese, Hindi, and English, increasing the fortunes of both Hollywood (Wildman & Siwek, 1988, 1993) and Bollywood (Kumar, 2006). However, television is still broadcast largely in the main national languages of various countries. Quite a few people—from India and Mexico to most of sub-Saharan Africa—are still isolated (or protected) from both national and global cultures by their exclusive use of local, subnational languages. That, again, is changing as production and transmission costs for television go down. It is gradually becoming more feasible to produce television in local languages. That tendency is most visible in India, where large regional-language communities support both film and television production (Kumar, 2006), but it is also quite evident in Great Britain, Spain, and some other parts of Europe, where local-language television for various subnational regional cultures, such as Wales or Catalonia, has been gradually increasing since the 1980s, often driven by increasingly autonomous regional governments (Moragas Spa, Garitaonaindia Garnacho, & Lopez, 1999). Such localization or regionalization of television production and distribution is also increasing among large minority populations in less wealthy countries, for example, some of the major language groups of India, such as Bengali, Telegu, or Tamil. But often even sizable groups of people who do not speak the dominant national language—for example, the Maya in Central America and southern Mexico, who often do not speak Spanish—still largely do not have much television in their local languages. The situation is worse for minority languages in the poorest countries, such as Mozambique, even where, as in that case, less than a third of the populace speaks the supposed national language, Portuguese. Radio is growing in some local languages there but seldom television, which remains too expensive.

Most people are increasingly pulled into using one of the world/main national languages, in some part precisely so that they can watch the available television programming. Others are hastening to learn English in particular so that they can have access to more material from countries on the Internet. A number of people are worried that this tendency is hastening the extinction of small indigenous languages. Hundreds of such languages disappear every year. "In the world, approximately 6,000 languages are spoken . . . of which only about 600 are confidently expected to survive this century" (MIT Indigenous Language Initiative, 2006). However, among other language groups, the native language remains the language of the family, the village, and, increasingly, the radio because radio is still much cheaper to produce, transmit, and receive than television. A well-documented case involves the indigenous-language radio stations that have sprung up in many Latin American cities, especially in Andean nations such as Peru and Central American nations such as Guatemala, to serve indigenous-language speakers who have migrated to the city for work.

One outcome of these processes is that different languages may become the mode of access to different media. I have interviewed people in Brazil who listen to radio for music in a local dialect that mixes Portuguese and indigenous languages, who watch television in the national version of

Portuguese, and who read materials in books or on the Internet in English. Lack of in-depth ability in English or other world languages limits access to a great deal of global media content. However, the lack of prevalent ability to understand English also provides an essential protection for many cultural markets in other languages.

# 6

# Producing National
# Television, Glocal, and Local

This chapter examines the context within which television producers, writers, and directors act as they create the range of programs that flow across the world to various audiences. I look at the structures within which producers work: the rules and resources that both constrain and enable their creation of television programs. In this chapter a theoretical and empirical discussion of television audiences begins: What do they choose to watch? What understandings do they share with the producers of the programs they watch? Those understandings form a crucial aspect of the context within which television producers work.

AUTHOR'S NOTE: The conceptual development of this chapter owes a great deal to several colleagues and students, specifically Scott Hammond (Utah Valley State College), Martha Fuentes, and Dan Abram (University of Texas–Austin), Caçilda Regô (Utah State University), and Heloisa Buarque de Almeida (University of São Paulo). As with most large empirical projects, the data reported in this chapter and in Chapter 7 also resulted from substantial amounts of work by collaborators, including Patricia McCormick (Howard University), Consuelo Campbell (Michigan State University), Sug-Min Youn (Seoul National University), Nobuya Inagaki (University of Texas), Luisa Ha (University of Oklahoma), Seema Shrikhande (Oglethorpe University), Michael Elasmar (Boston University), and Luiz Duarte, among others.

Overall, I consider three questions and related theories of how producers work within the world system of television. First, how do boundaries, rules, and resources (Giddens, 1984; Williams, 1980) structure the producer's world of work? Second, how do the producer and audience interact within a process characterized by continuing cultures modified first in creations by television producers, and then consumed, thought through, and reconfigured by audiences (Ricoeur, 1984)? Third, how do local or national producers indigenize or glocalize their productions to absorb and adapt ideas that circulate transnationally (Robertson, 1995)?

I consider several key issues as I examine these theories. How have the changing conditions for producers contributed to increased levels of national, local, translocal, transnational, and regional production? How much power and autonomy do producers have in their creative process compared with the immediate institutional structures in which they work; the power of global institutions over both them and local/national/regional institutions; and the power of global forms, genres, and cultural trends over them and their local/national institutions? How much of local culture is preserved or maintained in producers' cultural products? How much is adapted or copied from global ideas, genres, and trends in circulation? If adaptation seems inevitable for producers working within the flow of global and regional forces, then how can the nature of their products be characterized? Are they hybrid, glocalized, localized, or perhaps, in the case of those trying to create cultural products for export, delocalized? Can those products maintain some continuity or authenticity from the historical cultures that produced them? Not all of these questions can be easily answered, but they are important to keep in mind.

To structure this examination and to give it a rigorous empirical base, I will examine the flow of television programs among broadcast television producers and the most widely viewed stations (those with at least a 5% share of the broadcast audience) in 25 cultural markets, focusing on local and national production. I will look at the general trends in local and national production, with a closer examination of one specific case of the adaptation and localization of a major genre: the telenovela. Focusing first on Latin America, then Brazil, and finally, one specific production in 1995, I find examples of many issues I wish to examine.

## Structuring the Producers' World

Theoretically, this chapter starts with a reminder that the structures of television as a medium are linked to the agency of both individual producers and audiences. As Giddens (1984) warned, structures like those of television production should not be viewed as things that exist somehow apart from people. The important structure of a television network is not its buildings and cameras, nor even simply who owns it or manages it from the corner office suite. What is important is the rather more complex sum of the daily routines and creative work of its owners, managers, directors, writers, technicians, and actors, all of whom work within rules and using resources set down by those who own and run the structure. To understand structures, which seem so solid and visible, requires understanding the people who daily reprise all the acts of production that make up meaning. Both Williams (1980) and Giddens (1984) noted that social structures such as television networks constrain and enable, guide and direct those actors. Giddens also noted that structures are constituted or reproduced daily by the producers' social acts, so, in a very subtle way, the structures and the actions of their professional staffs intertwine to create or structure each other.

Professionals work in a context, a structure such as a TV network or film studio, but they also bring their own subjective interests and ideas to what they produce in a way that can ultimately change the structural context itself. Hollywood likes to think of itself, for example, as a stable, ongoing force, a set of companies that will continue to make money years from now. Much of the rest of the world sees Hollywood as both stable and powerful, almost omnipotent. However, seen from inside, Hollywood is constantly changing as the result of new people with new ideas. One example is prime-time television's enormous turn from scripted drama and comedy toward unscripted reality shows in the late 1990s and early 2000s. This trend, in turn, was partially reversed by the mid-2000s as Hollywood rediscovered (See *Variety,* various issues 2005–2006) that audiences still like scripted comedies, dramas, and even "new" (at least to English-speaking America) scripted forms such as Latin American-style prime-time soap operas (Bielby & Harrington, 2005).

In an even more subtle way, the television audience structures television networks and professionals by controlling the resources that they need. The money that pays for TV ultimately comes from the audience, through work, attention paid to advertising, consumption, and public contributions, taxes, or license fees. The audience is, in turn, shaped by what it is given to watch, but it also has underlying preferences that guide its choices (if it has some) among programs and channels. A program or channel that goes outside the cultural boundaries of what the audience is prepared to like or at least tolerate will go unwatched, particularly if there are other choices. Some television structures, particularly those strongly driven by an ideology, a religious orientation, or simply the will of a dictator, may not be influenced in the short run by whether people want to watch something or not. The idea is frequently to make them watch by eliminating alternatives. However, even these kinds of regimes for television will eventually direct resources toward programs that people will watch because resources are seldom unlimited. Gramsci (1971) insisted that pulling people into a hegemonic consensus is much more efficient for rulers than coercion, so over time, even dictators will often try to figure out how to deliver their message in ways that people will watch, read, or listen to. That is even more imperative as VCRs, DVDs, satellites, and the Internet all cumulatively tend to make it easier for audiences to find alternative "television" to watch, as Chapter 5 points out.

The audience also watches within social structures, and a structure of research and circulated interpretations links producer and audience. I will discuss that later in terms of theories applying ideas of Paul Ricoeur (1984) about how dramatist, drama, and audience interact over time.

## Television Genre and Structure

Genres are categories of television programming. Mittell (2004) argued that genres should account for the particularities of the medium (TV versus film), negotiate between specificity and generality, develop from discursive genealogies (such as the examination of telenovelas below), be understood in cultural practice, and be situated within larger systems of cultural hierarchies and power relations. Different groups—critics, producers, advertisers, distributors, programmers, and audiences—often structure genre categories differently (Feuer, 1992). Critics are usually aiming for theoretical understanding, either of artistic/cultural/textual forms in themselves (Mittell, 2004) or of the complex practices between industry and audiences. Feuer (1992) called the first focus aesthetic and sees the second as cultural ritual, producing common understandings between audiences and producers; she added a third focus on the ideological control of audiences through formulaic television. In this book, I incline toward the view of television as cultural ritual linking producer and audience, a cultural forum (Newcomb & Hirsch, 1983), where institutional control and constraint exist but where both producers and audiences strain against it, often successfully, to create challenging cultural understandings; where significant cultural discussion takes place alongside the propagation of ideology and advertising.

Producers use genre categories to try to figure out what institutional structures, such as network managers and advertisers, will let them produce while also generally trying to please audiences. They use genres as a way to understand the broad patterns of interest in both media systems and audiences, while still creating some small differences to make their new production stand out (Feuer, 1992; Schatz, 1981). Schatz (1981) made a distinction between the deep structure of a film genre, as a sort of social contract between industry and audience, and a genre film, a specific enactment or production of the genre; this is rather like comparing the rules of language with a specific speech act. Analogous might be the deep structure of melodrama as a sort of global metagenre, the telenovela as a region-specific deep structure of television genre, and *Ugly Betty (Yo soy Betty, la fea)* as a particularly popular enactment of the genre (produced in Colombia, exported widely, and remade in the United States).

Advertisers use genres as a categorical shorthand for anticipating what audiences will watch so they can decide where to place their advertisements. Genres tend to ensure "the advertisers of an audience for their messages" (Feuer, 1992, p. 145). Distributors use genre categories as marketing devices to sell shows or formats to network programmers, who likewise use genre categories as a way to anticipate audience responses to a given show (as an enactment of a genre). In theory, audience preferences have the last word in defining and redefining genre, but audience preferences are also shaped by what they are given to watch, in a complicated reciprocal process that I explore further below. Kumar (personal communication, 2006) observed that audiences' sense of identity and television program preference, even when complex and multilayered, is shaped by a variety of institutional, political, and economic pressures, such as schooling, class status, work, religion, and government campaigns. In specific practice, television industry distributors and programmers often assume they understand what audiences want, what drives them toward local versus foreign programs, toward certain genres, or toward a specific show in question (Harrington & Bielby, 2005). For example, Haven (2006) acknowledged that for audiences, cultural proximity toward local programs is a factor, but what often counts most in program decisions is the programmer's own understanding of what that means, their understanding of what the audience wants.

## Cultural Industry Producers

To understand the most fundamental levels of resources and restraints, I begin by reconsidering the political-economic structures within which both television producers and audiences work, watch, understand, and act. That structural context starts with the cultural industries in which television programs are created, programmed, and transmitted. The political economy of the cultural industries, described in detail in Chapter 3, also provides an

essential critical basis for examining the process. However, specific producers create specific television programs within subtle structures of work. Also,
both producers and viewers create and interpret programs within a common
cultural context. Furthermore, people express themselves with unique sub-
jectivity or ideas.

Early cultural industry theorists, such as Horkheimer and Adorno (2001)
did not think much about the specific actions of the professional producers within television or other cultural industries. Implicitly, at least, they
thought the particular producers had little autonomy. The perception was
that the logic of the capitalist industrial system essentially predetermined
what producers could do. In classic Marxist terms, they were part of an ideological superstructure whose production or content reflects the ideological
interests of those who own and control the overall means of production
(Williams, 1980).

In early versions of dependency theory, almost all national elites, whether
in the economy, politics, or cultural industry, were seen as strongly linked
to the economic interests of the core countries (dos Santos, 1973). However,
people began to observe that media producers in developing countries had
their own agency and interests, even though the structures they worked in
could constrain and guide what they were able to do. For example, looking
at Latin America, Salinas and Paldan (1979) observed that cultural producers developed their own interests, including conflicts of interest and ideology, and did not necessarily follow the directions of those who owned or
managed media or cultural industries.

## Economic Boundaries on Television
## Genre and Program Development

Commercial broadcasting is subject to pressure from advertisers, as
discussed in earlier chapters. So a principal question for assessing the relative independence of television producers is the location and nature of the
advertisers and commercially minded managers within the producers' own
company or network, who will push to make programming maximally
advertisement-friendly and appealing to the demographics advertisers desire
(Gitlin, 1990).

In television, like film before it, demands for commercial success lead
to the emergence and standardization of certain successful formulas. Schatz
(1988) noted that early Hollywood experimentation soon settled into a
pattern of standard formulas or genres for producing on an industrial scale
films that had the most predictable success with the audience. If both the

production companies and the genre formulas are viewed as social structures, then Giddens (1984) would point out that structures both bound and enable the agency of those who act within them. More specifically, commercial film studios and commercial television networks essentially require cultural producers to work within the boundaries of certain successful genres or formulas. However, within those structural boundaries, producers find not only constraints but resources (Giddens, 1984). Contrasting U.S. film studio formulas with the French notion of the film *auteur* as an artist, André Bazin (1968) observed that "the (American) tradition of genres is a base of operations for creative freedom" (p. 154). The sense of his argument is that within the seemingly strict commercial formula imposed by studios, creative directors could manipulate the resources placed at their disposal by the studios' commercial success to achieve substantial artistic creativity. Clearly, however, the history of both American film studios and of other subsequent commercial producers of culture is full of cases in which artists or producers were hamstrung by imposed limits, along with cases in which great and memorable cultural pieces of film, television, and music have been produced within strict commercial boundaries of both industry and formula (Schatz, 1988).

Commercial television systems follow an institutional imperative to buy or create programming that can attract a certain size or type of audience the advertiser desires (Sinclair, 1995). As I will argue later, this can be best explained in complexity theory terms: these factors constitute a system of attractors (Urry, 2003) around commercial television, which tend to (re)produce certain kinds of television programming, both imports such as *Dallas* or *Baywatch,* and local adaptations of successful commercial formulas or genres such as soap operas, variety shows, action shows, and game shows (Cooper-Chen, 1994; Oliveira, 1993). In this chapter, the enormous flow of genre ideas is discussed, and in Chapter 7, the more formalized flow of licensed television formats is described.

Economic considerations drive part of the key decision whether to import television programs or produce them locally. Moran (1998) asked, for example, why some countries produce their own version of *Wheel of Fortune* whereas others import and dub the U.S. production? He observed that for some broadcasters, financial considerations are overwhelming, and they will tend to import U.S. programs, which are usually sold quite cheaply. However, this dubbed version remains foreign—it has American contestants, draws on American cultural knowledge, gives American prizes, and so on. It will also probably not do as well in the ratings as a local version would, so if producers can afford a local version, it will probably make more money (Moran, 1998).

Commercial genres tend to carry a strong systemic bias toward promoting consumption of goods, both in general and in specific. One of the first major critical analyses of an imported commercial genre, *How to Read Donald Duck: Imperialist Ideology in the Disney Comic* (Dorfman & Mattelart, 1975), pointed out that the contents were inclined toward teaching Disney comics' readers a consumer view of the world. Television game shows across a number of countries usually emphasize prizes, another way to promote desire for prized objects (Cooper-Chen, 1994). In Brazil, television networks early on decided to insert product placements, known in Brazil as merchandizing, within the plots of programs (La Pastina, 2001; Ramos, 1987). As a result, prime-time programming showed poor immigrants in cities not only ways to use electronic banking but also the virtues of a specific bank where the lesson just happened to take place, as in the 1990 Brazilian telenovela, *Tieta*. This reflects both a general promotion of a certain kind of activity and the specific promotion of a certain bank for that activity.

Genres carry patterns or boundaries of restraint on certain kinds of themes. The pattern, the relatively consistent system and logic of commercial television, tends to place boundaries around its television production so that other kinds of programming, such as education, high culture, and extensive documentary production, are less likely to be produced than under noncommercial systems, where other kinds of economic foundations may focus on other kinds of patterns. Oliveira (1993) argued that in Brazil, for example, the *telenovela* adaptation of the soap opera genre pattern did not raise issues that were discomfiting to the government, the station owners, or major advertisers. This corresponded to the criticism by Herman and McChesney (1997) that commercial systems (and genres) often severely limit what can be debated in the public sphere, at least that aspect of the public sphere represented by the commercial media. Such limits, however, while real, are not complete or determinant. Brazilian telenovelas, to pick up that example, have criticized both local and national political bosses, raised ecological concerns, and discussed issues of homelessness and landlessness (La Pastina, 2004a). They did this within commercial constraints, clearly, and in some cases, specific themes, such as criticism of multinational company abuses, have been censored by broadcast firms under pressure from advertisers (Straubhaar, 1988).

Do imported genres consistently determine or limit messages? Does the insertion of local content into a genre form that is (re)produced locally balance this determinism, and if so, how? I argue that imported genre forms impose fairly effective boundary limits on certain kinds of content and that certain kinds of patterns, such as underlying consumption messages, are often replicated in local production. In a way, this may represent a form of media imperialism via genre, or genre imperialism, but it operates through the replication of patterns and boundaries, not with linear control or even predictability from the center of the global system to its edges in places like Brazil, or from one center of the system, such as the United States, to another, say Italy. To understand that process demands an awareness of the complex emergence of cultural patterns and boundaries, as well as the long, continuing process of the hybridization of imported genres or patterns with local cultures.

The global creation and flow of television genres and formats should be thought of as a complexly articulated, fluid process of hybridity whose integrative effects do not simply eliminate cultural difference and diversity but rather provide the context for the production of new cultural forms marked by local specificity. In this respect, Ang (1996) observed,

> What becomes increasingly "globalized" is not so much concrete cultural contents, but, more importantly and more structurally, the parameters and infrastructure which determine the conditions of existence for local cultures. It can be understood, for example, as the dissemination of a limited set of economic, political, ideological and pragmatic conventions and principles which govern and mould the accepted ways in which media production, circulation and consumption are organized throughout the modern world. (pp. 153–154)

I argue that genres are one of the principal sets of "pragmatic conventions and principles" of this flow of forms in television. I discuss their application to local and national production in this chapter and to global and cultural-linguistic or geocultural markets and spaces in the next chapter.

## Material Versus Symbolic Boundaries

In the discussion of cultural boundaries on phenomena such as genre development, one is forced to address the relationship between the material and the symbolic. Complexity theory transcends this question by arguing that culture has both symbolic and material aspects, which are both important. Complexity economist Brian Arthur (1990) drew a useful distinction between limits or boundaries that are resource based and those that are knowledge based.

Resource limits are somewhat more fixed by physical resource factors and wealth. Knowledge limits or factors are more open to increasing returns, and the number of people who can be included eventually is almost unlimited. However, patterns of knowledge limits become real—"this is the way we do things around here"—and can be become stable and hard to change.

Genre forms are an interesting example of the binding power of a form that is both cultural and material. Genres develop within material conditions defined by political economy, network structures, work routines, and so on. They also are bounded and shaped by cultural parameters that develop from older genres in other media; for example, melodramatic traditions in China versus Spain or England shape television soap operas that develop within those cultures. The idea of boundary conditions that limit the range of possibilities within nonlinear cultures helps us understand the role of genre patterns as bounding and limiting but not as determinant. A new imported television genre may bring powerful new patterns and messages into a culture but almost necessarily hybridizes with that which is local, even as it seems to impose new cultural patterns. Put another way, a global pattern must be performed or produced locally (Moran, 2004), so it is theoretically fruitful to put complexity together with hybridity theory, which argues for the persistence of local cultural content even as it hybridizes with imported genre forms, changed institutional forms, and content elements.

## Complexity, Patterns, and Genres

Complexity theory adds several other useful concepts to an understanding of the globalization of genres. Even global patterns seem to be reenacted locally in such a way that control is hard to determine. In specific, implying that foreign forms exert a linear control over local productions may overlook the strength of the local component and the transformation of the genre itself by local adaptation.

The complexity theory notion of self-organization as represented in fractals and replicating patterns fosters understanding of how television genres help create similar patterns in different cultures. Jorge González (1991) applied this idea to the development of the *telenovela* genre. Each telenovela is a fractal, a specific enactment of the Latin American telenovela tradition, which is itself a fractal subset of the larger genre of melodrama.

Various forms of television seem to function as what complexity theory terms attractors: conditions that tend to form the basis of a pattern. Attractors can be stable, holding a system in equilibrium or balance. New conditions introduced into a system, such as the introduction of a certain form of television, can change that balance, perhaps even to a catastrophic or system-changing extent. At a systemic level, commercial, advertising-supported television seems to function as an attractor across cultural systems, forming recognizable, but not entirely predictable patterns of television production as the forms of commercial television are transplanted and adapted in various cultures. At a more specific level, television genres such as soap opera or music video function as attractors, formulas that may be used in a number of settings, forming new hybrid patterns within each culture. In both cases, outcomes include elements of both the original pattern and the nonlinear, unpredictable variations.

The genealogies of commercial television soap operas in Brazil and Taiwan, for example, show adaptation of patterns that began in Europe with serial fiction; were shaped further in the United States, Great Britain, and elsewhere with radio and television soap operas; were adapted to Latin America in Cuba and to Asia in China and Hong Kong; and were further adapted in Brazil and Taiwan. Enduring aspects of the various earlier or preceding pattern transformations can be seen in Brazilian and Taiwanese soap operas, but the final results are still emerging and would not have been predictable from earlier variations of the serial pattern, such as the U.S. radio soap opera. The earlier patterns have set some boundaries, such as the need to achieve commercial success with a mass audience, the need to be compatible with commercial advertising messages, and the dramatic and thematic characteristics of the general genre or formula of melodrama, but the outcomes within these boundaries could not have been linearly predicted.

To use a different genre example, action shows often flow from a few producers, but those producers influence each other as the genre evolves as a global form. U.S. action genres such as westerns, police shows, detective shows, and suspense have influenced productions in the United Kingdom, Japan, and Hong Kong. Cowboy movies influenced samurai movies and series, and vice versa (Akira Kurosawa borrowed from John Ford, while George Lucas admits to borrowing from Kurosawa). Samurai movies and series influence kung fu movies and vice versa.

## Cultural Boundaries: Feedback to Producers

Cultural patterns form boundaries within which both producers and audiences for television make choices. Compare the United States, United Kingdom, and Brazil, for example. American television producers inherited from radio a set of political-economic boundaries, such as a commercial pattern of broadcasting, private ownership of stations, groups of stations formed into three dominant commercial networks, not to mention factors outside radio, such as private commercial film studios that were poised to provide television programming. U.S. producers also inherited a set of genres from both radio and film that occupied a middle ground between the political economy of television, which favored certain kinds of entertainment and information, and U.S. culture, which had favored themes, issues, and forms.

In general, as time elapses and television systems develop further, the relevance to local culture may give many kinds of local or national programming an advantage. In a study of television in Brazil, Kottak (1990) observed,

> Common to all mass culture successes, no matter what the country, the first requirement is that they fit the existing culture. They must be *preadapted* to their culture by virtue of *cultural appropriateness* [italics in the original]). If a product is to be a mass culture success, it must be immediately acceptable, understandable, familiar, and conducive to mass participation. (p. 43)

Two key theoretical approaches to the cultural boundaries placed on production, export, and flow of television are the cultural discount and cultural proximity, which were developed in Chapter 4. Cultural discounts create a barrier or boundary that may protect national, local, or regional programming as it develops (Hoskins et al., 1989). The idea of cultural proximity (Straubhaar, 1991), building on Pool (1977), is that audiences tend to prefer programming that is closest or most proximate to their own culture. Understanding cultural proximity is crucial for understanding television producers. Moragas Spa et al. (1999) noted that proximity for television has to do with "a scene of shared experiences" between producers and recipients. It also provides a boundary that gives incentives to local producers to create local productions.

It is clear that the expectations of audiences form boundaries within which producers work. Audiences also provide specific feedback to specific productions. Most countries have some kind of system for providing audience feedback to producers. The importance of such feedback is reinforced by the increasing redefinition of broadcast worldwide as a commercial enterprise. For commercial media markets to work, advertisers require evidence of how many people are reached by their ads. In response ratings research firms have developed, and commercial broadcasters have come to rely on ratings, both to sell their programming to advertisers and, internally, to guide their producers to create programming that is easiest to sell to advertisers. This kind of feedback powerfully reinforces the constraints on producers placed by the structure and nature of commercial broadcasting, per se.

Audience expectations are a strong part of genre formation (Feuer, 1992), as will be discussed more in Chapter 7. Audience preferences for local, national, or regional production can be a resource for would-be producers, creating a space in the programming marketplace for them. These preferences draw ratings that put advertising or other resources at a producer's disposal, as shown in the case study of Brazil later in this chapter. However, audience expectations of a genre production can also act as a limit on the producer, discouraging topics that break the mold of the genre. The Brazilian case of the telenovela, *The Cattle King,* cited below and in Chapter 8, provides a clear example of that; even when commercial production circumstances permitted a scriptwriter to insert a strong political message, parts of the audience felt the strong political theme was too much at odds with their expectations of the melodramatic basics of a telenovela. Perhaps conditioned by earlier, more commercially melodramatic telenovela productions, some of the audience found the new piece too didactic and not melodramatic enough.

## Complexity, Prefiguration, and Cultural Hybridity

Understanding how television producers work within a variety of levels of culture is further informed by two additional concepts, the first focusing on the individual as a source of culture and the second attempting to explain cultural behavior from a macroperspective. The first set of concepts comes from Ricoeur, who argued that people keep track of time through a nonlinear emplotment of their lives, building on Aristotle's concept of *mimesis.* The emplotment process involves prefiguration, configuration, and refiguration (Ricoeur, 1984). The major focus of my discussion will be prefiguration because that is the *phase space* where the patterns of meaning first become apparent. Ricoeur showed how the individual is coupled with culture; how the individual is a recursive symmetric scale of the culture, if you will.

The second concept, which I discussed in Chapter 2, is hybridization. More specifically, I will examine several theoretical variations on how a general theory such as hybridity may be applied to specific global and national actions, such as those of television producers. I will also refer to Ricoeur and use his notions of prefiguration, configuration, and refiguration to show how cultural patterns begin to emerge in complex, often hybrid cultural systems.

Combined with complexity, these concepts help show that beyond quantifiable, somewhat predictable effects of demographic factors on peoples' cultural choices within complex cultural systems, there are a number of far less linear cultural elements. These combine to create complex possibilities of cultural formations or patterns within cultural systems. These patterns or formations can be seen as the reflection of fractal patterns of strange—that is to say, nonlinear—attractors, using complexity theory terms. A wide variety of cultural elements combine to form patterns of cultural knowledge and cultural choices, such as those of television producers. These patterns depend on a specific context, which is itself constantly evolving in a process of hybridization of elements. Ricoeur (1984) termed this context a prefiguration to encounters with culture or communication acts.

## Complexity and Cultural Change

Within the emergence of culture are stable patterns. Once patterns are set, even within complex systems, they tend to create boundaries that maintain them. Arthur (1990) noted that "once random economic events select a particular path, the choice may become locked-in regardless of the advantages of alternatives. If one product or nation in a competitive marketplace gets ahead by 'chance,' it tends to stay ahead and even increase its lead" (p. 92). As an example, Arthur cited the success of the VHS videocassette recorder over the Betamax. Despite similar starting positions, better marketing of VHS increased its initial market share; this made it popular with rental shops, which reinforced its market share in a positive feedback loop.

In cultural terms, these relatively stable patterns can be seen as patterns within strange attractors. Prigogine and Stengers (1984) described how systems use communication to counter destabilizing forces and limit the impact of significant shifts in the external environment. Valdez (personal communication, June 8, 1997) saw cultural fractals as emerging within the kinds of parameters discussed above as boundaries. Valdez gave an example of how conditions like the rise of urban centers, which concentrate intellectual and economic resources, make certain kinds of cultural formations possible, such as the variety of artists who participated in a few centers to create and support the Latin American baroque period of music, architecture, sculpture, and literature. Certain conditions made cultural production possible. For example, the Baroque movement of Europe created an initial imported or received cultural condition within the Spanish and Portuguese colonial contexts. In Latin America, this movement drew on local elements as well to create patterns, which produced Baroque cultural products that resembled those of Europe but differed in many details (Valdez & Hutcheon, 1995).

González (1997) talked about cultural fronts, both in the sense of borders between cultures (that may be hybridizing) and in the sense of battlefronts, "fractal zones of intersection and interpenetration . . . resistance, 'capitulations,' negotiations and skirmishes" (p. 32; see also González, 2001). González saw networks of people drawn together in fronts. One example for him is the combination of genre traditions, television industry structures, television producers, and television audiences that produced the Latin American *telenovela,* a distinct variation on the rather globally dispersed notion of the soap opera. Producers drew on European serial novel traditions, American radio and television soaps, Cuban and other early Latin American adaptation of those genres, and emerging local and national cultural traditions that lent themselves to melodrama on television. Audience response ensured that advertisers would supply the economic resources for continued and expanded production of *telenovelas* in an increasing number of countries. Audience feedback shaped the productions away from elite-focused dramas toward a mass culture form that resonated more with a variety of traditions and plot devices and that could involve both men and women, peasants, urban workers, and the middle classes (Martín-Barbero, 1993). This cultural formation spread all over Latin America, with distinct adaptations or fractular variations, so that Brazilian *telenovelas* are quite different from those of Mexico (Hernandez, 2001). Earlier, I discussed the commercial television soap opera as a fractal or pattern; here, the effect of distinct national cultural formations of people, institutions, and resources makes for patterned but not particularly linear variations. The source of these patterns at the level of the individual is prefiguration.

## Ricoeur and the Hybridization Process

Ricoeur (1984) was trying to account for how humans create a time-based narrative for their own lives and also enter a discourse with a larger social group. His model is useful because it shows how individual narrative patterns may become part of a larger culture. Ricoeur (1984) focused on how narrative emerges over time and describes a *prefigured* time, where sense-making begins and patterns emerge; a *configured* time, which is the immediate social reality—the immediate experience of culture; and a *refigured* time, which is the projection of the narrative, both personal and collective, into the future (p. 54). Ricoeur's refigured time feeds back into the prefiguration, the context for configuration, and the immediate experience of culture. I argue that it also connects with a broader culture. The symmetrical patterns of individual prefigurations are also visible in a larger culture, just as the patterns of the larger culture are present at the level of the individual prefiguration. These are recursive layers in which the individual has exceptional experiences but also shares most of the broader cultural context, and indeed is constantly feeding parts of his or her own experience back into the cultural context via refiguration.

For communication scholars, in a social environment, prefiguration is the first evidence of cultural patterns. Ricoeur's (1984) language is similar to complexity theory in that he said prefigurative notions are held "within the field of our temporal experience." He suggested that the patterns emerge in an understanding of narrative plots. Plot, according to Ricoeur, is an "imitation of action," echoing and building on Aristotle's notion of *mimesis* (as explicated in Ricoeur, 1984). In other words, plot is both symbolic and real, acting as a kind of attractor for both meanings and behavior.

When applied to television, this echoes the point that genres are formulas for connecting the expectations and lived experiences of audiences with the creative direction and needs of producers (Allen, 1995). A television genre, such as soap opera or its specific fractular relative in the *telenovela*, is a concise formulation of expectations drawn out of a common prefigurative context by both audiences and producers. When writing melodrama, authors and producers draw on the prefigurative to anticipate the interests of their audiences. Audiences choose programs based on interests and images similarly drawn from the shared cultural prefiguration. The audience experiences the television program in the moment of configuration. Their satisfactions and dissatisfactions are communicated to each other and, through a variety of personal and mediated channels, enter the larger cultural context through refiguration, which then eventually (re)cycles into the prefigurative.

Ricoeur's ideas suggested how patterns, which are partially but not completely cultural, evoke a certain context for meaning as meaning emerges and as time moves from a prefigurative to a refigurative state. This prefiguration is generally the first sense of boundary and pattern that can be articulated in complex systems. Ricoeur (1984, p. 55) argued that once people see the pattern, they project it on others as a general assumption of understanding. Prefiguration is emergent, in that neither time nor this process is ever fixed. It is underdetermined, in that individuals can never be fully aware of what part of the pattern originated in the culture and what part may have originated in genetics, individual agency, and so on. It is holistic in that prefigurative ideas, regardless of their source, arise from individuals to impact the whole system in some way. Individual experience within the configurative stage takes place in interaction with other people and their ideas. The individual's interaction with others also then refigures the cultural context in a large summation, which forms and reforms holistic cultural patterns.

To analyze the process through which cultural formations, such as television genres, are created, Ricoeur's (1984) ideas of prefiguration, configuration, and refiguration are useful. He described the context in which someone receives a cultural artifact as the prefiguration, which includes cultural elements that form cultural knowledge. From a general pool of cultural knowledge, individuals draw a personal repertoire of symbols and interpretive understanding. Thus, television producers or writers sitting down to create a new melodrama in Brazil or Taiwan will draw on a pool of cultural knowledge. In fact, they will draw on several pools at several levels. The previous example shows that Brazilian serial producers took both global and regional Latin American models into account, drawing on new ideas that circulated at both levels, global and regional. More particularly, producers or writers know that the new television program must succeed with its original national audiences, even if they hope that it might later be exported to regional or global audiences as well. So the pool of understandings in Brazil or Taiwan about what makes for an interesting melodrama or soap opera is crucial. That pool of knowledge includes the writers' own previous work, things they wish to borrow from other parts of national culture, a sense of what a "Brazilian" or "Taiwanese" soap opera ought to be like, and feedback from the audience about what they like.

This prefigures or shapes the work of writers, producers, actors, and others in the production process. It provides boundaries and rules, as well as resources for the moment of creation. As producers create, they structure not only their work but also prefigure the viewing experience of the audience. That audience encounters a narrative that will inevitably have, to use Hall's (2001) idea, an intended reading included or encoded by the authors, a prefigured message that the producers hope to transmit to the audience. Such prefigured knowledge also affects another step in television, which is the cultural understandings of program distributors and programmers (Harrington & Bielby, 2005; Havens, 2006). In choosing what programs to buy, sell, and schedule, they also dip into the same pool of knowledge but make their own assumptions about what audiences like.

The prefigurative should not be seen as determinant. Bhabha (1994) noted:

> The representation of difference must not be read as the reflection of *pre-given* ethnic or cultural traits set in the fixed tablet of tradition. The social articulation of difference, from the minority perspective, is a complex, on-going negotiation that seeks to authorize cultural hybridities that emerge in moments of historical transformation. (p. 2)

Bhabha emphasized that culture is performed, or what Ricoeur would call configured, at the moment when an individual or group creates or encounters a work of culture.

People are thought of as consuming cultural products such as television programs. The moment of media consumption is the *configuration*. Individuals receive media within a cultural context and work within limits or boundaries imposed by economics, access to technology, and class-related demographic characteristics, such as education. Also, individuals employ cultural knowledge from the cultural prefiguration or context.

Individuals process media within a cultural context, making sense of media using cultural knowledge (Martín-Barbero, 1993). Much of the sense-making goes beyond the individual, however. People talk with others in a process of symbolic interaction and social construction, using interpretive communities to which they belong (Lindlof, Shatzer, & Wilkinson, 1988). Conversation selects elements, again within a cultural context, which are then added to the cultural context. This refiguration process, according to Ricoeur, reworks the cultural context, which then becomes the prefiguration for ongoing or further media consumption.

The idea of refiguration also provides a sense of how television producers learn from their audiences. People talk to each other and "word of mouth" develops about a television program that either excites or disappoints people. Often that word of mouth reaches producers directly as they try to find out what people think of their work. For example, several well-known Brazilian writers for telenovelas have said in newspaper interviews that they listen carefully to what their maids say about their shows and others to get direct feedback. Production houses and networks, particularly the dominant network, TV Globo, also run focus groups, do surveys, and look at ratings to get feedback about programs. At a less formal level, both ideas from television programs and audience reactions to them sink into the larger pool of shared culture. Characters are remembered as beloved or hated, influencing how writers develop new characters and how audiences interpret them. Certain social or political themes resonate and are expanded or avoided. For example, one Brazilian soap opera in 2001 started off to develop three themes: cloning of human beings (the soap title was *The Clone* or o Clone), how Arab-Brazilians were fitting in, and drug use among teenagers. As feedback came in to the writers and producers, it became clear that, after September 11, the second theme was more interesting to the audience than the first, and the third theme became so compelling that the show was followed frequently by short interview segments with real-life teenage drug users about their experiences to amplify the theme. All of these kinds of cultural waves refigure the larger pool of meanings. The next time someone either creates or watches a television program, the prefiguration of both creation and reception now includes these new meanings and symbols.

To understand more clearly how television producers and programmers work, it is helpful to review the notions of localization and glocalization, two specific forms of hybridization that I explored in Chapter 2. First, I look at how various national or local producers tend to take ideas they have seen in foreign genres or specific programs and adapt them for local productions, which I might characterize as glocalization (Robertson, 1995). Second, I examine the idea of localization of transnational formats. I will look first at the adaptation of global models to national and local production (Moran, 2004), which has been prevalent since 1950, and then later in Chapter 7 (Chalaby, 2002; 2005a), at how (in the United States, Europe, Australia, and Japan) global producers of television programs and channels intended for export have slowly worked toward adapting those cultural products toward new audiences other than those for which they were produced. Then, I test a new concept, delocalization, to look at how those in countries such as Brazil, Hong Kong, or Mexico, who have produced programs for a specific cultural or national audience, try to adapt them for global or regional audiences.

## Glocalization

The term glocalization originally derives from a Japanese marketing strategy of *global-localization* or *glocalization* (Robertson, 1995). It reflects how Japanese companies both incorporated foreign ideas into domestic cultural products and, acting transnationally, later adapted their Japanese cultural products to other cultures, instead of pressing for a global standardization, as many U.S. companies originally seem to have done.

Many of the more successful aspects of Hollywood programming formulas had already been adapted to local cultures by national and cultural-linguistic or geocultural producers. Robertson (1995) observed that national cultures and institutions tend to absorb and localize foreign influence in a process that he calls glocalization (Robertson, 1995). Glocalization is a blending of foreign and local.

Kraidy (1999) said that glocalization is a specific conceptualization of hybridity, a way to specify it and break it down for application to specific situations. It "is a more heuristic concept that takes into account the local, national, regional, and global contexts of intercultural communicative processes" (p. 472), he said. McAnany (2002) was critical of the concept of glocalization, thinking that it is often too vague and can be used hypocritically to reinforce a superficial multiculturalism that can simply reinforce (or obscure) the co-optation of those in power in local media. He was concerned that a neutral sounding term such as glocalization conceals power dynamics in which real local power is reduced.

Another important formulation of this general idea is the adaptation of foreign models, particularly foreign program formats, by regional, national, or local producers. Moran (2004) argued that there is a widespread push toward local production that can use locally originated concepts, program ideas from coproduction, and imported program format adaptation. Because many ideas and formats are available, very few television producers think of truly new, singular, local formats. This view is a specific version of the larger idea that almost all cultural products are hybrid because cultures have been interacting for so long that purity of cultural form is almost impossible (Nederveen Pieterse, 2004). However, as the example of the Latin American telenovela will show, quite distinct local versions may evolve from adapted forms. Moran (2004) observed that producers have been informally borrowing formats for a while, increasing coproduction, and particularly increasing the formal licensing of formats.

## Localization as Japanization or Brazilianization

Iwabuchi (2002) discussed how Japan localized U.S. culture in a process of Japanization. In this process, Japan selectively incorporated foreign elements of popular culture, technology, and economic technique into the still dominant mainstream of Japanese popular culture and Japanese cultural industry. Straubhaar (1981, 1984) wrote about how Brazilian television has Brazilianized foreign influences into a set of cultural industries and cultural forms, such as the telenovela, that are nationally distinct. The argument in both cases was that a strong national culture, supported by government policy and relying on dynamic cultural industries, successfully incorporated foreign influences into a continuity of national popular culture and national cultural industry. Both adapted foreign formats and made them over into something that seems nationally specific.

Regô (1988), Oliveira (1993), and others critiqued that argument about Brazil, arguing that Brazilian cultural industries could not be considered autonomously Brazilianized because they had become integrated parts of the world capitalist economy. Even if Brazilian commercial media created most of their own national cultural products, they still promoted consumption and brought Brazilians, both rich and poor, into accepting the world capitalist economy and their role in it. Critics felt that it didn't matter if the soap opera was now produced in Brazil as long as it copied American forms of soap opera and still sold Colgate-Palmolive soap (Oliveira, 1994). Although that critique is quite astute in terms of the media's role in economic globalization, it diminishes the role and importance of culture, per se. It leaves open the question of what happens to culture when foreign forms are adapted to local media and local cultures. In particular, it ignores the role of the actual cultural producers in places such as Japan or Brazil. As they borrow foreign forms and incorporate them in their own production, what explains their work process, and what can explain the larger impact on their local and national cultures? I turn now to examining Brazilian television, specifically its telenovelas, in terms of structuration (Giddens, 1984), localization in the sense that Iwabuchi (2002) used it, glocalization (also frequently used to analyze the Japanese case), Ricoeur's configuration process, and the larger framework of hybridity. I look closely at the case of the adaptation of the telenovela to Brazil and one case in particular.

## Structuration and Television Production in Brazil

There are several layers of actors with distinct interests in Brazilian television: the state, the advertisers (representing the global and national industrial economic elite), the television industry or network, the producers and writers within the network, and the audience. Although some of these clearly have more power than others, all are able to exercise some small degree of constraint over the others.

The state has had the most power, particularly when the military directly controlled the crucial telecommunications infrastructure and much of the advertising and enjoyed direct censorship power between 1964 and 1984. Even after the end of military rule, the state is still a power that broadcasters, particularly TV Globo, try very hard to please. It can still constrain or enable many of their actions. However, there is also countervailing power for television, which can enable or constrain politicians' access to the audience via news or other programs. In a democratic system, the government badly needs favorable coverage. So do other parties and political figures. A complex dance of mutual constraint extends between media, particularly major television networks, and the government. This applies to both television news operations and entertainment, particularly the telenovelas, which have carried political themes for many years (Porto, 2005; Straubhaar, 1989a).

Within the broadcast operation, there is also an uneven set of powers and constraints. TV Globo has considerable power to control agendas for content. However, Globo seems to delegate production of telenovelas and other programs to creative talent, who are relatively free as long as they stay within the parameters or boundaries for commercial success demanded by the company. Internal management expects a consistent level of production quality but provides the resources to enable high-quality productions, particularly for the telenovelas, which are the prime-time cash cow of the firm. More than anything, what is demanded and rewarded is commercial success, which is not surprising in a private commercial firm but which indicates that the firm is willing to push cultural, political, and moral boundaries as long as that content succeeds with the audience. That gives the audience a powerful but indirect constraint on the institutions of the broadcaster and the state.

## The Hybrid History of the Telenovela[1]

For the past 30-plus years, the telenovela has dominated prime-time television in Brazil and most Latin American countries, where such programs are often broadcast daily, 6 days a week. The Latin American telenovela is a serial narrative with roots that can be traced back to earlier melodramatic forms (theater, oral literature, etc.), including U.S. soap opera, which are a series of formula prefigurations of the genre. The example of the telenovela shows how a format may be taken from one region, the United States, to another, in Latin America, with complex steps, including the steps that preceded U.S. soap operas—earlier melodramas. The original format, as a prefiguration, impacts the results, but perhaps more powerful are the subsequent adaptations within geocultural regions, for example, the telenovela's history in Latin America or the idol drama in East Asia, which has passed from Japan to South Korea, China, Taiwan, and so on (Iwabuchi, 2002). Whereas this sort of adaptation is viewed as glocalization in Japan, it is usually discussed in terms of hybridization in Latin America (Lopez, 1995).

Across Latin America, the telenovela has a common history, but different countries employ varied themes, narrative styles, and production values. According to Lopez (1995), for example, Mexican telenovelas are the weepers, ahistorical telenovelas with no social context provided. Colombian telenovelas have more comedy and irony along with a greater concern for context. Venezuelan productions are more emotional but do not have the "baroqueness" of Mexican sets. Brazilian telenovelas are the most realistic, with historically based narratives that have a clear temporal and spatial contextualization (Lopez, 1995). These variations show how the common history, from European melodrama to Colgate-Palmolive soaps, has been adapted and reconfigured by producers interacting with distinct national cultures and audiences.

These divergent representations of the underlying telenovela format reflect considerable national adaptation of the regional genre, but all are faithful to the melodramatic roots of the genre. "The telenovela exploits personalization—the individualization of the social world—as an epistemology. It ceaselessly offers the audience dramas of recognition and re-cognition by locating social and political issues in personal and familial terms and thus making sense of an increasingly complex world" (Lopez, 1995, p. 258). The

Latin American telenovela, in almost all its variations, focuses on several central themes that were not central to American soap opera, and so it represents considerable adaptation (Moran, 2004) or reconfiguration (Ricoeur, 1984). These new themes include class roles and conflicts—for example, maids versus housewives as well as social mobility out of poverty.

Telenovelas evolved in Latin America from the U.S. radio soap model developed by Colgate-Palmolive, Proctor and Gamble, and Gessy-Lever. Seeing how it reached the targeted female consumer market for their products, these corporations then introduced the genre first in Cuba, later in the rest of Latin America. In Moran's (2004) terms, the telenovela was introduced as a sort of genre localization or coproduction between the outside sponsor, who brought in considerable genre and production knowledge, and local producers, who adapted or localized it to their circumstances and culture. The original genre pattern of radio soap opera passed indirectly from the United States to Brazil via prior cultural adaptations to more reconfigured and culturally proximate forms in Cuba, Argentina, and elsewhere in Latin America. In complexity theory terms, the telenovela acted as a fractal form, both replicated and adapted to fit local audiences and local cultural industries (Gónzalez, 1991). It created a new cultural pattern that took on a life of its own, replicated and adapted, which expands the sense of how such processes of hybridization work.

The radionovela reached Brazil in 1941. The first was produced by Colgate-Palmolive, showing how transnational actors, like sponsors, can (re)define cultural limits or bounds by providing resources for new types of production. The success of the genre on Brazilian radio stations led to an increasing amount of time and resources devoted to it. The leap from radio to television in Brazil took only a decade. Brazilian producers mostly adapted foreign literary works, following the melodramatic formula established by the Cuban radionovelas. Radionovelas and early serialized TV shows had a fundamental role as a breeding ground for the genre, creating a Brazilian television adaptation of melodrama that is hybrid but distinctive. Scriptwriters were trained in the melodramatic conventions and gradually adapted them to fit Brazil, reconfiguring both the U.S. and Latin American genres.

Telenovelas did not evolve only from the radio matrix; other traditions in serialized fiction affected the development of the genre in the region as well. From the serial fiction *fuilettons* in France and the centuries-old *cordel* (chapbook) literature in Brazil, the genre evolved in each country within Latin America with certain peculiarities (Martin-Barbero, 1993; Ortiz & Borelli, 1988), again reflecting the complexity of both telenovela origins and adaptations.

## Brazilianization as Hybridization

Since the late 1960s and early 1970s, the Brazilian telenovela has slowly evolved away from the general Latin American model. Straubhaar (1982, 1984) saw a "Brazilianization" of the genre in two senses: a significant amount of national production, as the telenovela came to fill 3 hours of prime time 6 nights a week, and an equally significant adaptation of the genre to reflect national culture. The TV Globo network, in particular, invested heavily in production values, such as the use of external shots that had previously been avoided due to production costs. Globo also promoted a modernization of the telenovela's themes to include current issues and appropriated texts produced by Brazilian writers, novelists, and playwrights. In this process, Globo created what it termed, in its own publicity, the "Padrão Globo de Qualidade" [The Globo Pattern of Quality] (Herold, 1986; Lopez, 1995; Straubhaar, 1982). This high level of production quality began to differentiate Brazilian telenovelas, particularly those of TV Globo, from others in the region and even more from the American soap opera. This shows reconfiguration in not only genre form but production quality as well.

These changes in style led Brazilian telenovelas to become more dynamic and more closely associated with current events in the life of the nation (e.g., thematic inclusion of elections, strikes, and scandals that were happening in "real" life). Attention to social events and issues, such as the telenovela about landless people discussed later, is one major development that differentiates Brazilian telenovelas from others in Latin America.

Brazilian telenovelas are "open works" or an "open genre" (Mattelart, 1990, p. 41). During production, creators receive direct and indirect input from viewers and fans, theatrical productions, commercials, elite and popular press, institutional networks, audience and marketing research organizations, and other social forces in society, such as the Catholic Church, the government, and activist groups (Hamburger, 1999). This responsiveness to audience input is stronger in Latin American telenovelas than in many other global forms of melodrama, and it is particularly notable in Brazil, where TV Globo has extensively developed its methods of researching, anticipating, and tracking audience preferences and reactions (Straubhaar, 1984).

This mode of production was influenced by the military regime's censorship practices, which slowly forced many writers to leave the theater and the feature film industry and find refuge in television. Television became a space in which, even if censored, writers managed to stretch the limits of what was acceptable in the repressive atmosphere of the 1970s. Telenovelas did not break completely with their melodramatic roots but rather incorporated a national voice. They introduced a popular language, using colloquialisms and characters rooted in the daily life of the Brazilian metropolis. But this process was limited by what was perceived to be the targeted audience's expectations. Klagsbrunn (1993) felt the incorporation of reality into Brazilian telenovelas was but a superficial image of the actual problems affecting the nation:

> The telenovela reflects social aspects and problems faced by Brazilian society superficially, not conclusively, as usually occurs in genres adopted to entertain the masses. Since social criticism and suggestions regarding the path to be taken are not the main target of telenovelas, as this would alienate a significant number of viewers, social and political problems are merely included in a secondary role. (p. 19, my translation)

The telenovela that started the redefinition of the genre in Brazil was *Beto Rockfeller,* aired by Rede Tupi in 1968 and 1969 (Mattelart & Mattelart, 1990; Ortiz & Borelli, 1988; Straubhaar, 1982). *Beto Rockfeller* escaped the traditional Latin American artificial dramatic attitudes and speech patterns. It used colloquial dialogue typical of Rio de Janeiro. The dramatic structure, narrative strategies, and production values were also modified. *Beto Rockfeller* was the story of a middle-class young man who worked for a shoe store but, with charm and wit, got himself mixed up with the upper class, passing himself off as a millionaire. The telenovela got very high audience ratings, leading the network to stretch it to almost 13 months, much longer than the usual 6 to 8 months (Fernandes, 1987).

TV Globo, which up to that point had followed a traditional style of telenovelas with exotic settings and plots, saw the audience interest in *Beto Rockfeller* and championed the style. In this process, the genre was reshaped, distancing the Brazilian telenovela from the Latin America model. Intentionally or not, Globo transformed the Brazilian telenovela into a forum for the discussion of Brazilian reality. Globo has brought into the majority of the Brazilian households current issues in the social and political arena. In a historical analysis of the development of telenovelas in Brazil, Hamburger (1999) argued that these texts have created a space to discuss the nation. They have become the way the nation is currently imagined (Anderson, 1983).

Beginning in the late 1980s, as a result of the political *abertura* (opening) that started with the transition from military to civilian government (Straubhaar, 1989a), and continuing now, telenovela writers have increased the visibility of their social agendas and included national political debates in their narratives (Porto, 2005). The commercial nature of telenovelas also evolved;

these texts were used to sell not only products targeting housewives, but sports cars, services, and many other products targeted to different audience segments. Although they are still have some room for creativity in plot lines, telenovela writers must now also bow to commercial imperatives and write such product placements into their scripts, in cooperation with network commercial departments. Even the commercial form of the soap opera has been reconfigured to exploit Brazilian culture and rules.

The "melodramatic glue" maintaining these texts' popularity with audiences has modernized. Still, these melodramas have remained loyal to traditional topics such as romantic desire and conflict, social mobility, and the expected happy ending. The genre structure of the telenovela constrains writers within the commercial and genre conventions, but also gives them resources with which to reach the audience with a message. This is reminiscent of Giddens's (1984) theories of how structure provides both constraints or limits and resources to social actors. One of the more socially minded telenovela authors, Benedito Rui Barbosa, who wrote *O Rei do Gado,* maximizes that space and resources to discuss land reform.

To take this telenovela as a central example, *O Rei do Gado* (The Cattle King) was broadcast from June 1996 to February 1997 in the 8:30 p.m. slot on Globo. The first week of a telenovela is traditionally designed to grab the audience with ravishing visuals and technical care. Toward the end of its run, *O Rei do Gado* was filmed further in advance than the typical few days to 2 weeks, and had higher production values. The first weeks of a telenovela also are used to evaluate it with focus groups and to provide preview screenings for the news media. Some writers dreaded these data from these focus groups and preferred to ignore them, but others perceived the feedback as a valuable tool (Hamburger, 1999). According to several anecdotes, some writers have had to change the fate of characters based on the evaluation of focus groups. In situations where focus group data and low ratings corroborated each other, dramatic measures such as the removal of the main writer might take place, which illustrates the potentially severe commercial restraints placed on the writer.

*O Rei do Gado* was a successful program, attracting an audience that hovered around 50% of all sets tuned in every evening. It promoted land reform, political integrity, and environmental issues through social merchandising. The main objective with this telenovela, however, as with any other Brazilian telenovela, was to create a space to promote commercial goods. Several companies committed to advertise in this telenovela based on the success of the writer, director, and leading actor in their previous collaborations, but also based on Globo's track record of delivering a sizable audience with desirable demographics (La Pastina, 2001).

Barbosa, *O Rei*'s author, wove the political narrative within the traditional melodramatic modes of love and betrayal, but with an added twist.

His hero, a wealthy cattle farmer, was vulnerable and understanding; the heroine, a landless peasant who inherits a fortune, never abandoned her roots. The landless people remained landless, and the honest politician was killed. Nevertheless, love prevailed. Those who never relinquished their love were rewarded with happiness after 9 months of tribulation, but the rest of the national problems remained as unsettled at the end as they had been at the beginning. According to the author, his message had come across loud and clear: Until land reform was taken seriously, the nation would remain under a cloud.

The writer, the news program of the broadcast network (TV Globo), newspapers, and several political figures from different parties all used the program to promote the idea of land reform and their own electoral prospects. The show's writer, by promoting this issue, challenged the interests of Brazil's agricultural elite, which in turn challenged somewhat the idea that mass communications are clearly structurally controlled. The interests of the commercial network may have bounded the writer's actions, but that same network also enabled the writer to reach millions of people with a potentially counterhegemonic message. In reaching millions of people, however, the author's message was bounded by viewers' ability and desire to engage with that particular socially relevant message. In part, this process may be explained by Giddens's structuration theory, which looks at institutions as both bounding and enabling the agency of individual actors. (See Chapters 8 and 9 for more on other audience reception issues.)

## National Television Flows and Production

This section has looked at an in-depth case study of the geocultural, regional, and national adaptation of a genre. To broaden understanding of how television programs are produced in the context of international flows of both programs and genres, the next section focuses on a very different kind of analysis of the flow of television programs and genre ideas. It looks at how genres have developed in several world regions and cultural-linguistic spaces. It focuses specifically on how programs have been produced and exported within genre categories, based on a quantitative study based in the television flow tradition that goes back to Nordenstreng and Varis (1974).

### Limits to Focusing on National Flows and Production

One of the limits of the empirical study of television production and flow contained in this chapter is that it focuses primarily on nations and on transnational geocultural or cultural-linguistic regions. Many smaller and larger cultural units are increasingly important, and so, in addition to a number of nations, this study also focuses on three significant subnational cultural spaces or markets: Anglophone Canada, Francophone Canada, and the Hispanic United States. These three units are bigger and richer than many nations. Sinclair (1999) broke the U.S. Latino market out as a major entity in his study of Latin American television, in a chapter called "The World's Richest Hispanics." Sinclair (2003) also focused on Miami as a major emerging television production center as well as a regional financial and cultural center. Curtin (2003) similarly considered Miami one of the major emerging media capitals, transnationally positioned in both the U.S. Latino market and Latin America. I want to recognize the complexity of the television markets and cultural spaces discussed here.

The research in the following section and in Chapter 7 was begun under much more traditional terms of debate, starting in the early 1980s when the discussion of television flows largely involved nations. I want to address that ongoing debate and to make the point that much of the world's television is still produced for, distributed within, and watched by audiences socialized into thinking of themselves as part of a nation. However, I will actively complicate that discussion by also focusing much more in the next chapter (Chapter 7) on production and flow within cultural-linguistic spaces and markets that are transnational, as well as those that are regions, physical or virtual, within nations, with the two closely interrelated. To show how much things changed from the 1960s to the 2000s, the following discussion is organized primarily by decade and secondarily by genre.

## TV Genres and TV Flow in the 1950s

Due to technological circumstances, television in the 1950s, where it existed, tended to be localized and even somewhat elitist. The equipment necessary for filming, taping, and networking TV stations together was expensive and rare outside of the United States and Europe. Televisions were also quite costly at the time; therefore, audiences were relatively small and restricted. Regardless, genre development in variety shows, soap operas, drama shows, and other important forms started occurring in several countries very early.

Television genres took shape in Latin America, North America, the larger Anglophone cultural-linguistic market, East and South Asia, Europe, the Middle East, Africa, and elsewhere. Their strong roots in both U.S. and European models are often evident. As discussed above in general and in the specific case of the telenovela, national television systems adapted genres for local production, particularly before television exports began to increase in the 1960s.

In Latin American countries, television genres developed slowly through the 1950s and 1960s. Variety shows, particularly the 4- to 8-hour marathons that still take place on Sunday afternoons and evenings in many Latin American countries, often include game show segments that seem to be copied directly from those in the United States.

Although Latin American countries developed their own specific styles, particularly in music and comedy, there was a remarkable amount of interchange and influence, particularly in the evening serial dramas known as telenovelas. In the 1950s and most of the 1960s, broadcast recording technology made it relatively difficult for Latin American countries to export programs to each other, but talent, scripts, and ideas flowed around the region. Scripts were often sold across borders, adapted, and translated (Straubhaar, 1982). If there was not yet a regional market for programming, therefore, a regional base for such a market was being formed by the development of common genres through sales of scripts.

In East Asia, soap operas or serials developed along similar lines, with influences from both national and imported programs However, initially, there was much less flow of scripts and professionals between countries within the region. Although the U.S. genre had some homogenizing influences, national traditions led serials in different directions over time. If some programs on East Asian networks are urban family dramas similar to U.S. soap operas, East Asians also see a variety of unique historical, costume, and martial arts dramas. Similarly, serial dramas have developed distinct forms in the Middle East and South Asia, where family dramas are still common but programs with overtly religious themes are much more widespread, along with historical and mythological epics.

## TV Genres and TV Flow in the 1960s

To flesh out the analysis of television program and genre development, I use data that students, colleagues, and I have gathered about television production and flow in terms of their genres and country/region of origin analysis as empirical evidence of developments over time. That data starts in 1962. This is then put in a context of genre evolution and adaptation. For reference, the cross-national Table A.1 in the Appendix shows the proportion of national programming between 1962 and 2001 that was broadcast in prime time and the number of hours in a total broadcast day. Cross-national Table A.2 shows the proportion of U.S. programming between 1962 and 2001 that was broadcast in prime time and the number of hours in a total broadcast day. Finally, cross-national Table A.3 shows the proportion of regional programming from 1962 through 2001 that was broadcast in prime time and the number of hours in a total broadcast day, and cross-national Table A.4 shows the proportion of international/unknown/other programming between 1962 and 2001 that was broadcast in prime time and the total broadcast day (There is also a full description of the methods employed in generating the data in Appendix A.)

Some countries produced only limited genres in the 1960s, but that was not true of the larger countries, or even some smaller countries with well-developed production capabilities. Throughout the whole study period in Japan, almost all genre models, including entertainment (movies, drama shows, soap operas, game shows, variety shows, music shows, comedy shows, and sports shows), information (news shows, discussion shows, secondary education shows, cultural shows, and documentaries), and children's programming (cartoon shows, children's educational shows, other children's programming shows) were kept in good balance (Takahashi, 1992). Ito (1991), Iwabuchi (2002), and others have pointed out how the Japanese often imported genre models from the United States or Great Britain, in the case of the public station NHK, but tended to indigenize or adapt them to Japanese culture. Indeed, the model for glocalization discussed above comes from the broader Japanese pattern of importing global models in various areas, then localizing them.

In Hong Kong, the production of serials, action shows, music shows, and so on developed early. Hong Kong also adapted some imported models but leaned perhaps even more on traditions and infrastructure from their own film industry, much of which had migrated to Hong Kong from Shanghai in the 1930s. That was particularly true for the dominant broadcast television producers, TVB, whose chairman is Sir Run Run Shaw, which developed from a base in the Shaw Brothers film studios (TVB interviews, June 22, 1999). TVB, therefore, presents an interesting history of blending mainland Chinese influences (it absorbed Chinese film traditions and cooperates on several levels with CCTV of China) and global/U.S. influences, with its own long history as a principal television producer for Asian markets. Taiwan and South Korea began to develop some dramatic programming in the 1960s, but they placed more emphasis on variety programs. Similar trends occurred in China, which also began slowly opening up to television programming imported from Hong Kong, at least into the Cantonese cultural-linguistic zone of southern China. Italy, France, South Korea, and Taiwan all started off making at least 70% of their own prime-time programs as early as 1962.

A number of countries, like Cameroon, Chile, Venezuela, and Nigeria, started from more limited ranges of genres in 1962 (moving to a broader range in the 1970s and 1980s). Low-cost genres, such as talk shows, music shows, and variety shows, accounted for most of the initial genre diversity, particularly in domestic programming of the 1960s.

The United States began to export a great deal in the late 1950s and early 1960s, a history described in the next chapter. However, many countries in this study (12 of 23 studied in 1962) created more than half of their production in both prime time and the total broadcast day in 1962 (Table A.1). Anglo-Canada produced more than half of its total broadcast day but imported most of its prime-time programming from the United States in 1962 (Table A.2).

## TV Genres and TV Flow in the 1970s

Overall, in the 1970s, while the outflow of U.S. programming to many countries continued to increase, a nationalization of programming swept a number of regions. According to Ito (1991), prior to 1970, Japan was an information-importing country (although the data in Table A.1 show it to have been self-sufficient in television even in 1962), became self-sufficient in the 1970s, and after 1980, was an information-exporting country. Sugiyama (1982) showed that Japan exported 4,585 hours of television programming to 58 countries in 1980, compared to about 2,200 hours of programming in 1971. In Taiwan, national prime-time programming went from 98.2% in 1972 to 89% in 1982 and 97.1% in 1991 (Table A.1). The main genres were local variety shows, soap operas, and news. India started broadcasting in 1972 and 1973, creating 81% of its own prime-time programs and 82% of its total broadcast hours. In prime time, Indian and U.S. feature films were most prominent, along with Indian news, information, youth programs, plays, and music. In the total broadcast day, educational programs were also notable in India, which initially focused television on development education (Kumar, 2006).

Perhaps somewhat more slowly and less completely, many of the larger or most-rapidly industrializing nations of the Third World also began to import less, produce more, and even began to export: countries such as Brazil, Colombia, Hong Kong, Israel, Mexico, and Nigeria, as our Table A.1 indicates, and also countries outside of this study, such as Argentina and Egypt. In Hong Kong, for example, the nationally produced proportion of prime time rose dramatically from 23% in 1962 to 64% in 1972 (Table A.1).

In the 1970s, the United States maintained its export presence in television action shows and cartoon shows, but in soap opera and drama shows, U.S. products were replaced by national or regional programming. This was true in Brazil, Chile, Colombia, Hong Kong, Israel, Mexico, South Korea, and Venezuela. The main East Asian and Latin American genres in 1972 were local variety shows, local soap operas (or telenovelas), and news shows.

As Hoskins (1991) might have predicted, outside of Indian, Japanese, and U.S. television self-sufficiency, most of the national productions in most regions in the 1970s concentrated their efforts in genres to which a heavy cultural discount applied; in other words, countries were focusing on formats where the local element was essential: news shows, talk shows, and variety shows, for example. In addition, a number of countries also began to adapt, localize, and experiment with the genres that they had been importing: comedy shows, soap operas, family dramas, and historical epics (Moran, 2004). A cultural discount can easily be perceived in comedy genres, which tend to have many local or at least intracultural references. The data suggest that local audiences were also beginning to seek cultural proximity (Straubhaar, 1991) in soap operas, drama shows, and other programming, where the United States was traditionally feared to have a "Wall-to-Wall *Dallas*" advantage (Collins, 1986).

## TV Genres and TV Flow in the 1980s

In the 1970s and 1980s, these data show a gradual proliferation and differentiation of television genres. A number of simple production formats—local news, talk shows, simple variety shows, and live music shows—seemed to occur in almost every country that I surveyed. With declining production equipment costs, even small, poor countries could produce many hours of these genres. Larger countries also manufactured these low-cost genres, but only to supplement their soap operas, drama shows, comedy shows, and complex variety shows. The largest countries began to add even more expensive genres, such as miniseries adaptations of Brazilian literary works in Brazil (Fernandes, 1987).

From the early 1970s to the early 1980s, in several East Asian countries, such as Hong Kong, South Korea, and Taiwan, television exhibited strong changes. The national proportions of prime-time and total programming increased to nearly 90% (Table A.1). Japan continued to produce in roughly the same proportions, with children's shows, news shows, educational shows, and various forms of soap operas and dramas being the most prominent. These high levels of national production were popular with audiences; however, they also reflected government policies designed to reduce imports and raise national production (Ito, 1991; Iwabuchi, 2002; Lee, 1980). Some mid-sized countries such as Chile, Colombia, and Venezuela began to create national versions of some genres, for example, telenovelas and the more lavish variety shows, which they had previously imported from regional producers.

However, some countries produced less in the 1980s. Chinese national production in 1982 dropped to about 80% of the total broadcast time and about

90% of the prime-time broadcasting, however, these portions are very high, consistent with the pattern for East Asian countries. In Europe in 1982, France and Italy were producing less national programming than they had in 1972.

## TV Genres and TV Flow in the 1990s

However, by the 1990s, some smaller countries such as Chile were producing more expensive genres such as telenovelas, whereas larger but poorer countries such as Nigeria were also producing more domestic drama. Domestic production of fiction, as well as new genres such as "reality" programs, was also notable in France and Italy (Bechelloni & Buonanno, 1997).

Many countries (9 of 24 studied in 1992) showed slight increases in national production from 1982 to 1992, but quite a few (7 of 24) showed slight decreases (Table A.1), so the period seemed to be one of consolidation rather than drastic change. A good example was Europe in 1991, where France and Italy still continued a marginal decline in national production, importing more from the United States, but still self-produced more than half of their prime-time programming. The Asian nations in this study, in contrast, all continued to produce nationally at very high levels (Table A.1). By 1991, local production continued to prosper in Hong Kong. India showed more dramatic series, soap operas, and Indian feature films in prime time. National production was still promoted or even required by most East Asian national policies in 1991 (Man Chan, 1994). In the Middle East, production was already strong in Lebanon and Egypt. Lebanon produced 66% of its own programs in prime time and 60% of its total broadcast hours (Table A.1). The African countries in this study continued to raise national production: three fourths of total broadcast time and nearly all of prime time in Nigeria, and two thirds of Cameroon's total programming.

## TV Genres and TV Flow in the 2000s

One of the notable trends in the 2001 data was the rise of the reality show genre in a number of countries. In several countries, such as France and Italy, locally produced versions of reality shows like *Big Brother* tended to replace imported programs on networks that had previously relied on imports. Because such reality shows were local productions of imported formats, I counted then as national productions, although that raised an interesting question for theoretical categorization.

By 2001, 16 of the 21 countries for which I had information were producing more than half of their own prime-time programming, In fact, 10 were producing more than 70% of their prime time, while 15 were producing more than half of the whole broadcast day. That indicates a strong push over time to nationalize schedules on the main broadcast channels, going well beyond the most popular hours in prime time to fill up much of the rest of the day, pushing out imports from the United States or elsewhere. For example, Italy pushed both U.S. dramas and Latin American telenovelas out of niches that they had previously occupied (Buonanno, 2002).

Several countries or cultural markets—Anglo Canada, Brazil, Chile, China, France, Francophone Canada, Ireland, Mexico, New Zealand, Nigeria, South Korea, and Taiwan—produced a greater proportion of their television programming nationally in 2001 than in 1991 (Table A.1). That was particularly true in prime time but also included the total broadcast day for most of them. Several countries—Australia, Colombia, Japan, and the United Kingdom—remained basically the same in national production in 2001, but all produced more than half of both prime time and the total broadcast day. Japan, South Korea, Taiwan, and the United States produced about 90% or more of both prime time and total hours for major broadcast networks (those with more than a 5% share of the audience, my criterion for who was included in this study).

## TV and Genre Flow Conclusions

In the Latin American countries that I studied, the data partially supported my expectation of increased localization or nationalization. Brazil, for example, dramatically increased its own national programming from 1972 to 2001. However, I did not witness the same trend in Chile, which exhibited a steady decline in total national programming until 1991, despite the growth of some strong national genres, such as prime-time telenovelas. Chile showed a resurgence in national programming in 2001, for both total time and prime time, which could be a signal of things to come. The results for Brazil and Chile supported the idea of cultural proximity—that when national production is available, audiences will prefer it; this was not true, however, for the U.S. Hispanic market, which seemed to prefer regional imports, particularly in prime time. This phenomenon has been noted by other industry and academic observers, who conclude that Hispanic people in the United States want to watch regionally produced Hispanic television to be in touch with their culture in parts of Latin America or, for recent immigrants, to continue watching shows that they watched while they lived in another country (Piñon, 2006).

As my data has revealed in East Asia, four decades of television programming in several countries, most notable South Korea, Taiwan, and

Japan, showed that national programming had increased dramatically. The pattern that these East Asian countries showed in my data is for strong nationalization and little or no importation, which firmly supports my expectations of an increase in national productions and a relatively greater national domination of prime time.

In Europe, data also confirmed expectations of increasing national production, particularly in prime time. The same was true of the African countries, Cameroon and Nigeria, where nationally produced total time and prime time proportions have been steadily rising. Similar national growth could be seen in Lebanon and Israel in the Middle East. As technological and human costs of production decline worldwide, the amount of local production seems to be increasing, as shown by increasing local production in Francophone Canada and, to lesser degree, the Hispanic United States.

Overall, Anglo-Canada tends to suffer from a reverse cultural proximity: Its audience is so culturally (but not necessarily politically) similar to the U.S. audience that it has been difficult for producers to mark out what is distinctly Canadian in entertainment genres. The proportion of Canadian national production in news is much higher; most of the Canadian production in prime time is news or public affairs (Abram, 2004), programming that is tied to the political issues and cultural ideas that make Canada quite distinct from the United States (Abram, 2004; Ferguson, 1995; Raboy, 1990).

Theoretically, there seems to be clear evidence for the concept of cultural proximity. In nearly all of the countries that I examined, national production increased over time, and national production was most clearly reflected in each country's prime-time programming. The placement of national programming in prime time was evidence for a tendency toward cultural proximity because the nationally produced programming was being aired in the times when most people were viewing and when concern over audience satisfaction, whether from institutional sponsors or from advertisers, was the highest. If the most popular programming went to prime time, then it seems that the most popular programming was national.

In a related theoretical vein, the framework of asymmetrical interdependence could also be applied in this instance. A broad spectrum of possibilities is observed in the national and regional production dynamics among a diverse set of Third World cultures. The outcomes of these industries are mostly dependent on the available resources. The more affluent East Asian countries and the poorer but larger Brazil were able to produce much more television, generally more quantity and more kinds of genres, than the smaller Latin American nations. However, as affluence rose in smaller nations such as Chile and Colombia over the course of my study, they too were able to produce much more of their own national prime-time programming.

Perhaps the idea of cultural proximity needs to be nuanced by other cultural variables. Populations may need both language and cultural barriers to U.S. programs, as are found in Latin America and East Asia, for a sense of cultural proximity to attach itself to their national or even their regional cultures. Until these ideas are more thoroughly explored, concrete expressions of cultural proximity are clearly limited by these cultures and countries' financial and occasionally even institutional constraints.

Television flows between countries are very different, depending on which television genre is at issue. Some forms or genres of programming seem to be almost inherently national in focus and scope, such as national and local news, talk shows, reality shows, game shows, variety shows, and live music, although these national or local programs may increasingly be adaptations or licensed versions of imported formats (Moran, 2004). That raises a more subtle issue of what national production means. In essence, I argue here that it means hybrid production in which imported elements, genres, and formats are adapted into national media systems and given national spins or interpretations. The outcome is neither national autonomy nor cultural imperialism. Perhaps it is what Nederveen Pieterse (1995, 2004) called the global mélange of global, geocultural, cultural linguistic, national, regional, and local, or, more simply, hybridity.

## Note

1. This section and the following one are rewritten from parts of two earlier papers, where coauthors were of enormous help in thinking through these issues: A. C. La Pastina, J. D. Straubhaar, and H. Buarque de Almeida, (2002), *Producers, audiences, and the limits of social marketing on television: The case of* The Cattle King, *a telenovela about land reform in Brazil,* unpublished paper, University of Texas, Austin; and A. C. La Pastina, C. Regô, and J. Straubhaar, "The centrality of telenovelas in Latin America's everyday life: Past tendencies, current knowledge, and future research," the online *Global Media Journal.*

# 7

# TV Exporters

## From American Empire to Cultural-Linguistic Markets

In Chapter 6, I pointed out how production of some genres, such as telenovelas, had changed over time in several of the countries examined. This chapter continues to focus on television production and producers in terms of globalization, U.S. dominance, transnationalization, localization, and delocalization. The uneven flow of television programs between countries has received considerable attention for decades. In this chapter, I argue that apart from the flow of television programming between countries, there is an even more important flow between countries of genres and models, or

AUTHOR'S NOTE: The conceptual development of this chapter owes a great deal to several colleagues and students, specifically Luiz Duarte (Ph.D., Michigan State University) and Martha Fuentes and Dan Abram (University of Texas, Austin). As with most large empirical projects, the data reported in this chapter resulted from substantial amounts of work by collaborators, including Patricia McCormick (Howard University), Consuelo Campbell (Michigan State University), Sug-Min Youn (Seoul National University), Nobuya Inagaki (University of Texas), Luisa Ha (University of Oklahoma), Seema Shrikhande (Oglethorpe University), and Michael Elasmar (Boston University).

patterns, for creating television programming. The use of foreign models seems to have accelerated with increasing transnational trade in the past few years of licensed formats such as *Survivor, Popstars,* or *Big Brother,* which are produced in dozens of countries (Moran, 2004).

## Genre Imperialism?

For many writers on media imperialism, foreign models for television were one major form of media imperialism (Lee, 1980). This line of analysis focuses on the political economy of importing system-level models, such as commercial versus public service broadcasting organizational forms. This is clearly important to program and genre choices. Countries that adopt a commercial model tend to use certain kinds of program forms or genres and neglect or even avoid others. Media imperialism analysis (Oliveira, 1993), however, may overstate somewhat the power of imported genres in terms of what they bring to the importing culture or television system. In dealing with the complexity of a cultural system like television, media imperialism explanations are often linear, emphasizing the determining power of the imported television form on the local cultural industry and the audience. Oliveira (1993), for example, argued that the commercial nature of imported genres overpowered the local aspects of culture inserted into the television program forms, even when the imported genre was transformed from soap opera to telenovela, for example.

The goal of this chapter is fivefold: First, I will continue to examine the flow of television programs among broadcast television producers and the most widely viewed stations (those with at least a 5% share of the broadcast audience), focusing in this chapter on global flows, U.S. exports, and flows among geocultural regions and transnational cultural-linguistic markets. Second, I will also broadly discuss how media genres and formats flow globally. Building on that, I will discuss how genre flows might best be theorized and understood, focusing in particular on complexity theory and hybridization. Third, I will look at the shift from informal copying of genres and programs to the increasingly formal business of legally licensing packaged television formats. Fourth, I ask how local or national producers delocalize their productions, or distance them from their original locations of production, to make them more saleable or acceptable across cultural borders (Iwabuchi, 2002). Fifth, I look at how global or transnational programmers begin to localize their production to make it fit the huge variety of world television cultural spaces and markets (Chalaby, 2002, 2005c).

## Genres Flowed Before Programs

In the 1950s, before the actual recording and flow of programs between countries was facilitated by cinescopes and videotape, there was already a flow of genres and genre ideas between countries. As soon as countries began to buy television production and reception equipment, they began to look for and borrow ideas about how to make and program television. In one example from Brazil, a radio and television entrepreneur named Assis Chateaubriand decided to start television in São Paulo in 1950. The first day's broadcast was full of opening spectacles and ceremonies. Reportedly, the next day the Brazilian staff turned to the U.S. RCA technicians who had installed the equipment and said, "What do we do next?"

Scripts for television programs such as dramas and soap operas were sold across borders, as described in Chapter 6 for Latin American telenovelas. Ideas for genre developments were "borrowed" and deliberately glocalized. Scriptwriters, directors, and entrepreneurs moved between countries. They had to adapt to new cultures, blending and hybridizing. In this chapter, I focus on the reverse process, the deliberate disembedding of a cultural product or genre from its culture, so that it can be exported.

## Delocalization

This section takes an idea from the general literature on globalization—the idea of globalization as delocalization—and redefines a new, specific role for it in the production of television. As John Gray (1998) has put it,

> Behind all these "meanings" of globalization is a single underlying idea which can be called "de-localization": the uprooting of activities and relationships from local origins and cultures. It means the displacement of activities that until recently were local, into networks of relationships whose reach is distant or worldwide. Domestic prices of consumer goods, financial assets such as stock and bonds, even labour are less and less governed by local and national conditions; they all fluctuate along with global market prices. Globalization means lifting social activities out of local knowledge and placing them in networks in which they are conditioned by, and condition, world-wide events. (p. 57)

As producers in a number of countries not only produce for their own markets but anticipate exporting their production, they must change local models to make them more exportable. This is taking place in the United States, where some television producers reportedly anticipate the characteristics required for export even as they produce originally for the U.S. market. It has been taking place in Japan for years. Iwabuchi (2002) described how Japanese producers deliberately minimized the "Japanese-ness" of many early cultural industry exports, such as anime cartoons and video games. He called this the process of making such Japanese exports culturally odorless so that they did not so clearly smell of Japanese culture and history.

In Brazil and Mexico, producers think about whether certain subgenres of telenovelas will export as well as others, recalling the spread of local varieties of telenovela noted in Chapter 6. This seems to require a new theorization, which I am tentatively calling delocalization. Delocalization consists of minimizing certain kinds of cultural specificities in a cultural product for export to lower the possibility of a cultural discount by the foreign audience. Such a cultural discount could be called forth by references to things that people are unfamiliar with, jokes that require cultural context to understand, visual environments that the audience might find confusing or unattractive, pacing that is unfamiliar or jarring, or dramatic themes that are too unfamiliar (Hoskins & Mirus, 1988).

For example, Japan produces and exports two rather distinct broad categories of cultural products, according to Iwabuchi (2002). One category is highly specific, almost idiosyncratic films and other products, which serve both internally and externally to establish Japan's cultural distinctiveness, the depth and uniqueness of its historical heritage. Iwabuchi noted that these "unique" exports often encountered a notable cultural discount in other countries (Hoskins & Mirus, 1988b). As a result, for years, Japanese companies focused on a second category, what Iwabuchi (2002) called culturally "odorless" commodities (pp. 24–30). For some observers, Japan was seen as manufacturing and exporting consumer entertainment hardware such as Sony products, but not software or programming (Nye, 1990). One could argue that these products were clearly delocalized. There was nothing specifically Japanese about them in any cultural sense, other than a general reputation for quality of design and manufacture.

In the 1990s, Japan exported another category of cultural products such as manga (comics), animated films/television, and computer games, which became "recognized as very 'Japanese' in a positive and affirmative sense in Western countries as well as non-Western countries" (Iwabuchi, 2002, p. 30). However, some Japanese critics still argued,

> The characters of Japanese animation and computer games for the most part do not look "Japanese." Such non-Japanese-ness is called *mokokuseki,* literally meaning "something or someone lacking any nationality," but also implying the erasure of racial or ethnic characteristics or a context, which does not imprint a particular culture or country with these features. (Iwabuchi, 2002, p. 28)

This also seems like delocalization. However, delocalization is relative to cultural relevance or proximity. Iwabuchi noted that Japan exports some cultural products, such as popular music, TV dramas, and fashion magazines, which are much more characteristically Japanese, only to other parts of Asia. Those exports are easier because of an increasing sense of cultural proximity between Japan and Taiwan or China, making delocalization of Japanese products less necessary.

Delocalization can go too far, resulting in programming that is too bland and not appealing to anyone. Some efforts to reach a pan-European audience were so watered down that some referred to them as Euro-pudding (Readhead, 2006). Once countries' cultural exports achieve a certain level of recognition and acceptance—for example, U.S. cartoons, U.S. action films, Japanese anime, Latin American telenovelas, or Asian martial arts dramas—their distinctive cultural characteristics are considered desirable. In fact, genres and countries become a combined brand in international television trade (Harrington & Bielby, 2005). Other countries might come to have aspects of what Gitlin (2001) called U.S. popular culture's familiarity as an appreciated second popular culture, not displacing home cultures but adding another layer of cultural identification and appreciation, as discussed in Chapter 9.

## Trends Toward Regionalization of Television

As noted earlier, an increase in the transnationalization of television into multicountry or regional markets linked by geography, language, and culture has been observed (Wilkinson, 1995). These markets might more accurately be called cultural-linguistic or geocultural markets rather than regional markets because not all these linked populations, markets, and cultures are geographically contiguous.

This regionalization of television rests on three levels of development, all of which diverge from many of the current commonplaces about globalization. First, many national television systems are far from being overwhelmed by global television imports. A number of countries in Latin America, Asia, and Europe produce most of their own programming, at least for broadcast television, which still dominates viewing in most places, as laid out in Chapter 6.

Second, a number of countries, including Argentina, Brazil, Mexico, Venezuela, India, Egypt, and Japan, or media capitals (Curtin, 2003) such as Beirut, Hong Kong, Miami, or Shanghai have gone beyond producing for their own publics and markets to exporting television in competition with the traditional exporters of North America and Europe. Much of this new exportation circulates largely within geocultural regions—the Spanish-speaking market of Latin America, the Arabic market of the Middle East, or the Chinese market of East and Southeast Asia—but some breaks into transnational cultural-linguistic or global markets as well. Brazil, for example, started by exporting to a multicontinent cultural-linguistic market in Angola, Mozambique, Portugal, and other Portuguese-speaking countries and regions, but fairly quickly exported to a truly global market of more than 100 countries in various language versions (Marques de Melo, 1992).

However, it has proven difficult for non-U.S. exporters to sustain truly global exports. Brazil and Mexico experienced considerable success as exporters of telenovelas in the late 1980s and early 1990s. However, in markets such as Western Europe, they never got more than 5% of the fiction market, compared to more than 50% for the United States (Biltereyst & Meers, 2000), and over time, their exports declined as countries such as Italy began to import less fiction and create more (Buonanno, 2004). Brazilian and Mexican exports were stronger and more sustained in southern Europe, where cultural proximity was relatively greater (Biltereyst & Meers, 2000).

Third, although subnational or local television broadcasting is far less well developed in many countries, it is beginning to grow. Local television often responds to an almost universal desire for local news and information, but in a number of situations, local entertainment also emerges, particularly to serve linguistic and cultural minorities. Some of this local growth often takes place within a context of economic and cultural regionalization at both supranational and subnational levels. The NAFTA area offers two examples: Hispanic Americans and French Canadians, which I examine later. In some cases, these minorities are also served as part of other cultural-linguistic markets, as with the dominance of Mexico in exporting television programs, or even entire channels such as Azteca America, which translocally extends TV Azteca from Mexico, to U.S. Hispanics. But sometimes, programming for minorities becomes more clearly differentiated or tied into other identities, as in Quebec, which imports some programming from other French-speaking countries but less than from the United States or English-speaking Canada.

Fourth, it is increasingly necessary to take into account the intermediaries in the international television trade process: distributors, program buyers, and programmers or schedulers. These are the people who concretely act to buy and schedule programs from other markets. They act, at least in theory, to please the audience, but their own perceptions of cultural issues and characteristics of producers, as well as their understanding of audience desires, are increasingly crucial (Harrington & Bielby, 2005; Havens, 2006). Intermediaries focus a great deal on genre to fit genres and audiences, but also on country reputations (the United States is tops for action shows, Brazil for telenovelas, for example), and producer or artist images and reputations (Harrington & Bielby, 2005).

# Flows of Television Programming and Genres in the 1960s

In the early 1960s, videotape and other recording technologies encouraged an enormous acceleration of U.S. television exports to the world. By the late 1950s, Hollywood studios were producing an enormous quantity of programs for the affluent North American market. Because their costs had been recovered at home, those same programs were sold cheaply abroad—much below the local costs of producing programming in the 1960s in most countries (Guback & Varis, 1986). A number of different genres of programming flooded out of the United States and into the world market: westerns, police shows, drama shows, situation comedies, musical shows, variety shows, and feature films. Because these programs were cheap and because programming in most countries was both scarce and expensive, almost all sold well. In 1974, Nordenstreng and Varis observed from an extensive survey of broadcast television schedules that most countries imported more than half of their programming, mostly from the United States. Smaller, poorer countries tended to import the most programming, whereas larger, more industrialized nations imported much less.

The data generated for this book, using the methods described in Appendix A, showed that of 25 countries or cultural markets studied in 1962, only 5 imported more than half of their broadcast television from the United States. Some imported more than half of their prime-time shows (Australia, Anglo-Canada, Hong Kong, Jamaica, and New Zealand), and some more than half of their total broadcast day (Australia, Hong Kong; Table A.2). By 1972, two countries imported more than half of their prime-time (Anglo Canada, Jamaica) and two (Australia, Hispanic United States) half or almost half of their total broadcast day (Table A.2). (Remember that this analysis distinguishes the Anglophone United States, seen here largely as an exporter, from the Hispanic United States—that is, the Spanish-language population of the United States and the stations and channels that broadcast to them—which is seen here largely as an importer of programming from within the Latin American geocultural region.)

Another pattern that becomes immediately clear is that the United States exports most to members of its own cultural-linguistic sphere, whether those are the other Anglophone nations or its own partially distinct, but still closely related Hispanic minority audience watching Spanish-language stations in the United States (where the U.S. programs are dubbed). The distinction between prime-time and total broadcast day is also useful because it shows that some countries were putting U.S. programs where the mass of the audience was (in prime time) whereas others were filling up the broadcast day with U.S. programs but putting other things in prime time, where audience numbers and attention are concentrated. For example, by 1972, Hispanic U.S. prime time was already filled 83% by programs imported from the larger Latin American cultural-linguistic television market (Table A.3), primarily telenovelas from Mexico. Australia was filling in prime time with 38% of its own production and 45% imported from Anglophone producers other than the United States (Table A.3).

Overall, the 1962 and 1972 results show an important dichotomy. Most countries produced at least half of their own programming, particularly for prime time (Table A.1), and imported most or all of the rest from the United States (Table A.2). Most countries (15 of 25) produced at least slightly more of their own prime time in 1972 than in 1962, although three decreased their prime-time production slightly in the same period (Table A.1). Slightly fewer imported most of either prime-time or total broadcast hours from the United States and created the rest for themselves. Few imported from anyone else. Those that did were clearly located in cultural-linguistic markets that were already well-developed and strong by the 1970s: Anglo-Canada, Australia, Ireland, Jamaica, and New Zealand in the Anglophone market, which already had strong producers in both the United Kingdom and United States; and Chile, Colombia, and the Hispanic U.S. audience in the Latin American market, which already had Mexico as a strong exporter by 1972 (Table A.3). While the United States was already a strong exporter in 1962, Mexico emerged as an exporter to other Spanish-speaking countries in the 1970s. (That cultural-linguistic market would continue to grow to include other exporters later.)

## Flows of Television Programming and Genres in the 1970s

Overall, in the 1970s, the increased outflow of U.S. programming to many countries continued, but a nationalization of programming swept a number of regions, as noted in the last chapter. In contrast, in Europe, both France and Italy began to import slightly more television programming in 1972, both from within their region and from the United States.

National production was consistently more prominent in most countries' prime time, while U.S. imports were relatively more prominent in the total broadcast day. But because the broadcast day was also being expanded to 24 hours in many countries around this time, U.S. exports increased notably (Miller et al., 2005). In other words, U.S. programs were increasingly being substituted as filler or used to expand broadcast hours, so its cultural impact was mixed. In countries like Brazil (Straubhaar, 1984) or Mexico and Chile

(Antola & Rogers 1984), where studies examined the actual audience hours spent with domestic production versus imports, it was clear that audience hours were climbing for national production, or in smaller countries, for regional production, and not for U.S. imports. By 1972, audience hours for those had dropped in Brazil (Straubhaar, 1984), and they continued to drop there and in other Latin American countries despite the increasing presence of U.S. programs in off hours (Straubhaar et al., 1992). The exceptions tended to be smaller countries in the cultural-linguistic export spheres of large exporters, as noted above.

Genre-specific import and export patterns in broadcast television also began to be apparent in the 1970s. The United States maintained its export presence in television action shows and cartoon shows, but national or regional programming became dominant in soap opera and drama shows. Mexico began to export telenovelas to Latin America, Brazil exported its first telenovelas (to Portugal, in an interesting reverse flow), and Hong Kong also began its notable role as a program exporter to other Asian countries.

## Flows of Television Programming and Genres in the 1980s

In the 1980s, some countries, such as Mexico, Brazil, Hong Kong, Egypt, and India (Abu-Lughod, 2005; Antola & Rogers, 1984; Boyd, 1993; Sinclair & Harrison, 2000), were also beginning to export more expensive genres, such as soap operas, drama shows, comedy shows, and complex variety shows regionally and, in the case of Brazil, Hong Kong, India, and Mexico, worldwide. These data show that when nationally produced genres were not readily available in certain genres, broadcasters were still using imports, but they were increasingly turning toward regionally imported genres when no locally produced ones were to be found. The U.S. genres that were most evident during prime time in the 1980s in most countries were comedy shows, cartoon shows, and movies.

From the early 1970s to the early 1980s in several East Asian countries, such as Hong Kong, South Korea, and Taiwan, U.S. programming decreased to about one tenth of total broadcast hours (Table A.2). This reflected government policies designed to reduce imports and raise national production (Ito, 1991; Iwabuchi, 2002; Lee, 1980). China still refused to import any programs from the United States, but it was gradually importing more programs from within its East Asian region (Man Chan, 1994).

In 1982, France and Italy both increased U.S. importation marginally and imported less than one tenth of their programming from within the European region. In contrast to the lack of intra-European television trade, the cultural-linguistic markets that emerged most strongly in the 1970s, the Anglophone and Spanish-speaking Latin American cultural spaces, continued to grow in the 1980s. Regional television imports were beginning in China and Hong Kong, but not yet in Japan, South Korea or Taiwan, which still had national policy barriers against such trade. However, for some mid-size countries such as Chile, Colombia, and Venezuela, regional imports declined in both prime time and total broadcast hours as regional telenovelas, variety shows, and other shows were largely replaced by national productions (Table A.3).

## Flows of Television Programming and Genres in the 1990s

Imports from the United States and other major international (nonregional) producers decreased overall from 1982 to 1992, but they remained relatively stronger in some genres, which were not widely produced locally or regionally. This was reflected in a decrease in the quantity and proportion of U.S. and other international productions in broadcast schedules, particularly in prime time (Table A.1). Nevertheless, some U.S./international genres remained relatively more prominent. Perhaps because of the greater associated costs, the production and exporting of documentaries, action adventures, cartoon shows, and feature films were still dominated by industrialized First World nations.

In 1991, France and Italy imported more from the United States but still self-produced more than half of prime time. Several of the smaller Anglophone nations (Ireland, Jamaica, and New Zealand) also increased their dependence on U.S. production slightly (Table A.2) and decreased national production slightly (Table A.1). Lebanon produced most of its own programs but still imported quite a bit from the United States (24% in prime time and 23% total hours; Table A.2); they also imported some other international programs but little from elsewhere in the Middle East. Israel imported quite a bit from other Middle Eastern countries for its own Arabic-language networks, somewhat analogous in scope to regional imports into U.S. Hispanic networks.

The Latin American market continued to grow in the 1990s (Table A.3). New stations in Brazil and other countries imported regional telenovelas when they could not afford to create them, but network consolidation in Mexico actually reduced regional imports. Some countries such as Chile and Colombia went from primarily importing telenovelas to also exporting them. For net importers such as the Hispanic U.S. networks, Latin American regional programs increased in total programming, primarily in daytime and evening telenovelas, feature films, children's entertainment shows, and sports shows. As U.S. Hispanics and smaller Latin American countries such as the Dominican Republic imported more such Latin American productions, they tended to substitute them for U.S. genres that had previously filled up off hours in the total broadcast day.

An Asian cultural-linguistic market began to be more visible in certain genres among some countries, but it continued to experience policy-imposed limits. China was one of the Asian first countries in my study that imported much, as it opened and decentralized its system (Man Chan, 1994); Taiwan and others began to do the same later in the 1990s. India limits imports from both the United States and potential regional exporters such as Pakistan, which shares elements of language and culture but which had strained political relations with India. However, Pakistani soap operas/serials are popular on videocasette in India (Shrikhande, 1992). Hong Kong became one of the major exporters of programs to its East and Southeast Asia neighbors, Taiwan, China, Thailand, Singapore, Malaysia, and other Chinese stations in the western countries. India had been exporting feature films for years and showed some potential for exported television programs with Asia and the Arab world, programs that were already popular on videocassette (Shrikande, 1992).

Japan became one of the main exporters in the Asian cultural-linguistic market, gradually increasing from the 1970s through the 1990s. Ito (1991) provided some reasons for the success of Japanese television programming exports in the overseas market. The first reason was the availability of Japanese television programming after 1975. At that time, many countries had become particularly wary of overdependence on American television programming, so they began to seek television programs from other countries that had a readily available supply. Naturally, importing from Japan, the second-largest television program-producing country at that time, increased.

The second factor in Japan's rising exports in East Asia and developing countries was due to a strong interest in Japan's economic and technological successes in the 1970s and 1980s. People in importing countries wanted to learn about Japanese history and society through Japanese television programming, hoping to use this information in a potential modernization model (Iwabuchi, 2002). As a result, East Asian governments and public broadcasting corporations sought Japanese drama shows that depicted the lives of ordinary citizens in the late 19th and early 20th centuries, when Japan was still a developing country. One good example is *Oshin,* a 15-minute drama series developed by NHK, whose heroically persistent female main character was popular in many countries, in Asia and elsewhere (Singhal & Udornpim, 1997; Svenkerud, Rahoie, & Singhal, 1995). The third factor that contributed to the rise of Japanese exports was the conscious export planning made by Japanese television stations and movie companies (Takahashi, 1992). Iwabuchi (2002) explained that Japanese television exporters targeted Asian markets, often minimizing the overt "Japaneseness" of programs such as anime cartoons to minimize any country-specific resentments related to memories of World War II and resulting fears of Japan.

## World, Regional, National, and Local
## Genres and Flows in the 2000s

In the 2001 data, one of the notable trends was the rise of the reality-show genre in a number of countries. In several countries, such as France and Italy, locally produced versions of imported, licensed reality shows like *Big Brother* tended to replace imported programs in networks that had previously relied on imports.

Italian productions pushed both U.S. dramas and Latin American telenovelas out of niches that they had previously occupied (Buonanno, 2002), but Italy still imported what remained from the United States rather than its European neighbors (Buonanno, 2004). A few countries, such as Chile, also imported more programming from the United States, especially in the total broadcast day. New Zealand imported more into prime time, not the total day, and the United Kingdom imported more in both (Table A.2). In Chile's case, as in others, this was because several new stations and networks entered the market in the 1990s, leading to an upturn in U.S. or regional imports (Wiley-Crofts, in press).

Regional imports went up slightly in Brazil, Ireland, and France (Table A.3). Ironically, regional imports in East Asia are reported up in the media (Faiola, 2006) and some academic studies (Dator & Seo, 2004) after 2002, driven by what is called the Korean Wave, an increased popularity of Korean dramas in China, Japan, Singapore, Taiwan, and elsewhere in Asia. (Ironic, because in my data, China decreased its imports, and Hong Kong data were flawed and not used; I did not catch the Korean Wave here.) Overall, there is a gradual strengthening of cultural-linguistic markets in some ways, but a falling back in others as more nations now produce genres, such as melodrama and drama, that they used to import from within cultural-linguistic markets or geocultural regions.

## Overall Trends in Broadcast Television Flows

My expectation that regional imports would be preferred to U.S. or other international imports was strongly supported by the data for several regions.

This regionalization trend was evident early in smaller Latin American or Asian countries, such as TVB exports of melodramas and comedies, for example, to Southeast Asian countries such as Indonesia and Malaysia. But it was also seen in Brazil, where regional programming began to appear in prime time in 1991, mostly in the form of evening telenovelas. Overall, some types of programs, such as soap operas and variety programs, seemed over the years of my study to primarily flow between countries within a geocultural or cultural-linguistic region, such as Latin America (Antola & Rogers, 1984; Sinclair, Jacka, & Cunningham, 1996), greater China (Chan, 1996), or the Arabic-speaking world (Boyd, 1993).

My expectation that U.S. or international programming would remain strong in certain genres was strongly supported by the data from Brazil and Chile, which revealed that U.S. genres too expensive for Latin American countries to mass produce, such as action movies, action shows, and cartoon shows, were still being predominantly imported from the United States. In addition, the second part of the theoretical prediction, an overall decline in imported U.S. programming, was also supported by the data from Brazil, Chile, and the U.S. Hispanic market.

As these data for East Asia have revealed, four decades of television programming in several countries, most notably South Korea, Taiwan, and Japan, showed U.S. programming has decreased in both total time and prime time and that international programming witnessed a small but noticeable increase by 2001. However, the regionalization of television trade that might be expected was not strongly apparent in my own East Asian data. The strongest genres among the limited regional trade were Japanese cartoons and Hong Kong martial arts dramas, along with a very recent rise in Korean dramas. This lends some support to the idea that regional genres are concentrated in genres that are relatively expensive or difficult for individual cultures or nations to produce, such as animation and highly produced melodramas or action/drama series. Furthermore, U.S. programming declined in the region and eventually included only high-cost productions, such as action series, documentaries, and movies.

In neither Africa nor Europe did my data reveal much evidence of a regional market. Schlesinger (1993) and others have noted the lack of linguistic and cultural coherence in Europe as a potential market, especially during the early stages of the changes that the European Union could bring to this market. The same could certainly be said of Africa, which is divided not only by its former colonial languages, English, French, and Portuguese, but also by the hundreds of dialects that are spoken throughout the region. In both the Europe and Africa, American imports were still used heavily in key genres that were not widely produced nationally.

My expectations of regional markets with regional cultural proximity were validated in Latin America and in the U.S. Hispanic market, but this trend was only beginning in East Asia. Perhaps the East Asian countries that I chose to review are, in fact, the television producers; if I had looked at other, less developed countries in the region, I might have found countries on the importing end of a regional market. Other research about Southeast Asia indicates that those countries imported more from other Asian producers (McDaniel, 1994, 2002). Also, a closer scrutiny of the East Asian countries in my survey showed many historical and political barriers to regional imports over the decades in my study. Many of these barriers were reduced by 2001, and perhaps that is why my data have reflected the very beginning of such a regional East Asian television marketplace.

## Global Flows

Some types of programs are created for and distributed to a truly global audience. The programs, films, and series that most often sell and flow directly across borders are usually precisely those that are the most expensive and the hardest to adapt as genres to national or regional production. The most widely sold programs are action series and films, news (usually footage not finished programs), dramas, soap operas, animation, documentaries, and music videos. Soap operas and music videos are also widely diffused as genres and widely produced at local levels; some genres also have relatively universal appeal, as well as being cheap and easy to produce (Singhal & Udornpim, 1997). With such genres, however, the trend is toward more regional and national production, even while some soaps and music videos still flow globally.

The United States still dominates the export of international news, action-adventure programs, drama, melodrama (both daytime soaps and evening programs such as *Dallas* or *Desperate Housewives*), scientific and historical documentaries, animation, music videos, and feature films, all of which require huge investments. Another factor in the exportability of action-adventure programs is that they don't require a great deal of cultural capital, language ability, or sophistication to understand.

Many other producers at various levels are beginning to compete with the United States as exporters. The Japanese have caught up fast in global exports of animation to many countries, even placing quite a few programs on both broadcast and specialty cable television channels in the United States. Hong Kong is cutting into the global market for action-adventure with both contemporary and costume martial arts dramas and serials. China, Great Britain, Japan, and Hong Kong produce a great deal of historical drama.

A comparative study of television fiction in five European countries (Germany, France, Italy, Spain, and Great Britain) showed that "fiction programmes from the US and Latin America, apart from no longer being at an advantage in terms of cost, are continuously losing favour with audiences" (Bechelloni, 1997, p. xvi). This suggests a change in the economics of television, favoring local production against the ongoing temptation to import what once seemed irresistibly cheap American imports (Allen, 1995). Another part of the trend shown in the five-country study in Europe was the movement toward adaptation and creation in Europe (and elsewhere) of usable genres (Buonanno, 2002). In fact, European producers see themselves competing with both American series and Latin American telenovelas, showing that Latin American producers, notably Mexico and Brazil, have succeeded in creating a genre that rivals American series in exports.

## From Program Genre and Idea Flows to Licensed Format Flows

Some new genres have become the focus for a global form of flow and adaptation, the licensed format trade. *Format,* in this sense, is a more specific framework for production than *genre.* According to Moran (1998), "a television format is that set of invariable elements in a program out of which the variable elements of an individual episode are produced" (p. 13). So a melodrama or prime-time serial is a genre. The concept, script, and production guidelines of *Desperate Housewives* constitute a specific format. This is so even if it is subtly transformed from the U.S. style of prime-time serial to, say, the distinctive Latin American telenovela, which some would argue is now a different genre (La Pastina, Regô, & Straubhaar, 2003). Moran (1998, 2004) observed that the two main kinds of formats are (1) drama, situation comedy, or scripted entertainment, and (2) reality shows, including game shows, talk shows, and live dramatic situations, such as MTV's *Real World.*

Licensing and importing formats is a convenient way of increasing or diversifying local, national, or geocultural production. Even the United States, which seldom imports finished television programs for its commercial broadcast networks, has imported a number of program formulas, from sitcoms such as *Three's Company* to reality shows such as *Survivor.* National and regional television industries have extensively recycled and adapted general genres or specific formulas for programs (Moran, 1998; Moran & Keane, 2004).

Culture exporters now sell relatively fewer television programs as direct exports and relatively more as formats to be produced locally. (See Table A.2

and discussion above for more detail about how U.S. exports have declined in many countries.) Because many program-purchasing countries are now producing more of their own programs, considerable interest has turned to selling them formats with which to produce local programs.

Developing countries once simply borrowed program formulas. A Brazilian network, for example, hired people in the United States to tape interesting game show ideas and send them the tapes to copy and adapt (my interviews with Brazilian TV network employees in 1998). Owners of copyrighted formats, such as *Big Brother* or the *Teletubbies,* have sued knock-off productions in Brazil, Mexico, and elsewhere (Kraidy, 2005).

American, Australian, British, and Dutch companies are all actively involved in licensing formats to a variety of producers around the world (Moran, 2004). The most globally visible examples, *Survivor* and *Jeopardy,* were created by the Dutch company Endemol and the U.S. company King World, respectively. These companies and others in the business of format-producing and licensing usually have a transnational orientation (Moran, 2000). Endemol, a merger of two companies, produced programs for transnational channels such as RTL (Radio TV Luxembourg) or Sky Channel.

Other format licensors include the BBC, which sells both programs and formats abroad. It also coproduces quite a bit of material, sometimes with networks such as the U.S. Public Broadcasting System, with PBS member stations such as WGBH in Boston, and with global networks like Discovery. Coproductions of documentaries and dramas are another interesting transnational variation on the transfer of formats, reflecting a much deeper involvement by the producer who is supplying the format. Granada Television in the United Kingdom does very similar kinds of format licensing and coproduction.

There are also format brokers, such as AAFI (All American Freemantle Inc.) or King World; the latter handles both export and licensing of two main game shows, *Wheel of Fortune* and *Jeopardy,* Even some developing countries have become successful format licensors. Building on its success, reputation, and commercial sales structure from globally exporting telenovelas, TV Globo of Brazil exported a novel format, a drama in which the audience could vote on two possible outcomes, called *Você Decide.* It sold 37 adaptations in Latin America, Europe, Middle East, Africa, and Asia (Moran, 1998).

## Localization of Global and Transnational Television Channels

Localization is the adaptation of globally produced television programs or channels to local audiences, according to Chalaby (2002). Both industry and academics use the term localization, although with somewhat different definitions. Some scholars, for example, Duarte (2001), use *adaptation* instead, and some scholars and industry groups talk about *customization* of global channels for segmented or local markets. The Turner Broadcasting Web site uses the term *customization*, for example. Discovery Channel materials talk about *reversioning* its product for local markets (Risch, 2003). Chen (2004) examined the *domestication* of foreign cable channels in Taiwan.

Both production of programming and packaging/distribution of programming are relevant to world television flows. I now focus on adaptation of global television channels, by groups like Murdoch and Time Warner, to various television audiences and markets, including regional markets like Southeast Asia or Latin America; cultural-linguistic markets that span regions, like greater China; and nations and localities, like Latinos in the U.S. Southwest. Global media firms often approach regional and national markets by making the most minimal adaptations to their existing television programming that they feel will sell. Their initial economic interest is to use as much of their existing programming and channel organization and design with as little extra expenditure as possible. In a way, what these global managers initially hoped to achieve was precisely what Boyd-Barrett (1977) or Chin-Chuan Lee (1980) might have called *media imperialism*. They wanted to maximize the export of their existing American (or British or Japanese) material to as many places as possible with as little change or modification as possible, to take advantage of economies of scale and maximize their profit, as standard business practice would dictate (Porter, 1998).

Theoretically, some of the literature on international marketing shows that foreign firms entering a local market must determine how much they are willing to adapt their products and procedures or whether they want to stick to exporting a standard product everywhere (Duarte, 2001). In the 1970s and 1980s, the growing interaction among people of all nations, spurred by cheaper and easier transportation as well as sophisticated communication technology, led many scholars to perceive a relative homogeneity between markets. According to Levitt (1983), "technology has been driving the world toward such commonality and the result is the emergence of global markets for standardized consumer products on a previously unimagined scale of magnitude" (p. 62). Marketing studies have highlighted the gains achievable through standardization, with economies of scale (Porter, 1998) and the potential to enhance product quality. Both of these were seen as significant advantages for Hollywood exports (Collins, 1986).

To attract larger audiences, global firms have had to make increasingly larger adaptations to local cultures, I believe, reflecting the theories of cultural proximity and the predominance of cultural-linguistic definition of markets. This process is often called *localization*. Chalaby (2005a) and

Straubhaar and Duarte (2005) both analyze how global companies, such as Murdoch, Hughes, Discovery, and others, have gone through a series of steps of localization as they tried to find audiences who would pay directly or indirectly for their channels. All of these producers have regionalized, using regional satellite systems, such as PanAmSat in Latin America, to carry their signals and opening regional offices to deal with national government rules for entry and operation, satellite carriers, and advertisers. Next, they have usually (often reluctantly) recognized the need to dub or subtitle their programming into local languages to increase their potential audience because not that many people speak English or other international languages well enough to watch without subtitles or dubbing.

Localization by transnational firms goes through four levels, according to a study of pan-European television channels by Chalaby (2002). First is creation of local advertising windows to bring in local commercial interests. Second is dubbing of television channels into local languages to make them more accessible to local audiences. Third is the incorporation of local programming services into the channel, focusing it more on the specificities of the local audience's culture. Fourth is breaking away from the centrally produced programming with local opt-outs where local programming is substituted for the central network channel programming, analogous to local affiliates opting away from central network programming in the United States.

Very few channels have gone to the last of Chalaby's four steps, genuine local production. One example in Latin America is a cartoon, *Mucha Lucha* (about Mexican wrestling, called *Lucha Libre*), created for Mexico and Mexican Americans; it appears only on the Mexican signal of Cartoon Network. Several examples exist in Asia. One of the first localized channels of Murdoch's Star TV was created for Taiwan, with extensive local news and debate, as well as local entertainment. It was sufficiently localized that Taiwanese referred to it as the "Fourth Channel," a popular supplement to the then-three government-controlled local television channels.

MTV is also an interesting example of considerable localization by local production. Its programmers originally thought they could send more or less the same U.S. signal everywhere but quickly discovered they had to localize or lose out to regional or local competitors, such as Channel V in Asia or several local music channels in Argentina. Chen (2004) argued that channels like MTV have been domesticated to fit markets such as Taiwan, where 70% of material is locally produced. To use Chalaby's (2006) categories, MTV now has a networked approach. It has 11 fully localized, differentiated channels just to cover Europe. They hybridize a mix of international and local contents, U.S. segments such as *Jackass* mixed with local music, in whatever degree of global versus local is deemed to be most successful in the local market. Chalaby (2006) argued that several U.S. companies are proving successful in localizing their products, adopting hybridization as a corporate strategy. In fact, Chalaby argued that European and other television companies will have to get out of their national silos and into thinking in similarly transnational terms in order to succeed.

Duarte (2001) and Straubhaar and Duarte (2005) created a somewhat different set of levels of localization. They focused on foreign firms' gradually increasing levels of commitment to local markets, reflected in increasingly expensive adaptations to the local market of their original imported programming. The first step was "changes in the original product to make it appear more like local ones" (Duarte, 2001, p. 82). Those steps include branding or rebranding channels in a more local way with interstitial images, promotions, and image adaptations, such as having Scooby Doo play soccer in Latin American promotions of the Cartoon Channel (Cornelio Mari, 2005). The second step was the use of local languages. The third step was employment of local talent, both in management and production (Duarte, 2001, pp. 164–165). The fourth step is the breakup of regionwide satellite channel feeds into subregional ones, targeted on specific subregions or countries. Examples might be the breakup of Star TV in Asia into dozens of channels specific to countries and languages, and the breakup of Sky Latin America into three feeds, to (1) Mexico, Central America, and northern South America; (2) Brazil; and (3) southern South America (each effectively headed by a key market: Mexico, Brazil, and Argentina or Chile, which present linguistic and cultural differences that had to be met by programming differentiation and localization). Duarte (2001) did not anticipate widespread local programming insertion or opt-outs, analogous to Chalaby's fourth step, so he did not create a specific step for them. Still a few channels, such as Discovery, have acquired local production staff and studios in larger markets like Brazil to produce local segments for Discovery productions (Risch, 2003), in addition to guaranteeing the quality of dubbing.

Instead of the fourth step of local program insert or acquisition anticipated by Chalaby (2002), what seems more frequent among some channels is international partnerships and coproduction. One example is the ongoing partnership and coproduction between Discovery Channel and the BBC. More relevant to the case of localization in a number of countries might be Discovery's more sporadic partnerships and coproductions with national broadcasters such as CCTV in China or government production funders such as the Media Development Authority in Singapore, with which Discovery cooperated on a 3-hour documentary history of Singapore, for example.

A number of channels seem to be not only localized, but perhaps more fully hybridized or glocalized. However, I argue that most of the truly glocalized or hybrid channels are produced by national or regional actors, not global ones, whose localization strategies tend to be conservative. Duarte (2001) noted that in Latin America, the most extensive changes in imported models and ideas come from local or national cable channels—for example, the extensive changes to formats such as the soap opera noted in Chapter 6—not from the global major channels. The latter are often unwilling to invest in unstable markets and perhaps also still underestimate the demand of national and regional audiences for cultural proximity and relevance.

Most localization strategies by global media firms and channels have been far more minimal. These networks have developed a variety of adaptation strategies, including language translations, production and coproductions at the local markets, multiple transmission feeds, and repackaging of programs and graphic vignettes. Some critics such as Cornelio Marí (2005) see these as a limited commercial customization by global operators to meet market demands. Certainly, it is difficult to look at the behavior of global firms and see much enthusiasm for creating new material to embrace and support local cultures. It seems they would prefer to indulge in straight-ahead media imperialism if only the audiences would go along.

If global channels were acting in a vacuum, they might be able to get away with cultural imperialism. However, a number of other actors at various levels—national television networks and regional and local networks and channels—have created programming that is far more localized, or perhaps more correctly, glocalized. Global channels faced severe difficulties competing against local, national, translocal, and geo-cultural regional producers, such as TVB in Hong Kong, Canal+ in France, Zee TV in India, Televisa in Mexico, or Al-Jazeera in Quatar. These latter producers continue to dominate the mass audience with greater local cultural appeal based in national and regional production.

## Broadcast Television Genre Flows Versus Satellite, Cable, and Internet Flows

How do several of these trends come together in the global flows of programs within genres and as part of genre-specific channels? These flows include not only individual programs, per se, but also the sale and flow of formatted programs, such as *Wheel of Fortune,* which can sell and flow either as a U.S. program export or as a licensed format. My discussion includes some transnational or global channels, such as MTV or Discovery, which are closely tied to the flow of both specific music videos and documentaries, as well as the genre ideas behind them, and concrete transnational coproductions in various countries of glocal videos and documentaries.

At the truly global level of television program flow and distribution, one of the most the most widely distributed and widely watched genres is action programs. These currently tend to be produced either in series formats (U.S. programs, such as *MacGyver,* reflected in the numbers in Table A.2) or in soap opera format, such as the martial arts dramas, often in historical costume form, produced by Hong Kong, China, and Taiwan (the various series that portray Shao-Lin Temple kung fu) and Japan (various samurai epics).

Despite apparent U.S. dominance of the action series genre, it is also one of the main areas in which other global producers are beginning to compete somewhat successfully compete with Hollywood. Chinese kung-fu and gangster series (from Hong Kong, China, and Taiwan) and Japanese samurai, animation, and superhero/science fiction series compete with and usually beat out U.S. action series in Asia, according to interviews by the author with television broadcasters in Taiwan and Indonesia in 1996 and in Singapore in 2006. Asian action series also compete with U.S. series in Latin America, South Asia, the Arab world, and elsewhere. Japanese animation and live-action fantasy hero shows (which often have plots similar to the animation) have been quite common on broadcast television for children in Brazil since the 1980s, because they are often cheaper than U.S. equivalents while being almost equally popular with children (my interviews in Brazil in 1990). German cop shows are one of the few European dramatic series that export well to other European countries, competing with U.S. cop shows (Buonanno, 2002).

Some countries that have experimented with television action series, such as Brazil with its late 1970s series *Plantão de Policia* (Police Beat), did not turn the genre into a mainstay of national production (Straubhaar, 1981). Audiences were more interested in other genres; the action-adventure genre was not well-suited to the national or local culture. Action stories involving heroes who use violence for good and bad guys who use action for evil are not a dominant cultural theme everywhere, at least not enough for this genre to become a dominant form of local production, particularly when they are expensive to produce. What many countries are doing, rather, is incorporating elements of the action-adventure genre into other genres such as melodrama. In both Latin America and Asia, for example, elements of action-adventure are often incorporated into soap operas. Brazilian telenovelas often have some conflict themes, which occasionally produce scenes of action adventure, within a story that is more likely to be dominated by traditional melodrama themes of family, upward mobility, and romance. One way that telenovela writers intend to keep male audiences involved with prime-time serial melodrama is by including thematic elements and key scenes that incorporate a good deal of action and conflict. Series and soaps from Hong Kong, Japan, Taiwan, and China likewise use elements of action-adventure themes and heroes such as kung fu experts or samurai in productions that otherwise emphasize family drama and history.

The other most widely distributed form is the feature film. Although these are not strictly speaking a television genre, they are widely syndicated and viewed on television channels. This includes both broadcast channels, which have shown more and more movies throughout the 1980s and 1990s, and transnational satellite or cable channels dedicated primarily to movies (such as Home Box Office). The most globally popular films also tend to be action-oriented. These two formats or genres are widely viewed by general audiences, which widely enjoy these two genres, regardless of age and social class or the cultural factors discussed earlier. As the television production and flow data in this chapter show, these are the imported programs that most often turn up on the most widely watched channels in the prime-time hours when most people watch. Action formats, high cost and technology intensive, are usually produced in the United States, China, Japan, and Hong Kong; and secondarily in Australia, Germany, Great Britain, and France.

There is also an enormous turn toward transnational coproduction, so that classifying the origin of films such as the *Lord of the Rings* trilogy can be difficult: The director, special effects team, locales, and many actors are from New Zealand; the books from which the films are adapted and many of the actors are British; and the financing and distribution are American. As Miller et al. (2005) pointed out, Hollywood is becoming less of a specific place and more of a global system of production.

The other most centrally produced global genre has been animation or cartoons. The cartoon as a genre was developed most prominently and earliest in the United States, which dominated global production and exports of the genre until the 1990s. U.S. ideas in the cartoon and animation genre clearly influenced Japanese and French producers. For example, Japanese animators reflect U.S. influences in action-oriented cartoons, such as science fiction and western, to some degree. Japanese science fiction cartoons, however, have taken different turns, including robots, futuristically armored heroes, and sexual comedy. Japanese animation also focuses on even more clearly local themes, such as high school life, high school romances, and— questionably, by U.S. broadcast standards—schoolgirl-focused soft-core pornography. Japan has competed quite effectively worldwide with animation (Iwabuchi, 2002). The U.S. animation industry, however, has also renovated its own output, coming up with shows such as *Sponge Bob Square Pants,* which is popular in many countries now, both on broadcast television and on cable channels like the Cartoon Network. There is also a considerable turn toward coproduction in animation, as Korean, Taiwanese, and Singaporean companies take over parts of the production process for U.S. or Japanese firms as a way to lower costs.

The next most popular global programs, those that flow to a number of countries from a limited number of producing nations, are international news, music videos, contemporary dramas, historical costume dramas, historical and contemporary soap operas, and documentaries on nature, science, or history. Audiences for these other global genres are more bounded by age, genre, and class limits than action shows and feature films. For example, Veii's (1988) study of audiences for imported American programs in Namibia showed that action programs such as *The A-Team* had the broadest audiences across class and age lines, in part because it was easy to understand and enjoy. On the other hand, imported soap operas such as *Falcon Crest* and situation comedies such as *The Cosby Show* required much greater verbal ability for comprehension and enjoyment, so their audiences tended to be higher class and better educated. These other global genres tend to show up on less widely popular channels, on targeted channels aimed at specific segmented audiences (such as CNN, which essentially targets globalized elites and international travelers in hotels), and at off-times, particularly daytime and late nights when smaller and less general audiences are watching.

Some of these genres are produced by only a few nations. International television news still tends to be dominated by the United States (CNN, APTV [Associated Press TV], CBS, ABC, and NBC) and the United Kingdom (BBC, Reuters Television, Sky News-Murdock). There is a newer global distribution of entire news channels, such as CNN, BBC, and others, primarily via satellite and cable television. Some of these channels gather quite a bit of their own news, particularly in the country or region where they are based, but they lean heavily on the news agency wholesalers for coverage, particularly video footage of events in other countries, particularly in developing world nations where even CNN and the NBC do not have bureaus to collect their own reports and footage (Paterson, 1996).

A number of regional news channels have, however, begun to rise in importance as part of the world television system. The most famous example in the early part of the new millennium is Al-Jazeera, a regional news channel based in Qatar and aimed at the Arabic-speaking region of the Middle East. Several regional news channels have also been tried in Asia and Latin America, although several of these have failed, for example, the Spanish-based ECO channel in Latin America. A new Latin America channel, TeleSur, explicitly modeled on Al-Jazeera as a successful alternative to U.S. and European news hegemony, was started in 2005 in Latin America, based in Venezuela and with principal support from Hugo Chavez, president of Venezuela (Calderón, 2005).

Documentary production is somewhat less dominated by a few producers, but the United States (PBS, Discovery Channel, History Channel, National Geographic), the United Kingdom (BBC, Granada, Channel Four), and Japan (NHK) produce or are at least partially involved in the coproduction of many of the documentaries that achieve global circulation. In documentaries, there has been a notable trend toward coproduction between one or more of the major global producers, broadcasters in other nations, and independent production companies (Hoskins, McFadyen, & Finn, 1997). The documentary channels are notable for the degree to which they have found a new audience segment in transnational satellite and satellite-to-cable television. Middle-class families—often those most able to afford pay-TV, satellite, or cable service—have greeted these channels with enthusiasm. A latent audience among poorer people awaits the time when such channels become affordable. Letalien (2002) discovered parents in a Rio de Janeiro *favela* (slum) prized the Discovery Channel because it was both educational and enjoyable for their children.

Discovery Channel programmers have found that transnational audiences want entertainment and education in the same package. They have also now begun to segment their audience within regions, targeting Singapore and Southeast Asia with material substantially different than Australia, for example. They are also taking advantage of increased channel capacities to target different lifestyle channels at men, women, travelers, and so on (my interviews at Discovery's Singapore office in 2006).

The United States and the United Kingdom initially dominated music videos, with distribution by MTV (Banks, 1996). After its successful development in the United States, MTV moved fairly quickly to establish channels abroad, usually in cooperation with local partners such as Star TV in Asia or TV Abril in Brazil. Even more interesting than the localization of various national and regional MTV versions are the growing number of local and regional music channels, which tend to adapt the music video genre much more extensively to local cultural preferences and to include much more local music. These are a good example of the tendency for locally originating channels, whether broadcast or satellite, to be extensively glocalized or hybridized compared with what comes from global conglomerates. Mexico- and Argentina-based and owned music channels on cable television have come to feature far more local music than the MTV Latino Channel, for example.

The localization and hybridization of music video production has proceeded rapidly, and the initial dominance of U.S.-based MTV channels declined much more quickly than U.S. prominence in news, documentaries, or cartoons. That seems to be due to both supply factors such as declining costs of production and growing music industries in many countries and to demand factors. Audiences seem to prefer a considerable quantity of local, national, and regional music in the adaptations of MTV in Asia, Europe, and Latin America.

Even the global or regionwide channels in the MTV style have had to localize more than some other kinds of genre channels. Star TV's Channel V, for instance, owned by Rupert Murdoch, has extensively localized the MTV formula. Maintaining MTV-style VJs and something of the distinctive MTV pattern of quick visual cuts and fast pacing, the channel has been split into multiple national or regional services, and content has been extensively localized with Japanese idol singers, Indian movie music, Cantonese pop ballads, and so on. The genre has been changed, too, as well as the cultural specifics of the content. Many more of the songs are slow romantic ballads, which lend themselves to slower pacing and different imagery (my interviews at Channel V in 2001).

Most European, Asian, Middle Eastern, and Latin American countries produce music videos. However, genre patterns flow globally and have considerable impact on the content, resulting in production of a hybrid. For example, by 2000, Turkey was programming and producing several different kinds of music videos, including imported MTV-Europe videos and local rock or pop videos made to look like them. There was also a local pop-music channel that produced Turkish pop videos, with MTV influences, similar to the local stations or networks that developed after the 1990s to produce and show local pop-music videos in Argentina, Mexico, and many other places. Perhaps most striking, Turkey had videos, filling most of a cable channel, that were cabaret music (what westerners might call belly-dancing) videos with a variety of more and less traditional dancers and music, shot with what seemed to be clear MTV influence in terms of pacing, shots, and so on. Music might vary from traditional to techno (Okur, 2000).

Music video has rapidly turned into a genre with a multilayered structure of production and distribution. Some videos, usually in English from U.S. or European groups, still circulate globally, distributed and promoted by the global music industry. Videos by popular Japanese or Cantonese music stars also circulate within both specific cultural-linguistic markets like greater China (Chan & Ma, 1996; Curtin, in press) and the larger geocultural market of East Asia (Iwabuchi, 2002). Many national music videos play only in Brazil or the United States or other places with fairly integrated national markets. Increasingly, videos cover a region within a nation, like the many regional music videos that interplay with song and dance numbers from regional films in India (Kumar, 2006). There are even fairly local videos, often based on live performance, that circulate in cities big enough to have a strong local music scene.

Costume dramas or historical dramas are a much more mixed phenomenon, produced at global, regional, and national levels. Some producing nations have achieved truly global markets and global general audiences for a limited number of productions. U.S. westerns were perhaps the first of these, but they have been supplemented by historical dramas from Hong Kong, Japan, Brazil, Mexico, Egypt, and India. These countries sell at least a few programs on a truly global level. They also sell a lot more programs to geocultural and increasingly transnational cultural-linguistic audiences, where culture and language proximities or similarities give them an advantage against other global producers.

One of the more dynamic current adaptations of the soap opera genre is the Asian historical-costume drama soap opera (which shows how genre lines can blur between cultures). Hong Kong and Japan have dominated global and regional production and sales in this arena. Both produce martial arts drama mixed with historical costume drama, as well as the latter by itself. The exports enjoy wide acceptance in an Asian market defined by the historical commonality of Chinese history and culture and the closely related adaptation of that culture to Japan (Iwabuchi, 2002). Historical costume drama has a regionwide cultural proximity for audiences. This might be seen as evidence of a broad cultural market based on the widely diffused Chinese cultural heritage. Most East and Southeast Asian countries are potential markets for the most popular costume dramas, particularly when dubbed into local languages or dialects (my interviews at TVB in 2001 and at MediaCorps in Singapore in 2006).

Other producers have entered into this regional market. China and Taiwan television stations export some of their best historical dramas and soap operas fairly widely. The immediate regional market is the cultural-linguistic market of greater China: China, Hong Kong, Singapore, and Taiwan (Chan, 1996). The programs can also be sold to regional satellite and cable stations. For example, both Chinese and Taiwanese soap operas about the only reigning Chinese empress have been exported throughout the regional market. Both Chinese and Hong Kong soap operas about a famously honest legendary Chinese judge, *Judge Bao,* have been exported to other Chinese-speaking countries such as Singapore (my interviews at MediaCorps in 2006).

On the other hand, there seems to be a clear preference for local versions of the classic Chinese historical drama form. Sylvia Liu at CTS, one of Taiwan's main broadcast networks, observed that "local productions are always more popular. They have more familiar faces with local stars. They seem more plausible to audiences. The Taiwanese production tempo is slower and more comfortable to the audience" (interview with author, June 1996). She noted that Taiwanese soap operas are less violent and less sexually explicit than Hong Kong productions, which suits the local audience better. Efforts have been made to sell the TVB or other Asian formats to other television producers in Southeast Asia or to coproduce channels in

Indonesia and other places that would take advantage of the formats' popularity while meeting demand for local production (my interviews at TVB in 2001). With a relatively small population, Singapore national television, for example, has found it useful to coproduce certain kinds of drama and other formats with producers from China or Taiwan (my interviews at MediaCorps in 2006).

As Table A.1 and discussion in Chapter 6 show, countries increasingly produce their own soap operas. They take the soap opera or melodrama genre idea and adapt it to local circumstances, as the telenovela example in Chapter 6 demonstrated. In regional genre production, a number of stories get copied and passed from one country to another. In Latin America, *Simplemente Maria,* about a servant girl who works her way up to be a seamstress (Singhal, Obregon, & Rogers, 1994), and *The Right to Be Born,* about a man trying to find out who his parents are, were both produced in a number of countries at various times, and different versions were made in the same countries over a period of time. However, some soap operas are still imported, both from global and regional producers. As discussed above, Table A.3 shows imports from regional producers.

There is also a growing format trade in melodrama. Scripts for melodrama have been marketed within regions such as Latin America or Asia for quite a long time: since the 1950s in Latin America, building on a 1930s and 1940s market for radionovela scripts. Full-fledged format sales are more recent. In 2006, U.S. television showed a production, called *Ugly Betty,* based on a popular 1999 Colombian telenovela, which had been exported to a number of markets, including the U.S. Hispanic market, as *Yo soy Betty, la fea (I am Ugly Betty).* Several Latin American adaptations have been made of *Desperate Housewives.* Whereas at one time melodrama plot ideas might simply have been borrowed across borders, producers now see advantages in paying for a licensed package that makes production quicker and easier.

# 8

# Multiple Proximities Between Television Genres and Audiences

## Choosing Between National, Transnational, and Global Television

What allows a reality show, telenovela, or game show to become a transnational hit? The concept of cultural proximity (Straubhaar, 1991, this volume) and previous success in the national market are preconditions but not completely accurate predictors of transnational success. As discussed in Chapter 2, the nature of cultural-linguistic markets (Sinclair, Jacka, & Cunningham, 1996; Wilkinson, 1995) helps explain some of the success of programs like the telenovela within Latin America, but not into new markets. Another useful idea is the emergence of subgenres within

AUTHOR'S NOTE: This chapter is coauthored by J. Straubhaar and A. C. La Pastina. Parts of this chapter are adapted from A. C. La Pastina and J. Straubhaar, "Multiple Proximities Between Television Genres and Audiences: The Schism Between Telenovelas' Global Distribution and Local Consumption," *Gazette, 67*(3), 271–288 (2005). Used with permission from Sage Publications.

the telenovela that speak to different audiences within both national and regional cultural-linguistic audiences (Hernandez, 2001).

How could a Mexican telenovela, produced in a foreign market, be more attractive to viewers than a national product that has better production values and a subtext that deals with important issues within the nation? This seems to be the dilemma of reception of transnational products. Most of the data indicates that viewers prefer locally produced programs to foreign imports (a line of inquiry started by de Sola Pool in the 1970s, which Straubhaar articulated as cultural proximity in 1991). Nevertheless, some of the transnational success of Brazilian (and Latin American) telenovelas seems to indicate a trend that could challenge this truism. Some of these programs were successful in spite of abundant local production in the receiving country—for example the Brazilian telenovela *Terra Nostra* in Italy.

We argue that audience preferences are indeed formed as part of the overall trend toward cultural proximity within both national and cultural-linguistic boundaries. However, as Iwabuchi (2002) pointed out, cultural proximity must be seen not as an essential quality of culture or audience orientation but rather as a shifting phenomenon in dialectical relation to other cultural forces. Within the logics of cultural proximity and cultural attraction in cultural-linguistic spaces, many other forces also apply. In this chapter, we examine several. First is the attraction or proximity of genres, from the virtually worldwide attraction of melodrama as an overall or macro genre (Martín-Barbero, 1993), to subgenres within the telenovela (already a subgenre of melodrama). Genres and subgenres can exert attractions to specific audiences that cross and even contradict the overall logic of cultural proximity, although genres tend to work within cultural proximity most of the time. Second is the sense of shared historical experience of specific groups within nations. For example, contemporary audiences in southern Italy seem to share a specific sense of cultural proximity to parts of Brazilian history defined by Italian immigrants who largely came from southern Italy. So those southern Italians might choose against their cultural proximity to national Italian production, preferring imported Brazilian telenovelas that focus on their shared history of emigration (from Italy) and immigration (to Brazil).

This study examines the interplay of several forces in international television. The primary focus is various competing, seemingly contradictory trends in television production and flow. Although many countries create more and more of their own television programs (Chapter 6), television programs continue to flow between countries (Chapter 7). Those flows include increasing numbers of telenovelas and other genres flowing to unusual cultural spaces and markets, beyond those predicted by a strict appeal to cultural similarity or proximity (Straubhaar, 1991). In this chapter, we also examine some of the complex, even contradictory forms and audience appeals of other kinds of proximity: genre proximity, value proximity, and thematic proximity. These theoretical categories for television flow are then considered within the context of an ongoing hybridization of television genres, which implies an underlying hybridization among their appeals to their audiences as well. To understand these new, more complex flows requires exploring and understanding multiple forms of proximity between the cultures—global, regional, and national—represented in imported television programs and the audiences that choose to watch them. Cultural and other proximities must be understood in terms of their relationship to cultural capital, so we explore these ideas both theoretically and empirically via interviews in Brazil.

Another major focus of this chapter is indeed the critical role of cultural capital (Bourdieu, 1984, 1986) in structuring interests and choices of television audiences. Reception of television is guided by various individual and cultural proximities to local and national cultures, values, and so on. But those proximities are structured by a variety of situations in which people find themselves. To paraphrase an often quoted line of Marx's 18th Brumaire, "People make choices but not in the circumstances of their choosing."[1] As in earlier sections of this book, Bourdieu's forms of capital, cultural, economic, and social are useful ways to represent the ways in which people's agency and choices work with resources and constraints based in class and other social formations. We will explore those ideas via a case study of Brazil.

## Culture-Bound Reception and Multiple Proximities

One way to begin thinking about the complex attractions between cultural texts and audiences is that cultural proximity has multiple levels. People have multilayered, complex cultural identities, which will be explored even further in the next chapter. Aspects of these identities are geographic or spatial: local, subnational regional, national, supranational regional. Other aspects are purely cultural or linguistic, as when migrants continue to have a strong layer of identity linked to their home language or culture. Other aspects might be religious, as when Catholic or Islamic messages or cultural products appeal across geographical and cultural boundaries. Others might be ethnic, as when various African-descendent subcultures across the Americas feel common ties because of their African heritage.

Much of a person's cultural identity continues to be local or linked to a subnational region. Texans are almost all proud of being Texans, but those in Austin and Dallas are likely to construct *Texan* differently and to be proud of their city/local identity as well. People actually born in the city of São Paulo distinguish themselves as *Paulistanos,* compared to *Paulistas* or people born in the state of São Paulo, even though those Paulistas may have lived in the capital city most of their lives. These definitions of locality and local identity are complex and subject to ongoing redefinition in the interaction of global, national, and local forces (Iwabuchi, 2002). For example, since Hong Kong became part of China, Chinese there have reconfigured their identity from simply identifying with greater China while affiliated more closely with their city to actually being Chinese citizens with a very special local history, along with government permission to have different local institutions.

In terms of television reception, the local culture or a religious or ethnic subculture, rather than at the national culture, may be the locus of proximity between a variety of television texts and viewers. Even within a country, local viewers may not understand or identity with all elements of the national culture as projected in national television. For example, Straubhaar is from Idaho, in the rural U.S. intermountain West. Many family members told him they did not like or identify with the popular *Seinfeld,* thinking it "much too New York." In one of the cases explored below in some depth, villagers in the rural northeast of Brazil found many barriers that kept them from identifying with national Brazilian television programming. In some cases, these Brazilians found imported Mexican programs more proximate, relevant, or appealing to their own tastes and sexual relationship values, which indicates the existence of complex, multiple proximities across both spatial relationships (local-national) and cultural relationships (traditional sexual values related to Latin American Catholicism).

There can be strong local values and historical alliances between the original culture of the television program's text and the local culture where it is received. Local values may more closely resemble values in other nations than the values represented in the core television-producing centers of the same nation. There can be a considerable gap between national cities, which have their own distinct cultural formations, and the rural and regional areas of their nations, which consume the television and other cultural products that the metropolis produces. Rural areas may have their own distinct subnational regional cultures; Hannerz (1996), for example, defines *locals* in contrast to *cosmopolitans,* who are more oriented to either national or global cultures. Rio de Janeiro, Brazil, produces much of the prime-time entertainment consumed on Brazilian television but has different values and mores than the rural interior of Brazil, which is noted for being far more socially conservative. Particularly within globalization, many major cities that are home to cultural industries become transnationalized as global cities (Sassen, 2004). They may be hybridizing or glocalizing global ideas in a manner quite distinct from the experience of some of the less urban (or less glocalized) audiences for which they produce cultural products.

People may look across national boundaries for ideological or historical content that fits their own values and beliefs. In one of the two cases noted below, southern Italians had specific cultural capital to draw on in their interpretations of the narratives they received, both from within Italy and from Brazil. In a similar case, southern Italians, particularly older women, identified more strongly with more traditional Catholic narratives in Argentine telenovelas than with much of the national production of Italian television (Del Negro, 2003). This raises the question of ideological, value-based, or thematic proximity across cultures and national borders. This study will explore some of those possible forms of proximity. It will focus on proximities based on topic or theme, on values, on ideology or world-view, on the qualities and characteristics of genres per se, and on ethnicity. It will also consider the attraction of television programs that are seen as cosmopolitan, modern, exotic, sexy and violently exciting. The relationship between locality, national identity, regional identities, and broad cultural-linguistic identities can be quite multilayered and complex. Much of the basic discussion of local, national, and cultural-linguistic proximities is discussed earlier in this book, so here we focus on competing proximities.

## Genre Proximity

Some genres are in themselves easy to share across diverse cultures. Rafael Obregon (1995) discussed the idea of genre proximity, emphasizing that the common structure of melodrama covers many cultures. Melodrama builds on underlying oral structures, formulas, and archetypes that can be shared by cultures. The underlying structure of melodrama has offshoots in almost all parts of world, so melodrama can reach past cultural differences. Many, if not most cultures seem to have experienced some form of serial storytelling rather like melodrama, even before television became available to them. These kinds of storytelling have flowed between countries for centuries before television in forms such as the chapbook (or *Cordel,* in Iberia and Latin America; see Martin-Barbero, 1993). The flow and adaptation of a new form of storytelling such as modern television soap opera is facilitated by the global spread of earlier roots of the same genre. An example that has been discussed in a number of publications is the successful transplant of the explicitly educational telenovela from Mexico to Asia (Singhal & Rogers, 1999).

Familiarity and a sense of proximity with relatively new genres can also be cultivated over time. For example, Hollywood has controlled global film distribution at key eras since World War I to such a degree that people who wanted to see movies often saw U.S. films, even if they might have preferred local, national, regional, or cultural-linguistic productions (Guback & Varis, 1986). Such prolonged exposure can create a sense of familiarity, so that aspects of U.S. culture became a sort of secondarily proximate culture for many people. Gitlin (2001) for example, talked about how the United States became a familiar second culture for many people around the world. Milly Buonanno (2002) observed that most European nations are producing more and more of their own prime-time programming, including drama, building on a fairly strong sense of national cultural proximity. However, she argued that cultural proximity as a trend among programmers, producers, and audiences was going to an extreme. People seem to want to watch their own culture on television, plus the second culture that became familiar during previous media exposure, that of the United States. Buonanno feared that other forms of possible proximity, such as historical ties to neighboring European nations, were being minimized in a sort of dualism between primary national cultural proximity and a sort of generalized secondary proximity felt with U.S. cultural products.

One strong secondary layer of proximity, depending on the television program genre, does seem to be programs from the United States. Again, the production and flow data in Chapter 7 show that the United States is still a strong exporter of feature films, action series, dramatic series, and cartoons to a number of countries. U.S. material does best in its own cultural-linguistic space or market, that of other English-speaking countries with strong Anglo-colonial heritages and strong historical migration from the United Kingdom, such as Australia, Canada, the English-speaking Caribbean, New Zealand, and the United States (Abram, 2004). Beyond that, however, the strong presence of U.S. cultural products in so many media over the years has created a sense of familiarity or proximity with them. So when genres are expensive or difficult to create, like animation or action series, or when they have become strongly identified with U.S. images and themes, like action series, then the sense of secondary proximity with U.S. cultural products can be maintained.

Another way to see this form of proximity, according to Iwabuchi (2002), is a desired proximity with modernity. In this analysis, U.S. cultural products represent a proximity based on not true cultural familiarity but desire or aspiration. People watched U.S. programs to see what global modernity looked like (Featherstone, 1990b).

## Cultural Shareability

A specific useful concept that to some degree opposes the notion of cultural proximity is cultural shareability, advanced by Singhal and Udornpim (1997). They noted that successfully exported television programs often share a language, such as the simplified export-oriented Spanish of *Simplemente María* (Singhal et al., 1994). Shareability refers to common values, images, archetypes and themes across cultures that permit programs to flow across cultural boundaries.

In an analysis of the globally marketed Japanese television soap opera *Oshin,* Singhal and Udornpim (1997) attributed part of that series' cultural shareability to its use of cultural archetypes that span a number of cultures. They built on psychologist Carl Jung's description of archetypes as independent of mediation, existing in individuals worldwide (p. 174). For *Oshin*'s broad cross-cultural appeal, Singhal and Udornpim cited the universal archetype of "self-seeking individuation," of self-determination, endurance, and strength. They also noted an archetype of the main character as a "disobedient female," a woman who defies oppressive social constraints. Third, they noted an archetype of "heroic struggle" and resistance against enemies, poverty, and misfortune until the heroine ultimately succeeded. We might add a fourth archetype common to soap operas in many cultures, the individual's or family's upward mobility from poverty to material success.

Cultural proximity as a force in media choices, then, exists in a dynamic tension with other motives and attractions. Cultural proximity is also limited by three other factors. First, there are material and structural limits at the production level on many cultures' ability to produce media products to meet the potential demand that cultural proximity might generate. Second, there are structural barriers of income or economic capital at the individual reception level, which keep many people from getting access to media, particularly new channels from satellite TV or the Internet (Mosco, 1996). Third, there are less tangible barriers of cultural capital at the individual level, which keep people from choosing or understanding some kinds of media, particularly those that use other languages or presume an in-depth knowledge of other cultures.

## Thematic Proximity

One clear factor that emerges from research on the flow of telenovelas and other kinds of television drama between countries is that certain themes and issues in telenovelas can appeal across cultures, particularly between developing countries. To some degree, the *Oshin* research shows that the themes of hard work and patience leading to upward mobility were appealing to people in many countries (Singhal & Udornpim, 1997).

People have wondered what audiences in eastern Europe, southern Europe, Africa, and China have found intriguing about telenovelas. Part of the appeal, certainly, is melodrama itself, according to research about the reception of Mexican telenovelas in Russia and Cameroon. Audiences identify with the romantic ups and downs of characters, along with the family drama that is featured in all melodrama (Tchouaffe, 2002).

However, some preliminary interviews by the authors with television professionals and audience members from eastern Europe also suggest that a number of themes in Latin American telenovelas are relevant to audiences in eastern Europe. These include commonalities of rural, regional pasts that appeal both to rural people and those who have migrated to cities. Related are themes and images of movement to cities, images of city life, and adjustment to city life, economic change, and industrial work. Most telenovelas show themes of families and love within urban stresses. Also prominent in most telenovelas are themes of upward mobility and hopeful images of middle-class life that people aspire to obtain.

## Value Proximity

Another telenovela appeal across cultures builds on shared values. Many telenovelas, both modern urban ones and historical, regional, or rural ones, show religion and other values under challenge from modern life. Many cultures facing rapid industrialization or economic change can relate to that.

Some cultures have a specific shared religious heritage such as Catholicism. At least one study has shown that Latin American telenovelas have considerable success in communicating common values with viewers of a conservative Catholic orientation in traditional sectors of Italian society, particularly in southern Italy (Del Negro, 2003). Globally diffused values of work and upward mobility go along with the themes mentioned here. For example, the Japanese soap *Oshin*, successful in many countries, showed a hard-working, survivor heroine (Singhal & Udornpim, 1997).

# Cultural Capital, Cultural Proximity, and the Audience

Cultural proximity builds on cultural capital, but it is a separate dimension of identity. Cultural capital focuses on the sources of knowledge that permit people to make choices among media and other sources of information and culture. Cultural proximity is more of a disposition or a tendency toward the use of cultural capital in a certain way. Forms of cultural capital, in terms of what people know about other countries and cultures, can lead them toward or away from cultural proximity, the tendency to prefer media products from their own culture or the most similar culture. This section builds on a series of in-depth interviews Straubhaar conducted in Brazil, 1989–2005.

Education is a principal source of cultural capital (Bourdieu, 1984). In the case of Brazil, basic education is often nationally focused, reflecting national languages, nationally authorized and focused textbooks, and teacher training to national standards. However, postsecondary education, as the interviews conducted in the Brazilian case reflect, tends to increase exposure to a more globally focused set of knowledge. Basic education might then accentuate an audience focus on cultural proximity whereas higher education might open interests to a more global view.

Family is the second principal source of cultural capital for Bourdieu (1984). Differences are particularly evident in families' daily routines and their daily cultural consumption. Various families emphasize different levels of culture—some very local, some national, some global. In the Brazilian case, differences were fairly consistent with social class stratification: Lower class families were more locally oriented in their knowledge and habits, working-class and middle-class families were more national, and elites were more global. In their media choices, lower-class, working-class and lower-middle-class viewers made more local and national choices, based on cultural proximity, than the upper middle classes and elites.

Families and schools, along with neighborhoods, are primary grounds of another source of cultural capital, personal and group networks. We particularly highlight peer networks, friendships, and continuing ties with schoolmates. British and American sociological work on television audiences and their choices highlights the importance of such networks (Morley, 1992), as does Latin American research on cultural choice and interpretation, or mediation (Martín-Barbero, 1993).

These personal networks are particularly important in Brazil, which is often characterized as a personalistic society where status and contacts matter greatly (Da Matta, 1997). At one extreme, lower class audiences have localized networks that stress localized cultural capital and a localized version of cultural proximity, preferring local music to national music, for example. At another extreme, elites often have family and school networks that are global, leading them to direct personal experience with global friends and contacts, perhaps to minimize cultural proximity, acquire a more globalized sense of personal identity, and pursue what they see as more cosmopolitan or global media choices.

Family income and interests often define another key source of cultural capital: travel. If some families never travel beyond their immediate locale while others get to know more of their nation by travel, then the former will have a more localized cultural capital while the latter are more nationalized in knowledge and interests. If some families can afford and have interest in international travel, that creates a globalized form of cultural capital that may, again, minimize national or local cultural proximity and stress more global interests.

Religion is another major source of cultural capital. Religion often cuts across social class lines in a unique manner, but actual religious practices in daily life tend to vary somewhat with social class, at least in Brazil. Although most Brazilians are at least nominally Catholic, actual forms of practice vary widely. Furthermore, lower class and working-class respondents are increasingly more likely either to be involved with syncretic religions that mix Catholicism with African traditions, such as *candomblé* or *macumba,* or to change religions and join the rapidly growing evangelical Protestant groups (Chestnut, 1997). Still, activity in most of these religions reinforces a certain sense of local or national tradition and values, which seems to reinforce a sense of cultural proximity. The exception may be some Protestant groups, which maintain very strong ties to U.S. churches.

Nonreligious associations such as unions, professional organizations, neighborhood associations, sports clubs, and hobby and interest groups also provide important inputs to cultural capital. In Latin America, Martín-Barbero (1993) indicated that most of these associations reinforce localized cultural dispositions and forms of knowledge, a conclusion that is confirmed in the authors' Brazilian interviews discussed later. However, some fraction of the viewing public is drawn into interpersonal associations that help create national, supranational, or global cultural capital, as when someone joins a national or international professional association. However, such direct global interpersonal interaction presupposes both economic capital or wealth and other forms of cultural capital, such as education and family connections.

These are the major channels of cultural capital: schooling, family practices, family networks, personal networks, travel, religion, groups, or associations. These help determine or mediate mass-media choices (Martín-Barbero 1993). However, the media themselves are also a source of cultural capital. The relationship is not a simple one of effects, either of media affecting values and ideas or even of values and ideas from other sources cleanly determining media choices and likewise determining interpretations of media contents. Mass media such as television are a source of cultural capital. However, other sources of cultural capital also mediate choices for mass media. The interaction is complex.

Together with education, family, networks, travel, and religion, media help construct meanings for three other principle bases of cultural capital that we wish to add to the discussion: ethnicity, age, and gender. Although ethnicity, age, and gender are in some ways physical characteristics, the meaning assigned to those characteristics is socially constructed (Lorber & Farrell, 1991) and becomes part of the cultural capital used by people in making media choices.

Ethnicity is important in the construction of national or regional cultural-linguistic markets. In fact, ethnic identity can be seen as constituting a type of cultural capital. The ethnic makeup of a television program's cast affects its visual appeal to audiences. If people can recognize themselves or a familiar or desired ethnic type on screen, then that would add to the cultural proximity of a program. Ethnic appeal can come from actual ethnicity or ethnic ideals. Within Brazil, for example, broadcasters differ over whether to broadcast an ethnic ideal that appeals to more affluent consumer classes, largely European in ethnicity, or whether to appeal to the larger television audience, which is about half Afro-Brazilian. The main network, TV Globo, has often been accused of underrepresenting Afro-Brazilians in both programming and commercials (Leslie, 1991). In an effort to segment the national audience and compete with the dominant national network, two other networks, SBT and Record, are creating interview, reality, game, and variety programming that addresses the working and lower classes' sense of identity or cultural capital. To do this they use participants who are ethnically more representative of the diversity of the Brazilian audience.

Age is sometimes seen as a crucial differentiating demographic characteristic in the preference for globalized culture, almost a basis of cultural capital in itself. Many observers have noted that younger people tend to be more involved in global or at least transnational cultural patterns than older people. Young people in Brazil are divided by class in terms of their television program preferences.

Gender images and concepts about gender roles are also elements of cultural capital that bear on preferences for cultural proximity or cosmopolitanism. If *Baywatch* shows roles for women that clash strongly with locally or nationally held ideas about how women ought to dress and behave, then those local traditions—reflected in and reinforced by religion, family practices, forms of education, and so on—function as forms of cultural capital that will likely lead many people to avoid the program. Those sorts of individual and household choices, accumulated across a culture and especially when articulated and reinforced by leaders like the Iranian clerics, can result in a violent rejection of imported culture, as during the Iranian revolution. On the other hand, many people like to watch *Baywatch,* as its export success shows, so contradictory and dialectic processes are at work within the audience between cultural proximity and the attraction of foreign cultural products.

Class and age seem to be directly related to general preferences for global, regional, national, or local culture. Gender is often tied to cultural use patterns that are less general, more specific to genre. Gender is a powerful factor in patterns of interest, use, and interpretation of a number of television genres, as shown powerfully in La Pastina's interviews in Macambira, Brazil, discussed later.

## Cultural Capital and Media Choices in Brazil

Cultural affinities create forms of cultural capital that inform cultural proximity. Such affinities may be specific factors such as linguistic commonalities, shared religious histories, gender roles, moral values, common aspirations, common histories with colonialism, shared art forms, shared music forms, similar forms of dress, character types and stereotypes, and ideas about genre, storytelling, and pacing. Perceived cultural similarities also might include ethnic types, gender types, dress, style, gestures, body language, and lifestyle. Perceived cultural relevance seems to include news and discussion topics, definitions of humor, familiar stars and actors, and audience knowledge about other lifestyles. Images and values include perceptions of other countries and peoples, opinions or evaluations of them, and values about marriage, family relationships, importance of material goods, work, and ideas about where and how to live. These specific kinds or forms of cultural capital add up. By interviewing audience members about what their knowledge and dispositions are in these terms, one can get a sense of their approach to media choices.

To examine cultural capital formation and its relation to television choices, Straubhaar has conducted a series of in-depth interviews in Brazil over a 15-year period, from 1989 through 2005. In São Paulo, he talked with working-class, lower-middle-class, middle-class, upper-middle-class, and upper-class people. He conducted interviews with the same range of classes, as well as urban and rural poor, in Salvador from 1989 through 1994 and 2003 through 2005 and in Ilheus, Bahia, from 1989 through 1994. These last two cities also provided an opportunity to compare Afro-Brazilians with people from São Paulo, who are disproportionately of European origin. He conducted almost 160 interviews from 1989 to 2005. About 45 people were reinterviewed at least once over the years. Thus, he had a chance to observe both some changes and, even more, consistencies in audience choices and class backgrounds.

In his study, the elite respondents are defined as those who have at least $2,500 a month in income and own all major consumer appliances and a nice car. Although some of the older elite are self-made and uneducated, the younger members almost all have university education. In terms most relevant to globalization of media and culture, they engage in international travel, learn foreign languages, and have access to satellite and cable television, to computers and the Internet, and to all print media, often including foreign-language media. The most distinguishing thing about them, from these interviews, is that they have direct, unmediated personal access to global culture via travel, work, education, and other direct experiences. They also often aspired to a lifestyle defined in global terms by both media and direct experience, such as travel to the United States or Europe. This group is potentially truly globalized, although many of the elite do not use their potential global access and have primarily national mediated and personal cultural and informational experience.

The upper middle class tends to have most of the same characteristics but lacks some of the economic capital that would provide access to frequent international travel and to the kind of private primary and secondary schooling that permits the elite to get into the best universities, including education abroad. Upper-middle-class people do not have the same access to global interpersonal connections, so their access to global information and culture is usually mediated via mass media and Brazilian schooling. This group may aspire to achieve more direct global experience by travel, education, and so on, and they also desire at least some of the lifestyle defined in part by global media images received at home via television and movies; they are more likely to pursue global media content within Brazil on radio, television, cable/satellite TV, the Internet, and film.

The middle class in Brazil is largely defined in national terms. The working definition emerging from interviews was that middle class has consistently meant a car, traditionally a landline telephone, recently mobile phones for most family members, a respectable dwelling (defined in fairly local terms), a few major appliances such as a refrigerator, and good prospects for at least a high school education, with hopes of university. Many would now have computers but not necessarily Internet access, although that is growing quickly. Middle-class people were nationally rather than globally focused in media consumption. Their material aspirations seem to be formed primarily by the dominant national media, such as television advertising, lifestyle images from telenovelas and variety shows, and, to lesser degree, international music and foreign movies that are televised after 10 p.m., although many middle-class people don't stay up for those. Their experience of the global is almost entirely filtered through Brazilian media, although some middle-class people are willing to spend scarce resources for international media such as pay-TV. Within Brazilian media, they are more likely to have access to print media, which carry more global content, as well as television and radio.

The lower middle class and working class are defined in terms of having decent housing (as defined locally), a fairly steady income and employment, a mobile phone, and usually some education. They often seek Internet access at free or cheap community technology centers, cyber cafés, or game-oriented LAN (local area network) houses. They aspire to the national middle-class lifestyle, largely as defined by what is shown in the telenovelas, especially a better house, a car, more appliances, and maybe a vacation. Their global images are formed almost exclusively by television and music because print media are usually priced out of their reach, although they often try to read them when they get access. The lower middle and working classes often do not realize which brands they aspire to are global—things are framed almost exclusively within a national context for them, in terms of both advertising and product placement with programs.

The poor earn little, often well under U.S.$100 a month, or less than the minimum wage. They can afford little consumption, although most of those who have a fixed dwelling also have a television. Many of their homes have a dirt floor, and relatively few have refrigerators or stoves, but most have a television. The poor aspire to the necessities of life, defined in local terms in style of food, clothing, toiletries, and so on. Few poor adults have anything beyond 4 years of primary education, although poor teenagers have begun to benefit from increased emphasis on public schools in the past 10 years under the Cardoso and Lula governments. Media access is either radio, which almost all have, or television: more than 60% of rural dwellers have a TV, compared to more than 90% of the urban poor. (Brazil is now 82% urban, which shifts the balance toward more ubiquitous television viewing.) Their media consumption tends to be local, provincial/regional, or national. They expressed little interest in foreign or global content in these interviews.

## Media Access, Cultural Capital, and Class in Brazil

Many rural and extremely poor urban Brazilians are only beginning to acquire cultural capital via media and schooling. As noted, however, even most poor Brazilians are coming into increasing contact with radio and television.

In rural areas, access to television varies with electrification, proximity to or coverage by broadcast television signals, access to satellite dishes, and economic capital or income. The very poorest 10% or so are not geographically stable, migrating to look for land or work. Increasingly, those who are stable on land or have a permanent urban dwelling have access to television. Recent migrants to urbanized areas acquire television before almost anything else. Rural dwellers are working hard to acquire television. For example, in the Cajueiro land reform community, which was settled about 20 years ago near Una and Ilheus, Bahia, less than a third of the 55 settled families in 1994 had television, although people could watch a solar-powered set in the settlement school sometimes.

The urban poor may have more contact with media, but it is often limited to watching television with neighbors or in public places. Like rural people, those without permanent dwellings are least drawn into media contact with either the national or the global. Interviews in 1989 and 1994 with homeless people in São Paulo showed that most of their cultural capital was based on interpersonal contacts within an oral culture context.

Interviews from 1989 to 2003 in São Paulo reflect that poor and working-class people often make television viewing choices that are somewhat different from the national majority. While they watch the dominant popular culture in TV Globo's telenovelas, they frequently turn away from TV Globo to watch other channels that target programs more directly at this very substantial number of urban poor, working poor, working-class, and lower-middle-class people. Interviews with poor people in Salvador, Bahia, found similar patterns, but even more turning away from TV Globo, except for its telenovelas and news. Poor people there were more likely to watch two networks, SBT and Record, which were targeting poor, working-class, and lower-middle-class viewers.

Media sources, particularly radio and television, are important for most working-class people as a primary source of cultural capital. Among those interviewed, almost all global and cultural-linguistic regional cultural capital comes to working-class or poor people via media or, to a lesser degree, formal schooling. Working-class schooling is often limited, however, to four to six years of primary school, which limits schooling's role in cultural capital formation. However, working-class parents and youth who have a certain amount of stability in the city often start focusing more on the school as a source of educational capital for upward mobility.

Working-class people, based on a locally or nationally oriented store of cultural capital, tend to make media choices that reinforce what is familiar or culturally proximate to them. Working-class people are much more likely to listen to radio stations that play only national or local music genres, such as *samba*, *forró* (northeastern dance music), *Axé* (samba plus reggae), or Musica Popular Brasileiro (MPB-Brazilian pop music), whereas upper-middle or upper-class interviewees were more likely to listen to stations that played either U.S./European pop music or a mixture of imported and Brazilian music.

Working-class print media exposure is much more limited and largely more national than the print media usage of the upper middle and upper class. Working-class people mostly read magazines and newspapers, rather than books, a trend noted across Latin America by Martin-Barbero (1993). The books read by working-class interviewees tended to be either national popular literature or popular U.S./European genre novels in translation.

Working-class Brazilians travel between cities by bus while the upper middle class and upper class go by airplane. It is revealing, therefore, to compare what is in a large bookstore or newsstand in a São Paulo bus station with what is in an equivalent shop in the São Paulo airport. The bus station shop has more magazines, comics, and cheaply printed chapbooks and pamphlets than books, although the book section is of a respectable size. Aside from the comics, many of which are Disney, Marvel, and D.C. translations, and the translated novels, almost everything else is national in origin. At the airport, the same national newspapers, magazines, and books are available, along with the translated comics and novels. The selection in the latter two is different, with more expensive book editions and more H.Q. or "high quality" comic translations. What is most noticeable is much more foreign literature in translation and a significant number of foreign-language books, magazines, and newspapers aimed at both international travelers and those Brazilians with elite cultural capital, such as sufficient foreign-language skills to read comfortably for pleasure in another language.

The cultural capital of those actually in the middle class still largely comes from television. Middle-class television choices are somewhat different; this audience may disdain the working class-oriented variety shows of SBT and focus much more on the telenovela-oriented contents of TV Globo. Middle-class cultural capital is more heavily supplemented beyond television, however, by education, print media use, personal contacts, and organizations such as churches, clubs, and networks of friends from school. Several newspaper critics and this study's interviewees noted that one of the key differences between working class and middle class is that the latter has more nonmediated options for information, entertainment, and leisure.

Middle-class Brazilians are somewhat more globalized than the working class in the kinds of media choices they make. Middle-class interviewees are much more likely to stay up after 10 p.m. so they can watch the American movies that are typically shown then on several channels. Such viewing expresses cultural capital already acquired through schooling and media and also reinforces a more globalized cultural capital. Movies in the cinema houses have become very expensive, so even middle-class people go to them fairly infrequently. But between late movies on television and rented movies on video or DVD, feature films seem to be an important source of American and global cultural capital for a fair number of middle-class Brazilians, whereas American or other imported movies do not seem as important to working-class or poor Brazilians, who generally prefer the national programs broadcast on television. However, even middle-class or upper-middle-class Brazilians usually prefer prime-time telenovelas to watching movies on video, even when they have the VCR or DVD sometimes gathering dust on a shelf. While some middle-class Brazilians have satellite dishes or cable connections, those interviewed for this study were more likely to use them to get a good-quality signal from TV Globo than to buy pay-TV packages that would deliver dozens of extra channels in English. (In comparison, elite Brazilians tend to use cable TV heavily to watch U.S. programming.)

A greater degree of globalization, both in media choices and in direct personal experience, is perhaps the main thing that divided upper-middle-class and upper-class interviewees from those in the middle class and working class. The upper class are characterized by a number of globalized attributes: language skills, particularly in English; higher education, including study abroad or aspirations to do so; international travel, particularly to the United States and Europe; occupations that lend themselves to contact with people in the United States and Europe or, increasingly, Asia; interest in U.S. and European lifestyles; knowledge of those lifestyles; identification with European standards of beauty, including ethnicity; detailed knowledge of both high culture and popular culture in the United States and Europe. Upper-class Brazilians are often divided about whether their global cultural capital is linked to Europe or to the United States, particularly those who were at least partially educated abroad and who learned English rather than another European language.

The upper-middle-class interviewees often aspire to this direct experience with global culture. Their actual experience is usually more heavily mediated, however. Most upper-middle-class Brazilians have visited Miami or Disneyworld, but they have otherwise traveled far less than the elite. Upper-middle-class global cultural capital is usually focused more on the United States and less on Europe, perhaps because travel to the United States is cheaper, study of English is more prevalent, and U.S. culture is much more widely available in mediated forms. Upper-middle-class interviewees seemed the most likely to watch American movies on video or to make use of the movie channels on pay-TV packages for satellite dishes or cable TV.

Language skill is one sharp division between the upper-class elite and the upper middle class. Comments by interviewees indicate that real skill in English, sufficient to watch and enjoy CNN, for example, is largely limited to the upper class. Middle-class people find language a major barrier to accessing globalized information. So do many in the upper middle class, but many of them have set a serious goal to acquire better English as a tool to attain elite-level media access to more global sources. Taking English-language classes is common among the upper middle class, de rigeur for their children. English and access to information through it are seen by many in the upper middle class as a crucial tool to be acquired. However, for most of them, it also remains a crucial barrier that ultimately reinforces their use of national media, particularly the telenovelas, music shows, variety shows, etc. and so on that are part of the broad national cultural capital.

## Cultural Capital in Rural Communities

In the case of the two rural communities researched by La Pastina, both the poverty of participants and the remote rural area where they lived were certainly constraining factors. Geography limits access to a broad range of networks, which may reduce economic access to a consumer culture and hinder the potential to reproduce lifestyles presented on television. The local political culture and the agrarian lifestyle were also elements that con-strained viewers' ability to participate in readings of the text. These same constraints created other social formations and forms of cultural capital that led viewers to alternative readings and interpretations of media texts.

La Pastina conducted fieldwork in two rural towns in northeastern Brazil in 1995, following up in the same locations for a year in 1996 and 1997. He focused a great deal on cultural capital and consumption. To be aware of new goods, as well as their social and cultural value, becomes important in maintaining one's cultural capital.

> This is particularly the case with aspiring groups who adopt a learning mode towards consumption and the cultivation of a lifestyle. It is for groups such as the new middle class, the new working class, and the new rich or upper class, that the consumer-culture magazines, newspapers, books, television and radio programmes . . . are more relevant. (Featherstone, 1991, p. 19)

Through these mechanisms, advertising has the potential to promote desire and create expectations about other worlds and realities. In the globalized contemporary world, images of consumer culture transcend the traditional local and national boundaries to become symbolic of a transnational reality. Geographic location becomes less relevant than access to the cultural and eco-nomic capital necessary to be part of these transnational communities. Thus, access to these different forms of capital allows a media consumer to become part of this transnational/national/regional community while not necessarily participating in a local shared community of meaning creation.

Consequently, the preferred reading of a message, inscribed by advertisers and media writers or producers, represents a certain constraining element, but viewers might not read that preferred message due to limits in their cultural capital (La Pastina, 1999, 2001). This does not suggest a system of classification in which certain viewers fare better than others. Meaning is assigned according to viewers' needs and values, their interest, their available textual and intertextual knowledge, and the cultural context in which viewers are immersed. Consequently, readings are culture bound. This notion allows for a better understanding of the process of telenovela reception and interpretation within a community routine outside the original terrain of the textual production. This process of reception constrained by the cultural terrain underlines the elements in the text and in viewers' everyday lives that may enable and constrain certain kinds of readings.

In the process of consuming media, viewers engage in a certain level of agency that allows them, in the case of telenovelas, to discard views conflicting with their own values and to accept, endorse, and appropriate other views they perceive to be useful or advantageous. To comprehend the reception process requires an understanding of how different realities are integrated in the everyday life of viewers and how viewers relate to the power structures that, for instance, privilege men over other groups, whites over people of color, and urban dwellers over rural residents.

In the two main reception cases discussed in this chapter—one of a Mexican telenovela in a small rural community in northeast Brazil and another of a Brazilian telenovela in two communities in Italy—the genre expectations played a role in the reception process, but the local culture and experiences bound viewers' willingness to engage with the text, interpretations, and potential for identification. The discussion that follows is based on La Pastina's fieldwork in rural northeastern Brazil.

## Layers of Reception Within Brazil and Italy

Reception of telenovelas within the diverse population of Brazil is not homogenous. La Pastina's work in rural communities in the northeast of Brazil, both in 1995 (when the main evening telenovela was *A Próxima Vítima*) and 1996 to 1997 (when the main evening telenovelas were *O Rei do Gado* and *Marimar*) seems to indicate that local viewers might lack some of the cultural capital to read some of the political and social subtexts in these telenovelas. Rural Brazilian viewers interpreted the telenovelas according to their own cultural context and available extratextual resources but also looked at these texts as a purveyor of an urban lifestyle, even when the telenovelas were set in rural areas (like *O Rei do Gado*). Viewing them did not necessarily strengthen their sense of belonging to the nation. In Macambira, where La Pastina conducted reception work in 1996 through 1997, many people watched *O Rei do Gado* regularly, but the popularity of this telenovela in the urban south, and its success with a more educated urban middle class, was challenged in this rural outback by *Marimar,* a Mexican melodrama named for its docile but vengeful heroine. In a third set of field-work by La Pastina, done in Italy, another case of complex proximity was examined with the appeal of the Brazilian telenovela *Terra Nostra* there.

This field research is related to the question of multiple proximities that might lead the viewer well beyond a simple sense of cultural proximity. The specific question explored here is how could a Mexican telenovela, produced in a foreign market, be more attractive to Brazilian viewers than a national Brazilian product that has better production values and a subtext that deals with important issues within Brazil? This seems to be the dilemma of reception of transnational products. Most of the data reviewed so far in this study indicates that viewers prefer locally produced programs to foreign imports; nevertheless, the transnational success of some Brazilian (and Latin American) telenovelas presents a potential challenge to this truism. Some of these programs, such as the Brazilian telenovela *Terra Nostra* in Italy, were successful even though they had competition from abundant local production.

## *Marimar* in Rural Northeast Brazil

Early in La Pastina's stay in Macambira, a small rural community in the *sertão do seridó* (chaparral) in Rio Grande do Norte, he visited Marta, a religious woman in her seventies who spent most afternoons quilting. She normally did not watch telenovelas but was now following *Maria Mercedes* because she had heard it was a "good and honest" telenovela. La Pastina asked Marta why she liked this telenovela and not the one from TV Globo. She replied that "this telenovela doesn't have all of that grabbing and non-sense you see in most of the others." Her moral views influenced her views of what she wanted to see on the screen; however, not only the perceived more morally conservative content of these narratives but also the traditional melodramatic structure of the Mexican telenovelas was an important factor attracting viewers in Macambira, particularly women.

Chica, in her sixties, was another example. She took care of the ranch house, cooked, and created beautiful objects combining natural products such as branches, stones, and flowers. She was religious and at least twice a day said the rosary. Like Marta, Chica did not care for television or telenovelas, but nevertheless, she was watching the current Mexican melodrama,

*Marimar.* Just before La Pastina ended his visit with her, she asked if he felt she was sinning because she was entertaining herself instead of praying.

*Marimar,* broadcast by SBT during most of the second half of La Pastina's stay in Macambira, was very popular. Unlike most Brazilians, such as the residents of Montes Claros and Vila Feliz (Almeida, 2003), however, Macambira viewers needed access to a satellite dish to watch shows like the Mexican telenovelas that were not aired on TV Globo, which was the only channel available to all viewers. Only 20% of the houses in Macambira owned a dish and thus had access to all the channels viewed in the two other communities. When La Pastina arrived in the first half of 1996, few homes owned a dish, and programs from other channels were not very popular. Due to a malfunction of Macambira's town-owned relay dish, most homes were without any signal for several months, and the desire to keep watching led many to purchase a dish. The drop in prices and the possibility of install-ment payments also facilitated this development.

Technological barriers, however, did not limit the visibility of *Marimar* among locals. Many returned to the habit of visiting a neighbor to watch television and saw *Marimar* as frequently as possible, many times running back home to watch *O Rei do Gado,* which was broadcast at Globo. SBT scheduled its telenovelas before and after Globo's programs to avoid a head-to-head competition for the audience.

*Marimar* is the story of a beautiful young woman wronged by greedy wealthy people. The man she falls in love with disdains her because she is poor. After a few episodes, she becomes wealthy and decides to destroy the family that abused her.

For most women whom La Pastina interviewed in Macambira, telenovelas were about romance. Men claimed they were following a telenovela because it was realistic or had a rural theme that appealed to them. Women liked those elements as well, but for them, the melodramatic plot was the key element. The modernization of the telenovela genre in Brazil, incorporating issues of con-temporary daily life in its narrative, seems to have been effective in attracting a male audience, at least in Macambira. But in doing so, these television texts seem to be distancing themselves from their melodramatic roots, raising complaints among woman viewers that Globo telenovelas are not romantic anymore. Katia was representative of the common complaint among women: "Globo's telenovelas have only sex and no romance anymore."

The Mexican telenovelas that SBT broadcast, on the other hand, were followed and admired by many female viewers for their romance, with lots of melodrama and little sex. A telenovela was expected to provide a romantic text, with couples struggling to fulfill their love. Longing and desire were important elements viewers expected to see. Most women viewers wanted to see the romantic couples struggling and developing a relationship at a certain pace. A common complaint against *O Rei do Gado* was that the couples were too quick to start kissing and having sex without developing intimacy.

Cota and Lucia, two women in their early twenties, liked the Mexican telenovelas. They mentioned *Topázio* and *Maria Mercedes* aired by SBT. In *Maria Mercedes,* "we didn't miss a day waiting for the first kiss. It was so romantic." They like this excessive melodramatic intensity. But at the same time, Cota, blushing and laughing, said that she didn't like it because "it never got to be really interesting." She was jokingly referring to the absence of sex and more explicit love that had been discussed regarding Globo's telenovelas, such as *Explode Coração* and *O Fim do Mundo.*

Celma, married to a powerful local politician, said that her 15-year-old daughter loved to watch *Maria Mercedes* with her. But they could only do it when her husband was not at home. "He wants to see the *Jornal Nacional* at Globo at the same time the telenovela is on the SBT." She also mentioned *Topázio* and said that she liked Mexican telenovelas on SBT for their romance and because "I don't feel ashamed in front of my daughter like I do when they have those sex scenes in the telenovelas at Globo."

For Junio, a young homosexual man, *Maria Mercedes* was wonderful. He enjoyed the drama and watched every time he could go to a house with a dish. The class ascension motif—the heroine is poor and the hero is rich—fascinated him in *Maria Mercedes* as well as it did later in *Marimar.*

Zé de Bia was an interesting case. He disliked telenovelas, and even though he owned the largest number of cattle in town, he did not follow *O Rei do Gado.* Several months into La Pastina's stay, SBT started airing *Marimar,* a Mexican telenovela. Zé de Bia used to watch the newscast on that station and one day decided to watch *Marimar,* after seeing commercials for it during the newscasts. Its viewers in the community—mostly women—saw *Marimar* as a good telenovela with strong romantic tension between the leading couple. Zé de Bia, however, read the telenovela as a realistic text discussing class mobility. He focused on Marimar's struggle to become respectable; overcoming her background as a poor orphan who suddenly inherited a fortune. He saw himself in her struggle. Orphaned at an early age, he had to fend for himself and today was one of the wealthiest men in town.

Zé de Bia's identificatory position—across gender and age and, if you will, national boundaries—is important to understand the pervasiveness of telenovelas in reaching broader segments of society. Engaging with the telenovela repertoire, Zé de Bia, a conservative older male who believes that the man should control the household and support his family, identified with a female character. He accepted and enjoyed the myth of class mobility and ultimate happiness of Marimar with the man she loves. Even though he abused her and she abused him, Zé de Bia wanted them to get together and be happy. Once, he started complaining that Marimar was becoming too greedy, like the people who had abused her, and that she was humiliating Sergio too much. Zé de Bia wanted her to teach him a lesson, but once that was done, she should submit to Sergio and declare her love for him so they would stay together. Zé de Bia's attention span for the long drawn-out telenovela was limited, and the inevitable secondary plot lines irritated him. He was clearly unfamiliar with the genre's conventions and unwilling to accept them.

Ozenildo, a small business owner in town, was one of the few men who watched *Marimar*. He started after casually seeing a couple of shows while his wife was watching it before *O Rei do Gado*. For him, *Marimar* was about class ascension, and he enjoyed the way it was represented. Ozenildo described Marimar in these terms:

> She came out of the mud, and she did it so fast and now is taking care of the whole thing with so much control and class and really managing of that business. And she is so beautiful and correct . . . Marimar is also too bright, because to come from where she did and became such an important woman so fast, really only on the telenovelas. . . . *O Rei do Gado* is much more part of our reality, but I think it is because *Marimar* is from Mexico. It was recorded in Mexico and it must be different there so the telenovela is really showing their life and their reality. (personal interview)

Other men were watching *Marimar,* but mostly those with a satellite dish. Unlike women, men had not left their homes to watch *Marimar,* La Pastina found, although some did go to the square or a friend's house to see *O Rei do Gado.* This paradoxical position by Ze de Bia and Ozenildo, in relation to the established discourse that regards telenovelas as female texts, points to a fascinating fissure in this established dichotomy between male and female viewers' taste. Most men used the argument that they enjoyed telenovelas that were perceived to be realistic. Several men in Macambira stretched this definition to justify including melodramatic texts in their male domain.

In the case of *Marimar,* viewers' local culture and the perceived challenge posed by urban Brazilian telenovelas to local values generated a positive atmosphere that facilitated the reception of a foreign text. The concept of cultural proximity (Straubhaar, 1991), in this case, could be stretched to mean not necessarily the text produced closer to home (i.e., in the urban south), but rather the text that provides local viewers with ideological content that does not challenge or stretch their own values and beliefs. Rather, it returns viewers to an idealized reception state in which telenovelas serve to provide a melodramatic cathartic space that does not question these viewers' attitudes. The next example, of a Brazilian telenovela, *Terra Nostra*, and its reception in Italy, seems to reinforce this idea of a transnational text that challenges local programs as it provides at least some viewers with a venue to deal with the sense of loss caused by the Italian diaspora.

## *Terra Nostra* in the Italy of the North and in the Italy of the South

Spending the first semester of 2002 in Italy, teaching on a study-abroad program at Texas A&M, La Pastina visited his aunt. He had last seen her in December 1999. This time, she had something new to talk about, *Terra Nostra:* a Brazilian telenovela, set during the earlier years of the 20th century, chronicling the saga of Italian immigration in that nation. Even though the telenovela's reality and the reality La Pastina's father and his brother experienced when they migrated to Brazil in the early 1950s were very different, and even though she had seen many other Brazilian telenovelas, *Terra Nostra* had touched on a primal necessity to connect to her brothers' experiences.

*Terra Nostra,* it seems, contextualized the Italian diaspora among residents of the small community of Castellabate, a southern Italian town where almost all families have relatives in Brazil. As in many other southern communities, immigration was more intense and widespread, than in the progressive northern regions such as Tuscany, where La Pastina was living during the period of this data collection. In the south, the telenovela rekindled memories and bridged informational gaps, even if through a fictionalized saga of success. In the north, the historical distance from actual immigration and the lack of closer family connections made the text a mythic narrative of othering, in which Italians are seen as the others in a distant land confronting the humiliation of an economic and military defeat.

Immigration has figured in the relationship between Italy and Brazil for a long time. With the first mass immigration from Italy in the mid- to late 1800s, the two nations became intrinsically linked in a flux and counterflux of diasporic identities and memories. La Pastina grew up in the middle of this pattern of images in flux, sensations, ideas, facts, myths, and desires of Italians in Brazil and Brazilians wanting to be in Italy. But for those who stayed in Italy and dreamed of the possibilities of another land, or who longed for their beloved ones, sons and daughters, brothers and sisters, fathers and mothers, the idea of Brazil was one of undefined contours, of riches and dangers.

After World War II, when the most recent wave of Italian immigrants left their country in an attempt to make it big in the New World, La Pastina's father, then 21, left a small costal village in Campagnia, an impoverish southern region of Italy. The family of seven could not survive with only the limited resources generated by their plot of land, and other choices were few.

The two younger sisters would marry and move, the oldest brother would stay with the parents and work on the land to survive, as tradition prescribed, while La Pastina's father and his other brother had to search for a future. Brazil, where many others from southern Italy had moved, was a dream holding the possibility of building a promising future.

La Pastina's aunt, now the only survivor of those five children, lives in a small hill town less than 3 miles away from where she was born. Every time La Pastina visited, she would talk about the sadness the family felt when his father left, the anxiety of not knowing what had happened to the ship, not knowing if he had arrived safely or found a job. It was painful to wait long days before a few lines would sporadically arrive and tell them all about his progress. After almost half a century, her eyes are still moist from the rupture in their family fabric. Her tears are from the death of her relatives but also from the years in which she longed to see her brothers. She only saw La Pastina's father four times during those 50 years, the first time 25 years after he had left. Technology, the lower cost of airfares, and telecommunications increased their contact as they aged, but still the memories and the fantasies of what her brother's life had been in Brazil was always one of difficulty, suffering, pain and distance, shrouded in mystery.

To residents of the Tuscan village, *Terra Nostra* was about Brazil: the land, the farms, the location, and also about the experience of "historical" Italians. Most viewers told La Pastina that they were from the south; very few people from Castiglione had migrated apparently. Using local history to guide the text, the Tuscan community was bounding the program very differently from the southern community, which read the show as the experience of their own people.

The Matarazzos—a wealthy Italian-Brazilian family mentioned in the telenovelas—had donated money and a building to the southern Italy community, increasing the sense of recognition of many viewers there. They felt an emotional, financial, physical, and historical connection to the characters' experiences and the narrative constructed on the screen. Among viewers in the north, the telenovela account was distant and dissociated from their experiences as Italians. This lack of recognition bound the readings and the cathartic potential of the narrative.

## Cultural Proximity Within Culturally Bound Reception Practices

As the two previous examples show, transnational narratives have the potential to motivate strong processes of identification. Cultural proximity seems to be an important concept in the process of reception. Nevertheless, in these two cases, the notion of cultural proximity must be discussed in terms of inherent local values and historical alliances between the original culture of the text and the local culture. In a broader sense, these two texts, although foreign, connected at some basic level to the viewers in Macambira (in the case of the Mexican melodrama) and the southern Italian viewers (in the case of *Terra Nostra*). In these cases, local culture, rather than the national culture, shows a proximity between these transnational texts and local viewers. Cultural and social capital was also central to the process of interpretation of these narratives, bounding and constraining the process of identification. Southern Italians had specific cultural capital to deploy in their interpretations of the narratives, at the same time that their level of emotional involvement allowed for identification to happen. More traditional Brazilians had value proximities that drew them to Mexican telenovelas with traditional values rather than to national Brazilian telenovelas with values they did not always share. Both built on various forms of cultural capital that people had acquired from their families, their local cultures, their religions, and their value traditions, which differentiates these viewers from those led by other sources of cultural capital, such as schooling and national media, which might lead them to prefer national media.

# Note

1. It reads, "Men make their own history, but they do not make it just as they please; they do not make it under circumstances chosen by themselves, but under circumstances directly encountered, given, and transmitted from the past" (Marx, 1977, p. 300).

# 9

# Making Sense of World Television

## Hybridization or Multilayered Cultural Identities?

There are many ways of looking at culture and the globalization of television. This last chapter looks at the aspect of culture that is the individual and collective synthesis of identity in interaction with media, particularly television. The movement from traditional local life to modern interaction with mass media has produced identities that are already multilayered with elements that are local, regional (subnational but larger than the very local), supranational, based on cultural-linguistic regions, and national (Anderson, 1983). In this study, I argue that television viewers around the world continue to strongly reflect these layers or aspects of identity while many also acquire new layers of identity that are transnational, or global. In this chapter, I examine the relationship between processes of hybridization of identity and culture over time and the buildup, maintenance, and even defense of various layers of multilayered identities. These layers of identity are articulated with media, such as television, but not in a

AUTHOR'S NOTE: This chapter was written with the participation, research, and conceptual understanding of Antonio La Pastina (Texas A&M University), Viviana Rojas (University of Texas at San Antonio), and Martha Fuentes-Bautista and Juan Piñon (University of Texas at Austin).

simple sense of being primarily influenced by television. Some layers of identity, such as those religious traditionalists hold, may actively resist many of the ideas most television channels carry.

Many people suppose that identities are rapidly globalizing. In this chapter, however, I argue, based on an analysis of in-depth interviews in Salvador (Bahia) and São Paulo, Brazil, and among Latinos in Austin, Texas, that the proportion of people whose identity is deeply globalized is actually quite small, that the traditional layers of identity at the local, subnational regional, and national levels are still the strongest for many people, with supranational or transnational cultural-linguistic regions rapidly becoming important for some cultures and some people.

These cultural-geographic levels of identity emerge as primary for almost all people, I found in my interviews, but other levels of identity emerge strongly for most people, as well. At a broad collective level, attention has focused for years on television viewing and identities framed by language and culture (Sinclair et al., 1996; Straubhaar & Duarte, 1997; Wilkinson, 1995). However, this volume has also focused considerable attention on social class, particularly in Bourdieu's (1984) sense of cultural capital, discussed in Chapter 8. I have also found strong layers of identity that guide viewing and interpreting of television in gender, ethnicity, age, and religion, among others. This chapter will focus on place, culture/language, and class as foci for multiple identifications and television viewing by audiences; these are the elements that emerged as fundamental in my interviews, as well as in a review of the evolving literature. I will examine the others more briefly as well. I recognize that these levels of identity are in large part structured for people by powerful institutions. Governments use schooling, maps, borders, and other forms of discourse to teach people to think in terms of cultural geography. A variety of economic forces structure people's positions in terms of class, economic, and cultural capital. Powerful cultural industries and many other social structures reinforce senses of cultural geography, class, gender, ethnicity, age, and religion. However, individual and group agency and action also construct and change these forces over time.

## From Local to Global

When local television is economically feasible, as is local news in the United States, it is popular because people live most of their lives within a locality, they want to know more about it, and they often identify with it quite strongly. Local identity also becomes a framework for mediating national television, as I showed in Chapter 8 and as I shall discuss later. In large nations, television is usually produced in a major city that is geographically and culturally distant from many of the places that view it. As a result, viewers may feel a critical distance from national television based on their awareness of the differences between their area of residence and the place where programs were produced. For example, Texans may be aware of how they differ culturally from people in New York or Los Angeles, just as people in northeast Brazil seem to be aware of how culturally different they are from fellow countrymen in Rio de Janeiro or São Paulo (La Pastina, 2004b). That awareness provides a critical frame with which to view national or global television.

Television produced in a core producing city that serves a subnational region with a coherent cultural or linguistic identity is becoming more common in southern China, Hong Kong, Catalonia (Spain), Scotland and Wales, Quebec, southern Brazil, and various parts of India; however, it is still limited to places populous or rich enough to afford it. Some of these production centers have emerged as global cities: media capitals (Curtin, 2003) that produce information, media, and other goods, not only for the city itself and the nation, but also for larger regional or global audiences (Sassen, 2004). There are examples of such global cities in China (Curtin, 2003), Mexico (Canclini, 2001), and elsewhere. They produce for themselves, their nations, and audiences across transnational cultural-linguistic markets that share their languages and cultures.

National television still seems to be the most common form, even at the beginning of the 21st century, when the seeming coherence of nations is breaking down in many ways. The nation-state, where it is strong, still has many tools and levers to shape television, as Chapters 3 and 6 discussed in detail. However, supranational or transnational cultural spaces and markets are also gaining considerable force, as Chapters 4 and 7 discussed in detail. Television producers almost always still produce for a specific national market because national markets continue to dominate commercial sales and advertising. Most television exporters still make more money in their national home market than in exports, including such visible examples as the United States, Brazil, and Mexico. National television spaces and focus also still correspond with the political desires or image-making needs of national governments, which control channel allocations, economic regulation, and their own advertising budgets. Increasingly, television producers also jump from those national bases to roles within larger spaces defined by linguistic and cultural similarities or proximities (Sinclair et al., 1996).

However, some analysts, such as Curtin (2003), have argued that nations are losing centrality to other logics of production, in which global cities or media capitals, for example, Hong Kong or Shanghai, produce for their own local markets, for national markets, and also for diaspora audiences, which are geographically distant but linked to the producing city by language and culture. In the United States, immigrants from China, India, and Mexico watch channels imported from back home, or in the case of Mexican Americans, a mix of programming from back home and programming produced in the United States in Spanish for their own specific needs. Some global producing cities such as Rio de Janeiro also produce for dispersed transnational audiences that still speak colonial languages like Portuguese that audiences have gradually acquired since the 1500s. So Curtin and others, for example, Canclini (2001) and Sassen (2004), argued for the increasing centrality of global cities in cultural industries and cultural production.

A strong producer in a global city or national market can first dominate the local or national market, then export programs, then export technology and know-how, and finally shape channels borne by satellite to cultural-linguistic markets that resemble the home market but are larger. Such operations include TVB (Hong Kong), TV Globo (Brazil), Televisa (Mexico), and All-Arab Television (Egypt). Exports from such nationally based groups pioneered cultural-linguistic markets, which are now courted by global groups like Murdoch and specifically regional groups like Al-Jazeera (Qatar), LBC (Lebanon), and Orbit (Saudi Arabia), which target regions like the Middle East where national television has left gaps in news or entertainment that regional groups move to fill.

In some parts of the world, particularly Latin America, the Arabic-speaking world, the Chinese-speaking world, and other parts of Asian and Central Asia, people increasingly experience a layer of culture defined both by geographic proximity and cultural-linguistic proximity. In 2002, when the new government in Afghanistan removed the Taliban's ban on reproduction of images of people, photos of actresses from Bollywood, not Hollywood, flooded into shops and homes, according to the news coverage at the time. Much of the world experiences various cultural aspects of global cultures produced in Hollywood, Europe, Japan, and elsewhere via television and other venues.

Some audiences are dispersed globally but still united by cultural-linguistic proximity. One example is people who learned colonial languages and still both import and produce in those languages. Former French colonies import programming from France and produce for themselves in French, creating a geographically dispersed transnational culture of *francophonie,* which supports film, television, and music production in a number of places, from Quebec to Senegal. Similarly, former Portuguese colonies are linked in a Lusophone culture, or *Lusofonia,* which centers on both Brazil and Portugal—Brazil dominates in terms of television production—but extends to East Timor and a number of African countries. Former British colonies are similarly linked, and as in the Lusophone cultures, television production is dominated not by the former colonial power but by a large former colony, the United States. Anglophone people, as well as those who speak Arabic, Chinese, Hindi, Persian, Turkish, and so on, have migrated globally in numbers large enough to create a diaspora of commercially attractive, transnational, cultural-linguistic audiences and markets.

The global level of television is clearly visible at two levels, one of structure and another of actual programming. Global corporations that are trying to operate in large parts of the world are easily identified. Groups like Murdoch's News Corporation have ambitions to own satellite/cable TV channels everywhere. These corporations powerfully reframe the political economy of how television works everywhere via ownership, advertising, actual program flow, and programming ideas.

The mass audience in most places tends to see quite a bit of glocal programming, globally inspired or even licensed but nationally or regionally produced. Although global flows of actual programs are visible, particularly via satellite and cable channels, they don't attract a majority of the audience in places where local, national, or regional material is available. Audience members in countries large or rich enough to produce quite a bit of programming are probably exposed more to locally produced versions of global genres and formats, such as *Big Brother,* than to direct flows of television from abroad. For example, Brazilians see little foreign television programming in prime time, but they are on their fifth version of *Big Brother,* which has been very popular. (See Chapters 6 and 7 for more analysis of the flow and export of genres.)

So audience members worldwide are now exposed to two distinct levels of global influence. One is the direct flow of television programs first highlighted by Nordenstreng and Varis in 1973 and examined in Chapters 6 and 7, along with the direct flow of complete channels via cable and satellite first highlighted by Schiller (1981) and discussed in Chapter 7. The other is the copying or licensing of foreign formats (Moran, 1998), which brings with it varied levels of cultural influence and ideology (such as a focus on aspiring to and taking on consumer roles; Fuller, 1992). That process of glocalization long took place informally, as when format ideas for soap operas flowed both globally and regionally (see Chapter 6). It has now taken a more formally licensed and traded form, with the increasingly global traffic in packaged formats, such as *Big Brother* or *Survivor* (Moran, 1998, 2004), which is examined in Chapter 7.

Audience members are also increasingly exposed to regional or geo-cultural flows of programs, such as the heavy regionwide flow of Mexican and Brazilian telenovelas, as well as regional satellite or cable channels in Latin

America. New phenomena arise, such as the apparent dominance of Al-Jazeera as a news source in the Arabic-speaking world and among the diaspora of Arabic speakers worldwide. As of this writing, Canada was debating whether to permit Al-Jazeera to be carried on Canadian cable services (Ignatius, 2006), weighing the competing demands of Arabic audiences and those upset by Al-Jazeera's critical coverage of actions and policies of the United States and the West, as well as leaders such as former U.S. Secretary of Defense Donald Rumsfeld and Vice President Richard Cheney. Al-Jazeera has become a notable precedent; Telesur, a pan–Latin American TV news channel that challenges a perceived U.S. news hegemony and was started by Venezuela and several other Latin American governments, is being called a "Latin American Al-Jazeera" (Calderón, 2005).

## Multiple Levels of Audience Identity and Cultural Choices

In Chapter 8, I focused on audience choices among geographically, linguistically, and class or cultural capital-defined levels of television to show how those levels of cultural experience shape television viewing. In fact, in the chapter, I argue that people's lives are shaped by various forces, such as class and their experience of cultural geography, which then shapes their viewing of television, particularly their choices of what to watch. People experience levels of identity and make television choices related to them, but it is harder for interviewees to reflect on what forces shape their choices. So I take very seriously the levels of identity that people articulate, but I also infer others from structural aspects of their lives.

In this chapter, I focus on the lived experience of audiences with various levels and forms of world television. In particular, I focus on audience identities and how people seem to form multiple identities that correspond in many ways to the multilayered cultural geography of television in the world. One explanation for this is that many of those levels of experience with cultural geography are broadly experienced by nearly the entire television audience. Everyone has experience of his or her city or locality, and this experience is increasingly addressed directly by local television production in many large cities or provinces. Although some people live isolated from any experience of nationality, most seem to be touched by national television as well as nationally defined schooling, newspapers, books, radio, government political campaigns, and so on, as shown in the Brazilian interviews reported in Chapter 8.

The other central argument of this chapter is that although identity for many people may be defined as increasingly hybrid, it is perhaps more clearly seen as multileveled. In fact, the two ideas are complementary. Hybridity is a long-term process in which all identities are constantly changing (Nederveen Pieterse, 2004); I argue here that, based on the interviews described in this chapter, most people experience identity as regards media in part as a series of cultural-geographic levels from local to global. Depending on the place and group, they also experience identity as related to language, class, culture, and religion. Also, identities and media uses are divided still further by ethnicity and gender. So the idea of levels of identity, per se, is a heuristic device for understanding the way that people seem to experience identity, particularly in relation to the complexity of world television.

Based on a review of the literature as well as fieldwork in Texas and Brazil, I find that people make sense of media first through a set of cultural identities based on space and place: local, regional, national, and global. Related to these are identities based on culture and language, which are usually linked to space and place but can be transnational. Examples are transnational, postcolonial, cultural-linguistic audiences, such as the Francophone, Anglophone, or Lusophone world; more contiguous geocultural audiences, such as those in the Arabic region, East or South Asia, and Latin America; or audiences composed of migrants or diasporic communities. These identities, which can define television viewing, can be maintained and re-created even after people have moved away from the place where the cultural-linguistic identity was first formed (Appadurai, 1996).

The next level of identity relates to social class, based on the idea of cultural capital and linked to experiences within the family, school, neighborhood, and social groups; it is shaped by economic class commonalities (Bourdieu, 1984) and a sense of group experience that solidifies into a class habitus (Bourdieu, 1984). Whether people verbalize in these terms or not, most also experience and interpret media through a sense of ethnicity or race, as it is culturally constructed in the place and time where they live.

Almost all people similarly experience media through an awareness of themselves and their identity in terms of gender. In some countries, people also have a distinct sense of identity related to their age group. In the United States, for example, media use and understanding are heavily segmented by age group. This may not be as true of other societies. In Brazil, upper-class youth are likely to have media uses that are very different from those of their parents, but such large differences (as reflected in interviews by the authors) are less common among the working class. Finally, almost everyone experiences media refracted through a sense of values shared with a community; this is most often expressed in terms of religious group identification, but it relates to other communities of values as well.

Depending on the circumstances of the individuals and the groups they are associated with, different levels of identity might be primary for experiencing and making sense of television and other media. For some, class identity might seem primary, as in some of the studies of the British working class (Morley, 1992). For others, as in studies related to the reaction to some Hollywood productions by audiences in the Islamic Middle East, religion might be a primary identity for interpreting media experiences (Chambers, 2002). For others, a primary identity for interpreting media might be ethnicity or gender, or both. For example, U.S. Latinas tend to view imported Mexican television in terms of their own experiences of class, gender, and ethnicity within the Latino minority in the United States (Rojas, 2001).

In this chapter, I first examine a variety of theoretical arguments about the audience experience of world television, culminating in my argument that this experience can be analyzed as mediated by an increasingly complex set of layers of identities. I then examine these arguments and theories using the case of Brazil, via fieldwork I conducted in the city of São Paulo and areas in and around Salvador, Bahia, and Ilheus, Bahia, in 1989 through 1990 and in the summers of 1991 through 1998; and continuing in Salvador in 2003 through 2005 and in East Austin, Texas, in 1999 through 2005. Viviana Rojas, Martha Fuentes, and Juan Piñon were crucial in developing and interpreting the fieldwork in East Austin. In this chapter, I also draw on fieldwork conducted by Antonio La Pastina in Brazil, as well as his writing and analysis of those interviews.

## The Process of Hybridization

I have presented the idea of hybridity as the historical axis of globalization (Nederveen Pieterse, 2004) in Chapter 2. This concept can be contrasted with the rapid spatial expansion of technological and economic changes to regions and countries most often considered the essential elements of recent globalization. Hybridity is the adaptation of these forces and changes into the local culture, economy, and social system. In some cases of genuine hybridity, substantially new cultures are synthesized out of the elements of previous cultures. In other cases, multiple layers are formed from substantial parts of the previous different cultures. In many cases, both occur.

To review, the process of hybridization begins with flows of people, technologies, economic systems, institutional and cultural models, religions, and recently, media. Nederveen Pieterse (2004) noted that such flows are normal and have always taken place. However, in current patterns of globalization, many of these flows are increasing, which leads people to worry about the increasing pace of change.

Second, these flows encounter cultures as they move into across borders, bringing ideas, images, values, and practices, often with extremely powerful impacts. Nederveen Pieterse (2004) also noted that intercultural contact, even heavy contact, is normal. Contact and change, hybridization, are normal, even inevitable.

Third, cultures interpenetrate and interact over time. While a few interactions are controlled by the receiving culture, in far more situations, the local culture loses official control under colonization but often maintains considerable continuity of culture anyway. In some cases, such as large parts of the Americas, indigenous or local cultures are heavily changed, if not virtually destroyed.

Fourth, I would argue that multiple layers of cultural identity form, especially on the receiving side, as new elements and ideas are incorporated. Even when the process seems overwhelming, as in the colonization of the Americas, local cultures often find ways to resist in part and preserve aspects or layers of their original culture and identity.

Fifth, there is some genuine mixture of these cultures, which is what many think of as the essence of hybridity. The obvious physical analogy is the mixing of races, which was fairly common in the Americas and elsewhere. Mixing of cultures was even more pervasive, involving everyone within reach of the colonists.

Sixth, many of those who are trying to preserve the continuity of their societies and cultures resist the new forces, ideas, and peoples, sometimes by using a layer of imported culture to mask the continuance of older cultures and identities. However, complete resistance to outside culture is almost impossible, so both mixture and the maintenance of older layers take place (Nederveen Pieterse, 1995).

The global flows of cultural artifacts and people provide models and ideas for these new hybrid forms and added layers of identity. These flows bring in new cultures to add to the existing mixtures and layers. Cultural products come in, and with even broader impact, so do more underlying sets of concepts, such as religions, adding new forms and ideas.

## Hybridization Versus Multiple Layers of Identity and Culture

Not all cultures are equally vulnerable to outside forces. Some sustain a fairly effective resistance to colonialism historically. Populations survive more or less intact. Local power structures are not completely broken. Many cultures achieve a great deal of continuity.

The nearly universal interpenetration of cultures does not mean that increasing homogenization, or even deep synthesis or hybridity takes place. Multiple cultural layers often form from the interaction of cultures, and those multiple layers persist, even as hybridization and mixture take place. Given the seeming ubiquity of hybridization as a process over time (Nederveen Pieterse, 2004), there will be layers of mixture as well.

There is often a superficial hybridity to mask these continuities. For years, outside scholars saw the Afro-Brazilian religion *candomblé* as the classic example of syncretism, mixing the *orixás* or spirits of Africa's Yoruba religion with Catholic saints to produce a new hybrid religion (Bastide, 1978). Some in Brazil, however, would argue that many forms of Afro-Brazilian candomblé actually represent a multilayered continuity. For example, one of the principal communities in Salvador, Brazil, Ilê Axé Opô Afonjá, issued a statement: "*Iansã* (a candomblé deity) is not Santa Barbara" (the Catholic saint with whom *Iansã* had often been syncretized; Afonjá, 1999). The group argued that syncretism was a protective overlay designed to conceal the ongoing worship of African religions and avoid persecution; today, the pretense of syncretism could be dropped in favor of a deliberate effort to return to the Yoruba roots of candomblé. Overlays of adopted culture can coexist with an inner core of traditional culture, with the adopted exterior perhaps serving as a mask to conceal the traditional core. Cultural elements sometimes survive as layers of culture and identity associated with social classes and groups. They can also survive as identities within individuals and various forms of collectivities.

## Multiple Identifications

In this emerging model, people increasingly identify with multiple cultures at various layers and levels. People can identify with multiple cultural groups in different fields of activity. People establish different identities at school and work, with family and friends. In the process of learning from others, people form multiple layers of cultural capital, often specific not only to a field of activity, as Bourdieu (1984) would predict, but to different subcultures or cultural layers. People form different dispositions to behave differently with various groups. Someone can be religious and traditional at home with their parents, adventurous and critical with some friends, sports-minded with others, and achievement-oriented with colleagues at work.

All of these different layers of identity and culture will have varied connections to global, cultural linguistic, national, and local spaces and forces.

Although few people reflect all these layers, I found in interviews that many people were indeed quite multilayered in both identity and media use. For example, a man interviewed in Salvador, Bahia, in 2004 and again in 2005 had a number of layers of identity corresponding to levels of attention to media and information. A former hotel accountant, he was then working as a taxi driver because it paid better. He gave some attention to global issues via Brazilian television news and newspapers; he knew enough about the war in Iraq to want to make jokes about President Bush, but he did not pay that much attention to a broad range of global issues. He was familiar with quite a bit of U.S. popular culture, mostly in music and feature films; the only U.S. television program he could remember was *The Simpsons*. He was somewhat conversant with a few bits of the Lusophone world; he knew about the recent independence of East Timor, for example, and some fragments of Portuguese history, but he mostly made jokes about the Portuguese. (Many Brazilians tell jokes about the Portuguese not unlike jokes often told in the United States about Polish immigrants.) He knew relatively more about Latin America in terms of news and events, knew some songs from other Latin American countries, and sometimes watched Mexican soap operas with his wife, who liked some of them (broadcast on SBT, the second most popular Brazilian network). He spent a lot of time with Brazilian national media, particularly newscasts, talk shows, telenovelas, sports, and music. He was passionate about national and local politics, talking about current national corruption scandals and giving local examples. He also knew a lot about the music of northeastern Brazil in general and the music of Bahia in specific. He considered himself an evangelical Christian but also seemed to know a lot about candomblé and some of the local music groups that used music from it. He considered himself lower middle class but sympathized a lot with the poor and working class, and he talked about class issues quite a bit. He had some college-level training in accountancy and clearly enjoyed talking with people he considered to be educated, but he also got along very well and talked a lot with fellow drivers, who had much less education. He is clearly of Afro-Brazilian descent and is proud of that in cultural terms but wary of talking about it in any way related to politics. He liked to talk about Afro-Brazilian music, but he was unwilling to talk about other aspects of racial issues, such as quotas for racial affirmative action, which are just being implemented in some Brazilian universities, including some in Salvador. Overall, his education probably permits him a greater level of complexity in terms of identity and media use than most Brazilians, but he is hardly a member of the global elite; he is consciously someone struggling to maintain a position in the lower reaches of the middle class. Thus, he is perhaps somewhat typical of what a large number of Brazilians would aspire to be and to do, in terms of identity and media use. He engages in media corresponding to several levels of identity, but locality, region, nation, class, and religion predominate.

## Researching Audiences and Their Identities

Overall, in the rest of this chapter, I analyze a variety of forms of hybridization and the formation and maintenance of multilayered identities as a way to understand the relationship between culture and television viewing in a complex world system. I will examine several areas where hybridization seems to be a dominant form of change in identities, and several in which the metaphor of multiple layers of identity seems more useful.

I will organize the rest of the chapter in terms of aspects or layers of identity. In part, this corresponds to theoretical concerns. In greater part, it reflects the way that people expressed their identities in the interviews that provide the empirical base for the rest of the chapter. The interviews come from Brazil and central Texas. In the case of Brazil, my students and I conducted fieldwork in the city of São Paulo and areas in and around Salvador, Bahia, and Ilheus, Bahia, in 1989 through 1990 and the summers of 1991 through 1998, continuing in Salvador in 2003 through 2005. In Texas, my students and I conducted interviews, primarily with Latinos, but also Anglos and African Americans, in East Austin, Texas, in 1999 through 2005. In 2004 through 2005, that interviewing focused on Mexican migrants to the United States. I will also draw heavily on fieldwork by Antonio La Pastina in Macambira, Rio Grande do Norte, Brazil, in 1994 through 1995, 1996, and 2002. In quite a bit of the Brazilian fieldwork, particularly La Pastina's, a number of interviews centered on the understanding and interpretations audiences gave to a specific telenovela, *The Cattle King* (O Rei do Gado), which was broadcast by TV Globo in 1994 through 1995. This provides continuity with my previous use of that telenovela as an example in Chapter 6.

In the following sections, I will first discuss space and place as anchoring points for flow of media, media consumption, and cultural identity. This layer emerged as primary in both my Brazilian interviews and my U.S. Latino interviews, although people differed in whether the spatial focus of identity was domestic or transnational. Next, I will discuss class, the second major layer for Brazilians and important for Latinos, too, although U.S. discourse tends to emphasize race and ethnicity over class as a marker of difference. Next, I will look at race and ethnicity as a fundamental layer of identity, particularly for U.S. Latinos; Brazilian social discourse tends to emphasize class over race as a contemporary marker of identity, even though

Brazilians talk freely about race mixing in the historical formation of Brazilian identities. I found that Brazilians also seem to talk about place in a way that is implicitly informed by racial identities. For example, in Brazil, a sense of place becomes a way to talk about race; informants in Salvador would discuss their differences from other parts and peoples of Brazil by talking about being *Baiano* (Bahian) rather than being black, but I often got the distinct feeling that they were talking about being black, too, using a less charged vocabulary. Related to ethnicity is language, too, particularly for U.S. Latinos. Finally, I look at religion and gender, which are fundamental layers of most individual identities.

## Cultural Geography: Cultural Distance, Global, National, and Local Identities

All audiences have a strong sense of local identity, as they live their daily lives in a specific place and time. Their interpretive community (Lindlof et al., 1988) is based in a family, local friends, neighbors, clubs, church congregations, sports groups, and so on. Most people also have a sense of region referring to an area larger than their immediate locale, but smaller than the nation.

Most of their day-to-day thought and interaction is still local, as the Brazilian interviews show, and much of the knowledge or cultural capital that people use in interpreting media, such as television, comes from their local experience of daily life in a specific culture shaped by their immediate environment, place, and time. Sometimes, the experience of locality sharpens a sense of difference between local life and what is shown of global or national scenes on television. For example, rural Brazilians observed and interviewed by La Pastina felt themselves to be on the periphery of Brazil, somewhat alienated from what they saw of urban Brazilian life on television (see Chapter 8).

The experience of locality is bound up with other layers of identity, such as ethnicity or language and culture. For example, Rosemary Alexander Isett (1995) found that Inuit interviewees in Alaska felt at considerable distance from the culture of the lower 48 U.S. states as portrayed on television. In fact, watching U.S. culture on television, they tended to be relieved that they lived in a rural area within their own ethnic culture. Latinos interviewed by my students and me in East Austin also tended to frame their identities in terms of local conditions, particularly neighborhoods and extended families. Like the Inuit, they often felt at considerable cultural distance from the U.S. mainstream, both in terms of language and culture. However, this sense of cultural distance varies greatly between generations and families. In fact, fieldwork with Latinos powerfully introduced the layer of family identity. Among Latinos, family often roots individuals in a specific neighborhood, but it can also connect them to extended family in Mexico. Thus, while family is often bound up with locality, that link is different with migrants, particularly those who see themselves as part of a temporary diaspora, with plans to permanently or cyclically return to what they consider a cultural homeland, such as Mexico or Central America.

I want to give weight to the relative solidity of the local, as many audiences experience it, without falling into what Nederveen Pieterse (2004) called "the reification of the local, sidelining the interplay between the local and the global" (p. 47). Well before the nation-state achieved relative primacy in institutional definitions of identity, local cultures generally had cultural exchange and interpenetration with larger cultural-linguistic regions. Local groups were part of larger language, culture, and ethnic groups such as the Inca or the Mayan cultures. These prenational cultures continue locally or subnationally in many parts of the world. In larger nations such as Brazil and China, or even medium-size nations such as Mozambique, coherent subnational regional identities often reflect these enduring hybrid forms of identity.

In fact, this balance of coexistence and conflict in the mix of local identity with national and transnational identities is one of the reasons that I focus here on multilayered identities alongside hybrid identities. Sometimes, the local changes with outside influence as a hybrid, and sometimes, elements of difference persist as a separate layer. My interviews in Brazil tend to show us both processes at work among most people.

In most places with relatively coherent, relatively powerful nation-states, people come to have a layer of identity that reflects an imagined national identity, as proposed by Anderson (1983). Historically, that process was experienced as beginning with the incursion into local places and cultures of national political institutions, such as the army, tax collectors, and governors. In many places, those national institutions left a relatively light footprint on a still largely local sense of identity. Urban elites have often been shocked at how many rural and small-town people are minimally involved with the nation. Correspondingly, those same urban elites have often radically misunderstood the local communities and identities constructed by people in the nation's periphery. When Peruvian novelist Vargas Llosa (1981) was looking for a metaphor or precedent to understand the enigmatic rural rebellion of the supposedly Maoist Shining Path in Peru, he looked at the striking example of a completely misunderstood religious community in rural Brazil. In the 1890s, this community's withdrawal into a mountain stronghold in southern Bahia at Canudos was (mis)interpreted by the national leadership as a monarchist revolt inspired by France, which led them to send several successive armies to level the place and movement, creating one of the classic, enduring narratives of regional versus national identity in Brazil (da Cunha, 1973).

## Rejecting Cosmopolitan Mores in National Television

In his work in the rural northeast of Brazil, La Pastina found that "things like that only happen in larger cities" was a common explanation for images of sex and gender relations on the major national network programming, telenovelas. Most viewers he interviewed in the small town that was called Macambira perceived a gap between the local set of norms, attitudes, and behaviors and those at work in the urban south represented in the telenovelas. These viewers, both men and women, saw the reality represented in the telenovelas as remote and uncharacteristic of their own lived experiences. This perceived gap was stressed by the conflict between morals and values presented in the telenovelas and those experienced in their own lives. For many, the core distinction between urban-rural lifestyles was located in the lack of privacy in small towns such as Macambira.

This difference between the two worlds—one urban and modern, the other rural and traditional—created a sense that they were in a peripheral state. Many saw Macambira at the edge of modernity *as seen on TV*. They could only glimpse the center of the nation through the screen. At the same time, these viewers were anxious to see these images from a different reality, to see telenovela characters engaging in activities perceived to be urban in nature and location. They were curious to see where these characters ate and entertained themselves and how they dressed, spoke, and worked. This desire informed their views of lifestyles as well as the perceived gap between their own choices and those in urban centers. Nevertheless, this gap between urban and rural attitudes and values underscored another split between viewers. Men and women did not necessarily share the same opinion on this perceived distance between their own lived experience and the life presented in the telenovelas. Many female viewers were more reluctant then male viewers to read those differences solely in terms of their geographical location. So we see here a differentiated interplay between the seemingly dominant discursive awareness of place and cultural-geographic distances within the nation and gender as perceived both locally and nationally.

Dinalva, a 27-year-old mother of two children, thought that women in larger cities could act more freely, like the women in the telenovelas.

In the larger cities the rights [between men and women] are more equal, there is not as much gossip. Here men and women have the same rights but men have more freedom; the woman is marked if she does anything, there is a lot of gossip.

For Dinalva, gossip exerts a damaging form of social control on women's lives in Macambira; she believes women in larger cities to be immune from those social pressures. For her, the distinction between men and women is much more dramatic than the difference between women in urban and rural communities. Equal rights are assumed but qualified: "Men have more freedom."

The telenovela seemed to reinforce this perception of a gap between norms and behaviors in urban and rural settings as well as a gap in gender relations. Men viewed the representation of urban norms and values as something distant and, in many ways, unacceptable. Alternatively, women perceived their constraints in comparison to those presented in the telenovelas. For men, this gap was about northeastern rural culture versus urban southern culture; for women, it was about freedom and equal rights.

Gedião believed the character of the adulterous wife, Leia (in the 1994 telenovela *The Cattle King*), was ripe for a polarized interpretation. As he saw it,

> If a woman "puts horns on his head" (makes him a cuckold), for the rest of his life he will be marked. There are things no one can accept here, you see. And in the south is not like that. I hear that there (in the south) it is common, the woman betrays him and the guy accepts her back.

It seems that television was the source for this reading of different levels of acceptance of betrayal between the urbanized south and Macambira.

Gedião also complained constantly about the representation of the northeast region in the news media. Several other informants in different situations critiqued the news media's recurrent representation of the northeastern Brazil as a poor, promiscuous, primitive, and backward place, and that a criticism sometimes reverted toward La Pastina as a potential promoter of false images of the community (La Pastina, 2004c).

The perception of distance between Macambira and the locus of modernity (in the south of Brazil) presented in telenovelas was manifest in the desire of some viewers to have the telenovelas present more of the lifestyles of the characters. At the same time, these images served as a reminder of their peripheral status, allowing for the circulation of new trends that could be absorbed and digested by the viewers. This distance also served to reinforce their identity as northeasterners, Sertanejos and small-towners: "I could never live in São Paulo, it is too dangerous, too big, too crazy," one person said. That was typical of local comments, at the same time people were talking about the amenities available for those living in urban centers: more leisure activities, greater shopping opportunities at cheaper costs, and anonymity. In this peripheral state, in which urbanness is perceived as central, viewers in Macambira are constructed as others by the television they watch. As media-defined others, these viewers consume modernity through the media at the same time they isolate what is perceived to be undesirable consequences of this modern reality. This dichotomy forced viewers to seek a position between the two realities, the peripheral but lived one and the central one that was only accessed through the screen.

## Language/Culture-Defined Spaces and Markets

Viewers can feel both distance from and proximity to what they see on television. People interviewed in Macambira can feel both cultural-geographic distance from their perceived position in the periphery and also proximity to a national culture to which they are exposed at multiple levels. While their perceived cultural distance is real, so is the lifelong cultivation of national identity that they receive through television, schooling, national music on the radio, national sports such as soccer, national symbols such as the flag, and so on.

Cultural proximity is based in a number of factors that work to overcome cultural distance. Cultural proximity is achieved at a number of levels: local, where shared experience is directly physical and personal; regional, where shared experience can be either direct or mediated; national, where experience comes mostly through media, as observed in Macambira; and transnational, where identities are based in shared language and history at a more removed, but perhaps still quite real level.

Transnational cultural proximity is perhaps derived most basically from language. However, besides language, there are other levels of similarity or proximity, based in cultural elements—dress, ethnic types, gestures, body language, definitions of humor, ideas about story pacing, music traditions, religious elements—that are often shared across national borders. Indian movies are popular in the Arab world because of such similarities; Brazilian telenovelas dubbed into Spanish are more popular than *Dallas* or *Dynasty* in small television-importing Latin American countries like the Dominican Republic, because of such similarities (Straubhaar & Viscasillas, 1991). Iwabuchi (1997, 2002) showed that Taiwanese young people often see Japanese television and music as culturally proximate, sharing a sense of Asian modernity, despite the language difference between Japanese and Chinese, a sense that evolves as modern Taiwanese come to feel more in common over time with modern Japan.

The creation of national borders and identities did not radically reduce existing supranational cultural-linguistic communities and identities, either. Most people in China, Hong Kong, Singapore, and Taiwan all thought of themselves as Chinese, even though those nations and autonomous provinces, as defined in the 20th century, were often in violent ideological or even military conflict.

## Multilevel Identities and Social Class

People identify with multiple cultural groups in various fields of struggle (Bourdieu, 1984). The idea of *field* is useful because people engage in multiple fields of activity and interest. Even within television, for example, people engage the field of entertainment quite differently than the field of news (Benson & Neveu, 2005). In Brazil, people were inclined to be more critical of television news—they were aware that it was censored and manipulated—than of telenovelas, even when both programs were produced by the same broadcaster, TV Globo, the dominant network in Brazil.

However, in my last two years of interviews in Salvador, a major city in the more Afro-Brazilian part of the northeast (in 2004 and 2005), building on La Pastina's (2004b) work in the rural northeast of Brazil, I found that a number of people were turning away from TV Globo's telenovelas. Interviewees continually said that they could not relate to them as well as they could to other kinds of programs on other networks. For example, I heard a recurrent phrase, "I don't see people like me on Globo" in several separate interviews in Salvador. In an interview in 2004, a working-class Afro-Brazilian taxi driver used that phrase to explain why he was increasingly watching SBT, instead of TV Globo (SBT, the No. 2 national network, has had an explicit strategy of targeting lower-middle-class, working-class and working-poor viewers across Brazil ever since the 1980s, when its management began to realize that it could not compete across the board for the general audience; Fadul, 1993). SBT's advertisements in media professional magazines clearly stressed that this audience was defined by class, but they did not make explicit that the working class and poor audience were largely Afro-Brazilian, given the strong demographic correlation that exists between class and race in Brazil (Crook & Johnson, 1999).

I asked the taxi driver if he meant that Globo did not have enough black people on screen and that SBT had more. He said that was part of it, but he wasn't able to elaborate much more; in fact, he seemed uncomfortable talking explicitly about race, as were several others when asked them what they meant by similar comments. They had a much easier time talking about how the people on TV Globo were always too rich, not like the people they knew. And they were able to articulate a sense of how Rio, where most of TV Globo's telenovelas and other programming is set, was a very different place than Salvador; that they were Baianos (people from Bahia) as opposed to Cariocas (people from Rio).

I have examined what people seemed to mean by this phrase. It seems to entail a varying combination of three layers of identity that emerged in the interviews. First, many people in Brazil are actively and consciously aware that most of the people portrayed on television, particularly on TV Globo, are much richer than they are. Interviewees openly articulated a sense of class difference with the people they saw on television. Second, they are openly aware of the same distance, based in cultural geography, which La Pastina found in more rural parts of northeast Brazil: that those people on screen live in a very different part of the country with a substantially different culture. Third, a few articulated the point that more people on screen were white than in Salvador, where most people are Afro-Brazilian.

## Hybridization and Social Class

The relations of social classes change, as groups get defined in class terms, as well as religious, ethnic, and other group differences. Subordinated groups are often moved into lower class status, with ethnicity and other differences serving as markers of class as well as other continuing differences. This reflects an expression of power over the changing political economies by dominant groups, but there is also usually hybridity and movement across class lines as well.

Spaces of interaction emerge between classes and ethnic groups where hybridization takes place (Vianna, 1999). Among cultural elites, some will seek out working-class or poor cultural producers across both class and ethnic lines. Numerous examples exist in Brazil and the United States, as well as elsewhere. In the United States, musical elites, such as those in the 1960s folk revival, crossed class and regional lines to appropriate ideas from gospel, bluegrass, and country music. More commercially minded rock musicians and producers have reached to minority and working-class cultural producers to appropriate elements from blues, rhythm and blues, soul, and hip-hop. From several directions, there is a role for cultural spaces or places where elites encounter the popular and for social mediators, people who put the two together (Vianna, 1999).

### Television, Cultural Geography, and Poor Brazilians

Many rural and extremely poor urban Brazilians still rely heavily on traditional oral cultures that are often very local, so many poor Brazilians are only somewhat inserted into the national cultural context. Radio is often a localizing force in terms of music, news, and talk. People in Salvador talked about listening to local and regional music (*axé, samba-reggae, baião, maracatu, forró*) on local radio channels, as well as national music, such as samba. They were conscious of the differences and were aware of what stations to tune in for local versus regional versus national music. However, television is very much a nationalizing force in the lives of poor people. Poor people receive relatively little global cultural influence. However, the vast majority of what little global influence reaches poor people does so through television.

Writing of the mid-1980s, Kottak (1990) noted that "rural Brazilians knowledge of the contemporary world . . . is certainly greater now than it was before television. By the mid-1980s, as a direct result of exposure to television, villagers had become much more world wise" (p. 134). Kottak (1990) observed that most of the content rural and poor people in Brazil learn from television and radio is nationally focused. People in my studies, as well as those of La Pastina and Kottak, spoke of national soccer, characters and themes on telenovelas, awareness of a few national political issues, and a general sense of what Brazilians have in common. Kottak (1990) noted that one of the primary impacts of television in Brazil has been to make previously isolated people feel comfortable with other Brazilians and with being Brazilian. Kottak gave the example of a shy rural woman who moved to a formerly isolated village on the outskirts of Salvador and remained isolated despite the move until her family got television. With television and more regular social opportunities, she gradually became more outgoing and socially integrated (pp. 133–134).

The results of both Kottak's study and the present one show that television tends to add a layer of national awareness to rural Brazilians. They become aware of Brazilian city life, as portrayed in the telenovelas, but the actual motivation to migrate to the city has much more to do with interpersonal contacts with migrants, particularly among their own families. They become aware of new ideas about race and gender roles, which tend to change locally held definitions and stereotypes. They become aware of national holidays, foods, sports, and music, and this knowledge gradually supplements traditional local activities and consumption. They also receive a very minimal global awareness.

The urban poor are mostly migrants to the city from rural areas and small towns. Much of their cultural identity is a hybrid of rural tradition and national urban culture. For example, the traditional music that rural migrants brought with them from northeastern Brazil to the major cities of the southeast, such as São Paulo, has been transformed into various hybrids that add electronic instruments, urban images and themes, industrial production, and marketing to rural tunes, stories, and images. According to my interviews in São Paulo, the migrants welcome, indeed help create, this kind of hybrid culture because it helps them adjust to life in the city while preserving a memory of the (oral) culture where they grew up. Some of these kinds of music, such as *forró*, have since become major regional cultural industries as well as partial successes within the national music market. Migrants from the northeast of Brazil use such music, related holidays, foods, and travel back to festivals in their hometowns to maintain a layer of regional identity even after decades of living in southern Brazilian cities.

Interviews with urban poor people in Brazil reflect a cultural identity that is in transition from the kind of local and traditional rural culture described earlier to the national televised common cultural identity. Since their move to the city, they have an increasing awareness of urban issues, of city and national leaders, of urban transport and working conditions, of working-class consumer aspirations (particularly in food, clothes, and basic household products), of national ethnic and religious images, of new urban gender roles, of less traditional sexual behavior and imagery, and—to a small degree—of global culture. Although much of this comes from national television, interviews show that the urban poor rely mostly on oral communication with the people and groups they know for essential cultural capital as they adjust to city life.

## Working-Class Cultural Identity

Not unlike the urban poor, from which they mostly come, working-class people in Brazil are focused on the local and the regional, to a lesser degree on the national, and fairly little on the international or global. Interviews in São Paulo and Salvador, Bahia, for this study show that the interpersonal sources of working-class culture involve the extended family, the neighborhood, groups of friends of the same age and gender, the workplace and union, and, most of all, the immediate nuclear family and the home. Jacks (1996) talks about the importance of the home and of daily life as the crux of people's reception and understanding of television in Brazil. This was true for most of those interviewed for this study, but it seemed particularly key for working-class people, who are working hard to establish and maintain a stable residence and home environment, aware of the danger of slipping back into the urban poor and maybe even into homelessness. Interviews from 1989 to 1995 evidenced a particularly strong sense of anxiety about this. The church, either Catholic or Protestant, is important for some but not all as an additional source of cultural capital. In fact, by the time of my interviews in 2003 through 2005, a number of working-class and poor Brazilians in Salvador were joining Pentecostal churches to get alternative forms of cultural capital to change their lives, both spiritually and economically (Chestnut, 1997).

Our interviews showed that working-class Brazilians primarily used television to learn about the nation and national culture in Brazil. Television itself is a considerable source of cultural capital for working-class Brazilians. In interviews, working-class people talked about things they had learned about other parts of Brazil and the world. Working-class men, in particular, talked about prime-time television news programs such as Globo's *Jornal Nacional* as a major source of information; this was true in my interviews, in work by La Pastina and Kottak (1990), and in various surveys over the years. In fact, in 2005, when I was specifically examining the idea that the poor and working-class black Brazilians might be moving away from TV Globo, most working-class and poor men I spoke with still watched *Jornal Nacional*. In part, television news still holds this niche because working-class and poor people can't afford newspapers, newsmagazines, or cable TV, and news on radio is seen as limited in quantity and depth. Like poor Brazilians, working-class Brazilians seem to have learned mostly about Brazil itself, although what they knew about the world also tended to come from television news, variety shows, and documentaries. For example, Ivan, whom I interviewed in both 2004 and 2005, was interested in what he had learned about U.S. politics from television news, but what he knew from the same source about Brazilian politics was far more detailed and nuanced.

An increasing number of programs on SBT and TV Record directly focus on working-class concerns, particularly a genre of issue-oriented reality shows that focus on and denounce real issues, such as the shortage of hospital beds in free public hospitals. On one of those shows on TV Record, an interviewer talked to people waiting in hospitals for operations or even just a bed. Watching the show with several working-class Afro-Brazilian people, mostly musicians, in Salvador in 2004, I was struck by how interested they were in the issues raised by the show. They repeatedly commented that the program was showing things the way they really were—hard—for poor people in Brazil. At the same time, people remarked that TV Globo did not show things like this, the things that interviewees cared about. Class awareness of issues can provide a critical filter for selecting, reading, and interpreting television programs for Brazil, just as Morley (1992) found for working-class people in Britain.

## Middle-Class Cultural Identity

Working-class Brazilians aspire to be middle class, at least lower middle class. That typically means a nicer dwelling, a car, more appliances, a telephone, and more and better education, aiming at completed secondary or maybe even university education. To the interviewees, it also implied an occupation with less physical labor, residence in different neighborhoods, opportunity to attend private schools, and adherence to what is seen as a more conventional set of values and mores.

An image of what it is to be middle class seems to be one of the main items of cultural capital that poor and working-class interviewees acquired from watching television, particularly the telenovelas. Although census statistics suggest that moving from working class or lower to the middle class is fairly hard to accomplish in real life in Brazil, this is very much the stuff of which telenovela plots are made, according to reviewers such as Artur da Távola (1984). Reviewing an ostensibly Americanized telenovela with discos, called *Dancin' Days,* in the late 1970s, da Távola observed that like most novelas, it was really about how to become middle class. The defining moment for him came not in the disco scenes, but when one of the characters asked his wife if she would like a refrigerator, and she burst into tears of joy (cited in Straubhaar, 1981).

My interviews over the years have supported this view. People interviewed think telenovelas mostly focus on romance, on getting ahead in life (upward mobility—*subir na vida*), and on the urban middle class, particularly the upper middle class in Rio de Janeiro. Aside from consumer items such as refrigerators, the Brazilian cultural capital understanding or perception of *middle class* focuses on education, family stability, a better and more varied diet, greater leisure options, better housing, and a sense of security, according to interviewees, both in the middle class and beneath it.

Considerable impacts on identity and behavior among Brazilians can flow from this TV definition of what it is to be middle class and from hints on televised programs, both telenovelas and others, about how people get there. A team of Brazilian and U.S. demographers saw a series of connections, including a high and significant statistical correlation in census data, between how long Brazilians had television and smaller family sizes (Faria & Potter, 1994). Although hard and fast conclusions about cause and effect were impossible, their overall conclusion from surveys, ethnographies, focus groups, and content studies was that telenovelas had consistently shown for decades that successful middle-class families had fewer children; the audience had learned that lesson (McAnany & Potter, in press).

## Upper-Middle- and Upper-Class Cultural Identity

Chapter 8 makes the point that upper-middle-class and upper-class Brazilians are more globalized in their television viewing because their life experience, reflected in their cultural capital, enables them to understand and enjoy globalized television more than working-class or poor Brazilians do. Through schooling, family travel, language education, personal networks, occupational experiences, and other direct personal experiences, the upper classes build both the cultural capital and the disposition to watch globalized television. They also have the economic capital to afford cable or satellite pay-TV, which is far more global than broadcast television. The number of Brazilian homes with cable or satellite pay-TV has slowly risen from 5% to just over 12% in the past 15 years.

Brazilian MTV provided an interesting case of globalization aimed at the upper, upper middle and some of the middle class through television in Brazil. MTV Brazil is a joint venture between MTV and the large publisher, Editor Abril. Its content started as 70% to 80% U.S. and European rock and pop music videos, although the Brazilian percentage has risen over the years. The program targeted only the upper 20% to 30% of the population, in terms of class status and buying power, according to interviews in 1994 and 1998 with MTV Brazil research and marketing staff members. The show reflected the need of advertisers to target the more affluent and the more globalized among Brazilian youth in terms of consumer preferences. MTV Brazil also targeted this group because it was the most interested in the U.S. and European music that MTV has to offer. The target was reached. A 1997 MARPLAN study of eight major urban markets in Brazil showed that 22% of MTV's audience was in Class A (upper class), 44% in Class B (upper middle class), 28% in Class C (middle class), 6% in Class D (working class), and none in Class D (the poor; MTV, 1997).

These middle-, upper-middle-, and upper-class youth have the cultural capital base that leads them away from a strictly national cultural identity and into a more globalized direction. They have a more elite education, which often includes serious study of English. They are more likely to have traveled abroad or to know people there. They are more likely to be aware of American and European brands, due in part to MTV's own role in building and focusing their cultural capital; magazines and radio stations that target this same elite youth audience also have an impact. The targeted audience is more likely to be aware of American stars, lifestyles, and images, again partially due to MTV, as well as movies, both at the theater and on video. However, even these more upper-class youth still usually like Brazilian music, particularly Brazilian urban rock, samba-reggae, rap, hip-hop, funk, and other global elements. Some Brazilian music is part of the broad cultural capital shared across class lines that was discussed earlier. These elite youth reflect the power of social structure in the very different access that their cultural and economic capital gives them to being global.

## Some Broadly Shared Globalization via Television

Although media exposure and use is enormously varied by social class, media exposure has produced some degree of globalization in almost all Brazilians. Very few have no global layer at all to their identity or cultural capital. At the simplest level, people are aware that there is an outside world, an America, a Japan, although "foreignness" is relative. More than one northeastern Brazilian interviewee thought Japan was down by São Paulo someplace and didn't realize that people speak languages other than Portuguese because everything on television is in Portuguese and the dubbing isn't always obvious to people.

This minimum globalization that almost all Brazilians have is almost entirely a result of media exposure, particularly radio, television, and movies on television. Interviews by my students and me showed that few Brazilians outside the upper middle and upper classes have any direct, unmediated contact with foreigners or with global culture. In contrast, my interviews in the Dominican Republic in 1987 through 1988 showed that almost everyone knew someone who had been in the United States to work or live, so Dominicans participated much more in the diasporic or migrant approach to globalization emphasized by scholars such as Bhabha (1994). In contrast, due to their geographic distance from the United States and the more self-contained economy of Brazil, the vast majority of Brazilians participate only in mediated and very limited globalization, acquiring relatively little global cultural capital.

# Hybridization: Race and Ethnic Identity

In this analysis, hybridization includes several key elements. The most basic is the movement, interaction, and interpenetration of human populations. Focusing on migration and the movement of peoples adds a racial or ethnic interpenetration via *mestizaje* or racial miscegenation. This was particularly true historically in the Americas. The element of migration also introduces the formation of diasporic communities, where the migrants often try to maintain their own ethnic definitions or constructions, along with a sense of cultural community. This is particularly true of recent patterns of global migration and of the migration of Asians, Latinos, Africans, and Middle Easterners, such as Turks and Arabs, to North America and Europe.

One current approach to hybridization would argue that ethnicity, like culture, is an evolving or hybridizing social construct (Nederveen Pieterse, 2004). Definitions of ethnicity may vary within a country, as they do in Brazil. They can be articulated by social class, as they are in Brazil, so that a richer, better dressed person would likely be considered 'whiter" than a poorer person of the same physical racial characteristics. Definitions can change over generations, as they have among U.S. Latinos. However, a contemporary sense of racial and ethnic identity exists for most people. For many, they are important mediators of watching television and other media. For migrant audiences in the diaspora, differences of ethnicity and of language are often the primary levels of identity mediating television choices.

U.S. Latinos are an interesting example of a migrant population and audience for television (Davila, 2001). Many Latinos have come to the United States and fully acculturated, following the old model of the U.S. melting pot. They intermarried with non-Latinos, learned to speak only English, and integrated fully in what is considered the dominant U.S. culture. However, many Latinos preserve a variety of aspects of Latino cultures (even those from Mexico come from a variety of regional subcultures, and many come from Central America or elsewhere). Many still speak Spanish, and some speak only Spanish. Thus, they present an interesting example of a group whose identities may be both hybridizing and forming multiple layers. Furthermore, many Latino immigrants come as part of a temporary diaspora, fully intending to go back home after making some money, getting an education, learning English, or seeing some new things. Former migrants have gone back home to run for political office in Zacatecas and other states in Mexico. Others come and go in a kind of circular diaspora, spending part of their time in the United States and part back in their home countries. Others represent a kind of split identity, working in the United States to support family members back home, forming some ties in the United States but still participating in the cultural life of villages, cities, and states back home. To some scholars, this complexity is less important than the perceived threat to U.S. cultural stability from the recent massive influx of immigrants who do not share the language (English), culture (Anglo), or dominant religion (Protestant) of the United States (Huntington, 2004). However, many others have noted that this view focuses on the large number of first-generation immigrants and that second- and third-generation immigrants from Latin America tend to learn English and adapt to the United States, just as earlier immigrants from other countries did.

U.S. Latinos present a mixed group of people. Some families have been in the United States, particularly California, New Mexico, and Texas, much longer than the Anglos who now consider themselves the dominant mainstream of those states. Most Latinos come more recently and from various Latin American countries. Those who have been in the United States for multiple generations may no longer speak Spanish as a first or primary language. The effort to scoop all these diverse people into a single Latino or

Hispanic television audience, based primarily on Spanish-language broadcasting, has been criticized as somewhat artificial (Rodriguez, 1999). More and more, this audience is fragmenting into more specific groups based on more specific layers of identity, including language and culture (Gardyn, 2001). Latinos are divided not only by language and linguistic capital, but also by culture, cultural capital, and their use of new technologies such as the Internet (Rojas et al., 2004).

In 2004, my colleagues and I interviewed a number of Latinos who had been in Austin, Texas, for at least 2 years but were otherwise diverse in terms of years in the United States, gender, age, and reliance on English or Spanish more in media use. Some Spanish speakers, particularly those older than 50 years, were similar in their use of Spanish-language television, even though they were otherwise divided by religion, gender, education, and political agenda. An older woman with the lowest education level in the entire group watches mostly Mexican telenovelas; a younger man with a college education and a strong political agenda as a Chicano, watches Spanish-language TV as a way to reinforce his cultural and linguistic ties. Three of four interviewees who had been born in Mexico watched Spanish-language television, such as telenovelas and news, to stay in touch with their homeland. Only the most highly educated first-generation Mexican immigrant, with a college degree from the Monterrey Institute of Technology, declared that he watched TV in English. Several younger interviewees were more likely to speak English and watch television in English.

In the 2004 interviews, we began to notice strong differences between generations of immigrants in terms of what kind of television they watched. In the 2005 study, then, we made a stronger effort to find both recent and longer term immigrants from Mexico and Central America. We built on the methodological ideas of Gonzalez (1986) and Bertaux and Thompson (1997), who emphasized the value of interviewing and tracking multiple generations of families to trace phenomena related to social class. Drawing on other ideas of Bertaux (1981) and Gonzalez (1986), we emphasized life history interviews with as many generations of families as I could locate. This gave us a particularly powerful look at the differences between generations of immigrants, as well as the commonalities in the trajectories of families as they struggled to acquire economical and cultural capital (Rojas et al., 2005).

We found that we had to be careful about two quite different sets of categories of generations. Much of the literature builds on the idea of comparing the experiences of first-generation immigrants, who often rely more on their native languages, with second- and third-generation immigrants, who may have adapted to their new environment and learned English, thus using more English-language media. However, the literature on U.S. media has increasingly emphasized generational differences between young, middle aged, and older people. As a result, we found it necessary to discuss both generation of immigration and literal age generation. In the latter, we grouped people as follows: young (18–29), parent generation (30–55), and grandparents generation or older (55 years or more). Anticipating differences based on age among Mexican immigrants as well as long-term U.S. residents and citizens, we built on the findings about differences between these three age groups in Mexico by Maass and Gonzaléz (2005).

In 2005, we interviewed several first-generation immigrants, people who had come across the border either by themselves or with their families. Some spoke only Spanish and were focused on Spanish-language television. However, several, particularly those with more years of education, had learned some English before coming to the United States and were using television in both languages. For example, Nora left Mexico after graduating from college; she watched entertainment programs in Spanish sometimes to relax, but she pushed herself to watch English programs to improve her English.

Generational age differences were in many ways more striking. Overall, younger people, both adolescents and those of college age, were more likely to watch either just English-language programming or both English and Spanish programming. Some younger Latinos who spoke Spanish still considered English their first language, considering themselves better educated in English than Spanish, so their television use, particularly for news and information, tilts toward English. Some of them consciously watched entertainment such as telenovelas in Spanish to maintain or improve their Spanish. For example, Steven and Joe felt embarrassed about their Spanish-language ability and saw Spanish-language television as one way to bolster it. One third-generation Latino in his 20s said, "I don't want Spanish speakers to think I am some kind of *pocho* [a derogatory term for an Americanized person of Mexican origin] who has forgotten everything about where he comes from." In another example, Stephen and Estrella had come to see learning and maintaining Spanish as part of a politically defined Chicano identity that was important to them. They tended to use English more but made a point of using Spanish-language television, too, deliberately to reinforce a sense of Chicano identity.

Some young Latinos who are also third-generation (or more) immigrants did not grow up speaking Spanish at all, particularly if their parents were encouraging them to go to college. Joe and Alberto, for example, were trying to learn Spanish as adults to reclaim that heritage. Others were simply assimilating into the Anglo population, using almost entirely English-language media.

Adults older than 30, even if they were second- or third-generation immigrants, were more likely to be proficient in Spanish. Several adults were specific in their media use: English for certain kinds of information or entertainment, Spanish for other kinds of information and entertainment. However, some adults did not watch television in Spanish, preferring both entertainment and information in English. Those in the older or grandparent generation, older than 55, were more likely to speak only Spanish or have only limited English ability, leading them to stress Spanish-language television more heavily.

In the 2005 interviewing, we also looked at differences in family trajectory. We found that families differed considerably in whether they encouraged younger generations to maintaining their Spanish-language skills. When families did so, it had considerable impact on whether younger members used Hispanic-oriented television. However, some were like the M family of West Austin, a neighborhood in what is considered the Anglo part of town. They maintained some ability in Spanish but made very little use of Spanish media. Other families, like Joseph's, pushed children to learn English, not Spanish; he is learning Spanish in college, after marrying a bilingual Spanish speaker.

In Brazil, my interviews found less evidence that race or ethnicity was a major conscious criterion in deciding what to watch on television. As noted earlier, people had a hard time sorting out their own identities between race and class. Does something interest them because they are black or because they are working class or poor? This reflects 20th-century Brazilian ideology that race is not a problem in mixed-race Brazil, but class is a real problem (Crook & Johnson 1999). As noted earlier, at least two networks target lower-middle-class, working-class, and working-poor Brazilians, who are much more likely to be African-descended, black, or mixed race, whereas middle-class and elite Brazilians tend to be European-descended or at the whiter end of mixed race.

Contemporary movements seek more awareness of race as a layer of identity in Brazil, particularly in Salvador, Bahia, where a number of well-known Carnival music groups have been notably Afrocentric in their themes, imagery, and discourse since the early 1980s (Guerreiro, 2000). This movement was reflected in my observation and interviewing in 2005. I watched a TV Globo national singing contest, FAMA (Fame), with a group of people at the Banda Femina Didá, an Afrocentric samba group for women. The group's lead singer was competing with seven others for one of three spots representing northeast Brazil. Only three contestants were Afro-descended, although most people in the region probably are. One black contestant, whom the Didá people called a *negão* (handsome black man), and two white people won. The Didá people were rooting for their singer and another mixed-race woman who had a lot of charisma and a great voice. As the other regions (north-central and south-southeast) also voted, the founder of Banda

Femina Didá, a musician widely known as Neguinho da Samba, became disgusted with the predominance of white singers in the winners circle. Two other probable Afro-descended contestants won among five from the south, making a total of three black winners out of twelve. (Census data, which depend on self-report, show that about half of Brazilians are Afro-descended.) Neguinho looked at me and said, "Look, Professor, at the bias that is still there in this country," then left the room.

## Gender Identity and Television

In highly segmented television systems like the cable and satellite TV systems common in North America, East Asia, and Europe, gender has often become one major means of splitting the audience into specific interest groups. Channels like Oxygen or Lifetime in the United States target women directly. In less segmented systems, the direct targeting of women as an audience is more subtly worked into the schedules of mass audience networks; for example, Univisión, which targets U.S. Hispanics, or TV Globo, which targets all classes of Brazilians. On such networks, women are targeted in certain talk shows and as a major part of the audience for telenovelas. Certain daytime hours are seen as key times for women-oriented programming.

During his interviews with people in Macambira in rural northeast Brazil, La Pastina found that gender, patriarchal culture, geographic isolation, and differing levels of cultural capital were central mediating factors influencing readings, interpretations, and occasional appropriations of the telenovela *The Cattle King*. Gender was central not only to the engagement and interpretation of the telenovela text but also to the shaping of cultural capital and other subject positions adopted by the viewers.

In many ways, established gender norms and attitudes in Macambira structured the levels of interaction between viewers and text. Women's increasing economic power, due to their work as embroiderers, and the increasing dependence among males on women's income, has created a fracture in the traditional male-female domination patterns in the area. This has allowed women to question their roles and men's roles in the household and community. Through the telenovela, women could observe alternatives, which they then appropriated to assess their own lives and the life of the community in relation to that of the characters in the south. La Pastina's finding supports earlier reception study findings by Leal (1986) and Vink (1988). Women viewers in Macambira perceived the melodramatic roots of the genre and expected the writers to follow conventions. Incorporating a more contemporary social context in the telenovela narrative seemed to distance these texts from their melodramatic roots, apparently making it harder for women to engage with the characters.

Males, on the other hand, saw these contemporary aspects as a bridge to what they perceived to be a realistic narrative, which is how they justified their viewing and enjoyment of the telenovela. Established norms and attitudes regarding gender roles in the community made it unlikely that men would acknowledge enjoying the melodrama. Telenovelas, for these males, were valued according to their perceived informational content and realism. Men felt that their masculinity, many times questioned by their inability to provide for their households, could be damaged even more by their association with a feminized text, such as a telenovela. When they watched telenovelas, men preferred to talk about issues that interested them; in the case of *O Rei do Gado,* it was land reform and the rural lifestyle (La Pastina, 1999). Even if the genre was perceived as feminine, males used the rural lifestyle and the political narrative to think about their lives in relation to the urban modern south (La Pastina, 2001). Their interest in these elements of the narrative seemed to indicate that perceived gender norms hindered male viewers' engagement with the more traditional melodramatic elements of class ascension, love, and betrayal. This, however, does not mean that men paid no attention to those elements. It means they took a greater interest in elements associated with the male sphere, such as politics and farm techniques, rather than engaging with elements normally associated with the female sphere, such as child rearing and romance.

## Telenovelas, Gender, Sexuality, National Values, and Local Values

Viewers in Macambira frequently blamed television for many problems in the community, especially the behavior of young people. Some complained about violence and drugs. Others said that children misbehaved and did not respect parents and elders anymore. But the most common accusation was that television, and telenovelas, in particular, were showing too much sex, making young children excited and prone to engage in it. Some in Macambira felt a conflict between a desire to see their children better informed and the need to hide and protect them from what some perceived to be difficult times, in which traditional sexual norms and roles had been challenged. As most parents and adults saw it, television led children and adolescents to become more aware of the world around them and therefore to be more demanding. In some cases women were also considered potential victims of television. It would seem that only adult males were perceived to be immune to the impact of television.

Augusto thought telenovelas showed the road to change in traditional social behaviors and adoption of behaviors he perceived to be more modern or civilized. He also believed that telenovelas could influence the way female adultery was perceived. He acknowledged that women's reputations were still much more vulnerable than those of men, but he thought that was changing. For him, women in the telenovelas, and consequently in larger urban centers, were already liberated and engaging in practices that were still perceived to be wrong in a small town such as Macambira. He believed that women, even in rural communities, had gained more freedom and that society was more accepting. This view was corroborated by many other accounts in the community, but the question that remained was how much of the perceived change affected women's rights and independence.

From the interviews La Pastina conducted it seemed clear that most viewers believed telenovelas had a role in promoting behavior that many deemed inappropriate. Ultimately, telenovelas seemed to be showing a society in which gender relations were different than what was accepted locally, and in doing so, they presented the danger of subverting established norms. This awareness of different lifestyles also highlights the distance between local viewers' perceived culture and the culture represented in the telenovela. In this process, the viewers in Macambira felt themselves to be on the periphery of an urban modern world broadcast daily in the telenovela.

## Layers of Identity as Boundaries for Choices and Understandings

Identities are clearly complex, even within an individual, much more so when aggregated to the level of collective identities in an even more complex culture. In my concluding thoughts, I return briefly to complexity theory, which I examined at the institutional and organizational level in earlier chapters. Increasing levels of identity seem likely to increase complexity at both individual and collective levels, leading to more complex, less easily predictable patterns of television choices and understandings by audiences. Viewers will share some layers of culture and identity, but it's unlikely that any will share all because they vary by gender, race, class, family background, language, and age. These all add different layers of experience and identity to guide choices and understandings among a set of television offerings, which are also increasingly multilayered and diverse. In fact, I have demonstrated in this chapter and the preceding one, in the case of Brazil, television helps form the cultural capital that works alongside identities to inform choices and understandings of television.

One useful aspect of complexity theory is the idea of recursivity (Balcazar, Diaz, & Gabarro, 1995; Kak, 2005). The idea is that patterns tend to repeat, that the whole of something develops or emerges from a process of repetition of many smaller, similar parts, like a computer program made up of many similar subprograms. In this sense, individuals in the same culture tend to share many of the same layers of culture. Many will share common experiences as women or Latinas; some will add having watched the same television programs, some not. As a combination of gender, ethnic, and cultural-linguistic identity, Latinas will have a lot of common patterns but also some variation—another key idea of complexity theory—that will emerge, change, and hybridize over time. Thus, the meaning of *Latina* is a constantly changing but still a recognizable cultural pattern or identity. Similarly, the larger culture will be made up of many people who share quite a few things, repeating patterns, but with a lot of variation. Some are watching television in English from within an Anglophone cultural-linguistic sphere dominated by the United States. Some, while living in the United States, are watching television in Spanish from within a Latin American culture-linguistic sphere dominated by Mexico. Both patterns are recursively performed or carried out by large numbers of people who sometimes interact more, sometimes less, but add to a collective pattern or identity for the United States.

Another related way of seeing the constellation of layers of identity for an individual or for a group is as a personal or collective set of boundaries that give some sense of the limits to what is likely in people's interests, choices, and understandings. If someone in the United States has a regional identity that is turned off by New York culture, they may draw a personal boundary that excludes *Seinfeld*. If they don't speak Spanish, then fairly clear boundaries are drawn around their viewing choices in terms of the languages and the large-scale cultural-linguistic, Anglophone versus Hispanic spheres of television in the United States.

On the other hand, interesting variations happen that cross such boundaries. For example, some primarily English-speaking television viewers in the United States found the Colombian telenovela *Yo soy Betty, la fea* (I am Ugly Betty) so interesting when it was broadcast in Spanish that they struggled to watch it. That caught the attention of U.S. broadcasters, who prepared a U.S. version, initiating what may be a significant cultural innovation, adapting the Latin American version of the soap opera back to the United States (Rivero, 2003). This may happen not only in the specific case of ABC's production of *Ugly Betty* but also the more general case of U.S. television networks adapting the format into more general English-language use for U.S. audiences (Bielby & Harrington, 2005). This is also an interesting example of recursion, in genres and formats rather than individual identities; it shows how examples recur and adapt over time, as Colgate-Palmolive deliberately localizes the soap opera in Cuba, whence the idea spreads to Colombia, where producers further adapt or glocalize the genre to fit Colombia, which produces a telenovela that concretizes a possibility of U.S. producers relocalizing the genre and the specific production in the United States. (See Chapter 6 for more discussion of localization and glocalization of the telenovela and other genres.)

## Layers of Identities as Mediators of Media Meaning

In this chapter, I have reviewed a number of the primary layers of identity that have influenced television viewing, particularly among people I interviewed in Brazil and among Latinos in Austin, Texas. People's senses of identity in terms of cultural geography, class, ethnicity, and gender guide their choices of what to watch on television. Those viewing choices are the most basic and perhaps most important way in which people interact with television. Multiple layers of identity also guide the ways that people make sense of television and the ways in which television seems to affect them.

For example, in 2004, I joined people from the Banda Feminina Didá to watch a television program denouncing inadequate medical care for poor people. Most but not all of the people shown on screen were Afro-descended. The commentary in the room at that point focused on the viewers' sense of solidarity with other poor or working-class people, like the ones on screen in hospitals and clinics. One could infer racial solidarity, too, but it was not the main issue at the moment, even though it was clearly the main issue for members of the same group a year later when they observed racial bias in a televised song contest. Clearly, people move among multiple senses of identity as frames of reference, as resources for understanding media, and as mediators of media content.

The idea of mediation has become a key theoretical principal in Latin American work about television, starting with Martin-Barbero (1993), who argued that the focus should move from the media themselves to the forces that mediate people's experiences with and understandings of media content. Both Martin-Barbero (1993) and Mexican media ethnographer Orozco (1993) argued for the importance of considering multiple sites of mediation. I would argue that this means consideration of mediation by multiple layers and sources of identity.

As La Pastina found in his fieldwork in Macambira, senses or layers of identity can be mediating forces that help people make sense of what they watch on television. In his work in this rural Brazilian community, he found that people expressed a sense of cultural distance from the television productions on TV Globo, reflecting life and values in the south of Brazil. That sense of significant difference in cultural geography between the local and the national corresponds to what I found while interviewing in Salvador, Bahia.

La Pastina also found in Macambira that gender, particularly the patriarchal culture of the town, its geographic isolation within Brazil, and people's differing levels of cultural capital, were central mediating factors influencing various individuals' readings, interpretations, and occasional appropriations of content. His fieldwork was focused on a specific telenovela, but these kinds of identities also provide filters and mediators for people's interactions with a variety of television content.

Much of this mediation process is local and interpersonal. In cases such as La Pastina's study of Macambira, local culture can be a significant mediator of national, regional, or global television viewing. However, this local process is also informed by previous exposure to television, to education, to travel and language learning, to advertising, to other media such as books and newspapers, and to a variety of personal experiences, all of this creating the cultural capital that mediates television viewing. This creates both a personal and shared cultural prefiguration. Much of that cultural exposure, especially to television programming, advertising, and education, is most often framed by a national process, guided in many nations by explicit state policy. So I must also put identity formation and maintenance in terms of power, as it is structured for people by national, local, and global institutions, by economic power, and by other social forces that construct race and ethnicity, for example.

These mediations or conversations can also be multiple, corresponding to multiple identities and groups' cultural habitus. These mediations select elements, again within a cultural context or contexts, which are then added to the ongoing larger cultural context(s). This refiguration process, according to Ricoeur (1984), refigures the cultural context(s), which then becomes the prefiguration(s) for ongoing or further media consumption.

## Reconfiguration and Synthesis of Identities

Ricoeur (1984) discussed a recursive cycle between producers and audiences of prefiguration, configuration, and refiguration. (He makes a specific use of the complexity idea of recursion discussed above.) As described in Chapter 6, the prefiguration is the context in which someone receives a cultural artifact such as a television program. I would argue now that these contexts are both shared and multiple. They include a variety of cultural elements from different layers (local to global, class-related, family-related, ethnic, etc.) that form cultural knowledge shared by individuals. There are general, interlinked pools of cultural knowledge from which individuals draw a personal repertoire of symbols and interpretive understanding.

The pool or layer of cultural knowledge most relevant to television is usually the national. This is the shared knowledge that both the writer of a national television network's soap opera and its viewers use to make sense of what is being said and shown. Some of this knowledge revolves around the definitions and conventions of the genre being produced or watched. However, much more general knowledge informs the specific content of the program: social references, historical situations or references, jokes, locations, ethnic definitions of beauty, culturally defined gender roles, national constructions of ethnicity, dominant religious sensibilities, and so on. Put another way, these are cultural definitions that also form the grounds for a viewer's feeling of cultural proximity with a program, which in television is probably most common again at the national culture level, despite all the other layers and levels I have discussed.

For Ricouer (1984), the moment of media or cultural consumption is the configuration of a cultural artifact such as a literary work by the person receiving and reading it. The individual receives media such as television within a cultural context, or as I argue here, multiple layers of culture and cultural identity that guide the processing of various forms of culture. The individual employs cultural knowledge from the cultural prefigurations or contexts, working within layers of identity that act as mediators for how to receive and interpret the new culture or information. These layers of identity also work within interpretive communities, from families to religious groups, friends, even formally structural groups like school classes. In this interpretive process, people not only rely on their own internalized layers of identity and cultural capital, but also interact with the broad pools of cultural knowledge available to them through media, through a variety of institutional channels such as schools and churches, and through interpretive communities based in a variety of social layers and spaces.

# Appendix

## Methods and Data for the Television Flow Study

This book rests in part on a foundation of data collected about television programming in several countries around the world. These data are discussed at length in Chapters 6 and 7.

## Methodology

The data for this study were generated through a simple content analysis of television listings in TV guides and newspapers during sample periods since 1962. Each program was categorized, and the number of minutes each program lasted were added up to create a total number of minutes for that category. Categories were located in a matrix between program types/genres (news shows, variety shows, etc.) and program sources (national, regional, U.S., other international, coproduction). The genre subcategories were originally developed during studies in the Dominican Republic and Brazil; the genre categories used by industry experts were compared with genre categories that emerged from in-depth interviews with audience members. The resulting list of genres was valid in terms of being accepted by both creators and consumers of television and reliable across interviewees in both countries. As countries were added to the sample, care was taken in further coding, particularly in countries outside Latin America, to make sure that the same overall genre categories still applied.

In the data, prime-time broadcasting is distinguished from the total broadcast day. This strategy permitted a rough measure of which programs were relatively more popular because in all countries used in the study, the most popular programming tended to be concentrated in that period of time when, by definition, the most people were watching. Local designations of prime time varied, depending on the national culture and habits, but they generally fell between 7 p.m. and 11 p.m. This prime time vs. total broadcast day distinction was used in a study of Brazil by Straubhaar (1981) and in the second round of the UNESCO study by Varis and Nordenstreng (1985). It has proven useful in isolating the programming intended to be most widely viewed, typically reflecting the programmer's anticipation of what will be most popular (Havens, 2006).

Participants or coders were selected for their familiarity with program names, types, and sources over time. Coders were trained in categorizing programs by genre and by country of origin. The coders were initially treated more as a panel of experts than as a set of interchangeable coders in a standard content analysis. They consulted with other people from their respective countries to make sure that the accepted definitions of genre categories applied within their country or culture. Substantial agreement was sought before coding the category definitions; in addition, an intercoder reliability analysis was conducted for subsamples of the coded schedule in all but two of the initial countries. Intercoder reliability exceeded 90%, which is not surprising, given that the coding was quite basic: simply categorizing programs by commonly accepted genre definitions and by country of origin. When coders had any doubts about how to identify or categorize a program by genre or origin, they contacted other people from that country to make sure that they had correctly identified the type and source of the program. A list of standard genre category descriptions, or coding instructions, was created and used, although for some countries, categories emerged that did not fit in the overall pattern of genres.

## Sample

Sample countries are drawn from six geocultural or cultural-linguistic areas: Latin America (including the U.S–Hispanic cultural market), the Anglophone (English-speaking) nations and cultural markets (including Anglo-Canada), Asia, Europe, the Middle East, and Africa. In Latin America, a regional market has been well-developed for decades; in East Asia, national production has been strong, and regional production seems to be developing; in Africa, a regional market might be logical, but as yet, countries are having little national production or regional exchange. Countries were selected to represent a diverse range of market sizes and production abilities within those six regions of the world.

The sample periods are one week in March or November in 1962, 1972, 1982, 1991/1992, and 2001/2002; that is, five 1-week periods. (When this project began in the early 1980s, a 1-week sample was considered adequate.

Some scholars now argue that at least 2 weeks per year is necessary, but lacking the staff or financial resources to redo early data, 1-week samples were used for comparability.) Some minor variations took place, particularly in the 1960s and again in 2001/2002. Data from Brazil were available for 1963, 1971, and 1981, not 1962, 1972, and 1982. Overall, the dates provide some comparability with the Nordenstreng and Varis UNESCO studies, done in 1972 and 1982. When a country did not yet have television in 1962, the first data were collected in the first year of broadcasting, whenever that was, and then in the ensuing regularly sampled year. Copies of TV guides and newspapers were obtained from libraries in hard copy or in microfilm/fiche. Some countries were coded during 1999, some in 2001, and a few in 2002, depending on material resources and when coders were available. Despite these minor variations, the data will be presented as though they were collected every 10 years beginning in 1962.

| Region | Sample Nations | Years When Data Were Collected |
|---|---|---|
| Latin America | Brazil | 1963, 1971, 1981, 1991, 2002 |
| | Chile | 1962, 1972, 1982, 1991, 2001 |
| | Columbia | 1962, 1972, 1982, 1991, 2001 |
| | Mexico | 1962, 1972, 1982, 1991, 2001 |
| | U.S.–Hispanic | 1972, 1982, 1991, 2001 |
| | Venezuela | 1962, 1972, 1982, 1991, 2002 |
| Anglophone | Australia | 1962, 1972, 1982, 1991, 2001 |
| | Anglo-Canada | 1962, 1972, 1982, 1991, 2001 |
| | Ireland | 1962, 1972, 1982, 1991, 2001 |
| | New Zealand | 1962, 1972, 1982, 1991, 2001 |
| | United Kingdom | 1962, 1972, 1982, 1991, 2001 |
| | United States | 1962, 1972, 1982, 1991, 2001 |
| East Asia | China | 1962, 1973, 1982, 1991, 1999 |
| | Hong Kong | 1962, 1972, 1982, 1991 |
| | India | 1972, 1982, 1991 |
| | Japan | 1962, 1972, 1982, 1991, 1999 |
| | South Korea | 1962, 1972, 1982, 1991, 1999 |
| | Taiwan | 1972, 1982, 1991, 1999 |

*(Continued)*

(Continued)

| Region | Sample Nations | Years When Data Were Collected |
|--------|----------------|-------------------------------|
| Europe | France | 1962, 1972, 1982, 1991, 2001 |
| | Italy | 1962, 1972, 1982, 1992, 1999 |
| | Franco–Canada | 1962, 1972, 1982, 1991, 2001 |
| Middle East | Israel | 1972, 1982, 1991 |
| | Lebanon | 1962, 1972, 1982, 1991 |
| Africa | Cameroon | 1991, 1999 |
| | Nigeria | 1962, 1982, 1991, 2001 |

Within each country, not all broadcasting stations are represented. One major city in each country was selected as a sample. Particularly in Latin America, some minor channels represented nonmainstream patterns of programming, which might distort the validity of the kinds of television that were actually being watched. Stations that had less than a 5% share of the audience, according to local ratings data, were therefore excluded. In Brazil, validity checks compared all stations with those that had more than a 5% audience share. The result was exclusion of some government stations, some educational stations, and some very minor, usually new, commercial stations, which did tend to use much more U.S. programming than other stations. I decided that including those stations would overstate the effective presence of U.S. programming in Brazil. For this very reason, some earlier research used weighted-measure audience hours to reflect media absorption more accurately, with hours being weighted by ratings to indicate actual audience viewing habits (Antola & Rogers, 1984; Straubhaar, 1981; 1984), but that measure was impractical in this phase of the study because the ratings data for all of the countries and years are not available. Readers may note that the trends seen here correlate with those observed in the audience-hour studies in Latin America (Antola & Rogers, 1984; Straubhaar, 1981; 1984), another indication of general validity. The U.S.–Hispanic data is based on Spanish-language Channel 26 in Chicago.

## Data and Analysis

The data are presented in the following tables. See Chapters 6 and 7 for further analysis.

**Table A.1**    Percentages of Prime-Time Television and Total Broadcast Day
Occupied by Nationally Produced Programs

| | 1962 | | 1972 | | 1982 | | 1991 | | 2001 | |
|---|---|---|---|---|---|---|---|---|---|---|
| | *Prime* | *Total* | *Prime* | *Total* | *Prime* | *Total* | *Prime* | *Total* | *Prime* | *Total* |
| *Latin America* | | | | | | | | | | |
| Brazil | 70 | 69 | 86 | 55 | 64 | 63 | 72 | 64 | 75 | 65 |
| Chile | 63 | 65 | 54 | 52 | 58 | 48 | 58 | 44 | 66 | 55 |
| Columbia | 65 | 77 | 81 | 75 | 83 | 66 | nd | nd | 83 | 67 |
| Mexico | 63 | 59 | 68 | 62 | 58 | 57 | 46 | 67 | 72 | 71 |
| U.S.–Hispanic | nd | nd | 3 | 66 | 14 | 43 | 0 | 43 | 75 | 38 |
| Venezuela | 57 | 53 | 40 | 51 | 44 | 59 | nd | nd | 42 | 47 |
| *Anglo-Speaking* | | | | | | | | | | |
| Australia | 26 | 34 | 38 | 43 | 51 | 53 | 53 | 57 | 52 | 52 |
| Canada–Anglo | 27 | 51 | 35 | 49 | 41 | 46 | 47 | 48 | 56 | 65 |
| Ireland | 17 | 16 | 14 | 14 | 13 | 19 | 15 | 22 | 20 | 24 |
| New Zealand | 13 | 11 | 28 | 18 | 33 | 38 | 12 | 20 | 26 | 46 |
| United Kingdom | 26 | 34 | 38 | 43 | 51 | 53 | 53 | 57 | 52 | 52 |
| U.S.–Anglo | 100 | 100 | 100 | 99 | 100 | 98 | 100 | 100 | 100 | 99 |
| Jamaica | 31 | 45 | 34 | 33 | 37 | 24 | 30 | 28 | 40 | 22 |
| *East Asia* | | | | | | | | | | |
| China | nd | nd | 87 | 92 | 86 | 80 | 64 | 78 | 79 | 85 |
| Hong Kong | 23 | 26 | 64 | 62 | 92 | 79 | 95 | 83 | nd | nd |
| India | nd | nd | 98 | 80 | 89 | 88 | 97 | 78 | nd | nd |
| Japan | 81 | 92 | 95 | 90 | 96 | 95 | 92 | 94 | 91 | 93 |
| South Korea | 73 | 76 | 80 | 79 | 89 | 87 | 89 | 86 | 100 | 92 |
| Taiwan | 74 | 64 | 98 | 79 | 89 | 88 | 97 | 78 | 98 | 89 |
| *Africa* | | | | | | | | | | |
| Cameroon | nd | nd | nd | nd | nd | nd | nd | 65 | nd | 62 |
| Nigeria | 67 | 66 | nd | nd | 95 | 65 | 92 | 77 | 93 | 82 |
| *Europe* | | | | | | | | | | |
| Canada–Franco | 26 | 32 | 33 | 33 | 29 | 32 | 30 | 27 | 36 | 40 |
| France | 100 | 100 | 87 | 88 | 83 | 82 | 60 | 66 | 65 | 78 |
| Italy | 99 | nd | 79 | nd | 69 | nd | 55 | nd | 66 | nd |
| *Middle East* | | | | | | | | | | |
| Israel | nd | nd | 63 | 69 | 72 | 71 | 67 | 57 | nd | nd |
| Lebanon | 66 | 60 | 46 | 38 | 37 | 34 | 34 | 24 | nd | nd |

Until 2002, at least, U.S.–Hispanic nationally produced programming was largely dubbed Anglo U.S.-produced
programming. So in these tables, the nationally produced programming is the same; and the same figures are
included in both Table A.1 and Table A.2.

**Table A.2**    Percentages of Prime-Time Television and Total Broadcast Day Occupied by U.S.-Produced Programs

| | 1962 | | 1972 | | 1982 | | 1991 | | 2001 | |
|---|---|---|---|---|---|---|---|---|---|---|
| | Prime | Total | Prime | Total | Prime | Total | Prime | Total | Prime | Total |
| *Latin America* | | | | | | | | | | |
| Brazil | 30% | 31% | 14% | 44% | 36% | 37% | 9% | 20% | 8% | 19% |
| Chile | 0 | 4 | 22 | 38 | 16 | 28 | 18 | 22 | 14 | 31 |
| Columbia | 31 | 18 | 11 | 10 | 14 | 23 | nd | nd | 13 | 21 |
| Mexico | 31 | 38 | 26 | 26 | 37 | 35 | 42 | 24 | 27 | 27 |
| U.S.–Hispanic | nd | nd | 3 | 66 | 14 | 43 | 0 | 43 | 75 | 38 |
| Venezuela | 37 | 40 | 38 | 39 | 42 | 36 | nd | nd | 42 | 32 |
| *Anglo-Speaking* | | | | | | | | | | |
| Australia | 51 | 53 | 16 | 48 | 36 | 42 | 35 | 36 | 36 | 29 |
| Canada–Anglo | 71 | 49 | 56 | 50 | 56 | 53 | 52 | 51 | 50 | 30 |
| Ireland | 33 | 24 | 31 | 20 | 17 | 14 | 27 | 30 | 18 | 24 |
| Jamaica | 56 | 45 | 66 | 62 | 39 | 61 | 65 | 66 | 61 | 53 |
| New Zealand | 51 | 42 | 23 | 41 | 33 | 32 | 43 | 49 | 51 | 33 |
| United Kingdom | 16 | 13 | 26 | 14 | 09 | 06 | 12 | 18 | 18 | 23 |
| U.S.–Anglo | 100 | 100 | 100 | 99 | 100 | 98 | 100 | 100 | 100 | 99 |
| *East Asia* | | | | | | | | | | |
| China | nd | nd | 0 | 0 | 0 | 0 | 0 | 3 | 0 | 9 |
| Hong Kong | 72 | 69 | 30 | 28 | 2 | 9 | 0 | 2 | nd | nd |
| India | nd | nd | 0 | 3 | 0 | 0 | 0 | 0 | nd | nd |
| Japan | 19 | 7 | 5 | 9 | 3 | 4 | 6 | 5 | 6 | 7 |
| South Korea | 27 | 24 | 20 | 19 | 7 | 10 | 5 | 9 | 0 | 6 |
| Taiwan | 26 | 36 | 2 | 21 | 6 | 9 | 3 | 20 | nd | nd |
| *Africa* | | | | | | | | | | |
| Cameroon | nd | nd | nd | nd | nd | nd | nd | 17 | nd | 13 |
| Nigeria | 23 | 33 | nd | nd | 0 | 21 | 8 | 12 | 5 | 10 |
| *Europe* | | | | | | | | | | |
| Canada–Franco | 35 | 35 | 42 | 38 | 37 | 38 | 41 | 39 | 39 | 23 |
| France | 0 | 0 | 8 | 3 | 7 | 6 | 33 | 22 | 28 | 18 |
| Italy | 0 | nd | 11 | nd | 17 | nd | 33 | nd | 28 | nd |
| *Middle East* | | | | | | | | | | |
| Israel | nd | nd | 16 | 13 | 19 | 14 | 21 | 18 | nd | nd |
| Lebanon | 24 | 23 | 40 | 41 | 22 | 34 | 29 | 29 | nd | nd |

The U.S.–Anglo and U.S.–Hispanic percentages for nationally produced programming and U.S.-produced programming refer to the same percentages; however, those figures are included in both Table A.1 and Table A.2 for clarity. When analyzing U.S.–Hispanic television programming, this study included Puerto Rican programs in the regionally produced programming.

For Canada–Anglo (Calgary stations), this study distinguished nationally produced programming (Canada), U.S.-produced programming, regionally produced programming, and internationally produced programming. There was no Canada–Franco material on regular broadcast channels—only on pay TV and cable.

For Canada–Franco (Quebec stations), this study distinguished nationally produced programming (Canada–Franco), U.S.-produced programming, regionally produced programming (Canada–Anglo), and internationally produced programming (including France).

**Table A.3**    Percentages of Prime-Time Television and Total Broadcast Day
Occupied by Cultural-Linguistic Regional Programs

| | 1962 | | 1972 | | 1982 | | 1991 | | 2001 | |
|---|---|---|---|---|---|---|---|---|---|---|
| | Prime | Total | Prime | Total | Prime | Total | Prime | Total | Prime | Total |
| *Latin America* | | | | | | | | | | |
| Brazil | 0% | 0% | 0% | 0% | 0% | 0% | 6% | 4% | 7% | 5% |
| Chile | 4 | 2 | 16 | 5 | 8 | 7 | 9 | 19 | 17 | 11 |
| Columbia | 0 | 0 | 8 | 10 | 2 | 5 | nd | nd | 3 | 10 |
| Mexico | 0 | 0 | 3 | 1 | 0 | 2 | 9 | 2 | 0 | 1 |
| U.S.–Hispanic | nd | nd | 83 | 32 | 71 | 53 | 100 | 55 | 25 | 62 |
| Venezuela | 1 | nd | 7 | 7 | 9 | 0 | nd | nd | 9 | 15 |
| *Anglo-Speaking* | | | | | | | | | | |
| Australia | 23 | 13 | 45 | 9 | 13 | 5 | 11 | 7 | 9 | 9 |
| Canada–Anglo | 2 | 1 | 2 | 1 | 1 | 1 | 0 | 1 | 1 | 5 |
| Ireland | 48 | 59 | 55 | 65 | 69 | 66 | 58 | 47 | 63 | 51 |
| Jamaica | 13 | 9 | 0 | 5 | 24 | 14 | 7 | 6 | 0 | 26 |
| New Zealand | 36 | 46 | 41 | 45 | 30 | 29 | 44 | 29 | 23 | 18 |
| United Kingdom | 2 | 1 | 0 | 2 | 3 | 4 | 2 | 3 | 1 | 1 |
| U.S.–Anglo | 0 | 0 | 0 | 1 | 0 | 0 | 0 | 0 | 0 | 0 |
| *East Asia* | | | | | | | | | | |
| China | nd | nd | 4 | 2 | 4 | 4 | 14 | 6 | 0 | 0 |
| Hong Kong | 0 | 0 | 31 | 7 | 3 | 11 | 4 | 15 | nd | nd |
| India | nd | nd | 0 | 0 | 0 | 0 | 0 | 0 | nd | nd |
| Japan | nd | nd | 0 | 0 | 0 | 0 | nd | nd | 0 | 1 |
| South Korea | 0 | 0 | 0 | 0 | 0 | 0 | 0 | 0 | 0 | 0 |
| Taiwan | 0 | 0 | 0 | 0 | 3 | 2 | 0 | 2 | nd | nd |
| *Africa* | | | | | | | | | | |
| Cameroon | nd | nd | nd | nd | nd | nd | nd | 5 | nd | 7 |
| Nigeria | 0 | 0 | nd | nd | nd | nd | nd | nd | nd | nd |
| *Europe* | | | | | | | | | | |
| Canada–Franco | nd | nd | nd | nd | nd | nd | nd | nd | nd | nd |
| France | 0 | 0 | 1 | 6 | 1 | 7 | 2 | 2 | 6 | 3 |
| Italy | 0 | nd | 6 | nd | 2 | nd | 3 | nd | 2 | nd |
| *Middle East* | | | | | | | | | | |
| Israel | nd | nd | 8 | 5 | 0 | 4 | 0 | 2 | nd | nd |
| Lebanon | 0 | 0 | 0 | 5 | 3 | 9 | 24 | 30 | nd | nd |

For both the Canada–Franco and the Canada–Anglo programming analysis, this study included each one's programming in the other region's cultural-linguistic regional program percentages.

For both the U.S.–Hispanic and the U.S.–Anglo programming analysis, this study included each area's programming in the other region's cultural-linguistic regional program percentages.

**Table A.4**    Percentages of Prime-Time Television and Total Broadcast Day Occupied by Internationally Produced/Origin Unknown Programs

| | 1962 | | 1972 | | 1982 | | 1991 | | 2001 | |
|---|---|---|---|---|---|---|---|---|---|---|
| | Prime | Total | Prime | Total | Prime | Total | Prime | Total | Prime | Total |
| *Latin America* | | | | | | | | | | |
| Brazil | 0% | 0% | 0% | 1% | 0% | 0% | 13% | 12% | nd | nd |
| Chile | 33 | 29 | 8 | 5 | 18 | 17 | 15 | 15 | 3 | 3 |
| Columbia | 4 | 5 | 0 | 5 | 1 | 6 | nd | nd | 1 | 2 |
| Mexico | 6 | 3 | 3 | 11 | 5 | 6 | 3 | 7 | 1 | 1 |
| U.S.–Hispanic | nd | nd | 14 | 2 | 15 | 4 | 0 | 2 | 0 | 0 |
| Venezuela | 5 | nd | 15 | 3 | 5 | 5 | nd | nd | 7 | 6 |
| *Anglo-Speaking* | | | | | | | | | | |
| Australia | 0 | 0 | 1 | 0 | 0 | 0 | 0 | 0 | 3 | 11 |
| Canada–Anglo | 2 | 1 | 2 | 1 | 1 | 1 | 1 | 1 | 0 | 0 |
| Ireland | 2 | 1 | 1 | 1 | 0 | 1 | 0 | 1 | 0 | 1 |
| Jamaica | 0 | 0 | 0 | 0 | 0 | 0 | 0 | 0 | 0 | 0 |
| New Zealand | 0 | 1 | 5 | 7 | 4 | 1 | 0 | 2 | 0 | 2 |
| United Kingdom | 1 | 1 | 0 | 0 | 0 | 2 | 1 | 2 | 0 | 1 |
| U.S.–Anglo | 0 | 0 | 0 | 0 | 0 | 2 | 0 | 0 | 0 | 1 |
| *East Asia* | | | | | | | | | | |
| China | nd | nd | 9 | 6 | 10 | 16 | 22 | 13 | 21 | 6 |
| Japan | nd | nd | 0 | 1 | 1 | 1 | nd | nd | nd | nd |
| South Korea | 0 | 0 | 0 | 2 | 4 | 3 | 6 | 5 | 0 | 2 |
| Taiwan | 0 | 0 | 0 | 0 | 1 | 1 | 6 | 3 | 0 | 2 |
| *Africa* | | | | | | | | | | |
| Cameroon | nd | nd | nd | nd | nd | nd | nd | 13 | nd | 18 |
| Nigeria | 10 | 11 | nd | nd | nd | nd | nd | nd | nd | nd |
| *Europe* | | | | | | | | | | |
| Canada–Franco | 11 | 9 | 12 | 10 | 12 | 10 | 13 | 12 | 0 | 4 |
| France | 0 | 0 | 4 | 3 | 9 | 5 | 5 | 0 | 1 | 1 |
| Italy | 1 | nd | 4 | nd | 12 | nd | 9 | nd | 4 | nd |

# References

Abram, D. J. (2004). *Four tiers of Anglophone television importing: A comparative analysis of television flows between the United States, the United Kingdom, Australia, Anglo-Canada, Jamaica, Ireland, and New Zealand from 1962–2001.* Unpublished master's thesis, University of Texas, Austin.

Abu-Lughod, J. L. (1991). *Before European hegemony: The world system A.D. 1250–1350.* Oxford, UK: Oxford University Press.

Abu-Lughod, L. (1993). Finding a place for Islam: Egyptian television serials and the national interest. In C. A. Breckenridge (Ed.), *Public culture* (pp. 494–512). Chicago: University of Chicago Press.

Abu-Lughod, L. (2005). *Dramas of nationhood: The politics of television in Egypt.* Chicago: University of Chicago Press.

Adorno, T. W. (1957). Television and the patterns of mass culture. In B. Rosenberg & D. W. White (Eds.), *Mass culture.* Glencoe, IL: Free Press.

Afonjá, I. A. O. (1999). Iansã is not St. Barbara. In R. M. Levine & J. J. Crocitti (Eds.), *The Brazil reader: History, culture, politics.* Durham, NC: Duke University Press.

Agger, G. (2001). Fictions of Europe. On "eurofiction"—a multinational research project. *Nordicom Review, 22*(1), 43–51.

Aksoy, A., & Robins, K. (2000). Thinking across spaces: Transnational television from Turkey. *European Journal of Cultural Studies, 3*(3), 343–365.

Allen, R. C. (1995). *To be continued: Soap operas around the world.* London: Routledge.

Allen, R. C. (2004). Frequently asked questions: A general introduction to the reader. In R. C. Allen & A. Hill (Eds.), *The television studies reader.* New York: Routledge.

Almeida, H. B. d. (2003). Telenovela and gender in Brazil. *Global Media Journal, 2*(2). Retrieved April 4, 2004, from http://lass.calumet.purdue.edu/cca/gmj/oldsite backup/submitteddocuments/archivedpapers/spring2003/almeida.htm

Alvarado, M. (1988). *Video world-wide.* London: John Libbey.

Anderson, B. (1983). *Imagined communities: Reflections on the origin and spread of nationalism.* New York: Verso.

Ang, I. (1996). *Living room wars: Rethinking media audiences for a postmodern world.* New York: Routledge.

Antola, A., & Rogers, E. M. (1984). Television flows in Latin America. *Communication Research, 11*(2), 183–202.

Appadurai, A. (1988). How to make a national cuisine: Cookbooks in contemporary India. *Comparative Studies in Society and History, 30*(1), 3–24.

Appadurai, A. (1990). Disjuncture and difference in the global cultural economy. *Public Culture, 2*(2), 1–24.

Appadurai, A. (1996). *Modernity at large: Cultural dimensions of globalization.* Minneapolis: University of Minnesota Press.

Arrighi, G. (2005, March–April). Hegemony unraveling–1. *New Left Review.* Retrieved November 25, 2005, from newleftreview.net

Arthur, B. (1990, February). Positive feedbacks in the economy. *Scientific American,* pp. 92–99.

Atwood, R., & Mattos, S. (1982). Mass media reform and social change: The Peruvian experience. *Communication Research, 32*(2), 33–45.

Axelrod, R., & Cohen, M. D. (2000). *Harnessing complexity: Organization implications of a scientific frontier.* New York: Basic Books.

Baer, W. (1989). *The Brazilian economy: Growth and development.* New York: Praeger.

Balcazar, J. L., Diaz, J., & Gabarro, J. (1995). *Structural complexity* (2nd ed., Vol. 1). New York: Springer-Verlag.

Baldwin, T., & McEvoy, S. (1988). *Cable communication.* New York: Prentice Hall.

Banks, J. (1996). *Monopoly television: MTV's quest to control the music.* Boulder, CO: Westview Press.

Banks, J. (1997). MTV and the globalization of popular culture. *Gazette: The International Journal for Communication Studies, 59*(1), 43–60.

Bannerjee, I. (2002). The locals strike back? Media globalization and localization in the new Asian television landscape. *Gazette: The International Journal for Communications Studies, 64*(6), 517–535.

Barbero, J. M. (1988). Communication from culture: The crisis of the national and emergence of the popular. *Media, Culture & Society, 10,* 447–465.

Barnouw, E. (1977). *Tube of plenty: The evolution of American television.* London: Oxford University Press.

Bastide, R. (1978). *The African religions of Brazil: Toward a sociology of the interpenetration of civilizations.* Baltimore: Johns Hopkins University Press.

Bazin, A. (1968). *Qu'est-ce que le cinema?* [What is cinema?] (H. Gray, Ed., Trans.). Berkeley: University of California Press.

Bechelloni, G. (1997). Introduction. In G. Bechelloni & M. Buonanno (Eds.), *Television fiction and identities: America, Europe, nations.* Naples, Italy: iperMedium.

Bechelloni, G., & Buonanno, M. (Eds.). (1997). *Television fiction and identities: America, Europe, nations.* Naples, Italy: iperMedium.

Beltran, L. R. (1978). TV etchings in the minds of Latin Americans: Conservatism, materialism, and conformism. *Gazette: The International Journal of Communication Studies, 24*(1), 61–65.

Beltran, L. R., & Fox de Cardona, E. (1979). Latin America and the United States: Flaws in the free flow of information. In K. Nordenstreng & H. I. Schiller (Eds.), *National sovereignty and international communications.* Norwood, NJ: Ablex.

Benson, R., & Neveu, E. (Eds.). (2005). *Bourdieu and the journalistic field.* New York: Polity Press.

Berger, P. L., & Luckmann, T. (1967). *The social construction of reality: A treatise in the sociology of knowledge.* Garden City, NY: Doubleday.

Bertaux, D. (Ed.). (1981). *Biography and society: The life history approach in the social sciences.* Beverly Hills, CA: Sage.

Bertaux, D., & Thompson, P. (1997). *Pathways to social class.* Oxford, UK: Clarendon Press.

Bhabha, H. (1990). *Nation and narration.* London: Routledge.

Bhabha, H. (1994). *The location of culture.* New York: Routledge.

Bielby, D. D., & Harrington, C. L. (2005). Opening America? The telenovela-ization of U.S. soap operas. *Television & New Media, 6*(4), 383–399.

Bourdieu, P. (1984). *Distinction: A social critique of the judgent of taste*. Cambridge, MA: Harvard University Press.

Bourdieu, P. (1986). The forms of capital. In J. G. Richardson (Ed.), *Handbook of theory and research for the sociology of education* (pp. 241–258). New York: Greenwood Press.

Bourdieu, P. (1998). *Practical reason: On the theory of action*. Stanford, CA: Stanford University Press.

Bourdieu, P., & Wacquant, L. (1999). On the cunning of imperialist reason. *Theory, Culture & Society, 16*(1), 41–58.

Boyd, D. A. (1993). *Broadcasting in the Arab world: A survey of the electronic media in the Middle East* (2nd ed.). Ames: Iowa State University Press.

Boyd, D. A., Straubhaar, J. D., & Lent, J. (1989). *The videocassette recorder in the third world*. New York: Longman.

Boyd-Barrett, O. (1977). Media imperialism: Towards an international framework for the analysis of media systems. In J. E. A. Curran (Ed.), *Mass communication and society*. London: Arnold.

Boyd-Barrett, O. (1980). *The international news agencies*. Beverly Hills, CA: Sage.

Boyne, R. (1990). Culture and the world system. *Theory, Culture & Society, 7*, 57–62.

Brants, K., & Siune, K. (1992). Public broadcasting in a state of flux. In K. Siune & W. Treutzschler (Eds.), *Dynamics of media politics*. London: Sage.

Briggs, A. (1995). *History of broadcasting in the United Kingdom* (Vol. 2). London: Oxford University Press.

Brown, A. (1987). *TV programming trends in the Anglophone Caribbean: The 1980s* (Occasional Paper No. 2). Kingston, Jamaica: University of the West Indies, Caribbean Institute of Mass Communication.

Browne, D. R. (1989). *Comparing broadcast systems: The experiences of six industrialized nations*. Ames: Iowa State University Press.

Buonanno, M. (Ed.). (2002). *Convergences: Eurofiction fourth report*. Napoli, Italy: Liguri.

Buonanno, M. (2004). Alem da proximidade cultural: Não contra a identidade mas a favor de alteridade [Beyond cultural proximity: Not against identity but in favor of alterity]. In M. I. Vassallo de Lopes (Ed.), *Telenovela—internacionalização e interculturalidade* (pp. 331–360). São Paulo, Brazil: Edições Loyola.

Calderón, C. A. (2005). Que es telesur? [What is Telesur?]. *Revista Latinoamericana de Comunicación Chasqui, 92*, 44–51.

Canclini, N. G. (1982). *Las culturas populares en el capitalismo*. Mexico City: Nueva Imagen.

Canclini, N. G. (1995). *Hybrid cultures: Strategies for entering and leaving modernity*. Minneapolis: University of Minnesota Press.

Canclini, N. G. (1997). Hybrid cultures and communicative strategies. *Media Development, 44*(1), 22–29.

Canclini, N. G. (2001). *Consumers and citizens: Globalization and multicultural conflicts*. Minneapolis: University of Minnesota Press.

Cardoso, F. H. (1970). *Dependencia e desenvolvimento na america latina*. Rio de Janeiro, Brazil: Zahar Editores.

Cardoso, F. H. (1973). Associated dependent-development: Theoretical and practical implications. In A. Stephan (Ed.), *Authoritarian Brazil*. New Haven, CT: Yale University Press.

Carey, J. W. (1989). *Communication as culture: Essays on media and society*. Boston: Unwin Hyman.

Castells, M. (1997). *The power of identity*. Malden, MA: Blackwell.

Castells, M. (2005). *Globalización, desarollo y democracia: Chile en el contexto mundial.* Santiago, Chile: Fondo de la Cultura Económica.

Chadha, K., & Kavoori, A. (2000). Media imperialism revisited: Some findings from the Asian case. *Media, Culture & Society, 22*(4), 415–432.

Chalaby, J. (2002). Transnational television in Europe: The role of pan-European channels. *European Journal of Communication, 17*(2), 183–203.

Chalaby, J. (2005a). Deconstructing the transnational: A typology of cross-border television channels in Europe. *New Media & Society, 7*(2), 155–175.

Chalaby, J. (2005b). From internationalization to transnationalization. *Global Media and Communication, 1*(1), 28–33.

Chalaby, J. (2005c). Towards an understanding of media transnationalism. In J. Chalaby (Ed.), *Transnational television worldwide: Towards a new media order* (pp. 1–13). London: I. B. Taurus.

Chalaby, J. K. (2006). American cultural primacy in a new media order: A European perspective. *International Communication Gazette, 68*(1), 33–51.

Chambers, D. (2002, Spring/Summer). Will Hollywood go to war? *Transborder Broadcasting Studies, 8.* Retrieved September 5, 2005, from http://www.tbs journal.com/Archives/Spring02/chambers.html

Chan, J. M. (1994). National responses and accessibility to Star TV in Asia. *Journal of Communication, 44*(3), 112–131.

Chan, J. M. (1996). Television development in greater China: Structure, exports, and market information. In J. Sinclair, E. Jacka, & S. Cunningham (Eds.), *New patterns in global television: Peripheral vision* (pp. 1–25). New York: Oxford University Press.

Chan, J. M., & Ma, E. K. W. (1996). Asian television: Global trends and local processes. *Gazette: The International Journal of Communication, 58,* 45–60.

Chen, P. H. (2004). Transnational cable channels in the Taiwanese market. *Gazette: The International Journal for Communication Studies, 66*(2), 167–183.

Chestnut, R. A. (1997). *Born again in Brazil: The pentecostal boom and the pathogens of poverty.* Rutgers, NJ: Rutgers University Press.

Collins, R. (1986, May–August). Wall-to-wall Dallas? The US-UK trade in television. *Screen,* pp. 66–77.

Commission of the European Communities. (1984). *Television without frontiers: Green paper on the establishment of the Common Market for broadcasting, especially by satellite and cable* (No. COM, 84, 300 final). Brussels: Author.

Cornelio Mari, E. M. (2005). *Mexican children's perception of cultural specificity in American cartoons.* Unpublished master's thesis, University of Texas, Austin.

Craddock, P. (2003, April). Radio listening survey. Retrieved August 25, 2006, from http://www.comminit.com/trends/ctrends2003/trends-115.html

Crook, L., & Johnson, R. (Eds.). (1999). *Black Brazil: Culture, identity, and social mobilization.* Los Angeles: University of California Press.

Cunningham, S. (2001). Popular media as public "sphericules" for diasporic communities. *International Journal of Cultural Studies, 4*(2), 131–147.

Curran, J. (1990). The new revisionism in mass communication research: A reappraisal. *European Journal of Communication, 5*(2–3), 135–164.

Curtin, M. (2003). Media capital: Towards the study of spatial flows. *International Journal of Cultural Studies, 6*(6), 202–228.

Curtin, M. (in press). Industry on fire: The cultural economy of Hong Kong media. *Post Script.*

da Cunha, E. (1973). *Os sertões [Rebellion in the backlands]* (Educational edition prepared by Alfredo Bosi). São Paulo, Brazil: Cultrix.

Da Matta, R. (1997). *Carnavais, malandros, e herois* [Carnivals, rounders, and heroes]. Rio de Janeiro, Brazil: Zahar.

Da Tavola, A. (1984). *Comunicação e mito* [Communication and myth]. Rio de Janeiro, Brazil: Zahar.

Darling-Wolf, P. (2006). *Getting over our "Illusion D"Optique": From Globalization to Mondialisation.* Global Fusion Conference, Chicago.

Dator, J., & Seo, Y. (2004). Korea as the wave of a future: The emerging dream society of icons and aesthetic experience. *Journal of Futures Studies, 9*(1), 31–44.

Datta-Ray, S. (2006). *Covering Asia—Singapore.* Retrieved September 3, 2006, from http://www.asianz.org.nz/node/181

Davila, A. (2001). *Latinos Inc.: The marketing and making of a people.* Berkeley: University of California Press.

Davis, M. (2006). Mitch Cavis on Mormon movies. *Meridian.* Retrieved September 2, 2006, from http://www.meridianmagazine.com/arts/041018Mitch2.html

de Sola Pool, I. (1977, Spring). The changing flow of television. *Journal of Communication,* pp. 139–149.

de Sola Pool, I. (1979). Direct broadcast satellites and the integrity of national cultures. In K. Nordenstreng & H. Schiller (Eds.), *National sovereignty and international communication.* Norwood, NJ: Ablex.

de Sola Pool, I. (1983). *Technologies of freedom.* Cambridge, MA: MIT Press.

Del Negro, G. P. (2003). Gender, class, and suffering in the Argentinean telenovela milagros: An Italian perspective. *Global Media Journal, 2*(2). Retrieved September 25, 2005, from http://lass.calumet.purdue.edu/cca/gmj/oldsitebackup/submitted-documents/archivedpapers/spring2003/delnegro.htm

Dirlik, A. (1994). The postcolonial aura: Third world criticism in the age of global capitalism. *Critical Inquiry, 20*(2), 328–356.

Dizard, W. P. (2004). *Inventing public diplomacy: The story of the U.S. Information Agency.* Boulder, CO: Westview Press.

Dobrow, J. R. (1989). Away from the mainstream? VCRs and ethnic identity. In M. Levy (Ed.), *The VCR age.* Newbury Park, CA: Sage.

Dorfman, A., & Mattelart, A. (1975). *How to read Donald Duck: Imperialist ideology in the Disney comic.* New York: International General.

Dos Santos, T. (1973). The crisis of development theory and problems of departure in Latin America. In H. Bernstein (Ed.), *Underdevelopment and development: The third world today.* Baltimore: Penguin.

Downing, J. D. H., with Villarreal, T., Ford, G. G., & Stein, L. (2001). *Radical media: Rebellious communication and social movements.* Thousand Oaks, CA: Sage.

Duarte, L. G. (1992). *Television segmentation: Will Brazil follow the American model.* Unpublished master's thesis, Michigan State University.

Duarte, L. G. (1997). *Social class as a mediator for patterns of viewership of international programs.* Unpublished manuscript, Michigan State University.

Duarte, L. G. (2001). *Due south: American television ventures into Latin America.* Unpublished doctoral dissertation, Michigan State University.

Dutton, W. H. (1999). *Society on the line: Information politics in the digital age.* New York: Oxford University Press.

El-Nawawy, M., & Iskandar, A. (2003). *Al-Jazeera: The story of the network that is rattling governments and redefining modern journalism.* Boulder, CO: Westview Press.

Evans, P. (1992). *High technology and third world industrialization: Brazilian computer policy in comparative perspective.* Berkeley: University of California at Berkeley, International and Area Studies.

Fadul, A. (1993). *The radio and television environment in Brazil.* Unpublished manuscript, University of São Paulo (Brazil), School of Communication and Arts.

Faiola, A. (2006, August 31). Japanese women catch the "Korean wave": Male celebrities just latest twist in Asia-wide craze. *Washington Post,* p. A01.

Fair, J. E. (2003). Francophonie and the national airwaves: A history of television in Senegal. In L. Parks & S. Kumar (Eds.), *Planet TV: A global television reader.* New York: New York University Press.

Faletto, E., & Cardoso, F. H. (1979). *Dependency and development in Latin America.* Berkeley: University of California Press.

Fanon, F. (1967). *Black faces, white masks.* New York: Grove Press.

Faria, V., & Potter, J. E. (1994). *Television, telenovelas, and fertility change in northeast Brazil.* Unpublished manuscript, University of Texas, Austin, Population Research Center.

Featherstone, M. (1990a). Global culture: An introduction. *Theory, Culture & Society, 7,* 1–15.

Featherstone, M. (1990b). *Global culture: Nationalism, globalization, and modernity.* Newbury Park, CA: Sage.

Featherstone, M. (1991). *Consumer culture and postmodernism.* London: Sage.

Featherstone, M., & Lash, S. (1995). An introduction. In M. Featherstone, S. Lash, & R. Robertson (Eds.), *Global modernities.* Thousand Oaks, CA: Sage.

Fejes, F. (1980). The growth of multinational advertising agencies in Latin America. *Journal of Communication, 30*(4), 36–49.

Fejes, F. (1981). Media imperialism: An assessment. *Media, Culture & Society, 3*(3), 281–289.

Ferguson, M. (1992). The mythology about globalization. *European Journal of Communication, 7,* 69–93.

Ferguson, M. (1995). Media, markets, and identities: Reflections on the global-local dialectic. *Canadian Journal of Communication, 20,* 439–459.

Fernandes, I. (1987). *Memoria da telenovela brasileira* (2nd ed.). São Paulo, Brazil: Brasiliense.

Fernández, C., & Paxman, A. (2001). *El tigre: Emilio Azcárraga y su imperio televisa* [The tiger: Emilio Azcárraga and his television empire] (Rev. ed.). Mexico City: Grijalbo Mondadori.

Fishman, J. (2000). *English: The killer language? Or a passing phase?* Retrieved October 25, 2000, from www.wholeearth.com/ArticleBin/

Fiske, J. (1987). *Television culture.* New York: Methuen.

Fox, E. (1975). Multinational television. *Journal of Communication, 25*(2), 122–127.

Fox, E. (1988). Media policies in Latin America: An overview. In E. Fox (Ed.), *Media and politics in Latin America: The struggle for democracy* (pp. 6–35). Newbury Park, CA: Sage.

Fox, E. (1992). *Cultural dependency thrice revisited.* Paper presented at the International Association for Mass Communication Research, Guarujá, Brazil.

Fox, E. (1997). *Latin American broadcasting.* Luton, UK: University of Luton Press.

Freyre, G. (1964). *The masters and the slaves* (S. Putnam, Trans.) (Abridged ed.). New York: Knopf.

Friedman, T. (1999). *The lexus and the olive tree.* New York: Farrar, Straus & Giroux.

Fuller, C. (1992, May 11). Dutch reformat, resell shows. *Variety Europe,* p. 75.

Galeano, E. H. (1988). *Memory of fire* (C. Belfrage, Trans.) (1st American ed.). New York: Pantheon Books.

Galperin, H. (1999). Cultural industries policy in regional trade agreements: The cases of NAFTA, the European Union, and Mercosur. *Media, Culture & Society, 21*(5), 627–648.

Galtung, J. (1971). A structural theory of imperialism. *Journal of Peace Research, 8*(2), 81–117.

Gardyn, R. (2001, April). Habla english? *American Demographics,* Retrieved April 4, 2003, from http://adage.com/results? search_offset=0&search_order_by= score&search_phrase=Se+habla+English&searcha-btn.x=19&searcha-btn.y=2

George, C. (2004). *Singapore: The air-conditioned nation: Essays on the politics of comfort and control, 1990–2000.* Singapore: Landmark.

Giddens, A. (1984). *The constitution of society: Outline of a theory of structuration.* Berkeley: University of California Press.

Giddens, A. (1991). *Modernity and self-identity.* Oxford: Polity.

Gitlin, T. (1990). *Inside prime time* (Rev. ed.). Berkeley: University of California Press.

Gitlin, T. (2001). *Media unlimited: How the torrent of images and sounds overwhelms our lives.* New York: Metropolitan Books.

Golding, P., & Murdock, G. (1997). *The political economy of the media.* Cheltenham, UK: Edward Elgar.

González, J. (1986). Y todo queda entre familia [Everything falls within the family]. *Estudios Sobre las Culturas Contemporáneas, 1*(1), 135–154.

González, J. (1987). Frentes culturales. *Estudios Sobre las Culturas Contemporáneas, 2*(4–5), 41–100.

González, J. (1991). La telenovela en familia, una mirada em busca de horizonte [The telenovela within the family: Viewing in search of perspective]. *Estudios Sobre las Culturas Contemporaneas, 4*(11), 217–228.

González, J. (1997). The willingness to weave: Cultural analysis, cultural fronts, and the networks of the future. *Media Development, 44*(1), 30–36.

González, J. (2001). Cultural fronts: Toward a dialogical understanding of contemporary cultures. In J. Lull (Ed.), *Culture in the communication age* (pp. 106–131). New York: Routledge.

Gramsci, A. (1971). *Selections from the prison notebooks* (Q. Hoare & G. M. Smith, Trans.). New York: International Publishers.

Grantham, B. (2000). *Some big bourgeois brothel: Contexts for France's culture wars with the U.S.* Luton, UK: University of Luton Press.

Gray, J. (1998). *False dawn: The delusions of global capitalism.* London: Granta Books.

Gray, J. (2003). From the great transformation to the global free market. In F. Lechner & J. Boli (Eds.), *The globalization reader* (2nd ed.). London: Blackwell.

Guback, T. (1984). International circulation of U.S. theatrical films and television programming. In G. Gerbner & M. Siefert (Eds.), *World communications* (pp. 153–163). New York: Lingman.

Guback, T., & Varis, T. (1986). *Transnational communication and cultural industries* (Reports and Papers on Mass Communication No. 92). Paris: UNESCO.

Guerreiro, G. (2000). *A trama dos tambores* [The web of the drums: The afro-pop music of Salvador] (R. J. Straubhaar, Trans.). São Paulo, Brazil: Editora 34.

Hall, S. (2001). Encoding/decoding. In G. Durham & D. Kellner (Eds.), *Key texts in media and cultural studies.* New York: Blackwell.

Hamburger, E. (1999). *Politics and intimacy in Brazilian telenovelas.* Unpublished doctoral dissertation, University of Chicago.

Hamelink, C. J. (1983). *Cultural autonomy in global communications.* New York: Longman.

Hannerz, U. (1996). *Transnational connections: Culture, people, places.* London: Routledge.

Hardt, M., & Negri, A. (2001). *Empire.* Cambridge, MA: Harvard University Press.

Hardt, M., & Negri, A. (2004). *Multitude: War and democracy in the age of empire.* New York: Penguin Press.

Harrington, L., & Bielby, D. (2005). Global television distribution: Implications of TV "traveling" for viewers, fans, and texts. *American Behavioral Scientist, 48*(7), 902–920.

Hartenberger, L. (2005). Mediating transition in Afghanistan, 2001–2004. Unpublished doctoral dissertation, University of Texas, Austin, Radio-Television-Film Department.

Harvey, D. (2005). *A brief history of neoliberalism.* Oxford, UK: Oxford University Press.

Havens, T. (2006). *Global television marketplace.* London: British Film Institute.

Head, S. (1974). *Broadcasting in Africa.* Philadelphia: Temple University Press.

Head, S. (1985). *World broadcasting systems: A comparative analysis.* Belmont, CA: Wadsworth.

Herman, E. S., & McChesney, R. W. (1997). *The global media: The new missionaries of global capitalism.* Washington, DC: Cassell.

Hernandez, O. D. (2001). *A case of global love: Telenovelas in transnational times.* Unpublished doctoral dissertation, University of Texas, Austin.

Hernández, O., & McAnany, E. (2001). Cultural industries in the free trade age: A look at Mexican television. In E. Zolov (Ed.), *Fragments of a golden age: The politics of culture in Mexico since 1940* (pp. 389–414). Durham, NC: Duke University Press.

Herold, C. (1986). *Brazilian television in the 1980s: The making of "Brazilianized" culture.* Unpublished master's thesis, University of Texas, Austin.

Hesmondalgh, D. (in press). *The cultural industries* (2nd ed.). London: Sage.

Hilmes, M. (2003). Who we are, who we are not. In L. Parks & S. Kumar (Eds.), *Planet TV: A global television reader.* New York: New York University Press.

Hoover, S., & Britto, P. (1990, May). *Communication, culture and development in the eastern Caribbean: Case studies in new technology and culture policy.* Paper presented at the International Communication Association, Dublin.

Horkheimer, M., & Adorno, T. (2001). The culture industry: Enlightenment as mass deception. In M. G. Durham & D. M. Kellner (Eds.), *Media and cultural studies: Keyworks.* Malden, MA: Blackwell.

Hoskins, C., & McFayden, S. (1991). The U.S. Competitive advantage in the global television market: Is it sustainable in the new broadcasting environment? *Canadian Journal of Communication, 16,* 207–224.

Hoskins, C., McFayden, S., & Finn, A. (1997). *Global television and film.* Oxford, UK: Clarendon Press.

Hoskins, C., & Mirus, R. (1988). Reasons for the U.S. dominance of the international trade in television programs. *Media, Culture and Society, 10,* 499–515.

Hoskins, C., Mirus, R., & Rozeboom, W. (1989, Spring). U.S. television programs in the international market: Unfair pricing? *Gazette,* pp. 55–75.

Hudson, H. E. (Ed.). (1985). *New directions in satellite communications: Challenges for north and south.* Dedham, MA: Artech House.

Hudson, H. E. (1990). *Communication satellites: Their development and impact.* New York: Free Press.

Huesca, R. (1985). *Low-powered television in rural Bolivia: New directions for democratic media practice.* Unpublished manuscript, Trinity University, San Antonio, TX.

Huntington, S. (2004). The Hispanic challenge. *Foreign Policy, 141,* 30–45.

Ignatius, D. (2006). Category: Al Jazeera intl. Retrieved September 11, 2006, from www.mediabistro.com/tvnewser/al_jazeera_intl/default.asp

Infopress. (2006). Televisão: Estação privada começa a funcionar em agosto em cabo verde. *Segunda, 08 Maio, 2006*. Retrieved May 13, 2006, from Infopress.unesco.org

Isett, R. A. (1995). *Publicly funded satellite television in Alaska: Lost in space*. Unpublished doctoral dissertation, Michigan State University.

Iskandar, A. (2006, December 1). *Spoonfeeding objectivity: Western media development initiatives to the Arab world*. Paper presented at the University of Texas.

Ito, Y. (1991). The trade winds shift—Japan's shift from an information importer to an information exporter. In J. Anderson (Ed.), *Communication yearbook* (Vol. 14, pp. 430–465). Newbury Park, CA: Sage.

ITU. (2006). *World telecommunication/ICT development report 2006: Measuring ICT for social and economic development* (8th ed.). Geneva: Author.

Iwabuchi, K. (1997). *The sweet scent of Asian modernity: The Japanese presence in the Asian audiovisual market*. Paper presented at the Fifth International Symposium on Film, Television and Video—Media Globalization the Asia-Pacific Region, Taipei.

Iwabuchi, K. (2002). *Recentering globalization: Popular culture and Japanese transnationalism*. Durham, NC: Duke University Press.

Jacks, N. (1996). Tendências Latino-Americanas nos estudos de recepção [Latin American tendencies in reception studies]. *Revista FAMECOS, Porto Alegre, 5*, 44–49.

Janus, N. (1977). Transnational advertising: The Latin American case. In G. Gerbner & M. Siefert (Eds.), *World communications* (pp. 137–143). New York: Longman.

Janus, N. (1981). Advertising and the mass media in the era of the global corporations. In E. McAnany & J. Schnitman (Eds.), *Communication and social structure: Critcal studies in mass media research*. New York: Praeger.

Janus, N. (1983, June 30). Advertising and global culture. In *Cultural survival quarterly, 7*(2). Retrieved September 4, 2004, from http://www.cs.org/publications/csq/csq-article.cfm?id=112&highlight=Janus

Jayakar, K. (1993). *National responses to international satellite television*. Paper presented at the Broadcast Education Association, Las Vegas, NV.

Johnson, R. (1993). Editor's introduction: Pierre Bourdieu on art, literature. In R. Johnson (Ed.), *The field of cultural production: Essays on art and literature/ Pierre Bourdieu*. New York: Columbia University Press.

Kak, S. (2005). *Recursionism and reality: Representing and understanding the world*. Retrieved September 9, 2006, from http://www.ece.lsu.edu/kak/RReality.pdf

Kalathil, S., & Boas, T. C. (2001). The Internet and state control in authoritarian regimes: China, Cuba, and the counterrevolution. *First Monday, 6*(8). Retrieved from www.firstmonday.org/issues/issue6_8/kalathil/

Katz, E., & Wedell, G. (1976). *Broadcasting in the third world*. Cambridge, MA: Harvard University Press.

Klagsbrunn, M. (1993). The Brazilian telenovela: A genre in development. In A. Fadul (Ed.), *Serial fiction in TV: The Latin American telenovelas*. São Paulo, Brazil: Robert M. Videira.

Kottak, C. (1990). *Prime-time society: An anthropological study of television and culture*. Belmont, CA: Wadsworth.

Kraidy, M. M. (2002). Arab satellite television between regionalization and globalization. *Global Media Journal, 1*(1). Retrieved January 5, 2007, from http://lass.calumet.purdue.edu/cca/gmj/OldSiteBackup/SubmittedDocuments/archive dpapers/fall2002/Kraidy.htm

Kraidy, M. M. (2005). *Hybridity, or the cultural logic of globalization*. Philadelphia: Temple University Press.

Kraidy, M. (2006). Popular culture as a political barometer: Lebanese-Syrian relations and superstar. *Transnational Broadcasting Studies, 16*. Retrieved from http://www.tbsjournal.com/Kraidy.html

Kumar, S. (2006). *Gandhi meets primetime*. Urbana: University of Illinois Press.

La Pastina, A. (1999). *The telenovela way of knowledge*. Unpublished doctoral dissertation, University of Texas, Austin.

La Pastina, A. (2001). Product placement in Brazilian prime-time television: The case of a telenovela reception. *Journal of Broadcasting & Electronic Media, 45*, 541–557.

La Pastina, A. (2004a). Selling political integrity: Telenovelas, intertextuality, and local elections in Brazil. *Journal of Broadcasting and Electronic Media, 48*, 302–325.

La Pastina, A. C. (2004b). *Telenovelas' reception and the schism between national production, global distribution and local consumption*. Unpublished manuscript.

La Pastina, A. (2004c). Telenovela reception in rural Brazil: Gendered readings and sexual mores. *Critical Studies in Media Communication, 21*(2), 162–181.

La Pastina, A., Regô, C., & Straubhaar, J. (2003). The centrality of telenovelas in Latin America's everyday life: Past tendencies, current knowledge, and future research. *Global Media Journal*.

La Pastina, A., & Straubhaar, J. (2005). Multiple proximities between television genres and audiences: The schism between telenovelas' global distribution and local consumption. *Gazette, 67*(3), 271–288.

La Pastina, A. C., Straubhaar, J. D., & Buarque de Almeida, H. (2002). *Producers, audiences, and the limits of social marketing on television: The case of* The Cattle King, *a telenovela about land reform in Brazil*. Unpublished paper, University of Texas, Austin.

Leal, O. F. (1986). *A leitura social da novela das oito* [The social reading of the eight pm telenovela]. Petropolis, Brazil: Editora Vozes.

Lee, C. (1980). *Media imperialism reconsidered*. Beverly Hills, CA: Sage.

Lent, J. (1978). *Broadcasting in Asia and the Pacific: A continental survey of radio and television*. Philadelphia: Temple University Press.

Lerner, D. (1958). *The passing of traditional society—modernizing the Middle East*. New York: Free Press.

Leslie, M. (1991, May). *Illusion and reality on commercial television: A comparison of Brazil and the U.S.* Paper presented at the International Communication Association, Chicago.

Letalien, B. (2002). *Does pay television viewership diminish cultural proximity? Evidence from a Rio de Janeiro shantytown*. Unpublished master's thesis, University of Texas, Austin.

Levitt, T. (1983, May–June). The globalization of markets. *Harvard Business Review*, pp. 2–11.

Lindlof, T. R., Shatzer, M. J., & Wilkinson, D. (1988). Accommodation of video and television in the American family. In J. Lull (Ed.), *World families watch television*. Newbury Park, CA: Sage.

Lopez, A. M. (1995). Our welcomed guests: Telenovelas in Latin America. In R. C. Allen (Ed.), *To be continued . . . soap operas around the world*. London: Routledge.

Lorber, J., & Farrell, S. A. (1991). *The social construction of gender*. Newbury Park, CA: Sage.

Maass, M., & González, J. A. (2005). Technology, global flows, and local memories: Media generations in global Mexico. *Global Media and Communication, 1*(1), 105–122.

MacBride, S. (1980). *Many voices, one world. Report by the International Commission for the Study of Communication*. Paris: UNESCO.

Magdoff, H. (1969). *The age of imperialism; the economics of U.S. foreign policy* (1st Modern Reader ed.). New York: Monthly Review Press.

Mallapragada, M. (2006). Home, homeland, homepage: Belonging and the Indian-American Web. *New Media and Society, 8*(2), 207–227.

Man Chan, J. (1994). Media internationalization in China: Processes and tensions. *Journal of Communication, 44*(3), 70–88.

Marlière, P. (1998). The rules of the journalistic field: Pierre Bourdieu's contribution to the sociology of the media. *European Journal of Communication, 13*(2), 219–234.

Marques de Melo, J. (1988). *As telenovelas da globo.* São Paulo, Brazil: Summus.

Marques de Melo, J. (1992). *Brazil's role as a television exporter within the Latin American regional market.* Paper presented at the International Communication Association, Miami.

Martín-Barbero, J. (1993). *Communication, culture, and hegemony: From the media to the mediations.* Newbury Park, CA: Sage.

Marx, K. (1977). *Karl Marx: Selected writings* (D. McLellan, Ed.). Oxford, UK: Oxford University Press.

Mattelart, A. (1991). *Advertising international: The privatization of public space.* New York: Routledge.

Mattelart, M., & Mattelart, A. (1990). *The carnival of images: Brazilian television fiction.* New York: Bergin & Garvey.

Mattelart, A., & Schmucler, H. (1985). *Communication and information technologies: Freedom of choice for Latin America?* (D. Bruxton, Trans.). Norwood, NJ: Ablex.

Mattos, S. (1982). *The Brazilian military and television.* Unpublished master's thesis, University of Texas, Austin.

Mattos, S. (1984). Advertising and government influences on Brazilian television. *Communication Research, 11*(2), 203–220.

McAnany, E. (1984). The logic of cultural industries in Latin America: The television industry in Brazil. In V. Mosco & J. Wasco (Eds.). *Critical communication review* (Vol. 2). Norwood, NJ: Ablex.

McAnany, E. (2002). Globalization and the media: The debate continues. *Communication Research Trends, 21*(4), 3–19.

McAnany, E., & Potter, J. (Eds.). (in press). *The role of television in the demographic transition in Brazil.* Austin: University of Texas Press.

McChesney, R. (1997). *Political economy and globalization.* Paper presented at the Association for Education in Journalism and Mass Communication, Chicago.

McChesney, R. (1999). *Rich media, poor democracy.* Champaign-Urbana: University of Illinois Press.

McDaniel, D. O. (1994). *Broadcasting in the Malay world.* Norwood, NJ: Ablex.

McDaniel, D. O. (2002). *Electronic tigers of Southeast Asia: The politics of media, technology, and national development.* Ames: Iowa State University Press.

McLuhan, M. (1994). *Understanding media: The extensions of man.* Cambridge, MA: MIT Press.

McPhail, T. (1989). *Electronic colonialism* (2nd ed.). Newbury Park, CA: Sage.

Meyer, W. J. (1980). The world polity and the authority of the nation state. In A. Bergesen (Ed.), *Studies of the modern world system.* New York: Academic Press.

Mickiewicz, E. P. (1988). *Split signals: Television and politics in the Soviet Union.* New York: Oxford University Press.

Miller, J. (2000). *Something completely different: British television and American culture.* Minneapolis: University of Minnesota Press.

Miller, T., Covin, N., McMurrin, J., Maxwell, R., & Wang, T. (2005). *Global Hollywood* (2nd ed.). London: BFI Publishing.

MIT Indigenous Language Initiative. (2006). *Language loss.* Retrieved December 5, 2006, from http://web.mit.edu/linguistics/www/mitili/language%20loss.html

Mittell, J. (2004). A cultural approach to television genre theory. In R. Allen & A. Hill (Eds.), *The television studies reader* (pp. 171–181). New York: Routledge.

Moore-Gilbert, B. (1997). *Postcolonial theory: Contexts, practice, politics.* New York: Verso.

Moragas Spa, M. d., Garitaonaindia Garnacho, C., & Lopez, B. (Eds.). (1999). *Television on your doorstep: Decentralization experiences in the European Union.* Luton, UK: University of Luton Press.

Moran, A. (1998). *Copycat television: Globalisation, program formats, and cultural identity.* Luton, Bedfordshire, UK: University of Luton Press.

Moran, A. (2000). *Copycat TV in the Asian/Pacific region? Australian pilot research.* Paper presented at the Political Economy Section of the 22nd General Assembly and Scientific Meeting of the International Association for Mass Communication Research, Singapore.

Moran, A. (2004). Television formats in the world/the world of television formats. In A. Moran & M. Keene (Eds.), *Television across Asia: Television industries, programme formats, and globalization* (pp. 1–8). London: RoutledgeCurzon.

Moran, A. K., & Keane, M. (Ed.). (2004). *Television across Asia: Television industries, programme formats, and globalisation.* London: RoutledgeCurzon.

Morley, D. (1992). *Television, audiences, and cultural spaces.* New York: Routledge.

Morris, N., & Waisbord, S. (Eds.). (2001). *Media and globalization: Why the state matters.* Lanham, MD: Rowman & Littlefield.

Mosco, V. (1996). Structuration. In *The political economy of communication: Rethinking and renewal* (pp. 212–245). Thousand Oaks, CA: Sage.

Mougayar, W. (2002, October 11). Small screen, smaller world. Retrieved August 25, 2006, from yaleglobal.yale.edu/display.article?id=204

MTV. (1997). *Perfil da penetração mtv* [Profile of MTV's market penetration]. São Paulo, Brazil: MTV Research.

Mydans, S. (2004, June 4). Russian TV newsman fired in media crackdown. *New York Times.* Retrieved from http://select.nytimes.com

Naficy, H. (1993). *The making of exile cultures: Iranian television in Los Angeles.* Minneapolis: University of Minnesota Press.

Nederveen Pieterse, J. (1995). Globalization as hybridization. In M. Featherstone, S. Lash, & R. Robertson (Eds.), *Global modernities* (pp. 45–68). Thousand Oaks, CA: Sage.

Nederveen Pieterse, J. (2004). *Globalization and culture.* Lanham, MD: Rowan & Littlefield.

Newcomb, H., & Hirsch, P. M. (1983). Television as a cultural forum: Implications for research. *Quarterly Review of Film Studies, 8*(3), 45–55.

Nordenstreng, K., & Schiller, H. I. (1979). *National sovereignty and international communications.* Norwood, NJ: Ablex.

Nordenstreng, K., & Varis, T. (1974). *Television traffic—a one-way street.* Paris: UNESCO.

Nye, J. S. J. (1990). The changing nature of world power. *Political Science Quarterly, 105*(2), 177–192.

Nye, J. (2004). *Soft power: The means to success in world politics*: New York: PublicAffairs (Perseus).

Oba, G., & Chan-Olmsted, S. M. (2005). The development of cable television in East Asian countries: A comparative analysis of determinants. *Gazette, 67*(3), 211–237.

Obregon, R. (1995). *Telenovelas: An exploration of genre proximity in international television.* Unpublished manuscript, Penn State University.

Okur, O. (2000). *Music television in Turkey.* Unpublished manuscript, University of Texas, Austin, Radio-Television-Film Department.

Oliveira, O. S. d. (1986). Satellite TV and dependency: An empirical approach. *Gazette, 38,* 127–145.

Oliveira, O. S. d. (1993). Brazilian soaps outshine Hollywood: Is cultural imperialism fading out? In K. Nordenstreng & H. Schiller (Eds.), *Beyond national sovereignty: International communication in the 1990s.* Norwood, NJ: Ablex.

Olsen, S. R. (1999). *Hollywood planet: Global media and the competitive advantage of narrative transparency.* Mahwah, NJ: Lawrence Erlbaum.

Olsen, S. R. (2002). Contaminations and hybrids: Indigenous identity and resistance to global media. *Studies in Media & Information Literacy Education, 2*(2).

Oncu, A. (2000). The banal and the subversive: Politics of language on Turkish television. *European Journal of Cultural Studies, 3*(3), 296–318.

Orozco, G. (1993). *Cultura y televisión: de las comunidades de referencia a la producción de sentido en el proceso de el consumo cultural en México* [Culture and television: From interpretive communities to the production of meaning in cultural consumption in Mexico]. Mexico City: CONACULTA.

Ortiz, R. (1994). *Mundialização e cultura* [Globalization and culture]. São Paulo, Brazil: Editora Brasiliense.

Ortiz, R. (2002). Cultural diversity and cosmopolitanism. In G. Stald & T. Tufte (Eds.), *Global encounters: Media and cultural transformation* (pp. 53–68). Luton, UK: University of Luton Press.

Ortiz Ramos, J. M., & Borelli, S. H. (1988). *Telenovela: história e produção* [Telenovelas: History and production]. São Paulo, Brazil: Brasiliense.

Page, D., & Crawley, W. (2001). *Satellites over South Asia: Broadcasting, culture, and the public interest.* Thousand Oaks, CA: Sage.

Parameswaran, R. E. (1995). *Colonial interventions and the postcolonial situation in India: The English language, mass media, and the articulation of class.* Paper presented at the AEJMC Conference, Washington, DC.

Pashupati, K., Sun, H. L., & McDowell, S. (2003). Guardians of culture, development communicators, or state capitalists? A comparative analysis of Indian and Chinese policy responses to broadcast, cable, and satellite television. *Gazette, 65*(3), 251–271.

Paterson, C. (1996). Global television news services. In D. Winseck, J. McKenna, & O. Boyd-Barrett (Eds.), *Media in global context.* London: Arnold.

Paulu, B. (1974). *Radio and television broadcasting in Eastern Europe.* Minneapolis: University of Minnesota Press.

Perrin, N. (1979). *Giving up the gun: Japan's reversion to the sword, 1543–1879.* Boston: D. R. Godine.

Piñon, J. (2006, September 29–October 1). Mexican TV Azteca's transnational expansion in America as part of its national competition. *Global Fusion: Nation, State & Culture in the Age of Globalization,* Chicago.

Pinto, M., & Sousa, H. (2004). Portugal. In M. Kelly, G. Maszoleni, & D. McQuail (Eds.), *The media in Europe, the Euromedia handbook.* London: Sage.

Porter, M. E. (1998). *On competition.* Cambridge, MA: Harvard Business School Press.

Portes, A., Guarnizo, L. E., & Landolt, P. (1999). Transnational communities. *Ethnic and Racial Studies, 22*(2), 217–233.

Porto, M. P. (2005). Political controversies in Brazilian television fiction: Viewers' interpretations of the telenova *Terra Nostra. Television & New Media, 6*(4), 342–359.

Postman, N. (1986). *Amusing ourselves to death: Public discourse in the age of show business*. New York: Penguin Books.

Prada, R. R., & Cuenco, N. T. (1986). *La television en bolivia*. La Paz, Bolivia: Editorial Quipus.

Price, M. (1999). Satellite broadcasting as trade routes in the sky. *Public Culture, 11*(2), 387–403.

Prigogine, I., & Stengers, I. (1984). *Order out of chaos: Man's new dialogue with nature*. New York: Bantam.

Public Broadcasting Service. (2002). Vivendi loses $12 billion: PBS Media Watch Online Focus. www.pbs.org/newshour/media/media_watch/july-dec02/vivendi_8-14.html

Raboy, M. (1990). *Missed opportunities—the story of Canada's broadcasting policy*. Montreal: McGill-Queen's University Press.

Ramos, R. (1987). *Gra-finos na Globo—Cultura e merchandising nas novellas* [TV Globo: Culture and product placement in the telenovelas]. Petropolis, Brazil: Editora Vozes.

Read, W. H. (1976). *America's mass media merchants*. Baltimore: Johns Hopkins University Press.

Readhead, P. (2006). "We don't want a `Euro-pudding' common culture," says EU Commissioner. *ESRC Society Today*. Retrieved December 30, 2006, from http://www.esrc.ac.uk/ESRCInfoCentre/about/CI/CP/Our_Society_Today/News_Articles_2006/europudding.aspx?ComponentId=13944&SourcePageId=13438

Research, M. M. (2006). *Radio trends in India and abroad: A Madison India study*. Retrieved August, 25, 2006, from http://www.exchange4media.com/e4m/radio/RadioTrendsinIndia.asp

Ricoeur, P. (1984). *Time and narrative* (Vol. 1). Chicago: University of Chicago Press.

Risch, E. (2003). *Discovery international* (unpublished paper). Austin: University of Texas.

Ritzer, G. (2004a). *The globalization of nothing*. Thousand Oaks, CA: Sage.

Ritzer, G. (2004b). *The McDonaldization of society* (rev. New Century ed.). Thousand Oaks, CA: Sage.

Rivero, Y. M. (2003). The performance and reception of televisual "ugliness" in *yo soy betty, la fea*. *Feminist Media Studies, 3*(1), 65–81.

Robertson, R. (1990). Mapping the global condition: Globalization as the central concept. *Theory, Culture & Society, 7*, 15–30.

Robertson, R. (1991). Social theory, cultural relativity and problem of globality. In A. D. King (Ed.), *Culture, globalization, and the world-system*. London: Macmillan.

Robertson, R. (1995). Globalization: Time-space and homogeneity-heterogeneity. In M. Featherstone, S. Lash, & R. Robertson (Eds.), *Global modernities* (pp. 25–44). Thousand Oaks, CA: Sage.

Rodriguez, A. (1999). *Making Latino news: Race, language, class*. Thousand Oaks, CA: Sage.

Rogers, E. (1983). *Diffusion of innovations* (3rd ed.). New York: Free Press.

Rogers, E., & Schement, J. (1984). Media flows in Latin America. *Communication Research, 11*(2), 305–319.

Rojas, V. (2001, May). *Latinas in el show de Cristina: Notes on representation within a framework of sexual labor*. Paper presented at the International Communication Association conference, Washington, DC.

Rojas, V., Straubhaar, J., Fuentes-Bautista, M., & Pinon, J. (2005). Still divided: Ethnicity, generation, cultural capital and new technologies. In O. Jambeiro &

J. Straubhaar (Eds.), *Políticas de informação e comunicação, jornalismo e inclusão digital: O local e o global em austin e salvador* [Information and communication policy, journalism and digital inclusion: The local and global in Austin and Salvador). Salvador: Federal University of Bahia Press.

Roncagliolo, R. (1995). Trade integration and communication networks in Latin America. *Canadian Journal of Communications, 20*(3). Retrieved September 20, 2005, from cjc.com.

Rowe, W., & Schelling, V. (1991). *Memory and modernity: Popular culture in Latin America.* London: Verso.

Ruiz, E. E. S. *Current aspects of the MacBride report: A Latin American viewpoint.* Retrieved January 8, 2007, from http://www.portalcomunicacion.com/informe_macbride/eng/articles.asp

Salinas, R., & Paldan, L. (1979). Culture in the process of dependent development: Theoretical perspectives. In K. Nordenstreng & H. I. Schiller (Eds.), *National sovereignty and international communiations.* Norwood, NJ: Ablex.

Sanchez-Ruiz, E. (2001). Globalization, cultural industries, and free trade: The Mexican audiovisual sector in the NAFTA age. In V. M. a. D. Schiller (Ed.), *Continental order? Integrating North America for cybercapitalism* (pp. 86–119). Boulder, CO: Rowman & Littlefield.

Sanchez-Ruiz, E. (2004). Current aspects of the Macbride Report: A Latin American viewpoint. *Twenty-five years of the MacBride Report: International communication and communication policies.* Retrieved June 5, 2006, from http://www.portalcomunicacion.com/informe_macbride/eng/autors_det.asp?id_autor=8

Santoro, L. F. (1989). *A imagem nas mãos—o video popular no brasil* [The image in our hands—popular video in Brazil] (Vol. 33). São Paulo, Brazil: Summus Editorial.

Santoro, L. F., & Festa, R. (1992). Experiments on audiovisual co-productions (cinema, video and TV) in Latin America: The Brazilian case. In J. Marques de Melo (Ed.), *Brazilian communication research yearbook* (Vol. 1, pp. 69–88). São Paulo, Brazil: University of São Paulo Press.

Sarti, I. (1981). Communication and cultural dependency: A misconception. In V. Mosco & J. Wasco (Eds.), *Communication and social structure.* New York: Praeger.

Sassen, S. (2004). *Global cities* (3rd ed.). Thousand Oaks, CA: Pine Forge.

Schatz, T. (1988). *The genius of the system: Hollywood filmmaking in the studio era.* New York: Pantheon.

Schiller, H. I. (1969). *Mass communication and American empire.* Boston: Beacon.

Schiller, H. I. (1976). *Communication and cultural domination.* White Plains, NY: International Arts and Sciences Press.

Schiller, H. I. (1981). *Who knows: Information in the age of the Fortune 500.* Norwood, NJ: Ablex.

Schiller, H. I. (1991). Not yet the post-imperialist era. *Critical Studies in Mass Communication, 8*(1), 13–28.

Schlesinger, P. (1987). On national identity: Some conceptions and misconceptions criticized. *Social Science Information, 26*(2), 219–264.

Schlesinger, P. (1993). Wishful thinking: Cultural politics, media, and collective identities in Europe. *Journal of Communication, 43*(2), 6–17.

Schnitman, J. A. (1984). *Film industries in Latin America—dependency and development.* Norwood, NJ: Ablex.

Schramm, W. (1964). *Mass media and national development.* Stanford, CA: Stanford University Press.

Schwoch, J. (1990). *The American radio industry and its Latin American activities, 1939–1990*. Chicago: University of Illinois Press.

Scott, J. C. (1999). *Domination and the arts of resistance: Hidden transcripts*. New Haven, CT: Yale University Press.

Semati, M. (2006, October). *Satellite television, cultural policy, and political discourse in Iran*. Paper presented at Global Fusion, Chicago.

Sengul, A. F. (2006). *Globalization and the reshaping of national identity in Turkish televisual space*. Unpublished paper, University of Texas, Austin, Radio-Television-Film Department.

Shrikhande, S. (1992). *Star TV: The age of pan-Asian television*. Unpublished doctoral dissertation, Michigan State University.

Sinclair, J. (1994). *Televisa-ization and Globo*. Unpublished manuscript.

Sinclair, J. (1995). Culture and trade: Some theoretical and practical considerations on "cultural industries." In E. McAnany & K. Wilkinson (Eds.), *Media, culture, and free trade: The impact of NAFTA on cultural industries in Canada, Mexico and the United States*. Austin: University of Texas Press.

Sinclair, J. (1999). *Latin American television: A global view*. New York: Oxford University Press.

Sinclair, J. (2001). NAFTA, culture, and trade. Unpublished manuscript, University of Texas, Austin.

Sinclair, J. (2003). The Hollywood of Latin America: Miami as regional center in television trade. *Television & New Media, 4*(3), 211–229.

Sinclair, J. (2005). Globalization and grassroots: Local cable television operators and their household subscribers in India. *Media Asia: An Asian Communication Quarterly, 32*(2), 69–77.

Sinclair, J., & Cunningham, S. (2000). Go with the flow: Diasporas and the media. *Television & New Media, 1*(1), 9–29.

Sinclair, J., & Harrison, M. (2000). Globalisation and television in Asia: The cases of India and China. Retrieved January 8, 2007, from http://www.dcita.gov.au/crf/papers2000/sinclair.pdf

Sinclair, J. S., Jacka, E., & Cunningham, S. (1996). Peripheral vision. In J. Sinclair, E. Jacka, & S. Cunningham (Eds.), *New patterns in global television* (pp. 1–15). New York: Oxford University Press.

Singhal, A., Obregon, R., & Rogers, E. M. (1994). Reconstructing the story of *Simplemente María*, the most popular *telenovela* in Latin America of all time. *Gazette, 54*(1), 1–15.

Singhal, A., & Rogers, E. M. (1989). *India's information revolution*. Newbury Park, CA: Sage.

Singhal, A., & Rogers, E. M. (1999). *Entertainment-education: A communication strategy for social change*. Mahwah, NJ: Lawrence Erlbaum.

Singhal, A., & Udornpim, K. (1997). Cultural shareability, archetypes, and television soaps: *Oshindrome* in Thailand. *Gazette, 59*(3), 171–188.

Smith, A. D. (1973). *The shadow in the cave*. Urbana: University of Illinois Press.

Smith, A. D. (1990). Towards a global culture. *Theory, Culture, and Society, 7*, 171–192.

Smith, A. D. (1993). *National identity*. Reno: University of Nevada Press.

Soh, F. (2005, July 22). Globalisation of the local. *Singapore Straits Times*, p. 29.

Sparks, C. (1998). Is there a global public sphere? In D. Thussu (Ed.), *Electronic empires* (pp. 108–224). London: Arnold.

Sparks, C. (2005, May). *What's wrong with globalization*. Paper presented at the International Communication Association, 2005 Annual Meeting, New York.

Stald, G., & Tufte, T. (2002). Introduction. In G. Stald & T. Tufte (Eds.), *Global encounters: Media and cultural transformation*. Luton, UK: University of Luton Press.

Stevenson, R. L., & Shaw, D. L. (1984). *Foreign news and the new world information order*. Ames: Iowa State University Press.

Straubhaar, J. (1981). *The transformation of cultural dependency: The decline of American influence on the Brazilian television industry*. Unpublished doctoral dissertation, Tufts University, Fletcher School of Law and Diplomacy.

Straubhaar, J. (1982). The development of the telenovela as the paramount form of popular culture in Brazil. *Studies in Latin American Popular Culture, 1,* 138–150.

Straubhaar, J. (1984). The decline of American influence on Brazilian television. *Communication Research, 11*(2), 221–240.

Straubhaar, J. (1988). A comparison of cable TV systems. In T. Baldwin & S. McEvoy (Eds.), *Cable communication*. Englewood Cliffs, NJ: Prentice Hall.

Straubhaar, J. (1989a). Television and video in the transition from military to civilian rule in Brazil. *Latin American Research Review, 24*(1), 140–154.

Straubhaar, J. (1989b, May). *The uses and effects of cable TV in the Dominican Republic*. Paper presented at the Intercultural and Development Division, International Communication Association.

Straubhaar, J. (1991). Beyond media imperialism: Asymmetrical interdependence and cultural proximity. *Critical Studies in Mass Communication, 8,* 1–11.

Straubhaar, J. (2003). Choosing national TV: Cultural capital, language, and cultural proximity in Brazil. In M. G. Elasmar (Ed.), *The impact of international television: A paradigm shift*. Mahwah, NJ: Lawrence Erlbaum.

Straubhaar, J., Campbell, C., Youn, S. M., Champagnie, K., Elasmar, M., & Castellon, L. (1992). *The emergence of a Latin American market for television programs*. Paper presented at the International Communication Association, Miami.

Straubhaar, J., & Duarte, L. G. (1997, April). *The emergence of a regional television market in Latin America: Broadcast television program trade vs. DBS/cable TV*. Paper presented at the Broadcast Education Association Conference International Division, Las Vegas.

Straubhaar, J., & Duarte, L. G. (2005). Adapting U.S. transnational television to a complex world: From cultural imperialism to localization to hybridization. In J. Chalaby (Ed.), *Transnational television worldwide: Towards a new media order* (pp. 216–253). London: I. B. Taurus.

Straubhaar, J., & Hammond, S. (1997). *Complex cultural systems and cultural hybridization*. Alta Conference on Communication and Complex Systems, Alta, Utah.

Straubhaar, J., & Viscasillas, G. (1991). Class, genre, and the regionalization of the television market in Latin America. *Journal of Communication, 41*(1), 53–69.

Streeter, T. (1996). *Selling the air: A critique of the policy of commercial broadcasting in the United States*. Chicago: University of Chicago Press.

Sugiyama, M. (1982). *Television programme imports—international television flow project*. Tokyo: NHK Public Opinion Research Institute.

Svenkerud, P., Rahoie, R., & Singhal, A. (1995). Incorporating ambiguity and archetypes in entertainment-education programming: Lessons learned from Oshin. *Gazette, 55,* 147–168.

Takahashi, M. (1992). *The development of Japanese television broadcasting and imported television programs*. Unpublished master's thesis, Michigan State University.

Tchouaffe, O. (2002). *Watching Marimar from Cameroon: Telenovelas and "parallel modernities" in Cameroon*. Unpublished manuscript, University of Texas, Austin.

Telles, E. E. (2004). *Race in another America: The significance of skin color in Brazil.* Princeton NJ: Princeton University Press.

Thussu, D. K. (1998). *Electronic empires: Global media and local resistance.* London: Arnold.

Thussu, D. K. (2005). The transnationalization of Indian television. In J. Chalaby (Ed.), *Transnational television worldwide: Towards a new media order* (pp. 156–172). London: I. B. Taurus.

Tomlinson, J. (1991). *Cultural imperialism.* Baltimore: Johns Hopkins University Press.

Tomlinson, J. (1999). Globalization and culture. In *Globalization and culture* (pp. 1–31). Chicago: University of Chicago Press.

Tunstall, J. (1977). *The media are American.* New York: Columbia University Press.

UNESCO. (1980). *Many voices, one world.* Paris: Author.

Urry, J. (2003). *Global complexity.* Cambridge, UK: Polity.

Valdez, M. (1997, June 8). Mapping a literary culture. Lecture, Brigham Young University, Provo, UT.

Valdez, M., & Hutcheon, L. (1995). *Rethinking literary history—comparatively.* New York: American Council of Learned Societies.

Vargas Llosa, M. (1981). *La guerra del fin del mundo.* Barcelona, Spain: Editorial Seix Barral.

Veii, V. S. (1988). *Foreign television entertainment programs viewing and cultural imperialism: A case study of U.S. television entertainment programs viewing in Windhoek, Namibia.* Unpublished doctoral dissertation, Michigan State University, Department of Sociology.

Vianna, H. (1999). *The mystery of samba.* Chapel Hill: University of North Carolina Press.

Vink, N. (1988). *The telenovela and emancipation: A study on TV and social change in Brazil.* Amsterdam: Royal Tropical Institute.

Wallerstein, I. (1976). *The modern world system.* New York: Academic Press.

Wallerstein, I. (1979). *The capitalist world economy.* Cambridge, UK: Cambridge University Press.

Wallerstein, I. (1991). *Geopolitics and geoculture—essays on the changing world system.* Cambridge, UK: Cambridge University Press.

Walters, G., Quinn, S. R., & Walters, L. M. (2005). Media life among Gen Zeds. *International Journal of Cultural Studies, 8*(1), 63–82.

Wang, G. (1993). Satellite television and the future of broadcast television in the Asia-Pacific. *Media Asia, 20*(3), 140–148.

Washington, A. U. (1964). *Area handbook for the United Arab Republic.* Washington, DC: Government Printing Office.

Waterman, D., & Rogers, E. (1994). The economics of television program production and trade in Far East Asia. *Journal of Communication, 44*(3), 89–111.

Wildman, S., & Siwek, S. (1988). *International trade in films and television programs.* Cambridge, MA: Ballinger.

Wildman, S. S., & Siwek, S. E. (1993). The economics of trade in recorded media products in a multilingual world: Implications for national media policies. In E. M. Noam & J. C. Millonzi (Eds.), *The international market in film and television programs.* Norwood, NJ: Ablex.

Wiley-Crofts, S. (in press). Transnation: Globalization and the reorganization of national media in Chile. *Journal of Broadcasting and Electronic Media.*

Wilkinson, K. (1995). *Where culture, language, and communication converge: The Latin-American cultural linguistic market.* Unpublished doctoral dissertation, University of Texas, Austin.

Williams, R. (1980). *Problems in materialism and culture.* London: Verso.

Wriston, W. B. (1988). Technology and sovereignty. *Foreign Affairs, 67*(2).

# Index

# About the Author

Joseph D. Straubhaar is the Amon G. Carter Professor of Communication in the Radio-TV-Film Department at the University of Texas. He was Director of the Brazil Center in the University of Texas Lozano Long Institute for Latin American Studies, 2002–2005. He previously was a Professor of Communications and Director of the Communications Research Center at the Department of Communications, Brigham Young University, and Professor in the Department of Telecommunication, Michigan State University. He has a Ph.D. in International Communication from the Fletcher School of Law and Diplomacy, Tufts University. He worked as a Foreign Service Officer, in Brazil and Washington, and as a research analyst for the U.S. Information Agency.

Much of Professor Straubhaar's work has focused on globalization of media, starting with the development of television in Brazil and the conceptual challenge it presented to then-dominant theories of dependence and imperialism. He has published extensively on international media, particularly Brazil and Latin America, including a number of articles and book chapters which have developed concepts of cultural proximity, asymmetrical interdependence, transnational cultural-linguistic markets, local vs. national vs. regional and global television markets, multiple television flows among global, regional, and national cultural markets, cultural hybridity, and multi-layered identities in the use of global cultural products.

He has also worked quite a bit on information technologies, and on development of information societies in both the United States and Latin America, particularly the issue of the digital divide among different social classes and ethnic groups. He has co-written *Media Now: Communication Media in the Information Society,* now in its third edition. He has written and consulted on telecommunications privatization and deregulation, including an edited book, *Telecommunications Politics: Ownership and Control of the Information Highway in Developing Countries.* On the digital divide, he is now doing comparative work on Brazil, Chile, and Mexico. He has edited a book comparing information society issues in Brazil and the USA with Othon Jambeiro, coeditor of *Políticas de informação e comunicação, jornalismo e inclusão digital: O Local e o Global em Austin e Salvador* (Information and communication policy, journalism and digital inclusion: The local and global in Austin and Salvador), published by Federal University of Bahia Press (2005). He is now finishing a book for the University of Texas Press, *The Persistence of Inequity in the Technopolis: Race, Class and the Digital Divide in Austin, Texas,* a case study of the digital divide persisting within a highly information-oriented city. He is also working on media and migration into Texas.

CPSIA information can be obtained
at www.ICGtesting.com
Printed in the USA
LVHW021915130222
710503LV00009B/144